Psycho/Analytic Psychoth

G000254814

Richard Morgan-Jones is a full member, a training therapist and supervisor at the London Centre for Psychotherapy. He has a private practice as a psychoanalytic psychotherapist in Eastbourne, where he works with individuals, groups and couples. He also works as an organisational consultant. He was formerly chair of the Brighton Association of Analytic Psychotherapists. Before he qualified as a psychotherapist in 1981 he worked at the National Institute for Social Work as a lecturer and consultant in group work and organisational development.

Jan Abram is a psychoanalytic psychotherapist in private practice in London and an associate member of the London Centre for Psychotherapy. Since 1989 she has worked on many courses and workshops for The *Squiggle* Foundation and was appointed Director between 1996 and 2000.

The author of many papers on the work of Winnicott, she is the author of the first edition of this book *Individual Psychotherapy Trainings: a guide* published by FAb in 1992. She is also the author of *The Language of Winnicott: a dictionary of Winnicott's use of words* by Karnac Books in 1996, and she is the editor of a collection of papers – *André Green at The Squiggle Foundation* by Karnac Books in 2000.

She is a training therapist, teacher and supervisor for many of the trainings described in this book and lectures widely in Britain and abroad. Currently she is following the training in psychoanalysis at the Institute of Psycho-Analysis.

Richard Morgan-Jones
with Jan Abram

PSYCHO/ANALYTIC
PSYCHOTHERAPY TRAININGS
A Guide

FREE ASSOCIATION BOOKS / LONDON / NEW YORK

First published in Great Britain 2001 by
FREE ASSOCIATION BOOKS
57 Warren Street, London W1T 5NR

Previously published in 1992 by Free Association Books as
Individual Psychotherapy Trainings: A guide by Jan Abram

A catalogue record for this book is available from the British Library

ISBN 1–85343–537–6 pbk

10 09 08 07 06 05 04 03 02 01
10 9 8 7 6 5 4 3 2 1

Produced for Free Association Books by
Chase Publishing Services, Fortescue, Sidmouth, EX10 9QG
Printed in the European Union by Antony Rowe, Chippenham, England

Contents

List of Figures

Richard Morgan-Jones

Acknowledgements

The idea for this book was the inspiration of Jan Abram who wrote its first edition nearly ten years ago. She has agreed to produce it with me, offering constant and substantial support borne of years of experience of living with these issues, developing the research needed and in producing and editing texts of many sorts for the benefit of analytic readers. My main appreciation is to her for her skill, support, experience and confrontation of my limitations in as humane a way as it is possible to imagine.

Many colleagues have offered comments on and contributions to different parts of the text. Views expressed are my own and not theirs, although they have informed me. They include Peter Addenbrooke, Fred Balfour, Ricky Emmanuel, Pam Howard, Darian Leader, Vivien Lewin, Leslie Murdin, Nancy Mackenzie and Hilde Rapp. Thanks also go to Donald Campbell (President of the BP-AS) and Jenniffer Johns (Editor) for permission to quote from the British Psycho-Analytic Society leaflet 'Psychoanalysis Today'. Permission was also gratefully received from Jonathan Pedder and the editor of the *British Journal of Psychotherapy*, Jean Arundale, on behalf of Artesian Books for permission to develop the diagram of the evolution of psycho/analytic psychotherapy trainings found on page 21.

Many others have contributed hugely over the years in the role of colleague, teacher, supervisor or analyst. I would particularly like to record my appreciation of the Brighton Association of Analytic Psychotherapists for many years of providing a local therapeutic and learning community for support, debate and challenge. As refugees from the steeper hierarchy of London trainings we seem to have created an ethos of sibling robustness without excessive rivalry in which to develop our diverse and mutually valued trainings across a wide field of application.

Beyond all these 'teachers' I am profoundly grateful to the patients and supervisees whose struggles with being psychotherapists-in-training have taught me much. Inspiring is their determination to find the ever-increasing resources needed to train. They have also demonstrated that difficult to assess ingredient in a suitable therapist, namely the determination to fight me for their corner within my limited understandings and frameworks that has stretched both me and this guide from what it might otherwise have been.

In addition to all these teachers has been the love and support of those nearest to me without whom none of this would have been possible. They have each recently shown what extraordinary things can be achieved with education and training. To them my part of this guide is dedicated.

Finally among these acknowledgements comes the list of those who contributed towards the entries in what is the largest part of this guide. Here is a list of those who wished to be known. They have all made a valuable contribution in their different roles to the awareness of analytic trainings through their contributions. They represent many more times their number who give freely of their time on committees and as learners to make psycho/analytic psychotherapy trainings a reality.

LIST OF CONTRIBUTORS IN THE ENTRIES SECTION OF THE GUIDE

Names will be given unless contributors have asked otherwise. Initials will be used for the organisations. Please refer to the contents list for their full names. First named will be representative(s) from the training committee. 'T:' will signify the beginning of the name(s) of trainee representatives. Those named are representative of the trainees. All consulted beyond themselves, some with every single current trainee. What they wrote is therefore a representation of diverse views across year groups or from within a trainee/student organisation, as some make clear.

Individual trainings
AGIP: Sue Corneck, Sian Ellis **T:** Mary Hughes, Mary Spencer
AIP: David Henderson **T:** Arthur Lockett, Jo Outray, Anne Martin
AJA: The Training Committee **T:** Penny Broadfield
ARBS: The Training Committee **T:** Rachel Searson
BAP: Viqui Rosenberg, Sharon Raeburn, Angela Bennett, Tim Fox, Heather Wood, Denise Taylor, Lydia Tischler, Verena Crick **T:** Sarah Nettleton, Adam Newman, Susan Hughes, Christina McNichol, Sarah Farmer, Steven Flour, Joy Smith, Debbie Bellman
CAPP: Susan vas Dias **T:** James Park
CFAR: Vivienne Bar **T:** Janet Low
CPP: Malka Hirsch-Napchan, Richard Tan **T:** Maria Parissis, Liza Catan
CSP: Rosemary Randall **T:** Glenys Plummer
GUILD: Sylvia Cohen, Haya Oakley **T:** Elisabeth Roddeck
IGAP: Eve Jackson **T:** Helen Brammer
Inst P-A: Michael Parsons **T:** Elizabeth Wolf, Susan Loden
IPSS: Veronica Norburn **T:** Mary Horton, Kevin Jones
LINC: John Lawrence, Angela Mynors **T:** Cynthia Dacre, Christine Smith, Carola Gross
LCP: Jennie McDonnell, Belinda Pethwick **T:** Valerie Scott, Rachel Adema, Sally Griffin, Sandra Wiener
NEATPP: Alison Cookson **T:** Christina Oliver, Peter Brumby
NIASP: Anne Anderson
PA: Paul Gordon **T:** Rosalind Mayo
SAP: Jane Knight **T:** Anna Bravesmith, Sandra Brown
SIHR: Denis Carpy **T:** Chris Brogan, Mark Cohen, Lynn Forsyth, Anne Patterson
SIPS: Glenys James **T:** Mark Bartlett, Marie Claire Diaz, Judi Brosnan
SITE: Noreen O'Connor, Joanna Ryan **T:** Stephen Gee, Maria Constantinou-Hickman
TAVI-Ad: David Millar **T:** Maxine Dennis
WPF: The Training Department **T:** Pat Gilliland, Caroline Morcom
WMIP-F: Michael Reynolds, Helen Lloyd **T:** Gloria Babiker
WMIP-J: Linda Hoag, Jenny Stokes **T:** Dorothy Holmes
WMIP-K: Shirley Truckle **T:** Sue Whitehouse, Debbie Willer, Elizabeth Dennis

Child trainings
AFC: Vivienne Green **T:** Michela Biseo

BAP-Ch: Monica Lanyado **T:** Linda Pae, Susan Turner, Judith Thorp, Caryn Onions
BTPP: Shirley Truckle **T:** Wendy Healey, Phillippa Willieris, Paula Land
SAP-Ch: Ian Williamson **T:** Joanna Goldsmith, Alessandra Cavalli, Jacqueline Cohen, Julia Shay
SIHR-Ch: Debbie Hindley, George Crawford **T:** Janet Sherrard
TAVI-Ch: Margaret Rustin **T:** Jane Ross
FAETT: Gillian Salmon **T:** Pamela Blakelock

Group and couple trainings
TMSI: Dorothy Judd
IGA: T: Barry Curnow
UL:G: Kevin Power **T:** Jud Stone, Rosemary Bodiam, Racarla Taylor
TURGAP: Sylvia Hutchinson **T:** Sheila Ritchie
WPF-Gp: The Training Department

Courses affiliated to universities and/or the NHS
CSPK: Georgia Lepper **T:** Avril Leonard
NWIPD: Alan Horne
ULDPD: Michael Jacobs, Gail King **T:** Rosemary Markham, Karinne Dummer
USCPS: Geraldine Shipton **T:** Stoya Wright
ULPD: Celly Rowe **T:** Krystal Brown
STTDP: Nicky Buckley, Geoff Fisk **T:** Lydia Holt-Garner

For Hilary, Pete, Tim, Lois and Grace

Introduction

This volume is the updated version of *Individual Psychotherapy Trainings: A guide* published by Free Association Books in 1992. In that first edition my attempt was to demystify the title 'psychotherapist' by comparing the requirements of training organisations that were members of the United Kingdom Standing Conference for Psychotherapy – now called the United Kingdom Conference for Psychotherapy (UKCP). I limited the book to one form of psychotherapy – individual psychotherapy for adults – and two of the most common types – analytic and humanistic. In 1990, when I began the research, there were 15 analytic trainings and 11 humanistic.

The British Confederation of Psychotherapists (BCP) was officially formed in 1993 and is now a registering body for psychoanalysts, analytical psychologists, and psychoanalytic psychotherapists. This has led to a sharper definition of what constitutes psychoanalytic psychotherapy. So when Trevor Brown of Free Association Books invited me to update the original, it seemed more pertinent in today's climate to be comparing the similarities and differences between the trainings belonging to the BCP and the trainings of the Psychoanalytic and Psychodynamic (PP) Section of the UKCP.

When Richard Morgan-Jones agreed to be the main author of this new edition, he suggested that ALL the trainings with psychoanalysis and analytical psychology at their root be included, and not just the adult trainings. Thus this volume presents the trainings in psychoanalysis, analytical psychology, psychoanalytic psycho-therapy, child psychotherapy, group analysis, group analytic psychotherapy, psychoanalytic psychotherapy with couples and psychoanalytically based educational therapy.

There has never been the opportunity to see in one volume a coherent demon-stration of the differences and similarities of trainings. I am grateful to Trevor Brown for commissioning this new edition, and to Richard Morgan-Jones for carrying out this huge task with such enthusiasm and patience. He has proved to be the open minded, thoughtful and sensitive person that was required. I had the privileged position of making comments and suggestions on the drafting of Part One and Morgan-Jones' Author's Comments.

As with the original there are two parts, and Morgan-Jones has extended and elaborated Part One. The evolution of the trainings provides an introduction to the historical evolution of training institutions in this country starting with The Institute of Psycho-Analysis in 1924. The reader is invited to trace the key thinkers in the early institutions and how they influenced the growth of new organisations which burgeoned from the late 1960s. The development of a profession: regulation and registration – covers the current issues concerning standards, regulation and registration. This is where the reader can learn about the background to the existence of two registering bodies and the nature of the debates concerning standards and registration.

In Part Two, as with the original, there is a common format for each training organisation detailing information on course requirements. There is also, as before, a response from trainees regarding their experience of the training. The original edition covered only 15 psycho/analytic training organisations – this volume includes 48 psycho/analytic courses from 37 different organisations – 24 from the UKCP and 13 from the BCP.

I think that the inclusion of all the analytic trainings, along with the extensive elaboration of Part One, the bibliography, the appendix of useful addresses of organisations related to the field, as well as Morgan-Jones' chart of requirements, makes this edition much more of a resource than the original. It is invaluable as a guide for the analysand seeking treatment, the student interested in following a training, and for all of us already in the profession. To have an awareness of the work of colleagues in other organisations is truly enlightening.

As with the original edition, the intention of this volume has been to present a picture that is as non-partisan as possible, whilst both of us realise that this is difficult, if not impossible, to achieve. It must be remembered that all of the entries have been prepared by the training committee members of the organisations, and the trainees have prepared their own accounts of their personal experiences. Inevitably, Part One and Author's Comments are coloured by our collaboration on how we see the development of the analytic world.

I wonder what Freud and his early colleagues would have thought. I think many of us are amazed by the almost over night preponderance of 'talking cures'. All the more reason for ways of distinguishing one type of psychotherapy from the other, as well as the organisations that train people, and the registering bodies that are working for sound practice, continuing professional development, and the protection of the public.

USE OF TERMS

Psychoanalysis is associated with the work of Freud and the post-Freudians. Those trained in psychoanalysis are qualified as psychoanalysts.

Analytical psychology is associated with the work of Carl Jung and his followers. Those trained in analytical psychology are qualified as analytical psychologists and/or Jungian analysts.

In recent years the term psychodynamic has come into use as a general term which serves to include the theories of both Freud and Jung. The term analytic or analytical also serves this purpose. This is why the use of the slash between psycho and analytic is used in the title of this volume. Please note that it is not in general use.

Many trainings refer to people-in-training as students or candidates. In the common format in Part Two everybody in training is referred to as a trainee.

The term personal therapy in the common format refers to the personal work the trainee has to undergo on herself as part of the training. This is often referred to as a training analysis, mostly with the BCP training organisations.

PART ONE: THE EVOLUTION OF TRAININGS

1.1   Psychoanalysis

The first training in the analytic field in the UK was established when the British Psycho-Analytical Society formed the Institute of Psycho-Analysis in London in 1924. Since then the Institute has trained individuals in psychoanalysis leading to the qualification of psychoanalyst. It remains the only training organisation in Britain whose training is recognised by the International Psycho-Analytical Association, which Sigmund Freud originally founded in 1910.

Classical Freudian psychoanalytic practice has created the foundation stone for all of the work described in this volume. Sigmund Freud's discovery of the technique of free association and the use of dreams as a means of accessing the unconscious mind was revolutionary. So was his insistence that current ways of relating could be understood by analysing the transference from the past experiences and relationships. His instinct theory provided an understanding of the way the frustrated aims of instincts were repressed by experiences with frustrating objects, usually parents. Freud's structural model of the tripartite division in the psyche between id, ego and super-ego has created a base for exploring the structure of the psyche and the task of analytic work in modifying the constraints of the patient's super-ego on their instinctual desires. Fundamental to all these discoveries were his theories of infantile sexuality and the way a child's inner psychic structure is shaped by the resolution of gender identity conflicts in relation to parental figures, illustrated by his use of the Oedipus myth to develop understanding of early childhood anxieties. These are described succinctly in Freud's *An Outline of Psycho-Analysis* (Freud 1940).

Along with these fundamentals has been the stance of the analyst's free floating attention and unobtrusive neutrality. Analysis of anxiety, defence and repressed impulse provide the context for reconstruction of the past and its reproduction in the transference relationship to both current relationships and the analyst (Strachey 1969, Malan 1979).

The early years of the British Psycho-Analytical Society from 1913 when it was founded, is of no more than a dozen men and women who were influenced by Freud and had at least begun some kind of analytic experience with him or one of his collaborators (Hinshelwood 1998). They were led by Ernest Jones. In the early days becoming a psychoanalyst depended on some personal analysis, but the requirement for it was not insisted on until later, a requirement encouraged first by Carl Jung (Falzeder 2000).

All these ideas were fostered by Freud's British collaborator in London, Ernest Jones. He was a founder member of the Institute of Psycho-Analysis, its president for 24 years and the man who encouraged key thinkers from Europe to flee Nazi Germany and Austria for the safety of England in the late 1930s. These included Melanie Klein in 1924 , Freud himself and his daughter Anna in 1936. Dr Eric Rayner, an Independent psychoanalyst, suggests that 'although rather autocratic by nature, Jones was a convinced egalitarian in his principles ... men and women were equally allowed to join from the start so the society became remarkably wide-based in skill and knowledge' (Rayner 1999).

Melanie Klein had begun working with children in the Berlin Psycho-Analytic Institute before she came to England. She and her followers argued that they followed Freud's development of his ideas from a purely instinct and drive model to one that explored the internal structure of the psyche. She furthered her analyst, Karl Abraham's work in developing analysis of the early and innate aggression of the infant and was one of the initiators of understanding the dynamics of internal objects within the psyche (Klein 1932). Her ideas were well received by a significant number of the British Psycho-Analytical Society, including Jones himself, in a way that created tension between the Vienna and London psychoanalytic circles. However, many British analysts were reserved about the single-minded passion of Klein and her followers, because of the exclusive focus on early infantile interpretations in analytic work and her exploration of primitive internal phantasies rather than exploring instinctual repressions effected by environmental deprivations and developments in the growing child.

Freud's daughter Anna developed her father's work, particularly in identifying the mechanisms of defence and producing a psychoanalytic theory of normal and pathological development (Freud 1936, 1965). Each of these she discovered and applied in the psychoanalysis of children. Her different approach based on the careful collection of data by a group of fellow researchers resulted in a more diffident stance that Edgecumbe suggests may have left her ideas less influential than Klein's (Edgecumbe 2000).

Conflict between these two European pioneers and their followers nearly led to a parting of the ways within the British Psycho-Analytical Society. The conflict was contained by insistence on a recorded debate between 1941 and 1945 which came to be referred to as 'The Controversial Discussions' (King and Steiner 1991). The urgency, ferocity and passion of the arguments between the émigrées from Berlin (Melanie Klein) and Vienna (Anna Freud) and their followers, alarmed and bemused British analysts who sought to persuade them to compromise rather than divide the Institute irrevocably. Rayner suggests that there were no more than a dozen analysts in each of the warring factions and that the majority belonged to neither group (Rayner 1999). These discussions concluded with a 'gentleman's agreement' (sometimes described as the 'ladies' agreement') between Melanie Klein, Anna Freud and Sylvia Payne. The latter was Jones' first successor as president of the Institute. A new era was established in UK psychoanalysis with the end of Jones' powerful 24 years as president of the Institute and this made way for new developments in psychoanalytic thinking and training.

The compromise produced two distinct groups of analysts, the A group – supporters of Melanie Klein, and the B group – supporters of Anna Freud and the classical Freudian analysts (Sandler and Sandler 1998:ix). A number of analysts did not wish to attach to either group. Initially they came to be known as the 'Middle Group'. It was not until the 1970s that they formed a third group known as the Group of Independent Psycho-Analysts (Kohon 1986). Meanwhile the B group had begun to move away from the classical Freudian position on instinct theory and the structural model of the psyche. They were very much influenced by the debates and discussions within the BP-AS about inner object relations and the internal structure of the psyche. This group became known as the Contemporary Freudians in 1987.

To this day there remains a small group of psychoanalysts within the BP-AS loyal to Anna Freud's views and style of treating patients, who are known as the Classical Freudians. Arthur Couch provides an illuminating description of his experience of his analysis with Anna Freud, her views and how they differ from the modernising trends within Freudian and Kleinian thinking (Couch 1995).

Since 1945 within the training of the Institute of Psycho-Analysis, there have been three different groups – they are currently called the Contemporary Freudian, Kleinian and the Independent groups. This means that despite having a common course of study a trainee psychoanalyst belongs to one of these three groups (Kohon 1986, Rayner 1990).

Prospective applicants to courses need to have some idea about the range of views taught on different courses described in this book as well as which approach they might wish to choose for their own training analyst or therapist. These three groups have clarified different approaches to psychoanalysis, inspired different emphases in clinical work and inspired different institutions in analytic training.

The Controversial Discussions within the British Society stopped further suggestions that Klein's supporters had no legitimate place in the Institute. Anna Freud and her followers had withdrawn increasingly from the debates, choosing not to cause further conflict by opposition at that point. Fortunately for British psychoanalysis Anna Freud did not follow up her idea of going to the US where she had a lot of supporters as she would not have been able to practise there as a non-medical lay analyst. Instead she furthered her work in the Hampstead Nurseries, set up during the Second World War and pioneered with Dorothy Burlingham (Freud 1946). This became the base for a child training, which absorbed her energies along with her work with her American following, but she was not at the heart of the Institute the way Melanie Klein was (Geissmann and Geissmann 1992).

The initial compromise agreement, following the controversial discussions, was that the first supervisor would be the same orientation as the candidate's analyst. The second supervisor had to come from one of the other groups. This agreement changed in the 1950s when the schools of thought tended to become more tightly defined and candidates chose both supervisors from their preferred group. Recently, with years of dialogue, debate and exchange of clinical material within the Institute, there has been some loosening of the group boundaries.

It is significant how far the competing groups that represent different schools of thought have come from personalised competition and antagonism of the war years. A *History of Child Psychoanalysis* written by two French child analysts from Bordeaux, covers the history of this period, the personalities and their professional views. This research was funded by both the Melanie Klein Trust and the Anna Freud Centre (Geissmann and Geissmann 1992). In this volume they quote the Contemporary Freudian psychoanalyst Anne-Marie Sandler, who chairs the child psychoanalytic training at the Institute: ' We can now listen to each other, from one group to another' (p. 248). Whether this is the case or not, the controversial discussions and their outcome continue to impact on all trainings.

CONTEMPORARY FREUDIANS

Two centres of research of psychoanalysis have been central to developments in contemporary Freudian thinking: the Anna Freud Centre in Hampstead and the University of London Psychoanalysis Unit. In Hampstead Anna Freud was able to develop her work of the different defence mechanisms and her theories of normal and pathological development (Freud 1936, 1965). Under the leadership of Joseph Sandler the Centre developed the Hampstead Index as a research tool, which had been started by Anna Freud and Dorothy Burlingham, to produce coherent definitions of psychoanalytic processes from closely recorded analytic sessions (Sandler 1962, Sandler et al. 1973).

The University of London Psychoanalysis Unit has been a centre of research and teaching under Joseph Sandler initially and now Peter Fonagy. It offers an introductory lecture series, taught by psychoanalysts, for those interested. Research has explored a wide range of issues, including the application of attachment theory to a range of clinical problems. These have been related to outcome predictors in child analysis (Fonagy et al. 1993, Fonagy and Target 1996).

In contemporary Freudian thinking, there is also much interest in object relations, inner object representations and the way in which they evoke role-responsiveness in the analyst (Sandler 1976). The importance of the setting is also emphasised as providing a 'background of safety' (Sandler 1987).

Contemporary Freudian analysis is characterised by the neutrality of the analyst and an interpretative style that aims to read the surface material of the real world as derivatives of unconscious structure and the internal world. This moves at a pace that is geared to the patient's increasing ego strength to deal with interpretations. There is also a focus on inner representations of internalised object relations, how they are related to the impulses and defences, as well as the current feeling state of the patient (Sandler and Sandler 1998). The classical Freudians distinguish a real relationship from the transference relationship as described by Greenson (Greenson 1978, Couch 1995).

KLEINIAN AND POST-KLEINIAN

Melanie Klein's work has had a huge impact on the whole field. Her exploration of the unconscious phantasies of young children has been as widely applied. So has her theoretical work leading to the paranoid-schizoid and depressive positions as a way of understanding the depths of human psychic experiences of mental pain and pleasure.

Although the earlier emphasis placed by Kleinians on the death instinct as the source of human destructiveness is no longer so widely accepted, this, along with the potential destructiveness of envy, has enabled Kleinians to explore the experience of human cruelty, sadism and persecution.

Post-Kleinians have relinquished an approach that interprets the phantasied use of part-objects so exclusively, in favour of close attention to the way parts of the infant mind are regulated by alteration of its structure using schizoid mechanisms (Hinshelwood 1994).

The work of Wilfred Bion and Herbert Rosenfeld, both analysed by Melanie Klein, explored the way psychotic and narcissistic aspects of the personality actively attack personal and emotional experience and the capacity to reflect upon it in thought, has been a fundamental addition to the understanding of psychic experience (Rosenfeld 1965, Bion 1967). This means that harder to reach patients and the more hidden aspects of otherwise well-functioning personalities have become more accessible to psychoanalytic work. Bion's understanding of psychotic aspects of the personality as attacks on relatedness and the capacity to use insight and relating has had a significant influence on psychoanalysis (Bion 1967).

Contemporary examples of Bion's thought include Rosenfeld's work with psychotic transferences and impasse in the analytic relationship (Rosenfeld 1987); Ronald Britton's work on the inner experience of the parental relationship (Britton 1989); Betty Joseph's 'The Patient who is Difficult to Reach' (Joseph 1989b) and 'Addiction to Near-Death' (Joseph 1989a); Donald Meltzer's understanding of claustrophobic states (Meltzer 1992) and of beauty and aesthetics (Meltzer and Williams 1988); John Steiner's work on *Psychic Retreats* (Steiner 1993); Ruth Reisenberg-Malcolm's work *On Bearing Unbearable States of Mind* (Riesenberg-Malcolm 1999); and Edna O'Shaugnessy's understanding of the abnormally mocking super-ego (O'Shaugnessy 1999). The student wishing to follow the development of Kleinian and post-Kleinian thinking can read Bob Hinshelwood's descriptions in *Clinical Klein* (Hinshelwood 1994).

INDEPENDENT (OR MIDDLE) GROUP

The Independent analyst Ronald Fairbairn, working in Scotland between the wars, had developed a theory of object relations independent of Freud's instinct theory (Fairbairn 1952). His analysis of schizoid, split-off aspects of the personality had influenced Klein in her choice of the phrase 'paranoid-schizoid' position. The Independent group of psychoanalysts were neither exclusively Kleinian nor Freudian. They agreed with some of Klein's theories about early childhood development and the importance of the relationship with mother in shaping inner templates of relations between subject and object. Fairbairn and Klein each developed a theory of the workings of the unconscious psyche that explored internalised objects. Klein explored the internal phantasies associated with these objects and developed an analysis based on deep unconscious interpretations of them, which she also related to Freud's instinct theory. Fairbairn explored the tensions between these internal objects and the mechanisms they commanded within the psyche and in doing so broke with Freud's instinct theory (Mitchell 1994).

The work of the Middle Group and their followers has done much to advance the understanding of inner psychic creativity and destructiveness and the way trauma is repeated and lays down a deep structure in the unconscious that determines relatedness to self and other.

In the disputes in the British Psycho-Analytic Society in the 1940s as already mentioned (p. 5f.) between the Kleinians and the Freudians this third group emerged influenced very much by object relations thinking of Klein and Fairbairn. They differed in technique from the Kleinians by interpreting human destructiveness as also being shaped by internalised experiences of environmental privation that structure the psyche into sabotaging both its own libido and its accompanying good objects. Fairbairn termed this internal object the 'internal saboteur' or the 'anti-libidinal ego' (Fairbairn 1952).

As well as these pioneers came the work of Donald Winnicott and Harry Guntrip (Guntrip 1973). Winnicott brought his paediatric experience to psychoanalysis and developed an understanding of the profound aspects of the child's relation with the mother and the child's need for gradual experiences of the loss of total presence and a 'holding environment' (Winnicott 1965). His work on transitional objects and space turned the analytic consulting room into a place for regressed experience and the analyst as a symbolic mother receiving the love and hate of the infant in the patient. He also distinguished between the 'true' instinctual and libidinal self and the protective caretaker 'false self'. An excellent description of the range and depth of Winnicott's work can be found in *The Language of Winnicott* (Abram 1996).

Guntrip articulated the significance for analysis of the historical shift in theory from instinct to object relating and analysed the nature of the schizoid splits within the psyche (Guntrip 1968). Michael Balint's work on benign as opposed to malignant regression as a means of bridging a 'basic fault', or vertical split within the psyche, established parameters for facilitating deeper work with more regressed aspects of narcissistic personalities (Balint 1968).

Independent Group successors to these thinkers have been characterised by their freedom from doctrinaire positions and a willingness to express creatively their experience of patients and theory in their own way. Pioneer Independents included Margaret Little, John Klauber and Marion Milner, each of whom developed and used theories of artistic creativity in their work with patients (Little 1986, Klauber et al. 1987, Milner 1987). Recent Independents include Christopher Bollas (Bollas 1987), Patrick Casement (Casement 1985), Nina Coltart (Coltart 1992), Gregorio Kohon (Kohon 1986, 1999), Michael Parsons (Parsons 2000), Harold Stewart (Stewart 1992), Neville Symington (Symington 1996), and Kenneth Wright (Wright 1991). A collection of the work of some of these thinkers can be found in Kohon (Kohon 1986), and a summary of their contribution can be found in Eric Rayner (Rayner 1990).

Ground-breaking clinical understandings can be found in Casement's theory of the internal supervisor (Casement 1985), Perelberg's work on violent and suicidal states (Perelberg 1999) and Bollas' work on hysteria (Bollas 1999). An excellent and easily understandable survey and integration of object relations thinkers both sides of the Atlantic can be found in Josephine Klein's *Our Need for Others and its Roots in Infancy* (Klein 1987).

DEVELOPMENTS IN THE US

Before leaving the field of psychoanalytic thinking, note should be taken of developments in the US that are taught at the Institute for Psycho-Analysis, presented and debated in the *International Journal of Psychoanalysis* and referred to in many psychoanalytical psychotherapy trainings.

Historically, a number of Viennese analysts fleeing Nazi German occupation chose the US rather than London as a home to flee to. Some of them had not been welcomed by Jones with his increasing interest in Klein's work. Many of them were loyal to Sigmund Freud and his daughter Anna who had a strong following in the US. US developments in Freudian thinking have emphasised ego psychology and the techniques of analysing the adapting ego against the onslaught of unconscious processes from the id and the super-ego that threaten to engulf (Greenson 1978).

In the past decade there has been increasing interest in British object relations thinking in the US as a counterpoint to ego psychology. Edith Jacobson developed an integrated model of object relations including early defence mechanisms, early instinctual development with the tripartite structural model (Jacobson 1964). Otto Kernberg has developed, over the past 20 years, an object relations approach that endeavours not to exclude drive theory and instincts and works out a framework for narcissistic and borderline personality organisation within diagnostic categories and prescriptions for different models and styles of therapeutic intervention (Kernberg 1976). Thomas Ogden has also incorporated object relations thinking into an American interactionist approach to understanding the replay of deeply laid psychic structures in the analytic encounter (Ogden 1982).

Heinz Kohut's self psychology has not as yet produced a training centre or school of thought in this country, although one clinician who has applied his ideas is Phil Mollon, an associate member of the BP-AS (Mollon 1993). Kohut's notion of the self was elusive, sometimes referring to the 'centre of the individual's universe' (Kohut 1971), sometimes less broadly as the experiencing self or the self as represented in the ego. He also described *selfobjects*, people who are experienced as part of the self for necessary development. However, his key concept was the idea that early failures of empathy and understanding in childhood could be changed through experiences of the therapist offering the chance for *transmuting internalisations*. This process offered the opportunity of a cohesive self that could ease the grandiose and omnipotent aspects of the narcissistic personality and transform them into something creative.

PSYCHOANALYSIS IN FRANCE

Exploration of French psychoanalysis has to begin with the influence of Jacques Lacan who has written extensively on his interpretation of Freud. Yet his emphasis was perhaps more on elements of Freudian theory than had been neglected or forgotten in contemporary psychoanalytic debate. In 1953 there was a split in the French psychoanalytic movement and there followed ten years of politicking, which resulted in Lacan setting up L'Ecole Freudienne de Paris in 1964, following his expulsion from the International Psycho-Analytic Association (Benvenuto and Kennedy 1986). The work of Lacan seems to be far more accepted outside the Anglo-Saxon world of psychoanalysis and psychotherapy, which retains a mixed response to the work of Lacan and Lacanians (Turkle 1992). Lacan's work is beginning to be studied more in UK analytic trainings. The Centre for Freudian Analysis and Research (CFAR) in London provides the only Lacanian training in the UK. Several members of CFAR give seminar series to other training groups and there is certainly some interest in Lacan in some areas of the Institute of Psycho-Analysis.

The influence of Lacanian thinking and practice in this country has been slow to develop. While the work of CFAR is the cornerstone of such interests, other writers have begun to make use of his theories rather than his methods of doing psychoanalytic work. His approach places emphasis on stability in the analytic setting, but with techniques that are very different from those described so far. The tradition has not specified frequency of sessions and their length is variable, sometimes more or less than 50 minutes in order to produce a kind of punctuation in the patient's speech so that his or her work continues in between sessions.

Despite the association between Lacanian thinking and cultural analysis, Lacan himself was a clinician. He was keenly aware of the power of specular images to captivate the human being and form the nucleus of the ego. He also explored how the child's sexual choices and orientations are shaped by his or her reaction to the parent's sexuality, constituted by the alienating experience of the subject's response to the ideals and fantasies of the parents. In this way he explored the way language that predates the individual, structures his conscious and unconscious life. He urged the significance of the symbolic import of the father as a symbolic role in separating the child from the mother.

Other French analysts have become important to the British scene. Jean Laplanche and J-B. Pontalis produced ground-breaking work in their *The Language of Psycho-Analysis* (Laplanche and Pontalis 1980), which provides an insight for both the beginner and the more experienced reader into the range and depth of the use of psychoanalytic terms.

Another French-based analyst published in the UK is Joyce McDougall, a New Zealander who began her analytic training at the Anna Freud Centre before moving to France and absorbing both the classical Freudian and the Lacanian approaches there. She has developed her own interest in the use of the metaphor of the theatre to describe the analytic stage in her books *Theatres of the Mind* (McDougall 1986) and *Theatres of the Body* (McDougall 1989). She has also developed a study of erotic life that moves on from Freud's theories of the perversions into what she describes as neo-sexualities (McDougall 1995).

Significant also is the work of André Green whose work on the Dead Mother has attracted so much interest and discussion in recent years (Green 1987). Many of the translations of his work have recently been published. Most recently a collection on Green's theories edited by Kohon, *The Dead Mother* (Kohon 1999) and a Winnicott Studies monograph, *André Green at the Squiggle Foundation* edited by Abram (Abram 2000). Another original contribution was made by Christiane Olivier whose re-working of Freud's theory of the Oedipus complex explores how the 'imprint of the mother' can have such a devastating different effect on men and women and hence upon the relationship between them (Olivier 1980).

DEFINITIONS

Having explored some of the history of important thinkers in the field, this guide now turns to more precise definitions: what is psychoanalysis; what is a psychoanalyst; how is the title defined, delimited and disputed?

> Psychoanalysis is a specific approach to the understanding and treatment of mental functioning and disturbance. Freud showed that consciousness is not all of the mind; we have impulses, feelings and thoughts that we are not at the time, or ever, aware of. This knowledge has become part of our culture and our view of the mind. He also introduced us to the understanding that apparently

meaningless symptoms have a psychic meaning, of which the patient is not aware, but of which he or she can become aware by the psychoanalytic method. (British Psycho-Analytical Society 1997)

This definition illustrates some of the core discoveries in depth psychology that have influenced all the psychotherapies particularly the analytic ones. It is the setting of analytic work that has most influenced and characterised the nature of the analytic therapies.

THE PSYCHO-ANALYTIC SETTING

The physical aspects of the psychoanalytical setting have not changed much since Freud's day. The patient comes to daily sessions at pre-arranged times and lies on the couch while the analyst sits in a chair just behind the couch. The analyst does not make notes in the patient's presence, as this would interfere with the analyst's capacity to given proper attention to what the patient is conveying. Notes are sometimes made after the sessions. It is the analyst's responsibility to provide a consulting room that is comfortable, quiet, and as free from interruption as possible. Every session lasts 50 minutes and the analyst starts and ends on time. The establishment of this secure setting, together with reliable and predictable adherence to it by the psychoanalyst, is very important as it provides a containing structure within which the patient and analyst are able to explore and think about the patient's difficulties. (BP-AS 1997)

TITLES

A hyphen between 'psycho' and 'analyst', Psycho-Analyst, denotes the qualification recognised by the International Psycho-Analytical Association. Depending on the context, many analysts nowadays drop the hyphen for the words psychoanalysis and psychoanalyst, and the 'psycho' may often be dropped too. Writers and publishers use different forms, but as for the label 'psychotherapist', there is at present no statutory legislation limiting use of the title.

The official position of the Institute of Psycho-Analysis is:

The term 'psychoanalyst' is often used rather indiscriminately. Strictly speaking, a psychoanalyst must have undergone and completed a training approved by the International Psychoanalytical Association (IPA). This is a world-wide body whose role is to maintain professional and training standards. In the UK full psychoanalytic training, recognised by the IPA, is provided and run only by the British Psycho-Analytical Society, which was founded in 1919. (BP-AS 1997)

Most analysts differentiate between psychoanalysis and psychotherapy and see their training as enabling them to practise either. However, there are many psychoanalytic psychotherapists who see their training and depth of work as equivalent to that of many analysts. This issue will be discussed below in exploring how psychoanalysis and psychoanalytic psychotherapy can be distinguished. The dispute over title will be described later (p. 24f.).

1.2 Analytical Psychology

Carl Jung was one of the first dissenters from Freud (Jones 1957). Jung had been a key member of Freud's inner circle, relieving him of his sense of isolation from psychiatry in Vienna in the first decade of the twentieth century. Jung was Swiss and was working in a psychiatric hospital where Freud's ideas were used with patients and where Jung's scientific interests had led to his word association test as a tool for analytic diagnosis. Jung had accompanied Freud to the US on a lecture tour, which began to establish psychoanalysis in that continent.

The final dividing of the ways between Freud and Jung occurred in 1914 when Jung resigned as the President of the International Psycho-Analytical Association. Their disagreement focused on the nature of the unconscious (Jung 1916, Kovel 1976). Jung disagreed with Freud about the unconscious, and he saw libido as not just sexual, but also creative and relating to others through complex collective forms that shaped individual experience and needed individuation. These ideas formed the seeds of current rapprochement between Jungians and object relations thinkers. Early Jungians were much influenced by Jung's later writings that explored the archetypal aspects of collective unconscious experience and the analysis of personality based on Jung's research into four personality types: thinking, feeling, intuition and sensation; with the task of analysis as individuation, integrating undeveloped aspects of the personality.

Most Freudians see Jung's development of theories from psychoanalysis as a diversion, whereas some Jungians would see it as evolving beyond psychoanalysis. Nevertheless, the separation of these two men created two separate international organisations – the International Association of Psycho-Analysis (IAP – Freud) and the International Association of Analytical Psychology (IAAP – Jung).

JUNGIAN VIEWS, CLASSICAL AND CONTEMPORARY

Classical Jungians followed Jung closely in laying emphasis on the Self and Individuation and in separating the individual out from the collective myths that seemed to have shaped the psyche. They explored psychic conflicts with the notion of the patient's complex and related to transference as an impediment to analysis. Instincts were seen as having a biological aspect as well as an archetypal or mythological one and appeared when there was the experience of emotional overwhelm.

A key development of Jung's thinking in the Society of Analytical Psychology was the work of Michael Fordham in applying Jung's theories to child analysis. He used psychoanalytic theories and techniques to produce an approach to analysis and therapy that was rooted in early childhood experience and postulated the concept of a 'Primary Self' (Fordham 1969). Since then there have been a number of varying views about the balance between developmental and archetypal approaches to Jungian analysis (Samuels 1985).

Developmental Jungians in the UK followed the pioneering application of Kleinian and object relations ideas in child analysis by Michael Fordham, so rolling back the years of Jungian antagonism to psychoanalysis. Fordham's idea that the child is born with a level of instinctual competence and integration which he or she deintegrates in order to relate to an other provides the cornerstone of his theories (Fordham 1988). Jung was the first analyst to begin to use the counter-transference as a means for understanding the patient. Jungians believe that therapeutic transformation can only take place if the analyst is influenced and changed internally by the patient (Fordham 1978).

Archetypal Jungians, who developed the popular de-mythologising task in Jung's later work, were mainly interested in the process of amplification that involves patient and analyst exploring mythological, narrative, cultural, religious and symbolic material to give meaning and context to a patient's material. In this country there are few Jungians whose work is single-mindedly archetypal, although an interesting development is in the analysis of post-modern society using mythological analysis (Hauke 1998). A significant example of how archetypal thinking can be integrated with transference analysis and produce a new understanding of the psychology of human self-destructiveness can be found in Kalsched's understanding of self-attack as defence against the terrors of early childhood trauma (Kalsched 1996).

Within the Jungian fold there is enormous richness and diversity. Comparison and history of their differences can be found in Samuels' *Jung and the Post-Jungians* (Samuels 1985). Jungian trainees are given an experience of the dialogue and debate between these different Jungian and non-Jungian traditions. Those who wish to explore this range further should read Casement's (Casement 1998) and Alistair and Hauke's (1998) compilations of modern Jungian thought.

JUNGIAN TRAININGS

A small group of people in London who had been influenced by Jung established the Analytical Psychology Club in 1922. The Society of Analytical Psychology (SAP) was founded and began the first Jungian training in 1946. There are now over 150 SAP-trained analysts. Its founders had been applying Jung's teaching within a society despite the fact that Jung was wary of being the figurehead for a school of thought.

Differing views within the SAP produced the formation of two further Jungian training societies: the Association of Jungian Analysts (AJA), founded in 1977, and the Independent Group of Analytical Psychologists (IGAP), which was founded in the early 1980s and produced a training in 1985.

These three trainings, along with the British Association of Psychotherapists Jungian training, which began in 1963, are recognised by the International Association of Analytical Psychologists (IAAP) and have been members of the Analytical Psychology section of the UKCP. In 1999 the SAP withdrew following the insistence by the BCP on its single-member policy (see pp. 38–9). There is one other exclusively Jungian training in the UK, at the West Midlands Institute for

Psychotherapy (see p. 217). It will be noted that there seems to be more impact from Kleinian thinking on these trainings than the other schools, although they too are studied.

TITLES AND DEFINITIONS WITHIN ANALYTIC PSYCHOLOGY/PSYCHOTHERAPY

Within the Jungian tradition there is a wide variety of practice. Jung's followers in Zurich and originally in the London-based Society for Analytical Psychology use the term 'analytical psychologist'. They also refer to themselves as 'Jungian analysts'. In the US there are Jungians with a strong connection to object relations thinking calling themselves 'Jungian psychoanalysts'. This title has not been used in the UK. Since there is widespread acceptance in the Jungian trainings that the analysis practised is also a form of psychotherapy, it is common for Jungian analysts as well as for psychotherapists to describe themselves as 'Jungian psychotherapists' or 'analytical psychotherapists'. Ann Casement, the chair of the UKCP, points out that since all the Jungian members of the UKCP are members of the International Association of Analytical Psychologists (IAAP), there is no problem about all its members in that section being registered under the title 'Analytical psychologist-Jungian analyst' (Casement 1995).

DEFINITION OF ANALYTICAL PSYCHOLOGY AND ANALYTICAL PSYCHOTHERAPY (JUNGIAN)

This (the section) stems from the work of C.G. Jung. The central idea is that what we do and feel how we think of ourselves and other people, depend upon forces and processes we are not aware of – 'the unconscious'. These may be part of our common human nature or particular to the individual. (Flag statement of the Analytical Psychology Section of the UKCP. (UKCP 1998))

1.3   Psychoanalytic Psychotherapy

Each of the psychotherapy trainings described in this guide has developed its own flavour and slant, often dominated by one of the three psychoanalytic groups (see pp. 6–8). However, those that draw on the analytic tradition share a common characteristic.

The training requirements of the Institute of Psycho-Analysis have evolved out of the early years of the developments of psychoanalysis (Balint 1953), that became established first in 1920 at the Berlin Institute for Psycho-Analysis. They cover three main areas: personal analysis or therapy ('a training analysis'), supervision of clinical work ('control analysis') and theoretical courses and seminars (Falzeder 2000). These components are interrelated, working in dynamic relationship to each other, with self-knowledge at the very heart. They have now become the unequivocal fundamentals of every psycho/analytical psychotherapy training (see Figure 1.3.1).

Figure 1.3.1   Fundamentals of every psycho/analytical psychotherapy training (from original edition)

There appear to be two main streams of influence and context for psychoanalytic psychotherapy training in the post-war years. One is in the development of private psychotherapy trainings, self-funding and developed through the work of those whose convictions, beliefs and positions enabled them to give generously of their time in developing new institutions and new training organisations. The other is the application of psychoanalytic thinking and clinical work within the public sector, provided by government funding. These have mainly been linked to the National Health Service, but some have been developed in a University setting. In both the NHS and universities the staff are paid by the institution and there may be some grants or training posts that assist with fees or facilities, however much there is pressure in these public bodies to recoup their costs.

Details of the history of these courses can be found in the first section of each training course's entries in Part Two of the guide. This section will explore how some of these trainings evolved and the ideas that shaped them.

PSYCHOTHERAPY TRAINING IN THE PRIVATE SECTOR

Within the private sector, for the first half of the twentieth century the Freudian Institute of Psycho-Analysis (1919) and the Jungian Society for Analytical Psychology (1946) were the only training organisations in London. In 1951 a small group of people come together to form the Association of Psychotherapists. They had generally undergone personal analysis and supervision with members of the Institute of Psycho-Analysis and/or the Society for Analytical Psychology (Herman 1989).

They were individuals all interested in practising psychotherapy at their places of work or in private practice (Scarlett 1991). They were motivated by what was experienced as the elitism and exclusiveness of the IPA and the SAP and the wish to offer therapy and training for therapy on a one-, two- or three-weekly session basis. Many of these courses were inspired by the people who were working partly privately, partly in the public sector or in a charitable organisation. The vision was to create trained psychotherapists for a wider social influence.

In 1964 the Association of Psychotherapists formed its own training organisa-tion, the British Association of Psychotherapists (BAP), with a separate Freudian and Jungian stream. In 1974 divisions within the BAP resulted in two more training organisations: the London Centre for Psychotherapy and the Association for Group and Individual Psychotherapy.

Meanwhile other training organisations had developed, the Lincoln Clinic and Centre for Psychotherapy in 1967, the Westminster Pastoral Foundation (WPF) in 1970. Both were influenced by liberal and religious pastoral care and counselling ideals. The Guild of Psychotherapists was founded in 1972, the Centre for Analytic Psychotherapy in 1979, now known as the Centre for Psychoanalytic Psychother-apy. All these organisations were committed to offering training for those who would be able to offer lower-cost analytic psychotherapy whether within their associated clinics, in voluntary organisations or in the public services. It was only later that they developed as trainings almost exclusively for those wishing to practise privately.

The Philadelphia Association (1965) and subsequently the Arbours Association (1970) had developed from R.D. Laing's work with schizoid personalities using phe-nomenology and existentialism and his methods in creating a non-medical therapeutic community as an alternative asylum for psychotic patients.

In the early days of its life as well as currently the Guild has a number of teachers and trainers with an existential or phenomenological perspective. A training founded in 1999 and set up by therapists originally involved in the Philadelphia Association called 'the Site for Contemporary Psychoanalysis' has developed this approach. It includes more radical critical thinking from sociology, post-modern ideas and feminism, that provide a radical critique of the way the development and use of psychoanalytic ideas is shaped by a social context with a variety of unconscious messages which can further discrimination, prejudice and unequal power relations.

In 1980 a group of therapists in Cambridge organised a course based on a non-hierarchical structure. This aimed to encourage trainees to begin their learning from their own and each other's resources. This became the Cambridge Society for Psychotherapy.

Although it is much more psychoanalytic now, the Institute for Psychotherapy and Social Studies (IPSS), founded in 1978, was originally inspired by a mix of humanistic and analytic therapy and a concern to apply them to the social context. This social application theme is one that has endured in the increasingly psycho-analytic changes within IPSS.

All of these courses have changed over the years and come a long way since their original ethos and standards trained existing psychotherapists. The whole debate about standards, frequency and intensity of training will be discussed below (p. 37f.).

One training that was begun in the mid 1990s was designed by members of the BP-AS in South-East London. It is called the South of England School for Psychoanalytic Psychotherapy (SESPP). The only reason it does not appear in this guide is because it has not been established long enough to produce the graduate learned society that it needs to qualify as a member organisation of the BCP. Its standards and training requirements are within the BCP guidelines, and as an intensive course in a region of London with no other courses it is likely to attract interest (address in appendix).

PSYCHOTHERAPY TRAINING IN THE PUBLIC SECTOR

The Tavistock Clinic

The first trainings in psychotherapy using analytic ideas were at the Tavistock and were seen as postgraduate trainings on differentiated courses initially for psychia-trists, and later for psychologists and social workers. They are now unified in the one adult psychotherapy interdisciplinary course.

After the Second World War the flagship developments at the Tavistock Clinic (founded in 1920) provided an important focus for the training and development of psychotherapists within the newly formed public services employing psychiatrists and psychologists within a National Health Service (NHS) (Dicks 1970).

Leaders in applying psychoanalytic ideas at the Tavistock, such as Ian Suttie, were suspect to the BP-AS as they had connections to the Hungarian analyst Ferenczi whose work Freud had rejected (Suttie 1935). Malcolm Pines suggests that it was not until after the Second World War that Ernest Jones' mandate against psycho-analysts working at the Tavistock clinic was lifted so that they could begin to establish a base outside the Institute from which to apply their thinking to psychotherapeutic work and training (Pines 1998). It could be argued that it was not until then that a scientific research tradition from medicine could be applied to psychoanalysis.

Part of the fallout from the controversial discussions at the British Psycho-Analytical Society was John Bowlby's development of a different paradigm for analytic findings. He was looking for a more scientific approach than the intrapsychic explorations of the object relations approach. While at the Maudsley Hospital he had researched the attachment process in research done into the grieving process following the epidemic of loss after the First World War. Bowlby and his colleagues developed research on attachment, grief and loss. This was taken further by James and Joyce Robertsons' research films showing children briefly separated from parents, which did so much to influence managers of hospitals and their policies regarding access to hospitals by parents of sick children and indeed all visiting hours (Bowlby 1969, Robertson and Robertson 1989).

The Tavistock became the centre for a number of important developments. Wilfred Bion and Henry Ezriel developed analytic work in groups (Ezriel 1950, Bion 1961). David Malan and Michael Balint developed models and research into brief psychotherapy (Malan 1963, Balint et al. 1972). Balint also developed a method for offering analytic consultations to groups of GPs, thereby taking psychoanalytic thinking into a wider sphere of social psychiatry and medicine (Balint 1957).

Further developments included R.D. Laing's work at the Tavistock applying the existential and phenomenological approaches of European philosophy to the experience and analysis of schizoid personalities (Laing 1959). This created huge popular interest with psychological experience being de-pathologised and taken away from an exclusively medical framework (Van Deurzen 1998). Laing's ideas not only became the focus for the development of therapeutic communities, they also became the focus for psychotherapy trainings (Arbours and Philadelphia Association) based on his approach.

The work of the Tavistock also has extended to other arenas of development. There have been trainings in both child and adult psychotherapy. In 1948, the Tavistock Marital Studies Institute was formed out of the Family Discussion Bureau in offering training research and a clinical service to couples. As an Institution the Tavistock has played a key role in developing infant observation as an integral part of many psychotherapy trainings (see p. 27). In recent years it has made a notable contribution in research into autism and the autistic aspects of neurotic personalities (Tustin 1981, Alvarez 1992, Alvarez and Reid 1999). There has also been a group researching into the use of psychotherapy for people with learning difficulties and other forms of mental handicap (Sinason 1992). In making analytic thinking and practice more available it has produced a Channel 4 TV series with an accompanying book entitled *Talking Cure* (Taylor 1999). It also has a unit specialising in the research and treatment of post-traumatic stress syndrome and has supported teams of counsellors working in post-disaster situations (Garland 1999) and a course for bereavement counselling run by Dr Goldie.

The Tavistock was not the only centre for the development of and training in analytic ideas in psychiatry. Other London and regional teaching hospitals have offered a variety of trainings in psychotherapy, often taught by analysts with training registrar posts and clinical work within a psychotherapy unit in the hospital. The Maudsley, St Thomas's, St Bartholomew's hospitals in London and Leeds, Birmingham, Oxford, Liverpool, and the Cassell hospitals, among others, have all offered such training opportunities, authorised by the Joint Committee on Higher Psychiatric Training and assisted by the Association of University Teachers of Psychotherapy. A specialised development within the NHS has been the work of the Portman Clinic, now linked with the Tavistock as a single trust, in offering psycho-analytically based treatment, training and research into criminal and anti-social behaviour.

Regional trainings

Many of the regional trainings have grown out of training courses offered alongside an NHS department of psychotherapy, although they have all developed into courses offering training for private practice.

Jock Sutherland moved from being Director of the Tavistock in 1967 and set up the Scottish Institute for Human Relations in Edinburgh, known to some as the 'Mac Tavi'! The training at the Uffculme Clinic in Birmingham which had originally been for psychiatrists developed into training for psychotherapists, formed the West Midlands Institute of Psychotherapy in 1981 and eventually divided into three different trainings: Contemporary and Independent Freudian, Kleinian and Jungian. Following the Severnside example in Bristol, which had established a training in 1985, a group of therapists formed the North East Association for Training in Psychoanalytic Psychotherapy (NEATPP) in 1993 and increased its standards to join the BCP in 1999. Tom Freeman began a similar development in Northern Ireland where the Northern Ireland Association for the Study of Psycho-Analysis was formed in 1989 building on an established course at Queen's University, Belfast. This association has been a member of the BCP since 1996 and a study group of the Institute of Psycho-Analysis since 1998.

University trainings

(See Universities Psychotherapy Association, pp. 35–6.) A number of University trainings in psychodynamic or psychoanalytic psychotherapy have developed over the years. These are often associated with particular departments within the university whose professional and vocational orientation has shaped the course in preparing people to practise as psychotherapists within the health services. Indeed, many of them are specifically connected to NHS psychotherapy departments. Most of these courses have a strong research element that insists on teaching research methodology that may or may not be clinically related. Some critics feel that as academic courses they fail to emphasise the centrality of the clinical task. However, it is important to note the significant contribution they can make to organised research in the therapeutic field as well as to applying analytic approaches to public services.

In 1985 the Centre for the Study of Psychotherapy grew out of work with a local alcohol rehabilitation unit and counselling courses at the University of Kent, and since 1991 psychodynamic psychotherapy has become a recognised area of study at the University.

The University of Leeds ran a two-year diploma in psychotherapy alongside a psychotherapy clinic from 1974. In 1987 this was turned into a three-year Masters, increasing to four years in 1998 and recognised by the UKCP.

The University of Leicester ran a psychodynamic psychotherapy training in 1991 which was developed and recognised by the UKCP in 1993. The Leicester course has aimed at people who wanted to progress with their counselling skills to a deeper level of work.

In 1993 the University of Sheffield replaced its Diploma in Psychotherapy within the Department of Psychiatry with a UKCP-recognised course in its own Centre for Psychotherapeutic Studies.

NHS courses

In addition to these university courses there are those developed outside a university context within the NHS. Those accredited by the UKCP PP section include the North West Institute for Psychodynamic Psychotherapy, founded in 1987 in Manchester, and the South Trent Training in Dynamic Psychotherapy in Nottingham, which since 1982 has provided training for the psychotherapy services in Derby, Leicestershire, Nottingham and Lincolnshire.

Courses from universities and/or with NHS links, seeking possible UKCP accreditation as psychodynamic courses in the next few years, include the following:

*   Southern Counties Psychodynamic Psychotherapy Training at Oxford Brookes University

*   The Psychodynamic Psychotherapy in Practice course run by the University of Derby and the Southern Derbyshire Mental Health Trust

*   The Oxford University Department of Continuing Education Master's Programme in Psychodynamic Studies

*   The University of Lincolnshire/Doncaster Health Care NHS Trust course in psychodynamic psychotherapy.

Addresses for these courses can be found in the appendix and a summary of their requirements in the chart on p. 354.

These courses have the dilemma of seeking to train staff for work in the public sector that requires the skills of assessment and short-term work, as well as developing the depth needed for longer-term work of the sort for which the UKCP provides recognition. This makes the dilemma of clinical requirements difficult. There is some debate about both NHS and UPA courses as to whether they need to have PP section standards to be accredited by both the UPA, which itself accredits them as members of UKCP.

WHAT ARE THE DIFFERENCES BETWEEN PSYCHOANALYSIS AND PSYCHOANALYTIC PSYCHOTHERAPY?

The difference between the practice of psychoanalysis and Jungian analysis on the one hand and psychoanalytic psychotherapy on the other, becomes very complicated. There are psychoanalytic psychotherapists whose personal analysis, supervision and theoretical learning is on a par with somebody who has trained at the Institute of Psycho-Analysis or the Society of Analytical Psychology. They very often see patients four or five times a week over a period of several years. They have often been analysed, supervised and taught by analysts. Meanwhile, there are many analysts who see people once or twice weekly for shorter periods of time. Teaching curricula described in this guide can be compared and many will be found to cover

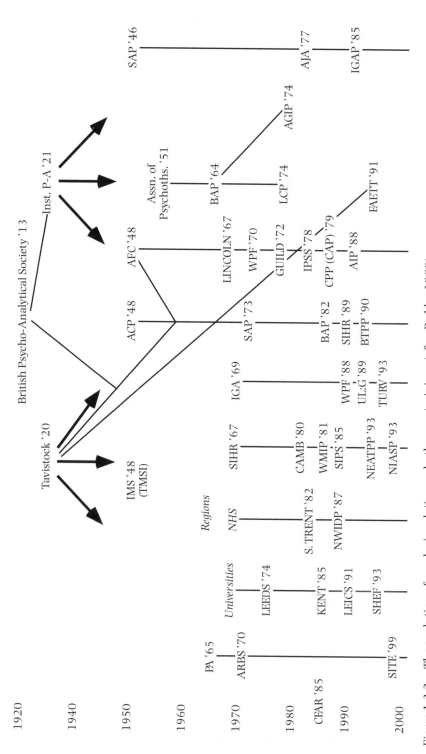

Figure 1.3.2 The evolution of psycho/analytic psychotherapy trainings (after Pedder 1989)

the same ground. This presents the question: who practises psycho/analysis and who practises psychotherapy?

In trying to make the distinction between the two, it is possible to look at the external factors, such as the five-times-weekly sessions that emphasise the analytic task and maximise the conditions for gathering the transference and processing it. These can be distinguished from internal factors: the analysis of the regressive trans-ference, the interpretation of deep-seated internal objects, the neutrality of the psychoanalyst (Sandler 1988, Kernberg 1999). Yet both these approaches are used by psychoanalytic psychotherapists.

Joseph Sandler has suggested that where the theory of the therapy is based on the direct analysis of unconscious phantasies, then the practice of therapy and analysis will be more similar. Where the emphasis is on moving from the surface to the deeper in offering interpretations, therapy and analysis will differ. He acknowl-edges that status and length of training are connected and that further training is needed for analysts to do psychotherapy, and concludes that the differences between the two are blurred (Sandler 1988).

It is possible to distinguish between work that is systematically interpretative (psy-choanalytic) and work with more narcissistic or borderline patients where a more expressive approach (psychotherapeutic) to analytic work is undertaken bearing in mind the patients need for ego integration and de-fragmentation. As a third point on this continuum from analysis to therapy, supportive psychotherapy offers cognitive support for patients in helping them explore how best to adapt to their internal and external worlds. This work is often a feature of weekly psychotherapy, psychodynamic counselling as well as of some supervision and colleague relating (Kernberg 1999).

Debate on these issues suggests a range of approaches along this continuum conducted by psychoanalysts believing they were doing psychoanalysis as well as among psychotherapists believing they were doing psychotherapy. A third point of view comes from patients who often wonder whether what they are participating in is analysis or therapy, given their experience that they find interventions from the whole range of theories confronting or supportive depending on their experiences. These issues will be taken up in the discussion of the debates between the registering bodies, the United Kingdom Council for Psychotherapy (UKCP) and the British Con-federation of Psychotherapists (BCP) (see p. 37f.)

DEFINITION OF PSYCHOANALYTIC PSYCHOTHERAPY FROM THE BRITISH PSYCHO-ANALYTIC SOCIETY

Psychoanalytic psychotherapy is a less intensive form of psychoanalysis; for example the patient having psychotherapy may have one, two or three sessions a week; a full psychoanalysis means that the patient attends daily sessions, usually five days a week, sometimes four. Some psychoanalysts practice psychotherapy; some do not. (British Psycho-Analytic Society 1997, *Psychoanalysis Today*)

The British Confederation of Psychotherapists has urged a differentiation in the demands and standards of training from the more inclusive, less demanding UKCP requirements. In their leaflet on Psychoanalytic Psychotherapy the BCP make the point:

Psychoanalytic psychotherapy differs from most other therapies in aiming for deep seated change in personality and emotional development. Psychoanalytic Psychotherapy draws on theories and practices of analytical psychology and psychoanalysis. It is a therapeutic process which helps patients understand and resolve their problems by increasing awareness of their inner world and its influence over relationships both past and present.

The relationship with the therapist is a crucial element in the therapy. The therapist offers a confidential and private setting where unconscious patterns of the patient's inner world become reflected in the patient's relationship with the therapist (transference). This process helps patients gradually to identify these patterns and, in becoming conscious of them, to develop the capacity to understand and change them. (BCP leaflet 'Psychoanalytic Psychotherapy')

In defining Psychoanalytic Psychotherapy as opposed to other psychotherapies, more tightly the 'flag statement' of the Psychoanalytic and Psychodynamic section of the United Kingdom Council for Psychotherapy states:

These therapies are based on psychoanalytic theory and practice. They may take place one-to-one or in a group. They may be of long or short duration. The central principle is that much distress has been caused by events in early life of which we are no longer aware. The therapy offers a reliable setting for the patient to explore free associations, memories, phantasies, feelings and dreams, to do with past and present. Particular attention is given to the interaction with the therapist, through which the patient may relive situations from their early life, the 'transference'. In these ways, the patient may achieve a new and better resolution of longstanding conflicts. (UKCP 1998:xix)

THE PRAGMATICS OF ANALYTIC PRACTICE

Whatever the formal definitions may suggest, the practical realities of analytic work inevitably shift our perspective. Both analysts and therapists are at the behest of the uncertain nature of their own sources of referral for the service they offer. Some may well be able to offer analysis only four to five times per week. Others may differentiate clearly between the five-times-weekly analysis they offer and the three-times-weekly psychotherapy.

For most psychotherapists and several psychoanalysts, the picture is different. Patients often do not arrive for an assessment with a clear idea of what they might want or be looking for. They may be psychologically minded but in no way knowledgeable about analysis or therapy. The clinician has to be flexible. Initial consultations may be accompanied by a patient's hesitancy about committing to a contract. Time from work and financial resources may be limited or uncertain. However good an assessment is done, work may only slowly proceed to one year or two of once-weekly psychotherapy. For the patient this may be manageable. Only then might the work deepen and intensify as the patient gathers resources, psychological and financial, and begins to use the therapist, beginning more intensive and frequent sessions with greater commitment and meaning.

All this suggests that the frameworks of analysis and therapy are shaped too by the patient and their readiness. Joseph Sandler tells of his psychoanalysis with a patient who was a pilot requiring him to be away for a week at a time. In presenting this case to colleagues there was no question about whether the six weekly sessions punctuated by a whole week's absence from analysis was proper psychoanalytic work (Sandler 1988).

TITLES

From these definitions and discussions it can be seen that the psychoanalytic and psychodynamic psychotherapies use the same theory as is taught in training analysts. Looking back at the history of titles, before the 1960s the term 'psychotherapist' could be applied to all psychological treatments that were not psychoanalysis. With the growth of the humanistic and other psychotherapies the term 'analytic psychotherapist' came into use. In 1992 just before the BCP was formed (from some of the organisations from the Analytic section of the UKCP), this section renamed itself the Psychoanalytic and Psychodynamic Psychotherapy section. This clarified that Jungians were not included and that a statement was being made that no single organisation should have a monopoly on the title 'psychoanalytic psychotherapist'.

Disputes over the title 'psychoanalyst'

The Centre for Freudian Analysis and Research describes its graduates as psychoanalysts and its training as a training in psychoanalysis. Some of its members also call themselves psychoanalytic psychotherapists as well as psychoanalysts.

A few psychotherapists disagree about the exclusive use of the title 'psychoanalyst' by members of the British Psycho-Analytical Society. Some believe they should not have exclusive use of the title as the International Psycho Analytic Association has made its policy.

The BP-AS exclusive position on title has been disputed by CFAR as well as by other psychotherapy bodies inspired by psychoanalytic thinking. In 1999 the UKCP Psychoanalytic and Psychodynamic Section agreed, with the support of the UKCP, that organisational members of this section should be able to decide for themselves whether their members can use the title 'psychoanalyst' in their work. In 1999 it was decided that the title 'psychoanalyst' would appear by the names of the 62 members who wished to use the title and whose organisations approved its use. In 2000 it was agreed that it should not appear beside the name, but that an asterisk would signify that the person was entitled to use the title 'psychoanalyst'. The issue is still under debate within the UKCP. By 1999, CFAR, the Site for Contemporary Psychoanalysis and the Guild of Psychotherapists were the only trainings who had permitted their graduates to use the title 'psychoanalyst'.

The response from the Institute for Psycho-Analysis has been that the president has written to the chair of the UKCP, as well as the chairs of all the organisations in the PP section. He makes it clear that according to the constitution of the International Psycho-Analytic Association, BP-AS psycho-analysts are not permitted to work with people who call themselves psychoanalysts who have not completed the training approved by the International Psycho-Analytic Association. In view of this, should the title be used, all members and associate members of the BP-AS would have to withdraw their professional contact from these organisations. The president, Donald Campbell, finishes the letter by conveying his concern that this issue could affect the talks planned between the UKCP and the BCP and his hope that splits could be healed in a search for common ground.

Psychodynamic psychotherapy
The title 'psychodynamic psychotherapist' has been widely used to describe anyone making use of psychodynamic or psychoanalytic ideas within psychotherapy. In recent years it has been associated with work in the NHS or with trainings that denote a training therapy of only once-weekly sessions and a less intensive requirement for clinical work with each individual patient.

1.4   Child Analysis/Psychotherapy

With Anna Freud and Melanie Klein arriving in the UK, analytic work with children expanded (see p. 3f.) Wartime offered the chance for the development of work with evacuated and traumatised children developed by both women and by the paediatrician and psychoanalyst Donald Winnicott. The Hampstead Nurseries (p. 5) founded by Anna Freud became the Anna Freud Centre and to this date offers training in child analysis. Its graduates are known as 'child psychotherapists'. The graduates of the Institute for Psycho-Analysis and those who work with children as further training at the Anna Freud Centre are known as 'child psychoanalysts'.

The Association of Child Psychotherapists(ACP) was formed in 1948. There are now six members. (see pp. 39f. and 237f.). A 'child psychotherapist' is trained in one of these six child psychotherapy trainings described in this guide under the standards and auspices of the ACP. The ACP has achieved recognition of the role, training and a pay-scale within the NHS as well as being the body recognised within the UK for registering child psychotherapists who have trained abroad.

It is significant that there is no rivalry with other methods of psychotherapy so the term 'analytic' is dropped. Sometimes the title 'child analyst' is used for those who have trained at the BP-AS and the SAP.

CHILD ANALYSIS AND THERAPY AND STUDIES IN CHILD DEVELOPMENT AND CHILD OBSERVATION

In many ways the key ideas that contribute to child psychotherapy training have already been described. The Anna Freud Centre works mainly within the Contemporary Freudian tradition; the Tavistock, mainly in the Kleinian, neo-Kleinian and object relations traditions; and the Jungian child training is inspired by Fordham's developmental rapprochement with psychoanalysis. Beyond that all the trainings include thinking based on Bowlby's theories of attachment which are taught in almost all the trainings in this guide.

ATTACHMENT THEORY

John Bowlby's pioneering work on attachment theory, largely at the Tavistock Clinic, opened up a whole new perspective on psychoanalysis in a different key. Bowlby reacted against Kleinian preoccupation with inner object relations and phantasies and explored in detail ethological studies of the survival function of attachment behaviour in animals to provide a methodology and framework for analytic studies of attachment (Bowlby 1969), separation (Bowlby 1973) and loss (Bowlby 1980). Freud and Klein had put the issue of attachment and loss on the analytic map by exploring types of attachment (Freud 1914), melancholia and grief

(Freud 1917, Klein 1940), but little had been done to relate it to developmental studies of children's behaviour. This work was taken further at the Tavistock Clinic (p. 17f.) (Bowlby 1977, Robertson and Robertson 1989).

It is significant how many training supervisors, from many theoretical approaches, emphasise the importance of the beginnings and ends of sessions, analytic weeks and terms as well as unexpected analytic breaks (Meltzer 1967). Following Bowlby's advice each offers the chance to re-visit how the patient deals with these experiences of finding and losing a secure base (Bowlby 1988).

Interesting application of this work on attachment can be seen in Marrone's work on groups (Marrone 1998) and the work of the Infant attachment network and PIPPIN in relation to services to families with new babies (see appendix).

INFANT AND CHILD OBSERVATION SEMINARS

At the Tavistock Institute and the other child therapy trainings, as well as many of the adult trainings, child observation seminars have become the norm. The student is asked to visit a mother and child for an hour weekly as an observer, making notes on the child's behaviour and experience and its interaction with the mother. Presenting these notes and discussing them in a small group becomes the task of these seminars.

The experience is one that prepares for the analytic clinical situation in having to sit with powerful feelings without intervening. Seminar leaders use the experience in different ways depending on their orientation. Most use it as a chance to illustrate understandings of primitive infant emotional states and interactions between mother and child. Others include reference to child development research and emphasise the contrasts between the following: the observed infant, the recon-structed child in analytic theory, the observed child in developmental research, and the child in the imagination of the adult patient. Other seminar leaders include an opportunity for participants to explore their own 'counter-transference' response to the whole situation as a resource for developing counter-transference respon-siveness with patients. Many incidents in the process of observation stimulate issues for the student's personal therapy (Miller et al. 1989).

COMPETENT INFANT RESEARCH

Other theories are also relevant to child therapists as well as having some influence on adult psychotherapy trainings. These are the findings about infant behaviour and development researched by child and infant developmental psychologists that explore what is often described as 'Competent Infant Research'. This includes studies on the growth and development of children as competent in seeking for objects and maternal recognition. These studies also explore sensory development and deprivation, the development of sensory cross-referencing, and visual and spatial awareness to which adults regress with concrete thinking (Rey 1979, Hindle and Smith 1999). The tradition of child observation as part of training can cover all these areas and is discussed below under teaching methods (p. 51).

One of the most significant areas of new ground in the field of infant and child analysis and therapy has been the development of Francis Tustin's work in describing work with autistic child patients. This has been carried forward in the Tavistock autism workshop lead by Anne Alvarez and Sue Reid (Alvarez 1992, Alvarez and Reid 1999). Their findings have opened up the possibility of treating children as well as adults whose experience of primitive infant trauma results in wooden or rigid defences which freeze out contact with their own and other's experience of emotion.

1.5 Group Analysis and Group-Analytic Psychotherapy

Perhaps the most pervasive influence in analytic trainings that focuses on social and interpersonal issues is the Group-Analytic movement. Developed by a German psychoanalyst Michael Foulkes, who moved to England before the war, group-analytic training offers an approach that views the personal as social (Foulkes 1964, Brown and Zinkin 1994).

Foulkes was among the pioneers of the therapeutic community movement in the UK and was a psychoanalyst interested in field theory and social systems. After working at the Northfield experiment (Harrison 1999), he enlisted and trained a number of other colleagues, including psychoanalysts, psychiatrists and therapists. In 1969 a group of them founded the Institute for Group Analysis. Details of the Institute and its courses, as well as the regional development of Introductory and block training courses, can be found in Part Two.

Less intensive trainings, that nevertheless use a group-analytic approach, developed at the Westminster Pastoral Foundation initially for individual therapists and later as a group psychotherapy training in its own right. Current trainings in analytic group psychotherapy are described in Part Two, one at the University of London, Goldsmiths', and the Turvey course.

Malcolm Pines and other colleagues have expanded and developed Foulkes' thinking through the Institute for Group-Analysis in London, the Group-analytic Society and the Group-analytic Practice (Roberts and Pines 1991). The Practice is a clinical base for senior practitioners in the field, one of several offering Group Analytic treatment in London (address in appendix).

Group-analytic ideas are widely used in other trainings. A number include an experiential group for trainees on the basis that it offers a chance to experience group dynamics, dealing with multiple transferences and their relevance in other fields; for example, staff groups, organisational consultancy, and so on.

Earlier in this guide the idea was mentioned that analytic work has moved beyond the primacy of insight as a means of therapy. Many people have insights. What matters is how they live in relationships where the feelings and emotions opened up can be lived with insightfully and experienced in relatedness. A group analytic process involves precisely this possibility.

The leader of a group is described as a conductor. This term describes the way that he/she addresses and maintains conscious awareness in the group of boundary issues, the safe and private nature of the setting, the membership of the group and its comings and goings. This is like an orchestral or choral conductor, bringing in voices in the group to illustrate restricting and creative elements. In this context the group can freely associate in such a way that each member's contribution can be an echo or a counterpoint to others.

A group-analytic approach makes it clear that therapy is not through analysis of the group *per se*, nor merely analysis of the individuals in the group, but of both. Interventions that bridge these two foci are the essence of group-analytic work. Such interventions are encouraged by members too as they become self-aware and insightful. It is this that makes it such a good training ground for prospective group-analysts and therapists who then have to negotiate their personal responses with those of others within the development of the group matrix.

The concept of the matrix within the group comprises the total sum of conscious and unconscious relationships, processes and membership that shapes and forms the group and gives to group analysis its unique stance from which to explore the intersection between the 'inner' and 'outer' realities of the group.

Some critics of groups for analysis and therapy suggest that there is no way a group can contain or resolve the deeper psychotic, narcissistic and borderline trans-ferences that have to be addressed by students for the safety of their future patients. Recent clinical writing in group analysis contradicts this view. A telling description of work with these aspects of personality is in a book entitled *Ring of Fire: Primitive Affects and Object Relations in Group Psychotherapy* (Schermer and Pines 1994). A proposition that such destructive forces within a group can be harnessed for therapeutic effect can be found in 'The Anti-Group' (Nitsun 1996).

TITLES

A 'group analyst' is trained at the Institute of Group Analysis (IGA) in London, or at one of its regional centres. The title is distinguished from a 'group analytic psycho-therapist', which describes someone trained at one of the other less intensive group psychotherapy trainings described in this guide. These trainings are inspired by group analytic ideas and often include trainers from the IGA, but differ in terms of volume of group analytic therapy and length of training.

1.6   Psychoanalytic Couple Psychotherapy

The Institute of Marital Studies was begun at the Tavistock in 1948. It was a development of the work of the Family Discussion Bureau, which Enid Balint had helped in developing. The Bureau initiated work with couples and wanted to combine a therapeutic service with research and training.

A psychoanalytic couple or marital psychotherapist is one who is a member of the Society of Psychoanalytical Marital Psychotherapists. These are in the main graduates from the Tavistock Marital Studies Institute (TMSI), as the Institute for Marital Studies was renamed, although others with similar training or background in the work are accepted as affiliated members.

All training analyses engage in the exploration of the unconscious forces and structures in the psyche that shape the choice of partners. Freud's analysis of object choices that are narcissistic (like me) or anaclitic (what he/she does for or to me) underlies the neurotic and sometimes psychotic aspects of intimate relations (Freud 1914). At the Tavistock, Henry Dicks pioneered understanding of three levels of marital interaction: (1) the public shared norms and social perceptions, (2) the personal values, judgements and expectations, and (3) the unconscious transactions (Dicks 1967). Further analysis of unconscious transactions has lead to understanding the unconscious collusion between couples where one projects unwanted emotions and personality traits into the other to destructively idealise or denigrate them.

Training in how to observe, engage with and analyse the complexities of couple symptoms and collusions is described in the Tavistock Marital Studies Institute training and elsewhere (Ruszczynski 1993, Ruszczynski and Fisher 1995).

Other ideas come from systems thinking applied to couples as well as group analytic formulations with Robin Skynner's idea of the object relations contained within a 'marital fit' and the notion of the couple relationship as a matrix that contains regressive projections as well as developmental opportunities (Skynner 1989).

More complex couple interactions involving the seemingly intractable 'grid-locked' (Morgan 1995) relationship between couples with borderline and narcissistic aspects to their personalities are described in *The Uninvited Guest* (Fisher 1999).

1.7   Educational Therapy

The Forum for the Advancement of Educational Therapy and Therapeutic Teaching, founded in 1991, developed out of the work of the educational psychologist Irene Caspari at the Tavistock Clinic. The task of Educational therapy is to work with individuals and groups of children who present difficulties in learning that have a significant emotional component in their aetiology. The method of educational therapy involves both the exploration of emotional factors that inhibit learning or give rise to disruptive behaviour at school as well as developing new ways of offering teaching that is sensitive to the difficulties that children may have.

In offering educational therapy there is awareness of the factors that can adversely affect the development of the capacity to learn: early loss or privation, abusive experience, and social and emotional factors in family life (Caspari 1974).

A number of local education authorities offer posts to educational therapists who are employed in that role in specialist remedial teams or attached to special units. It should be distinguished from Educational Psychology in that educational therapists are experienced teachers who have received specialist clinical training, whereas educational psychologists, whilst having a teaching qualification in addition to a psychology degree, are primarily involved in assessment and consultation work across every area of difficulty.

The training for these posts is described in Part Two of this guide. It draws upon experienced teachers who wish to develop analytic ways of understanding and respond to children who find learning emotionally distressing. The training is described under the section that describes work with children although it is a lot less intense than child psychotherapy training. Nevertheless like all the other trainings in this guide it does require a personal therapy or analysis.

Understandings from educational therapy developed at the Forum may make a fundamental contribution to the understanding of psychotherapy trainees who encounter blocks to their own learning and writing.

1.8 The Development of a Profession: Regulation and Registration

THE CURRENT SITUATION

Currently there are three umbrella organisations that represent training organisations in the field of psycho/analytic psychotherapy in the UK. The longest standing is the Association of Child Psychotherapists (ACP) founded in 1948. In 2000 it had 457 members, of whom 75 are overseas. It is the registering body for all child psychotherapists, as has been described above (p. 26). The United Kindgom Council for Psychotherapy (UKCP) developed out of the UK Standing Conference for Psychotherapy (UKSCP), which had been formed in 1989. It represents many forms of psychotherapy, as has been stated above. In June 2000 there were 4,856 registered members. This included 173 in the Analytical Psychology section, 1,470 in the psychoanalytic and psychodynamic section and 275 in the Psychoanalytically-based therapy with children section. The British Confederation of Psychotherapists (BCP) was formed in 1993. It represents twelve training organisations . It includes the Institute for Psycho-Analysis, the Society for Analytical Psychology and the other training organisations in psychoanalytical psychotherapy who train for more intensive therapy of three weekly sessions or more. In June 2000 it had about 1,355 members.

Each of these umbrella organisations has a register of analysts/therapists who have been accredited by their training organisations. There are about 120 members of both the UKCP and the BCP, who belong to more than one professional psychotherapy organisation, and where the different organisations to which they belong are members of different umbrella organisations. This gives an approximate number of registered psychotherapists in 2000, of 6,211, of whom about 3,153 (about half) work within the psycho/analytic traditions, whose training organisations are described in this guide. The number is increasing each year as more trainees qualify. It is reduced annually by those who die, retire or who are struck off a register for gross professional misconduct.

The first reading of a private member's bill was introduced in Autumn 2000 seeking to establish a statutory register of psychotherapists to make its standards, ethics and practice a matter of law and to ban unlawful use of the title 'psychotherapist'. All three umbrella organisations (ACP, BCP, UKCP) are committed to work together, to see if they can agree its process up to at least a first reading stage. This section of the guide describes some of the key issues and developments in the history of evolving the profession of psychotherapy up to 2000.

DEVELOPMENTS IN THE ORGANISATION AND RECOGNITION OF PSYCHOTHERAPY AS A PROFESSION

The evolution of the UKCP and the BCP

Prompted by the negative experiences some people had had with scientology, the Foster 'Enquiry into the Practice and Effects of Scientology' concluded that the profession of psychotherapy should be controlled by legislation. In 1974 the Institute for Psycho-Analysis convened a meeting with seven psychotherapy organisations and DHSS representatives to discuss a psychotherapy register. In 1975, following the Foster Report (Foster 1971), a committee was set-up known as the Sieghart Committee, named after its chairman. The representatives on that committee were from the British Psycho-Analytical Society, the Society of Analytical Psychology, the Institute of Group Analysis, the British Association for Psychotherapists, the British Association of Behavioural Psychotherapists, the Association of Child Psychotherapists, the Royal College of Psychiatrists, the British Psychological Society and the British Association of Social Workers. Perceiving that there was some conflict amongst psychotherapists (essentially between the analytic and behavioural) the DHSS stated that legislation would not be possible until a coherent picture of psychotherapy could be presented.

This fundamental message was repeated in 1993: 'Before official recognition can be considered we will need to be satisfied that it represents all the major psychotherapeutic approaches' (Pokorny 1995).

A private member's bill had been introduced by Graham Bright MP to regulate the practice of psychotherapy in 1981. This had failed at the second reading due to a technicality, leaving the work on registration still to be done.

It was not until 1982 that interested parties, representing the whole spectrum of psychotherapy, gathered together to discuss the issue of registration and legislation, facilitated by the British Association of Counselling (BAC). Apart from the clear need to form a regulated profession in order to protect the public from abuse, there was real concern about the forthcoming changes due in 1992 concerning European legislation on the interchangeability of professions – European psychotherapists coming to work here and British psychotherapists going to work in Europe. Nobody looked forward to a European Community dictating how psychotherapists should train and practise in this country, nor what kind of qualification, usually medicine or psychology, they should have as a prerequisite to becoming a psychotherapist (as is the case in many European countries).

It was agreed that energy should first of all be directed into forming a conference for psychotherapy that would represent all forms and types of psychotherapy. The issue of registration was for the moment put on hold. This Conference, meeting annually, became known as the Rugby Psychotherapy Conference. The first meeting was held in Rugby under the aegis of the British Association of Counselling (BAC). Seven years and an enormous amount of hard work later, the Rugby Psychotherapy Conference was ready to inaugurate the United Kingdom Standing Conference for Psychotherapy (UKSCP) in January 1989.

In 1984 there were 30 institutions involved in the Rugby Conference, by 1992, 123 delegates representing 68 organisations attended the UKSCP Conference. All the members either represented training organisations or groups of psychotherapists who had formed an association or society.

The first tasks of the UKSCP Council

The Council was strengthened and legitimated by giving a seat to the Tavistock Clinic and the Association of University Teachers in Psychiatry. Agreement was made on a formula for appointing a Registration Board, which would be powerful enough to run a register and could not be interfered with by either Council or the AGM. Conference also agreed that trainings should be at a postgraduate level with content roughly equivalent to a Master's degree, and with a requirement for appropriate personal therapy. Conference asked the Council to produce documents outlining detailed structure and functions of a Registration Board, a Training Committee, an Appeals Committee and an Ethical Committee. By January 1993 the Registration Board and other Committees were to be set up and the Council had been re-named the United Kingdom Council for Psychotherapy (UKCP). So far the Conference has divided itself into eight sections. These sections are a way of qualifying and grouping the types of psychotherapy taught and practised. Each section is responsible for monitoring its member organisations to ensure they meet the standard of training required within that section, before being placed on a register.

In addition the Conference finalised a Master Code of Ethics which each member organisation will have to include within its own ethical code. The register will therefore indicate a measure of the training the therapist has received as well as introducing a concept of a disciplinary procedure for any registered therapist who does not comply with the UKSCP's Code of Ethics (see below p. 36f.).

The current sections of the UKCP are as follows:

- Analytical Psychotherapy
- Behavioural Psychotherapy
- Experiential Constructivist Therapies
- Family, Marital and Sexual Therapy
- Humanistic and Integrative Psychotherapy
- Hypnotherapy
- Psychoanalytic and Psychodynamic
- Psychoanalytical-based Therapy with Children.

This book covers the training organisations that are members of three of these sections: Analytical Psychotherapy, Psychoanalytic and Psychodynamic Psychotherapy and Psychoanalytical-based Therapy with Children. They are the sections containing the largest number of societies, associations and training establishments.

Universities Psychotherapy Association (UPA)

There is one other important member organisation of the UKCP in this guide. The UPA is one of the 'Institutional members' of the UKCP along with the Tavistock Clinic and the Association of University Teachers of Psychiatry. These bodies cover 'psychotherapy organisations whose large size and complexity make it inappropriate for their membership to be confined to any individual section' (UKCP Register 1998).

The UPA accredits University courses in psychotherapy. So far these have been either humanistic or psychodynamic. Member organisations (namely, Courses) of UPA are either affiliated members or accredited members. Accredited members go through a process of accreditation that involves an inspection with two representatives from the UPA and two from the UKCP section that bears the title of the orientation of the course (namely, Psychodynamic or humanistic). The successful courses are then accredited via the section but are members of the UPA and not of that section. The UPA has a representative within each of these two sections in order to liaise.

So far the psychodynamic accredited courses are: Psychodynamic – Sheffield, University, Goldsmiths College, Leeds University.

The affiliated members who are planning psychodynamic accreditation in the next few years are Derby University, Oxford University Centre for Continuing Education, Oxford Brookes University 'The Southern Counties Course', and Lincoln University (see chart pp. 354–8 for details).

University courses that are members of the PP section but not of UPA are Kent, Liverpool and Leicester.

Most of these psychodynamic courses have close affiliations to the NHS. This means that their staff usually have a core professional identity beyond being psychotherapists. Not all the staff of all these courses are within the PP section of UKCP and some do not have UKCP membership at all.

The UPA provides an important grouping for University psychotherapy training. There is through them an increasing recognition of a career pathway in the NHS for Adult psychotherapists. Recently the UPA has made it clear that it is open to accrediting university courses in therapeutic counselling. This seems to open up a way in which courses in counselling can change their title and seek psychotherapy status within UKCP, which will be controversial.

ETHICS, CODES OF PRACTICE AND DISCIPLINARY PROCEDURES

Before going into details of the next stages in the development of professional representation of psychotherapy nationally, it is worth pausing to emphasise the importance of ethical codes of practice. When psychotherapy trainings first established themselves, it was thought generally unnecessary to have codes of ethics. Either a version of professional standards of relationship was thought to exist or medical models were called upon. It was not least under pressure and example of the BAC, that the need for codes of ethics for psychotherapy was first expressed. Each member organisation of the UKCP now has its own ethical code, as do members of the BCP.

Until this was done there were only informal complaints procedures and it was not uncommon for many training organisations in the 1970s and 1980s to be concealing malpractice, exploitation of patients and failure to take up complaints, along with an ethos that discouraged confronting malpractice. What the UKCP has achieved is that ethical guidelines are in place along with complaints procedures in each member organisation. These are backed up by dissatisfied complainants being able to appeal to the UKCP. Members of the UKCP register are also informed about members who have been withdrawn from the register on ethical grounds. All this has come a long way towards establishing the profession as one that is safe in the eyes and experience of both the public and psychotherapists.

A further consequence of these procedures is that there has been a growing body of advice, experience and 'case law' for those who have to go through the painful experience of being involved in a complaint, whether as complainer or accused person. Fiona Palmer Barnes, who has been chair of the ethics committee of the UKCP for some years developed her experience from having held a similar post in the BAC. She has produced a handbook of ethical practice entitled *Complaints, and Grievances in Psychotherapy* (Palmer-Barnes 1998).

This book offers clear and precise definitions, descriptions of complaints and how they can be dealt with by a training organisation. It distinguishes carefully between 'mistakes', 'poor practice', 'negligence' and 'malpractice' (emotional, financial, physical and sexual). It also deals with poor practice by trainers and supervisors as well as with 'protecting the fair name of the profession'. Finally it addresses the range of possible outcomes of a grievance or complaints procedure; from dismissal to warnings, insistence on further supervision and/or therapy or removal from membership of the UKCP register following removal from membership of a member organisation. The book concludes with an appendix containing sample letters to be used in different situations at different stages of a complaint.

Ethical issues are not just limited to clinical practice. The umbrella groups are only just beginning to address the ethics of training particularly around equal opportunities. (See discussion of access to the profession below, p. 55.)

UKCP, BCP AND THE DEBATE OVER STANDARDS AND ASSESSMENT

In March 1992 when the first edition of this book was going to press, four member organisations of the Analytical psychotherapy section (as it was then known) of the UKSCP, announced their intention to resign. These included: the Scottish Institute of Human Relations, the British Psycho-Analytical Society, the Association of Psychoanalytical Psychotherapists in the NHS and the Society of Psycho-Analytical Psychotherapists (Tavistock). They decided to form the British Confederation of Psychotherapists (BCP). They were initially joined by the Association of Child Psychotherapists, the British Association of Psychotherapists, the Lincoln Centre and Institute for Psychotherapy, the Tavistock Clinic and the Society of Analytical Psychology, all of whom remained members of UKSCP. They were also joined by the Scottish Association of Psychoanalytic Psychotherapists who had never been a member of the UKSCP. Since then, the BCP has formed its own ethical guidelines and register of psychotherapists and been active in negotiating with government bodies the possible future registration of psychotherapy in the UK. It has also been joined by the Northern Ireland Association for the Study of Psycho-Analysis (NIASP) (1998), the London Centre for Psychotherapy (LCP 1999) and the North East Association for Training in Psychoanalytic Psychotherapy (NEATPP 2000).

The main issues that lead to this departure focused upon the concern of representatives of these organisations that the UKCP were not willing to recognise varieties of standards within the Analytical psychotherapy section of the UKSCP. These organisations did not believe that they would have sufficient political representation on their own to outweigh the views of others involved in deciding upon this issue.

The issue of standards was twofold. In the first place there were concerns about the lack of recognition of the different standards of those trainings that required of trainees that they see two patients intensively for two years and eighteen months respectively at least at three times a week frequency. In order to be able to do such intensive work these trainings also insist on personal therapy with the same frequency. The second concern was about the need for training therapists and supervisors to be adequately experienced to be on a list of trainers. This involved a minimum of five years' post-qualification experience, and in some trainings even more stringent application process and criteria involving much more clinical experience. Many trainings did not insist on these standards and the future members of the BCP came to believe that the standards statements of individual training organisations (now in the UKCP) was not sufficient to protect the public's interest.

This issue of standards continues to be the significant difference between the two umbrella organisations. The UKCP has denied that there is a significant difference in the work of members of the PP section and that of BCP members. Meanwhile the BCP has attracted members from the UKCP as well as stimulated the interest of trainings that have considered increasing their standards to be able to apply to the BCP.

Members of the BCP had sought to have a section within the UKCP that distinguished the psychoanalytic component rather than being part of a 30-organisation section, which they thought too large and diverse. These organisations had found the widening and inclusive culture of the UKCP created a push for immediate registration with little discrimination between the organisations and their different standards. Certainly for some members of the BP-AS, particularly its representatives, the right of each member organisation to choose its own title did violence to their position of protector in the UK of the title 'psycho-analyst', according to the constitution of the International Psycho-Analytic Association.

Beside this key issue there have been two other points through which the BCP has sought to distinguish its position from the UKCP. One is over the UKCP working with the Lead Body on Advice, Guidance and Counselling, which will be discussed below (see p. 40f.). The other is the rejection of the idea that all UKCP trainings work towards the Accreditation of Prior Experiential Learning (APEL) and the use of Credit Accumulation Transfer System (CATS). These procedures are used increasingly by Higher and Further Education colleges in the UK to foster modular training in a way that the BCP feels undermines the coherence, integrity and containing qualities of complete and better boundaried courses.

In pursuit of clarifying their aims and boundaries, the BCP has come to insist on a single 'umbrella group' membership policy. This has meant that organisations that have been members of both the BCP and the UKCP have been asked to choose between them. The BCP has insisted that this policy is to clarify and distinguish points of principle between the two organisations. Within dual member organisations there has been strong feeling, as many members have wished to belong to both and be on both registers. Voting in the different organisations on this issue has been narrowly won, as many members of these organisations have wanted to continue to be represented in both umbrella organisations and be on both registers. The Lincoln, the Association of Child Psychotherapists, the Society of Analytical Psychology and the British Association of Psychotherapists have had to decide, as have those organisations who have raised their standards of training to BCP levels and have wished to apply to the BCP (London Centre for Psychotherapy and North of England Association for Training in Psychoanalytical Psychotherapy). Other organisations have considered whether they should change their standards and apply to the BCP.

The current position is that both organisations attempt to respect each other's right to exist and represent their members. They are currently working together in pursuing the aim of statutory registration. The tension between them has continued. On the one hand there is an umbrella organisation, the UKCP, that has sought to be all inclusive to push for statutory registration on behalf of *all* psychotherapists. On the other hand, there is a federation of organisations, the BCP, that seeks to differ-entiate training by title, standards and recognition. The negotiations between these bodies who both wish for statutory registration, albeit on different terms, is in progress as this guide goes to press. If and when statutory registration does come in, the character of both organisations will change as their registration tasks, possibly some aspects of their work to establish or protect title will be taken over by a statutory council.

Effects of the BCP single membership policy

One of the consequences of the BCP's stand on single membership has been that those who wished to support both UKCP and BCP and to be on both registers are now unable to do so. This has been one of the factors behind the formation of two new professional psycho/analytic psychotherapy organisations, neither of which support a training. The Forum for Independent Psychotherapists (address in appendix) was formed in 1998. It is a member of the Psychoanalytic and Psycho-dynamic Section of UKCP and has a number of members from Arbours, the BAP, the PA, the LCP and the SAP. The other organisation is the Confederation of Analytical Psychologists. It is a member of the Analytical Psychology section of the UKCP. Members from the BAP, SAP, IGAP and AJA may belong. At present there are about 230 members.

The Position of the Association of Child Psychotherapists (ACP)

The ACP is in a position that is unique in the professional world of psychotherapy. It acts as the umbrella organisations for the six child psychotherapy organisations described in Part Two of this guide. It also has a position to be envied by both the UKCP and the BCP in that it is recognised as the registering body by the NHS for child psychotherapists. It also acts as the validating body for child psychotherapists from Europe who wish to practise in the UK. This means that there is a career structure for child psychotherapists within the Health Service. In addition to that it has high standards of training that are more demanding than those required by the BCP minimum requirement (see p. 237f.).

One issue that the BCP has had to resolve over the single membership policy was the position of the Association of Child Psychotherapists. In upholding its distinctive training standards it was natural that the ACP should be members of the BCP as their training requirements demanded the more intensive personal therapy and clinical requirements. Furthermore the ACP contains the vast majority of child psychotherapists working in and recognised by the NHS. In this they are paralleled by the Association of Psychoanalytic Psychotherapists (APP), also a member of the BCP. Members of the APP work as adult psychotherapists in the NHS and most of them have membership of other organisations registered with the BCP. Here then is the joint platform upon which the BCP argues for high standards in psychoanalytic psychotherapists working in the NHS.

The ACP also has membership of the UKCP, which it did not want to give up as it is the main member of the Child psychotherapy section of the UKCP and hold for the Department of Health a key accrediting role. It has wanted to stay within the UKCP to fulfil this function in relation to other child psychotherapies. In resolving this situation the BCP and the ACP sought the facilitation of an organisational consultant who helped the two bodies sort out the different tasks and functions they performed. The upshot has been that the ACP has withdrawn from the BCP, chosen to remain members of the UKCP; meanwhile the BCP will continue to have a section in its register for ACP members to keep together practitioners who have trained to BCP standards.

UKCP Position on Standards

Within the UKCP it is argued that each training is quite able to represent its own standards for the public to examine when seeking a therapist and that it is inevitable that within its eight sections there is going to be a variety of standards and experience. The 'Analytical psychotherapy' section, at the time when the BCP's formation was being contemplated, renamed itself the 'Psychoanalytic and Psychodynamic Psychotherapy section'. It also agreed in 1999, that its member organisations may use the title 'Psychoanalyst' on the grounds that this title is used by trainings in Europe that have similar requirements to their own, such as thrice-weekly analysis, and that the International Psycho-Analytic Association founded by Freud and represented in the UK by the BP-AS, did not have the monopoly on title, nor in developing Freud's theories and clinical practices. The PP section has always encouraged a variety of standards and depths of training as well as self-determination by its members of their title, course, learning objectives and theoretical base so long as they fell within the PP section framework and its minimum standards of weekly personal therapy throughout training.

Standards and NVQs

In 1996 the UKCP decided to join the government's lead body in Advice, Guidance and Counselling to add the title 'Psychotherapy' and to establish a coherent list of competencies for the practice of all the psychotherapies. This involved articulating minimum standards based on what psychotherapists did. It was to produce a process of qualification, not just a training course based on functional mapping.

The BCP argued strongly against the use of functional mapping as a means of describing what psychotherapists do. There were also deep reservations within the UKCP about competencies being used as a checklist against which competency could be measured without any integration of theory with practice, let alone with experience of personal therapy. The fear was that those who satisfy the examiner might not be able to demonstrate the ability to think clinically when working with a patient (Randall 1995). So much is 'done' through the thoughtful processing of unconscious material as it appears in the patient's material and the process of relating between patient and therapist.

Within the UKCP there was a wish to articulate what different psychotherapies actually trained people to do. The UKCP hoped that employers in the public and voluntary services would be encouraged by a set of criteria that established standards of work in detail. It was not the aim that there should be government standardisation of all trainings.

In 1998 the newly named lead body for Counselling, Advice, Mediation, Psychotherapy, Advocacy and Guidance (CAMPAG) completed its work in mapping competencies for the whole range of psychotherapies. By 1999 a considerable amount of work had been done in articulating standards via distinctive routes for Counselling, Couple Counselling and the different Psychotherapies. Representatives from UKCP were involved in this work in helping to distinguish counselling from psychotherapy.

In 2000 CAMPAG was no longer recognised as the lead body in the field of Psychotherapy. The Department of Education developed a new structure to replace lead bodies. These were to be known as National Training Organisations (NTOs). These NTOs were to be funded by and accountable to the Qualifications Curriculum Authority (QCA). The new NTO for healthcare professions funded by the QCA was to be an organisation called 'Healthwork UK'. Their initial task was to fund mapping exercises within each healthcare profession including psychotherapy.

Many psychotherapists from the UKCP had had profound reservations about the NVQ approach. A key area was the resistance by the mapping facilitators to giving adequate acknowledgement to the way in which different theories of the mind and theories of the therapeutic process shaped competency and therefore standards of work that could be assessed.

The new process under Healthwork UK will begin by differentiating the different models and theories of the mind and of the therapeutic process. This will assist in differentiating the different kinds of psychotherapy and enable standards to be based upon approaches that are much closer to the practice and thinking processes of practitioners. This should help distinguish each of the psychotherapies. It will certainly help clarify the nature of analytic thinking and processing.

For readers who are students or contemplating training, it is of great importance how judgements are to be made about their suitability to train and to move on to clinical work with patients and eventually qualify. The stimulus of the assessment debate has meant that some trainings have begun to clarify the criteria in use in making such judgements. A number do not, using phrases like 'personal and professional readiness' without spelling these out in greater detail (see Part Two). This is part of an ongoing debate about how to articulate standards and how to practice fair assessments within psychotherapy training.

The work of the BCP and the UKCP
In addition to the massive amount of work in ensuring ethical guidelines are in place within the member organisations of BCP and UKCP, the work of these bodies has not been confined only to managing their relations with each other.

Both organisations have external relations committees that deal with the media and the press in relation to public issues or about the psychotherapy field as a whole. They have done much work to clarify the nature of psychotherapy and how it relates to the activities of other bodies, particularly within the mental health field. They have encouraged member organisations in establishing their own networks of information and referral. The UKCP sends out lists of regional therapists from its register database and the BCP has set up a regional initiative for callers wanting contact with someone in their region looking for a therapist (see telephone numbers in appendix). Both are engaged with European organisations seeking to further the recognition of psychotherapy in Europe.

Both organisations have web pages on the internet as do a number of their member organisations. Both have been involved with various government departments in seeking for recognition, resources and possible registration. Both run conferences and lectures and address issues within the profession. Both umbrella organisations have achieved a great deal with a huge amount of freely given labour by their officers.

Tasks and functions of the two organisations

In sorting out the complexities of the interorganisational relationships between the BCP and the UKCP, it is important to bear in mind their different tasks and functions and what each represents. In structure they are very different. The UKCP is a Council that was set up to initiate an umbrella organisation for the whole of psychotherapy in the UK. The BCP is a federation formed out of mutual interest with a different federal structure.

The great achievement in the UKCP has been to initiate and create a focus for the regulation of psychotherapy in the UK. In achieving this they have succeeded in coming to represent all the modes of psychotherapy across the wide range of different practices, theoretical and practical orientations and treatment protocols. They have established a common framework for a code of ethics in each member organisation in the service of protecting the public. They have created an enriching dialogue between the therapies and furthered exchange on professional and clinical issues that could not otherwise have happened. They have significantly moved the issue of statutory registration to the foreground.

Inevitably this has shaped one of the key survival tasks of the UKCP, namely to be able to contain the conflicts between the different psychotherapy orientations.

They failed to do this completely enough for BCP member organisations who have formed a federation with a different task that has recruited a lot of support. The BCP's task has been to represent the interests of those who wanted a boundary around the traditions and practices of the psycho/analytic therapies that demanded longer, more intensive therapy to be able to deal with the yet more disturbed aspects of patients' personalities. This has shaped their survival task, namely to insist that each organisation only belong to BCP as a way of preserving a voice on behalf of their work.

ARGUMENTS FOR AND AGAINST STATUTORY REGISTRATION

The main argument that has been put forward for the statutory registration of psychotherapists has been that it will protect the public. While this is a likely benefit it will not guarantee total protection. Voluntary registration has already begun the process, but clearly not all abusers of professional ethics and practice are discovered and dealt with.

A further consequence of registration is the probability that the profession will gain in resources, recognition and status. The consequences of this gain will be both professional and political. These consequences suggest why the issue is of such importance to current members. There are also concerns that a simple accreditation of all existing types and modalities of psychotherapy will reduce public discrimination in judging between different approaches and that all the psychotherapies and all psychotherapists will be giving each other recognition by association under the one register.

Possible advantages of registration will include: clear minimum standards, increased interest in psychotherapy by psychiatrists, increased recognition and payment of psychotherapy within the NHS, consultation of psychotherapists as a body by government over psychological issues. All of these have been achieved in Austria since statutory registration of psychotherapists in 1990 (Pritz 1998).

Developments in Europe

From the beginning of the UKCP it was clear that the issue of professional recognition had to take into account the views of the European Commission on the movement and mutual recognition of professionals as one aspect of encouraging mobility of labour within the EC. For this reason the UKCP fitted itself into the EC's 'First Directive on the Liberal, Independent and Social professions' in deciding that the profession would have a postgraduate entry with specific entry requirements.

The 'postgraduate' requirement has been interpreted flexibly. Some courses bill their training as 'postgraduate level work'; others have sought affiliation to a university so that an MA degree can be attained for those who do not have a first degree by extending the academic requirements of the course. Other courses include professional training as an appropriate basis for entry claiming that this is equivalent to degree status. There is also the practice of giving access to those with neither profession nor academic backgrounds on condition that their academic work in the form of papers reaches postgraduate standards.

In 1997 the BCP initiated a conference on 'Facts and fantasies about the regulation of Psychotherapy in Europe'. A representative of the EC made clear the position that there is no wish to intervene in the development of each nation's approach to deciding whether to regulate or not regulate the profession and practice of psychotherapy. There are 'General System directives' for the mutual recognition of qualifications between nation states that leave the authority up to the host state of a migrating psychotherapist to deem any possible control or restriction over practice. There is no plan at present to bring psychotherapy as a profession or as a practice within other professions within a harmonising directive. Any organisation that produces a Europe-wide organisation has no authority other than that it secures by its own reputation.

European Psychotherapy Organisations

The UKCP is currently exploring possible viable psychotherapy organisation in Europe. It has regular contact with the European Psychotherapy Association (EAP) from 1991 when it was formed. The EAP has its own journal, the *International Journal of Psychotherapy*. The UKCP has had considerable influence in this development, not least in providing a model of an umbrella organisation across the modalities of psychotherapy that has been useful in the development of similar organisations in other European countries. The EAP developed a European Certificate of Psychotherapy which could be granted to psychotherapy trainings across Europe in different modalities of psychotherapy. The UKCP has established a procedure whereby its training member organisations can apply to have their training recognised for this further European qualification. They became the National Awarding Organisation in the UK (Tantam and Van Deurzen 1998).

This was the position up to the summer of 1999 when UKCP delegates to the EAP became increasingly concerned at the unprofessional management of the EAP and the way they felt it centralised all dealings on a single person. The UKCP has voted to withdraw delegates, support and recognition of the ECP as a qualification. The delegates are now searching to understand what developments are taking place in Europe in each nation and for possible ways towards establishing a trustworthy European focus for psychotherapy (Casement, Chair's report in the *Psychotherapist*, issue 13, Autumn 1999). The work on the European Certificate of Psychotherapy remains as a collaborative resource to be drawn upon within an appropriate European psychotherapy organisation.

The BCP has also been engaged in relation to Europe in that the Association of Psychoanalytic Psychotherapists (APP) in the NHS, which is a BCP member organisation, has membership of the European Federation for Psychoanalytic Psychotherapy in the Public Sector (EFPP). The BCP is jointly represented with the APP. This has produced a rich professional exchange, reassurance that there is no plan for an EC-wide organisation (such as the EAP) becoming the only recognised psychotherapy umbrella, a series of annual international conferences and a book series that draws on international clinical experience. The EFPP runs annual conferences on the theme of psychoanalytic psychotherapy in the public sector, and has its own book series on this theme with Europe-wide contributions (Martindale et al. 1997, Pestalozzi et al. 1998).

Voices against statutory registration within psychotherapy

Within the analytic world there are few voices against seeking statutory registration other than the reservation of those who feel uncertain about being on the same register as those with different standards and approaches to the work. There is the occasional complaint against the fear of state involvement that might demand more bureaucratic procedures such as has happened in dentistry or general medicine, but that involves management procedures and complex methods of payment within the NHS.

Beyond the analytic world and beyond the debates within BCP and UKCP, there are voices against statutory registration for psychotherapy. Most of the critiques are based upon an analysis of power that seeks to capitalise on the economic, status and territorial dominance of professions as a minority group who can control other practitioners as well as exploit patients as helpless members of the public. This attempts to deny, so proponents argue, the fundamental ethical commitment of psychotherapy to encouraging power within people and the collaborative power of working with people rather than having power over people in their vulnerable psychological state of needing help.

These views suggest that registration will trap knowledge about the human condition within a closed economic and social elite who exploit knowledge and uniqueness for gain (Mowbray 1995, Postle 1995).

The same critique might be made of any of the professions offering a service. Psychotherapists should be aware of some of the self perpetuating aspects of their own work discussed in section below in the introduction to Part Two (p. 55f.).

Statutory registration of psychotherapy in the UK: the situation in 2000

The current situation within the UK is that the UKCP has made some recent moves to re-initiate the statutory registration of psychotherapists. Three routes are being explored:

1. The first is another attempt at a private member's bill to be introduced to the House of Lords by Lord Alderdice. This is supported by Lord Clinton-Davies who has gathered an all-party working group of peers to steer it through the house. This bill would set up a Psychotherapy Council composed initially of those organisations with an interest in the field. After three years they would be elected by members of the register. Those who could prove that they had been in psycho-therapy practice for three out of the past five years would be eligible to be on the register. There would be four Committees: Education, Health, Professional Conduct and Ethics.

The UKCP and the BCP are collaborating with Lord Alderdice in seeing the bill through its first reading in the House of Lords. Although it will probably fail to reach the second or third reading required by statute, it will put a framework for such legislation on the map and establish precedents for demonstrating cooperation between the interested parties. These also included the ACP, the APP, the BP-AS, the British Psychological Society, the Royal College of Psychiatrists and the Tavistock Clinic. This process will also offer the chance of difficulties being ironed out through the committee stages of the bill.

2. The second possibility is through the Council for Professions Supplementary to Medicine (CPSM). At present nine professions belong to this body, including the arts therapies, physiotherapists, optometrists and chiropractors. There is room for twelve. The disadvantage of this process is that it will take time for legislation to be passed to include psychotherapy as a profession and that it will involve a single body or college being ready to represent the profession as a whole.

Lord Alderdice has suggested that this might be a less beneficial way of proceeding because many practitioners of psychotherapy work privately and not in the NHS.

3. A third possibility is available without new legislation. The new Health Bill went through the House of Lords and reached Royal Assent in the summer of 2000. This is the Bill the Labour government has conceived to do away with GP fundholding and which aims to integrate the NHS as 'A First Class Service', based on the government's papers such as 'Modernising Mental Health Services'. This framework seeks evidence-based standards for service and seeks from profes-sional and national training bodies programmes to develop 'lifelong learning and reflective practice'. There is a much debated section of this bill in which the independence of recognised professions, including medicine, are recognised as self-regulating in producing registers of competent trained and recognised prac-titioners, able to claim title, competence and conditions of entry for their own profession in relation to the public. Establishment of such professions can be by orders in council as it will be the Privy Council and not Parliament that will have the authority to legislate about such matters.

This means that there is space within this bill for the statutory registration of psychotherapists to take place without further legislation. The disadvantage will be in the time required to initiate the Orders in Council required. The Clinical Psychologists are first in the queue. They are intent on creating a 'Psychologists Registration Council'. This might be possible by Easter 2001.

A similar registration body would be required by Psychotherapists. This is crucial. At present GPs can only refer to professions who have state registration or else they carry the burden of responsibility for the treatment. This restricts referrals. Statutory registration of psychotherapists would enable such referrals to take place and be funded within the NHS. This of course begs the question of funding for psychotherapy within other mental health services, but a first step needs to be the recognition of adult psychotherapy as a registered profession for such referrals to take place. Child psychotherapy is already recognised and registered in the NHS through the ACP and has been for the past 50 years.

PART TWO: THE TRAININGS

2.1 Introduction to the Format of the Course Entries

THE FORMAT AND METHODOLOGY

Each training was invited to use a common format in describing their course. The first four sections comprise headings addressed to the training committee. The first edition of the guide had involved the author (Jan Abram) interviewing 26 groups of trainees and their respective training committees. In this edition, the chair of each of the 48 training committees was contacted and asked to provide an entry for this guide under the four headings described above. The format has been arranged to cover as many aspects of the training as possible, including those which are not normally covered in a prospectus or brochure. In some cases this work was delegated to one or two individuals; in others the whole committee had an input.

Each training was also asked for the name of a trainee representative who could be contacted to put together a trainee response for the guide. Trainee representatives of the course provided comments for the fifth section. Some kept responses within the questions. Others used the questions as a stimulus and responded with their own framework and style. In some cases the trainees collecting responses were representatives of a standing trainee organisation. In other cases the training committee chose whom to contact.

Each trainee representative was invited to form a single one-off meeting with four to six representatives from across years and views and to record the views of that meeting, within the framework and under the headings described above. Not all were able to do this, given a variety of constraints of deadlines, geographical spread of colleagues or the structure of organisations. Some used the phone, e-mail or post to gather views. Some turned the exercise into a concerted piece of research and development, contacting every current trainee in the organisation. In many cases the methods used by the representatives reflected the stage of development of a formal trainee organisation and system of representation and feedback to the training committee.

The entries for this part of the guide were collected between May 1999 and April 2000. A list of the contributors who wished their names to appear is on pages x–xi.

These descriptions are the authorship of and responsibility of the training committee of that particular training and the trainee representative(s).

In the Author's Comments the attempt has been to summarise reflections and questions on each particular training: to open doors rather than to close them and to reflect on some of the issues raised in the guide.

MODELS OF ANALYTIC EDUCATION

Within the analytic world there is some debate about the philosophy of education that is being applied in different courses and about what approach is most helpful. You do not have to be an educationist to know that people learn differently. All have learning difficulties and learning strengths. Some are better at learning from books with detailed and complex ideas; others feel they can only learn by discussion and concepts being made alive through example, narrative or their own experience. Analytic trainings tend to include many styles of learning, thereby exposing trainees to both their strengths and their weaknesses. In their own therapies as well as in the course group and tutorials they can explore these issues and the way they interrelate with aspects of their own personality and capacity to be creative.

There has been some debate about the way in which an analytic education can offer a limiting and authority based vision of analytic education by restricting the responsiveness of trainees who bring their own expressiveness, curiosity and responsiveness to learning experiences (Symington 1996). (See the rationale for the Cambridge course below p. 105f.). Kernberg, for instance produces a list of 'Thirty Methods to Destroy the Creativity of Psychoanalytic Candidates' (Kernberg 1996).

There is also debate about different models or philosophies of educational institution that shape different analytic trainings. Kernberg describes four competing models (Kernberg 1986): the Art Academy, the Technical or Trade School, the Religious Seminary and the Graduate University Department. He wants to go for an approach that is open about its philosophy, its criteria for assessment and its encouragement of critical research shaped by the student (Kernberg 1986).

The idea in the Apprenticeship model describes much of what happens in UK analytic education. It is not the slavish indoctrination into a method or approach. Its essence seems to lie in the ability of the 'master-craftsman', having shown the apprentice some of what there is in the tradition, to allow the apprentice to use his or her own hunger and curiosity to shape the search for what can work and what can make sense.

An apprenticeship involves serving time in mastering a complex discipline. What is internalised is not a literal list of rules and theories with which to approach the work. Instead it is the capacity of an observer to understand, feel into and think about the complexity of communications in the analytic setting within whatever limits of personality, framework or experience that person has.

TEACHING METHODS

Within the section that describes the theoretical orientation and curriculum a number of different teaching methods are referred to. The following teaching methods are used across the trainings, each with its own rationale and emphasis.

Theoretical lectures
The lecture provides the opportunity for inspiration. Its aim is to be the presentation of coherent thought argued and explained by a well seasoned clinical practitioner who can make theory come alive with illustration and understanding of how the work of key theoretical thinkers can be applied in the analytic setting.

When well done, it can bring alive the ideas and writing of the analytic pioneers, related to clinical practice.

Clinical seminars

Clinical seminars focus on presentation by the students in turn, of their work with patients, in a way that provides an overview of a case and how it is developing. Encouragement and insight can flow when the seminar is run in such a way that supportiveness does not lead to cosiness and challenge does not lead to persecution.

Reading seminars

Reading seminars allow students to present their own interpretation and experience of authors. The discussion allows for internalisation and clarification of complex ideas often learned by speaking them. The value of these experiences of learning is underlined by the number of qualified therapists and analysts who continue to belong to reading groups.

Infant and child observation seminars (see pp. 27–8)

At the Tavistock Institute and the other child therapy trainings, as well as many of the adult trainings, a child observation seminar has become the norm. The student is asked to visit a mother and child for an hour weekly as an observer, making notes on the child's behaviour and experience and his or her interaction with the mother. Presenting these notes and discussing them in a small group becomes the task of these seminars.

The experience is one that prepares for the analytic clinical situation in having to sit with powerful feelings without intervening. Seminar leaders use the experience in different ways depending on their orientation. Most use it as a chance to illustrate understandings of primitive infant emotional states and interactions between mother and child. Others include reference to child development research and emphasise the contrasts between the following: the observed infant, the reconstructed child in analytic theory, the observed child in developmental research, and the child in the imagination of the adult patient. Other seminar leaders include an opportunity for participants to explore their own 'counter-transference' response to the whole situation as a resource for developing counter-transference responsiveness with patients. Many incidents in the process of observation stimulate issues for the trainee's personal therapy (Miller et al. 1989).

Tutorials

The importance given to tutorials varies between the trainings and among tutors and tutees. Getting a good fit can make all the difference. Some tutors will be able to help with writing blocks, some with explaining theoretical or clinical issues that a tutee is struggling with. Others will be able to have an overview of issues and developments in the tutee's learning without turning it into therapy or supervision. Colleague therapists-in-training also provide each other with what can be the beginnings of life-long peer tutorial and supervisory relationships.

Experiential groups

The inclusion of experiential groups on training courses has been partly inspired by the idea that trainees have to be able to deal with staff groups, networks of referrals as well as their own colleagues in the group situation. Groups also stimulate experiences of emotional relatedness that individual therapy can overlook. Groups often throw up personal issues as well as offering a container for interpersonal issues that otherwise might inhibit seminar and collaborative work on a course. Many courses employ group analysts to run these groups thus ensuring a measure of professional competence in the leaders.

However, these groups can be problematic. They are not always easy experiences as the group sets the agenda not the leader and because the group is an open system in the sense that it is not a stranger group like a patient group is. The crossover of members in different learning contexts punctuates boundaries of confidentiality so that already people know and like or dislike each other. This means that the group leader will need to be able to deal with the competition, rivalry, envy and uncertainty within the trainee group, over issues like 'who is doing well?' and 'who is more in touch and sensitive?'. To have a containing experience of such processes can do a lot for integrating learning as well as for future containing capacity of the membership of an analytic society. However, when the experience is not contained it may be felt to be as undermining to both individuals and the wider learning community.

HEADINGS GIVEN TO THE TRAINING COMMITTEES

Title and contact information
1. History of the organisation
2. Theoretical orientation and curriculum
   Mention if there is an introductory or pre-clinical course
3. Training structure
   3.1 Training committee
   3.2 Selection procedure and admission
        Include criteria for admission. What equal opportunities policy do you have for admissions and during the training?
   3.3 Time commitment per week and length of training
        Mention policy for post-curricular trainees
   3.4 Financial cost of training at different stages
   3.5 Interruptions in training
        What is permissible? For example, illness, pregnancy, other
   3.6 Graduating and beginning a career
        Postgraduate qualification and learned society – what opportunities are there for involvement in the organisation?
        What do you expect your graduates to be doing five years after graduation?
   3.7 Numbers of students per intake
4. Clinical and academic requirements
   4.1 Personal therapy
   4.2 Clinical requirements
        What help is there with referring training patients?
   4.3 Supervision
   4.4 Written work and course attendance
   4.5 Assessment, standards and ethical requirements
        What are the assessment procedures?
        What criteria for assessment are used?

5. Trainee response: readings given to trainees –
   1. Why this course was chosen
      1.1. What made people decide to train?
      1.2 What were the aspects of this course that were most attractive?
      1.3 What was your experience of the selection procedure?
      1.4 Before the start of the course, how informed did you feel about each stage of the training?
   2. The atmosphere of the course
      2.1 How do you feel about the way in which information is communicated?
      2.2 What do you find the most confusing aspect of the training?
      2.3 How much opportunity do you have to share thoughts and feelings with fellow trainees?
      2.4 What do you feel about the methods of teaching?
      2.5 What did you think about the way assessments were done to allow you to progress to the next stages of training?
      2.6 Has the course met your expectations?
      2.7 How do you feel about your future with the organisation?
      2.8 What plans do trainees have for future practice and possible balance of different sorts of work in their career?

TITLE AND CONTACT INFORMATION

Some trainings have a different organisation for their graduate or learned society. It may be the name of the organisation that originally formed and developed a training as a later activity. It may be the name of the society of a course's graduates. The first named is the training organisation.

After the title is included the abbreviation by which the training organisation is referred to in the text and its membership of the BCP or the UKCP, together with the section initials for the UKCP. (APS = Analytical Psychology section, PP = Psychoanalytical Psychotherapy section, PTCS = Psychoanalytically-based Therapy with Children section, UPA = Universities Psychotherapy Association).

1. HISTORY

This describes how the organisation came into being, its aims and objectives and how they have developed to date. Some organisations have chosen to go into more detail than others. Readers may like to cross-reference the history sections of each training with the section in Part One that describes the evolution of the trainings.

2. THEORETICAL ORIENTATION AND CURRICULUM

This heading in the format of responses from the trainings is in some way inextricable from their history. Some outline of the founders and their approach is described in the History responses, some in this section. The entries describe the philosophy, theory and practice of the psychotherapy taught on each specific course.

Those seeking to understand the wider canvas of theories and their origins are referred to Part One of this guide where the basic ideas of different theories are outlined along with an account of how they emerged out of and alongside others.

In choosing a course, one of the key issues is to understand how controversies between different schools of thought might be dealt with on a particular course. This leads to questions about possible incompatibilities of thought and practice in work with patients. It also leads to issues about how much time the course provides for integrating divergent theories and practices in a discriminating way. In the Author's Comments twin concerns are expressed. One is where courses attempt such a wide range of theories that it may be that trainees do not have the space, time and support to integrate them into theories of practice that support clinical interventions. This applies to the pluralist and eclectic trainings. The other is where the courses focus on a narrow band of theory without being open to criticisms that trainees might need encouragement to engage with from other sources.

3. TRAINING STRUCTURE

3.1 Training committee

The tasks of the Training Committee have already been described, although a few organisations use a different title. In most of the longer-standing trainings a democratic process is in place and members of the various committees are elected by the organisation's membership. Some training organisations are oligarchies, where the membership of the Association has no vote and no channel to contribute to the decision-making.

3.2 Selection procedure and admission

Each organisation has a specific entry procedure with requirements, like an age limit and academic qualifications.

What sorts of people are able to train to do this work?
The cost of training and the time required to do it makes huge demands upon those who consider training. This inevitably restricts access to the profession for many who may be suitable. However, their life experience, class, racial, geographical and cultural background could enable them to attune to people from a wider section of the population and so widen psychotherapy services.

Despite all this there are many from less advantaged backgrounds who train and there are some trainings that encourage them by giving not just access but consideration and differentiated support. There are a few trainees from the above groups whose determination to find the needed resources overcomes the difficulties. This may be seen as a testimony to their courage and aspirations, which needs to be understood and supported by trainers and tutors.

The age at which people train is a personal issue and yet one shaped by social and economic factors, about which there are no current statistics. For example, many psychotherapy trainings in this book appear to be populated by people in their forties and fifties who are seeking a second career, building on their first one in one of the helping professions and/or returning to paid work after having responsibility for young children. In the current social and economic climate this means that most of them are women. The increased demands of the trainings suggest that one solution is to be single or benefit from being well supported by others. In the light of this it is striking how many people train by making sacrifices that strain their own resources and those of their families.

Significantly it is the child psychotherapy trainings that attract people in their twenties and thirties looking to establish themselves in this particular field of work in the public services. The lack of such a route for adult psychotherapists seems to skew the age of the intake, as there is no clear route for someone becoming a breadwinner through a slowly developing private practice.

Training in psychoanalysis would seem to be more populated by academics and professional people in medicine with more balance between numbers of men and women. There may be more who are able to use their current professional position for time or funds to support their training.

It has been suggested that the emphasis on training being a postgraduate as well as a second professional qualification has meant that many analysts and therapists have a primary commitment to a previous professional identity (Johns 2000). This means that they begin their analytic training later in life in a way that foreshortens their analytic career and makes for older membership of analytic societies. Only a few who embark early on analytic training can benefit from longer careers and provide a longer commitment to the profession.

Access to analytic training: equal opportunities, institutional prejudice and homosexuality

Within the UKCP debate about equal opportunities issues has provoked the proposal that the following statement be included within the UKCP Code of Ethics to be implemented by each member training organisation:

> Teachers will not withhold training opportunities either at selection or subse-
> quently on grounds of prejudice including such grounds as gender, race, culture,
> class, sexuality, religion or other personal differences unrelated to competence to
> practise psychotherapy.

Likewise the majority of BCP member organisations are committed to equality of opportunity at the point of access to their training.

The area of equal opportunities takes the issue of access further into the realm of fairness and social justice. What is at stake is the ability of the profession to train therapists and analysts from a wider cross-section of society in order to be able to develop services and practices attuned to people with a wider range of values, backgrounds and cultural and racial origins.

Nafsiyat (address in appendix), a psychotherapy service for people from many ethnic backgrounds, has for a number of years offered not only an analytic therapy service sensitive to cultural and racial issues, but also training in intercultural therapy where the members of the therapeutic pair or group come from different cultures. Their service to clients of many cultures is supported by a service to therapists in opening up their own prejudices and in examining the important language and cultural differences in family norms and dynamics, child-rearing practices and mental health issues. They provide a valuable resource for trainings that wish to address these issues.

Sexual orientation

Within the analytic world there has been a reappraisal of the issue of sexual orientation. Traditionally, psychoanalysis saw homosexuality as pathology. In 1910 Freud delineated different sorts of homosexuality (at that time known as inversion) (Freud 1905). Some sorts of homosexuality were seen to be more treatable than others, but the general view of the psychoanalytic world was that a homosexual should not become a psychoanalyst or psychotherapist. This implied that homosexuality equalled pathology and as such it would interfere with the practitioner's ability to work effectively. This has meant historically that homosexuals have been precluded from psychotherapy training establishments. The issue of homosexuality is one of great controversy amongst psychoanalysts and psychotherapists world-wide.

In an informal enquiry among current psychotherapy trainees, only one in seven felt that the issue was being addressed thoroughly on their course, suggesting how the issues may be avoided in many current trainings (Leeburn 1999, private communication). In 1979, Meltzer, a Kleinian psychoanalyst, suggested that homosexuality be removed as a diagnostic and pathological framework (Meltzer 1979). In summarising the debate over homosexuality, Mendoza suggests that there is now acknowledgement that the Oedipus complex involves same sex as well as other sex identifications and attachments of an erotic nature, as Freud had outlined. The same point is made by West (1999, private communication), who suggests that post-Jungians have discovered both the animus and the anima archetypes in both sexes in a way that makes the opposite sexual compensation a redundant idea. Mendoza suggests that Meltzer is saying that it is no longer possible to distinguish homosexuality as perverse in the sense of needing 'to control the object out of fear or to punish it sadistically in a retaliatory and envious way'(Mendoza 1997, p. 386).

The majority of trainings discussed in this book say they would not exclude an applicant solely on the grounds of homosexuality. But it is true to say that there are some analytic trainings which contain a divided opinion in their membership as to an applicant's suitability to train, consequently conveying a confused and confusing stance (Ellis 1994).

3.3 Time commitment per week and length of training

Not all trainings can provide an exact guide to how many hours a week must be available to train, because it depends upon which stage of training a trainee has reached. However, in general, an estimated 15–25 hours per week is the sort of contact time commitment required, meaning time spent with colleagues, teachers, patients and supervisors. In some cases this may be less; in others, more.

These issues are important to the applicant who is trying to discover what the demands of a particular training will be at different stages and how it might fit with existing commitments. Both the course entries and often comments by trainees indicate what is expected in different organisations.

There is also the issue of travel. Within London, travel to and from a session or a seminar can take an hour. Those who live outside London but who are training in London need to at least double that time. This may involve 3–6 hours per analytic session, which creates long hours and demands a strong stamina to endure whether on the roads, or by public transport. The logistics and access to means of easy transport as well as the funds to pay for them are also important.

3.4 Financial cost of training at different stages

Training is an expensive business and it is important for the trainee to gauge the extent of the cost throughout and beyond training. Training fees do not cover individual therapy and supervision, except where mentioned.

How much does it cost to be in analysis or therapy?

In their recent leaflet entitled 'Psychoanalytic Psychotherapy', the British Confederation of Psychotherapists suggests that 'Prospective patients in the UK might expect to find fees per session for private treatment to be within the range of £30 to £45.' Possibly the range within the UKCP is lower and wider, perhaps £25–40. Outside London, fees are sometimes lower, but not necessarily so. Regional counsellors can sometimes charge as much as London analysts. The Institute for Psycho-Analysis in writing to prospective applicants suggests that the fee is 'usually between £25 and £50 per 50 minute session depending on the circumstances of the student'. If there is an average of £38 for each of three sessions per week over a 42-week analytic year, the annual cost will be £4,788. If the fee is £35, five times weekly, the cost over the same year will be £7,350 annually.

Just as some practitioners charge lower fees there are some who charge higher. Those who have a psychiatric training are used to charging £80–120 for private fees, particularly when paid for by an insurance company. Some analysts use this model as a basis for their fee structure and command the exclusiveness of the clientele who can afford such fees four or five times per week. Some suggest that £38 is charged by a number of experienced analysts for five sessions per week. Others charge more (1999–2000).

Within both the BCP and the UKCP, there are analysts and psychotherapists whose range of fees is wider than the figures above suggest. Many take on a small number of low-fee patients for £10–15 per session or less akin to the fees paid to trainees when they are referred training patients through clinics of training. Within the SAP and among many other practitioners there is the tradition that analysts are expected to take one clinic patient into analysis, who pays no fee.

There is a variety of practice among analysts and therapists about fixing their fees. Some have a fixed fee and make no allowance for the circumstances of the patient, whether training or not. Many have a scale of fees within which they negotiate with their patient. Some have no range, but a single higher and a single lower fee.

If the circumstances of the patient change during the course of an analysis or therapy both parties have a dilemma. This can happen to a trainee as much as to any other patient, and for a trainee, continuing in therapy will be a condition of the course which cannot be interrupted if the trainee is seeing patients under supervision. Continuing the work may be impossible at that fee for the patient. Lowering the fee may be impossible for the therapist. Some training institutes have a clinic fund to assist with this problem and support the patient with fees for a limited period. With job uncertainties, redundancies and 'downsizing' in organisations this is a real possibility that needs to be thought about, although transference issues need to be addressed.

3.5 Interruptions in training

Some trainings would not expect a trainee to take any time out, whilst others may encourage an interruption when more personal therapy is seen to be needed, or when personal health or circumstances take priority. Pregnancy is accommodated in all trainings.

3.6 Graduating and beginning a career

Postgraduate qualification and learned society – what opportunities are there for involvement in the organisation?
An essential element in the newly qualified therapist's professional life is a place to share the demands of clinical work. What can qualified trainees expect from the organisation with whom they have trained?

What do you expect your graduates to be doing five years after graduation?
Most trainings will include seminars and workshops on setting up in practice, although not all trainees wish to set up in full-time private practice. They also provide in many cases ongoing seminars post-curriculum and/or post-qualification. This is increasingly important where students finish the curricular aspect of the course, but have not completed their clinical or their written requirements. Teaching and supervision are areas that many therapists will be doing after several years of experience. It is worth noting what opportunities are available in each organisation.

What can an analyst or therapist expect to earn?
Those who work in GP practices as counsellors or psychotherapists are often paid on a scale that makes their hourly fee as low as £15 per hour. Other professions have an existing salary as psychiatrists, clinical psychologists or nurses, who are able to offer psychotherapy sessions within the NHS in their original profession. The same is true for those in statutory or voluntary social services, such as in day centres, residential units or the NSPCC. There is no salary for adult psychotherapists. Child psychotherapists are recognised in the NHS. Their salary scale is £16,500–40,666. Qualified child psychotherapists begin above the bottom of this scale. There are some trainee posts at £14,270–17,301 (1997 figures).

From the figures above it is possible to work out how much it might be possible to earn as an analyst or psychotherapist. Working for 30–40 hours per week with an average fee of £32 per hour, earnings amount to £40–54,000 gross of taxes and professional expenses. It should be remembered that ongoing professional expenses can be significant with continuing supervision, further therapy, room hire or use, and could take 15–30 per cent or more of an income, albeit these are expenses that can reduce the tax bill. Based on these figures it is difficult for a psychotherapist to earn more than a senior social worker, clinical psychologist or teacher. This could result in a full-time income of £32–48,000.

Clearly, a newly qualified person will take some time to build up a private practice depending on what access they have to good and regular sources of referral. It is not surprising then that many psychotherapists have other forms of employment that may or may not make use of their analytic training. These may include teaching, consultancy or something related to a former employment. If there is the flexibility, these 'portfolio careers', as they have come to be called, can provide some accommodation depending upon how much clinical work is available.

In the majority of organisations, trainees are expected to see training patients for a low fee. The newly qualified therapist will very often continue to see patients for a low fee. This brings in a limited amount of income to cover expenses. Some organisations will have consulting rooms available for hire. Occasionally there are bursaries or loans.

3.7 Numbers of students per intake

Some trainings take only a small number each year. Others postpone a year's intake until there is a viable group. This flexibility is becoming an important feature of trainings, as there is more competition to recruit good trainees. This section should provide some clues about the importance of the group of students. Some trainings provide group and seminar experience that crosses years, others keep the year groups distinct and separate. The general answers to these questions in this guide may not provide specific information about the particular year when a student applies.

4. CLINICAL AND ACADEMIC REQUIREMENTS

4.1 Personal therapy

Requirements of trainings for personal therapy
As has already been stated, the emphasis of every training therapy is on the trainee's psychological growth and personal process – reflecting the point of view that therapists must be aware of their own unconscious and their own pathology.

The purpose of this requirement is stated differently by each training. However, its general purpose is twofold. First, there is the opportunity for the prospective trainee to experience the analytic relationship at first hand as a way of ensuring it is work they want to undertake. Second, there is a chance to begin to explore the sensitivities and pathologies that have bought a person to seek analytic training in the first place. The principle is that nobody should, as a psychotherapist, put a patient through a process that they themselves have not been through.

From the point of view of the trainings this also provides some safeguards in that there is a vehicle for protecting the training from candidates who may have passed an interview and who yet may not be suitable for the work. Many of the trainings invite reports from training analysts at specific points during the training to confirm that they have no reservations about the candidate pursuing the course. Usually these happen at three points: when the trainee is about to embark on the course, when they are about to receive their first training patient and embark on therapeutic work under supervision and when the requirements of the course have been completed prior to final qualification.

This provides a safeguard for organisations against the psychological damage that might be done to future generations of patients by the limitations of their trainees. It can also be seen as part of an ethical requirement found in all analytic institutions that confidentiality could be broken when a patient may be at risk of doing danger to themselves or to others. In this case the others are the patients the trainee will be permitted to treat if their own therapy has not sufficiently resolved personal pathologies.

This reporting element in a training therapy marks it out as different from other therapies as boundaries of confidentiality are different. It is common practice nevertheless for training therapists to be discreet about the information divulged and to give no more than their view to the training committee, without personal details that could harm the confidentiality of the existing therapeutic relationship.

This process is not always straightforward. Some trainings and some training therapists feel that a reporting analysis is inappropriate. Where there is reporting the trainee depends upon the integrity of the training therapist to be professional and non-partisan.

Most training organisations endeavour to protect trainees from these experiences by vetting their training therapists with care and if need be, to challenge existing analytic relationships if the psychotherapist is not recognised as having the necessary experience or professional skills and attitudes. In these situations aspiring trainees have to consider carefully whether they need to find a different therapist who *is* recognised, which may be a difficult and painful decision.

For most of the analytic trainings a frequency of two to three times weekly is a requirement, and sometimes before starting the training. The personal therapy of the analytic trainee will usually last for years and, more often than not, beyond qualification. In the majority of cases this will be conducted with the same therapist. The Institute of Psycho-Analysis requires five weekly sessions; the Society for Analytical Psychology, four; and most of the BCP member organisations have trainees regularly in four or five weekly sessions even though some only require a minimum of three. There is a generally accepted rule of thumb that future clinical work should not be at a greater intensity than the therapist's own personal therapy.

There is a difference of opinion amongst the trainings as to whether or not members of the Training Committee should also be training therapists or supervisors for trainees. This issue is linked with boundaries and confidentiality, as trainees are exposed to limited choice and to being judged for suitability by their therapist. It also has to do with the size and history of the organisation. Regional trainings for example may only have a few experienced analysts and therapists to draw upon and they may additionally make up the committee.

One of the key issues about standards is the requirement of trainees to choose a training therapist/analyst from their accredited list. Where there are specific restrictions these are mentioned in the text from the trainings. Many but not all the trainings insist on five years' post-qualifying experience before a person becomes a training therapist or supervisor. Others have more stringent requirements.

Where there is no requirement for the standards of training and experience of the training therapist, the training trusts the trainee to choose someone who will be sufficiently challenging. On the other hand, the trainee may not have important aspects of their experience analysed to the cost of their own development and in a way that exposes fellow trainees with seeing difficulties that are not being addressed. These standards and requirements then also protect the whole course as they insist that all trainees are working at a similar depth.

4.2 Clinical and academic requirements

Depending on the applicant's previous experience some organisations will require their trainees to complete a psychiatric placement. This often involves half a day weekly for six months as an observer in a psychiatric unit.

In order to qualify for any training, the trainee will have to have seen a certain number of patients/clients, or have worked a specified number of clinical hours. The general rule is that the trainee must have seen at least two training patients for a required amount of time.

For organisations that are a part of the UKCP PP section, the minimum requirement is two patients each seen once weekly over eighteen months, with weekly supervision for each.

The BCP has a minimum requirement of two patients seen three times weekly over two years and eighteen months respectively, each under weekly supervision.

'Medical cover' is required by some trainings. This means that a medical practitioner (usually the patient's GP) has agreed to liaise with the psychotherapist about the welfare of the patient if medical intervention is necessary. Sometimes trainings will provide a psychiatrist who is analytically trained to provide consultation for a patient if the trainee and supervisor think it necessary. Malpractice insurance is a necessity now for every trainee and practitioner.

Referrals

This is very frequently an area of much concern and anxiety for trainees, because their future qualification depends on keeping patients/clients in therapy for a certain amount of time. The range of patients referred is also of some importance. Many training organisations offer a low-fee scheme, matching patients with restricted resources with trainees seeking clinical experience for their course. For the patients this is often a very good source of psychotherapy that might be otherwise impossible. Its quality is often excellent because of the previous experience and maturity of the trainee and the support of an experienced supervisor.

Most training organisations aim to provide their trainees with training patients who are not as disturbed as a borderline or psychotic patient. This is not always possible. Experienced practitioners acknowedge that it is very difficult to assess borderline conditions in a one-interview assessment.

Beyond qualification therapists need good sources of referrals, depending on how large a practice is desired. They are dependent upon their own networks, their contacts and their reputation for being professional, available and reliable.

4.3 Supervision

Supervision is seen by all trainings as a crucial aspect of training (see Figure 1.3.1, p. 15). What form the supervision takes, group or individual, will depend on the attitude adopted by each organisation.

The central tradition in psycho/analytic supervision is upon a detailed process record of a session by the therapist. Often a key element is in exploring the analytic setting and noticing the way the patient relates to and uses the beginnings and endings of sessions, weeks and terms of therapy. Any changes to the therapeutic frame are crucial to understand their impact upon the patient and any unconscious communication about how they have responded to such changes (Langs 1978, Livingston Smith 1991, Gray 1994).

Some supervisors emphasise the process of inner supervision and lend themselves alternately to therapist and patient, understanding how the one relates to and experiences the other. Casement has described developing this process within the therapist as developing an internal supervisor (Casement 1985).

Still other supervisors put their emphasis upon the counter-transference and explore what the patient evokes in the therapist that is difficult to manage. This provides rich material for personal development and an agenda for personal therapy. Other supervisors feel this is intrusive and only mention the counter-transference when the therapist brings it in.

Whatever style of supervision made available and however varied the views of supervisors about priorities, theories and reconstructions of the patient's past, the therapist receives another approach to thinking about the patient and another model for support in the work, understanding and intervening.

4.4 Written work

Some trainings have a minimal requirement for written work, such as a final reading-in paper that combines description of a long piece of clinical work with theoretical and technical reflections. There may still be a lot of writing throughout the course because of clinical presentations at seminars and written reports on training patients as well as other assignments.

Writing papers

Most courses require trainees to demonstrate in a paper their ability to relate theoretical ideas to their actual clinical work with a training patient. The task daunts many trainees. Some are not familiar with academic writing and balk at being judged for their competence at articulating theory, let alone illustrating it. Some courses offer seminar and tutorial help with writing. As adults returning to the learning situation some may be vulnerable to experiencing critical judgements as infantilising.

Writing challenges the therapist-in-training to deal with the capacity to develop links within the self as well as between therapist and patient. For many trainees the task of writing in which connection between clinical experience and theory has to be made, brings up personal issues, which the task of writing insists they confront in the act of going public (publication), albeit to a restricted audience. For this reason some trainings insist that personal therapy continue until the final paper is complete.

Some courses offer a degree qualification in conjunction with a clinical training. Sometimes this is not a requirement, but an option. This is increasingly a feature of the courses described in this guide. Where this is the case written papers will be shaped by academic requirements and standards. Some papers may be dedicated to research projects using qualitative and/or quantitative research methodologies related to clinical or psychological issues. These too will shape the training and the nature of the writing experience.

4.5 Assessment, standards and ethical requirements

Different courses deal with this issue in different ways. Varieties of transparency and openness about feedback are to be found. It seems that the debate about standards and the influence of practice more widely in training and education in other fields has made for more open reporting so that trainees will receive more direct and frequent feedback and assessment than they did a decade ago.

Most trainings not only have their procedures for assessment, they also have appeals procedures and make use of external examiners, as is common practice in higher and further education. This provides a corrective checking procedure for common standards as well as a means of dealing with disputed or borderline decisions and appeals.

Trainings vary in their practice. Some are extremely explicit, offering close guidelines and marking specific criteria for papers and clinical expectations. Others are less explicit. This can offer trainees the chance of being creative and individual in the way they respond. It may also provide an experience of mystification where criteria are hidden, individualised, which may leave a trainee floundering about what is expected.

5. TRAINEE RESPONSE

This is the section that endeavoured to produce some 'consumer feedback'. The aim in seeking these responses was to provide some clues about why a particular course was chosen and to describe something of the atmosphere of the course. The questions were designed to provide not just an idea of what drew people to the course but what they experienced and what hopes they had for the future. This should help readers to gauge the sort of work a course trains people for.

Inevitably the particular group of trainees contacted has shaped the issues current at the time. However, this should provide enough clues for possible applicants to be able to ask informed questions.

Most training bodies experience regular conflicts between the staff group and the trainee group for many good reasons. These may be covert and signalled by absence and disaffection or overt and signalled by confrontation and demand.

These inevitable signs of vitality and robustness need to be seen in context. There are always practical issues within trainees' demands and appreciations that need to be addressed. They may be about the quality of information, the changing of goal posts in training requirements, shifts in assessment methods or whatever. They may reveal unattended gaps in provision or injustice and need to be considered and weighed up. There are examples of them in the responses of trainee groups on their courses in this guide. The responses also contain clues about the frontier or stage of development of the course group and its ability to test its own authority or confront what they feel is missing on the course. They may also contain clues about the dynamics of the training body and how it is resolving its internal conflicts. They provide perspectives about the profession as a whole.

Trainee responses will be partly a reflection of the dynamics of staff trainee relations with all their multiple transferences, and partly individual. It is worth noting how positive or negative the trainees' answers seem to be. The ability to criticise can be a sign of a healthy and robust organisation; on the other hand, very negative or very positive feedback may indicate the trainees' transference towards their training organisation (parental/authority figures). Are they able to criticise the training or are they obliged to gloss over difficulties? Attitudes to authority can be revealed in the process of change. It should also be emphasised that the lack of conflict or positive appreciation in these comments may not signify absence of conflict on the course.

AUTHOR'S COMMENTS

The aim here is to outline issues mentioned in this guide that may be raised by a particular training and the trainee responses, in order to evoke as much thought as possible about the choice of training and the limitations and possibilities of each.

2.2   Adult Trainings

THE ARBOURS ASSOCIATION TRAINING PROGRAMME (ARBS – UKCP/PPS)

6 Church Lane, London N8 7BU
Tel. 020 8341 0916 Fax. 020 8341 5822
Web sites: <www.arbours.dircon.co.uk> and <www.arbourscentre.org.uk>
E-mail: arbours@dircon.co.uk

1. HISTORY OF THE ORGANISATION

The Arbours Association is a registered charity founded in 1970 in order to provide personal, psychotherapeutic and emotional support and places to live outside of psychiatric hospitals for people in emotional distress. Individuals and families who use Arbours' services include those with a wide range of psychological difficulties.

Since the first Arbours Community opened in 1970, the organisation has slowly expanded to provide three Therapeutic Communities, a Crisis Centre, a Training Programme in Psychoanalytic Psychotherapy (founded 1974), a Psychotherapy Service and the Association of Arbours Psychotherapists.

The work of the whole of the Arbours Association, its origins and development including the Psychotherapy Training Programme is described in the book, *Sanctuary – The Arbours Experience of Alternative Community Care*, edited by Joseph Berke, Chandra Masoliver and Thomas J. Ryan (Process Press, 1995).

2. THEORETICAL ORIENTATION AND CURRICULUM

The Arbours Training Programme critically studies and evaluates the main schools of psychoanalytic psychotherapy with a perspective on contemporary practice. In addition, the programme uniquely offers a broad clinical training experience by providing the opportunity of two extensive supervised placements, one in an Arbours Therapeutic Community and the other at the Arbours Crisis Centre. The placements are an integral part of the programme and combined with the theoretical curriculum provide a thorough training experience for the trainee.

The Arbours Training Programme consists of a one year introductory course, the Associate Programme, which is complete in itself, and the Full Training Programme, which is a minimum of three years.

- Associate Year Curriculum:
  The Arbours Experience
  Introduction to Psychoanalytic Psychotherapy
  Stages of Life

64

States of Mind
Art in the Communities
Experiential Group
Fortnightly Clinical Seminar

- Full Training Year One Curriculum:
Freud
Klein
Object Relations Theory
Introduction to Psychopathology
Child and Adolescent Development
Group Dynamics
Twice-termly Experiential Group
Fortnightly Clinical Seminar

- Full Training Year Two Curriculum:
Bion
Searles
Jung
Gender and Sexuality
Intercultural Perspectives
Borderline Psychopathology
Psychosomatics
Eating Disorders and Self-Harm
Twice-termly Experiential Group
Fortnightly Clinical Seminar

- Full Training Year Three Curriculum:
Practice of Psychotherapy
Transference and Counter-Transference
Containing/Holding
Interpretation of Dreams
Assessment
Brief Psychotherapy
Weekly Group Supervision
Fortnightly Clinical Seminar

- Full Training Mature Year:
Weekly Group Supervision

The Training Committee reserves the right to make any changes to the curriculum that it deems necessary.

3. TRAINING STRUCTURE

3.1 Training committee
The Training Committee is made up of ten senior psychotherapists and a part-time administrator. The Committee has an elected chairperson and members are elected for a set number of years. Various sub-committees contribute to the overall

management of the training. The Training Committee meets on a regular basis to discuss admissions, trainee progress and curriculum.

3.2 Selection procedure and admission

The Training Programme is committed to an equal opportunities policy and encourages applications from ethnic minorities. Applicants to the Associate Programme have to provide two names of referees who have known the applicant for at least one year. Applicants are interviewed by two, occasionally three, members of the Training Committee, and will be expected to satisfy the interviewers as to their personal maturity, motivation and competence. Acceptance is subject to the decision of the Training Committee.

At the end of the Associate Programme trainees can apply for admission to the Full Training Programme. Applicants must hold a university degree or equivalent. The Training Committee depending on the trainee's personal suitability, motivation and potential for psychoanalytic work, and the satisfactory completion of the Associate Programme decides their admission.

3.3 Time commitment and length of training

The Associate Programme is one year. Seminars and the Experiential Group are held on a Monday evening, fortnightly Clinical Seminars on a Tuesday evening and a minimum of two Saturday workshops per term.

The Full Training Programme is three years. Seminars are held on Monday and Thursday evenings with additional workshops on Saturdays and the fortnightly Clinical Seminar.

Trainees undertake two clinical placements prior to starting with training patients: the first is in an Arbours Therapeutic Community and is between six months and one year, depending on the trainee's circumstances and availability. The second placement is at the Arbours Crisis Centre for six months part-time.

The course is designed so that trainees are able to continue to work full-time. However, a degree of flexibility is essential to be able to undertake the two clinical placements.

Although the length of training varies individually, in total it is no less than four to five years, which includes a Mature Year during which time trainees complete their clinical requirements and take part in weekly Group Supervision.

3.4 Financial cost of training at different stages

Training fees are reviewed every two years.

Current fees:
Associate Programme: £1,380 per annum
Full training programme: £470 per term (covering placement supervision).

The fees do not include personal therapy costs or supervision for training patients in the third year of training.

After completion of the Full Training Programme a fee is payable to cover Group Supervision and tutorials until qualification.

Trainees can charge training patients up to £10 per session.

3.5 Interruptions in training
Arbours' policy is to accommodate interruptions due to personal circumstances including illness, bereavement or pregnancy provided the trainee remains in contact with their Personal Tutor.

3.6 Graduating and beginning a career
The newly qualified Arbours Psychotherapist is entitled to be placed on the UKCP register, in the Psychoanalytic and Psychodynamic Psychotherapy section. S/he is also entitled to become a Full Member of the Association of Arbours Psychothera-pists (AAP) which organises meetings, study groups, workshops and occasional conferences. She/he can also subscribe to the Arbours Referral Service.

Careers vary among individuals; some senior Arbours Psychotherapists are working in other facilities of the Arbours, or get actively involved with the AAP. Some work as psychotherapists in NHS Departments or other public and private psychotherapy services. Others teach in universities. All generally have their own private practice.

3.7 Number of trainees per intake
There is a maximum number of fifteen places for the Associate Year and ten places for each year on the Full Training Programme.

4. CLINICAL AND ACADEMIC REQUIREMENTS

4.1 Personal therapy
Associates are required to be in individual psychoanalytic psychotherapy at least once a week.

Trainees on the Full Training Programme are required to be in individual psycho-analytic psychotherapy at least three times per week throughout their training with a psychotherapist who is approved by the Training Committee.

4.2 Clinical requirements
All trainees must complete the Associate Year before starting the Full Training Programme.

All trainees are required to undertake two clinical placements (see Curriculum). The aim is to develop awareness of psychodynamic and interactional processes, as well as to give the trainee the opportunity to become aware of his/her own personal experience of them and to enable him/her to think conceptually about these experiences.

After successful completion of both clinical placements, which includes writing and presenting a paper on each, trainees can apply to the Training Committee for permission to start with their first training patient.

For qualification trainees are required to have worked with two training patients. The first training patient must be seen at least on a twice-weekly basis for a minimum of one year, and the second training patient also twice weekly for a minimum of six months. The trainee can then apply to the Training Committee for permission to start writing their final clinical paper.

4.3 Supervision
Trainees are required to have weekly individual supervision for all aspects of clinical work throughout their training.

4.4 Written work and course attendance
Trainees on the Full Training Programme are required to write three clinical papers during the course of their training which are presented at the fortnightly clinical seminar.

Trainees must complete all parts of the training programme. They are required to attend all lectures, seminars, fortnightly clinical seminars, workshops and trainee meetings. Trainees are required to meet at least once a month with their Personal Tutor and are expected to attend all supervisions of their clinical work throughout the duration of their training.

4.5 Assessment, standards and ethical requirements
Each trainee's ability to undertake clinical work is carefully monitored by the Training Committee on an ongoing basis throughout the training. The Training Committee receives regular reports about the clinical work and academic performance of each trainee from their Personal Tutor (who is a member of the Training Committee), from Supervisors, Seminar Leaders, and the leader of the Experiential Group. The trainee's ability to continue training is considered at every stage of the training, and is subject to the decision of the Training Committee. Important criteria include the trainee's ability to think psychoanalytically about his/her clinical experience and his/her potential for learning from the experience.

The Clinical supervisor and the Personal Tutor approve the final draft of the trainee's case presentation and together with a third therapist comprise a panel of readers who report to the Training Committee about the trainee's readiness to qualify.

All training standards are in accordance with the UKCP's training requirements.

The procedures and criteria for assessment are as transparent as possible. Each trainee is given the Handbook of the Arbours Association Training Programme upon admission which describes in detail all training and qualification requirements, assessment procedures and criteria, as well as the role and responsibilities of the Personal Tutor. It also contains a copy of the Code of Ethics of the Arbours Association, the Code of Practice of the Arbours Training Programme, and the Code of Practice of the Association of Arbours Psychotherapists for the practice of psychoanalytic psychotherapy.

5. TRAINEE RESPONSE

1. Why this course was chosen

1.1 What made people decide to train?
and 1.2 What were the aspects of this course that were most attractive?
One of the most important aspects that differentiates the Arbours training from others is that it is a practising body providing placement experiences in the long-term therapeutic communities and the Crisis Centre. The placements offer a working model that psychoanalytic thinking goes beyond the 50-minute hour. Some trainees

embarked upon a placement prior to considering the training programme, having then experienced the organisation and the supervision received, they then applied. One student was three years in another psychoanalytic course and changed her training school to Arbours, having done a placement in an Arbours community, preferring the experiential learning rather that an intellectual theoretical approach. 'You feel you can do the job, other trainings you learn after you qualify.' The Arbours is appealing in its approach and treatment of psychotic processes; the placement experiences allow a contained opportunity for students to process the feelings and anxiety that such distressed individuals present and project, thus providing a firm base for the eventual work as individual practitioners.

The theoretical approach is eclectic giving a broad overview of all theoretical models together with a historical sequence and context for a rounded understanding.

1. 3 What was your experience of the selection procedure?
The process by which one makes the transition from the Associate year to the full training is a competitive one. The Associate year is a time when each student is under assessment. Training committee members are tutors, supervisors in community placements and are involved in the weekly experiential group. Information about the selection does not focus upon procedure and details of prac-ticalities, instead adopting a more free-flowing approach. This method at times renders the student rather paranoid and anxious. However, it is preferred to the group interviews people had experienced in other training institutions. The process was summed-up by one student who said: 'It's all about bearing the anxiety, at least you can be yourself.'

1.4 Before the start of the course, how informed did you feel about each stage of the training?
The brochure about the training gives a comprehensive overview of the course which is a useful reference for later on in the training.

2. The atmosphere of the course

2.1 How do you feel about the way in which information is communicated?
Communication of information on the whole was very good. There are termly meetings within each year group with a member of the training committee as well as a student representative forum where all aspects of the training programme can be discussed and 'they really take notice'. Matters discussed are acted upon. Sometimes there have been administrative difficulties but they have been rare.

2.2 What do you find the most confusing aspect of the training?
There isn't much confusion as such, the statement that the course can be done whilst working full time irritates students when trying to negotiate placement hours because it is difficult to combine with other commitments of work and family.

2.3 How much opportunity do you have to share thoughts and feelings with fellow trainees?
Opportunities for sharing with fellow trainees: In the associate year there is a weekly experiential group. As a consequence the relationships that form at this stage

provide a solid base for the years ahead. In subsequent years, as well as the biweekly seminars there are termly experiential groups as well as other non-academic meetings. Bimonthly there are clinical seminars where a student presents a piece of clinical work to all members of the student body; here there is a formal and informal opportunity to meet those from other year groups.

2.4 What do you feel about the methods of teaching?
Students are given a reading list of papers to be read for discussion at each seminar and led by those who 'really know their stuff'. The most striking feature that is appreciated by students is the small seminar groups and relaxed atmosphere. There is plenty of space to think together without pressure to be intelligent. They are not rigid or restricted, they allow for spontaneity and a high level of participation.

2.5 What did you think about the way assessments were done to allow you to progress to the next stages of training?
Seminar leaders feed back to the Training Committee and then to students via their personal tutors and placement supervisors. Students are unaware if there is any formal appraisal criteria in terms of a 'person specification' as it were and acknowledge different tutors have different approaches but on the whole it is felt to work well. The clinical stages are two placements and then training patients. Supervision is continuous during these times and if things were not proceeding as well as they should, creative options are sought. Decisions regarding progress within the programme have a certain degree of mutuality and it may be useful for placements to be suspended, extended or students may take time off the course.

2.6 Has the course met your expectations?
Yes.

2.7 How do you feel about your future with the organisation?
Because Arbours is a relatively small organisation with an emphasis on personal experience, a sense of affiliation is generated. Most students interviewed felt keen to continue their connection within the organisation especially those involved in the new development of a consultancy service based in South London.

2.8 What plans do trainees have for future practice and possible balance of different sorts of work in their career?
The students interviewed all wanted to have some future practice but also acknowledged that the Arbours training has a broad base that makes the skills transferable to many related professions and settings, psychoanalytic thought can be of great usefulness in alternative specialist agencies.

AUTHOR'S COMMENTS

The anti-psychiatry work of Joseph Berke continues to pervade the Arbours course and its philosophy of engaging with psychoanalytic psychotherapy, both in the consulting room and in the Arbours Crisis Centre. Some trainees begin with placements in a therapeutic community and in the crisis centre prior to applying for the formal training. Those who undertake the training have to embark on two placements which they write up, before taking on individual clinical work. These placements enable participant-observer experience, exposure to mental breakdown and mental states that require non-medical asylum and care as an alternative context for managing breakdown and an experience much valued by the trainees. This is the learning model aimed at containment and understanding being developed. Connection with social context and its critique is also shown by how many training committee members have belonged to the Women's Therapy Centre.

It should be noted that the clinical requirements of twice weekly therapy of two patients for a year and six months is less than the norm for the Psychoanalytic and Psychodynamic section of the UKCP courses. Does this indicate that this is the norm, or perhaps that the placement experiences are valued above the individual therapy? Enquirers might need to explore what the relationship is between these two experiences of clinical work to discover what mix of work they are being trained for.

The training is taught by experienced analysts and therapists seemingly in a way that engages the responses of trainees within a fairly small group. The theoretical orientation is psychoanalytic with a recurring anti-psychiatry critique of medicalising solutions for mental health.

It sounded from the trainee response as though the demands of the training can be understated and not easy to fit in with inflexible employment. Many graduates are involved in applying psychoanalytic psychotherapy in contexts wider than the consulting room as well as having their own practices.

ASSOCIATION FOR GROUP AND INDIVIDUAL PSYCHOTHERAPY (AGIP – UKCP/PPS)

1 Fairbridge Road, London N19 3EW
Tel. 020 7272 7013 Fax. 020 7272 6945

1. HISTORY OF THE ORGANISATION

AGIP's institutional roots lie with the Association of Psychotherapists and its own Constitution was drawn up in 1974. The founding members envisaged a training that was to be psychoanalytic but which would also employ other approaches within the psychoanalytic framework. Underlying their philosophy was the belief that experienced psychotherapists integrate different orientations in their practice as they mature and that this implicit concept of a personal synthesis could become an explicit training principle.

The idea of a personal synthesis, the use of groupwork in an individual training, the critical bringing together of different theoretical and clinical approaches within a psychoanalytic tradition have remained at the centre of AGIP's work.

2. THEORETICAL ORIENTATION AND CURRICULUM

The overall aim of the training is to prepare trainees to work responsibly and independently as individual psychotherapists. The theoretical orientation is psychoanalytic, encompassing Freudian, Kleinian, Jungian and object relations schools of thought. Links to contemporary developments within the field are part of the fourth year curriculum and continue after that via AGIP's continuing professional development programme (CPD).

The four-year course includes theoretical seminars, written work, group experiences and supervised clinical work.

The curriculum is set out as follows:

- Year One – Psychodynamic Observation; Freud, Klein; Jung; Theory as Metaphor. This year concentrates on establishing a firm grounding in psychoanalytic theory and on the linking of theory with clinical practice.
- Year Two – The Fairy Tale (a means of exploring the application of Freudian, Kleinian and Jungian theory); Object Relations; Transference/Counter-transference; Beginning Work; Symptoms and Diagnosis; Approaches to Narcissism; Further Freud; Further Jung. This year concentrates on clinical work and on developing a critical, comparative attitude towards theory.
- Years Three and Four – Psyche-Soma; Groups and Institutions; Race in Psychotherapy; Winnicott; Bion; Comparative Psychoanalytic Technique; Clinical seminars; Further Transference/Counter-transference, Assessment for Psychotherapy, Contemporary Issues and Developments in Psychoanalysis/Psychotherapy, final long essay.

The format of these years emphasises the evaluation of theory and practice and continues to build upon the clinical experiences of the trainees. The seminars rely on trainee input and there is a continual review of psychoanalytic theory in relation to clinical experiences, enabling trainees to find an actively synthesising approach towards knowledge and practice in psychotherapy. Work on the final paper begins and there are seminars to support this process.

Throughout the first three years, trainees attend a weekly, closed analytic group. In addition, they attend approximately six all-day groups per year. AGIP believes that groups are vital to the training of psychotherapists – they highlight intrapsychic dynamics; they broaden the context from which to examine psychoanalytic thinking; they provide a place to work through the range of responses the trainees may have to the pressures of training and starting work with patients.

AGIP is fully aware of the value of Infant Observation in a psychotherapy training. The present policy is to encourage students to pursue it independently at a suitable point.

There are many channels for trainees to air any difficulties. Each person is assigned a Personal Tutor and a Senior Tutor coordinates the tutors' work. There is an opportunity each year for training groups to meet with members of the Training committee.

3. TRAINING STRUCTURE

3.1 Training committee
Council holds the ultimate authority in AGIP and all committees, including the Training committee, are sub-committees of Council. The Training Committee members are mostly, but not exclusively, members of AGIP.

3.2 Selection procedure and admission

Applicants must be at least 28 years old. Previous qualifications, education, experience and training (particularly in allied fields) are taken into consideration but AGIP looks primarily for evidence of personal and professional qualities that make for a reliable and effective psychotherapist. The course runs at a postgraduate level and there are considerable academic demands. Some experience of work in the field is desirable. There is an application form to be submitted with two referees.

If selected for interview, each applicant will have two individual interviews. These are normally followed by a group interview. A range of qualities and experiences are evaluated as being relevant to the process of becoming a psychotherapist based upon the interviewers' collective experience.

It is difficult to join AGIP's training course from another training because of the analytic group component and the integrated nature of the curriculum. AGIP welcomes applications from all sections of the community.

3.3 Time commitment per week and length of training

(a) Seminars and Analytic Group – one evening per week for three ten-week terms for four years. The analytic group ends after three years to allow time for the preparation of the final paper.
(b) Day Groups – two one-day groups per term, held on separate weekends, for three years.
(c) Personal Psychotherapy – at least two sessions a week until Professional membership, including a substantial period at a higher frequency.
(d) Training Patients – from the second year at least two patients seen twice weekly, plus time for writing up clinical notes. Additional time required to build up a caseload (usually from the third or fourth year).
(e) Supervision – one weekly individual session and one weekly group session until acceptance for Professional membership.
(f) Private Study and Written Work – allow about five hours study time per week for the first three years, plus additional time for written papers. Allow substantial time during the fourth year for the final paper.

3.4 Financial costs of training at different stages

Approximately £1,400 per year for the four years (excluding therapy and supervision). Fees must be checked at time of application to allow for changes.

3.5 Interruptions in training

Interruptions are difficult to accommodate due to the analytic group. However, there are exceptions and each case is dealt with individually.

3.6 Graduating and beginning a career

Once qualified, trainees become Professional Members of AGIP. Two further categories exist at the present time: Fellow of AGIP – for a Professional member who has made a significant contribution to AGIP's development; and Honorary member – for a person who has made a significant contribution both to AGIP and to the wider field of psychotherapy.

AGIP has an active CPD programme of events to support its members' continuing development as psychotherapists. There is a clear policy which sets out the means by which AGIP can encourage and monitor members' professional development both internally within AGIP and externally within the wider field as appropriate.

AGIP is currently involved in planning a Masters in Research with Goldsmiths' College, University of London. Future developments could include extending this into doctoral research.

3.7 Numbers of students per intake

Twelve students are usually accepted as the maximum per intake. Five would be the minimum in order to allow for a viable analytic group.

4. CLINICAL AND ACADEMIC REQUIREMENTS

4.1 Personal therapy

Trainees must be in therapy for a year before starting the course. The therapist must be validated by the Training committee according to its set criteria. Therapy up to Professional membership must be at least twice weekly, with a substantial period at a higher frequency.

4.2 Clinical requirements

Training patients can be seen from the second year. The minimum requirement is that the first training patient is seen for at least two years and the second training patient is seen for at least eighteen months, both at a minimum of twice a week. Training members must also acquire a caseload of several other patients (body of work) before applying for Professional membership.

4.3 Supervision

There must be individual supervision for the first training patient and group supervision for the second. Supervisors need to be approved by the Training committee.

4.4 Written work and course attendance

There are four major essays. The first is submitted during the first year. The second at the beginning of the second year. The third is submitted at the start of the third year. The fourth and final paper is usually started during the fourth year and needs to be submitted within four years of completing the seminar course. Additional, shorter papers on specific topics and presentations to the group on overall themes may also be required.

For attendance see above, section 3.3.

4.5 Assessments, standards and ethical requirements

AGIP's Code of Ethics covers all the sections required by the UKCP. AGIP is committed to maintaining high standards and various forms of assessment are used during the training period.

There is continuous assessment in the form of written papers, seminar presentations and regular reports from tutors and supervisors. The training therapist, tutor and both group leaders are consulted about readiness to work with patients. The final paper is assessed by two readers and there is a moderation process to ensure consistency.

5. TRAINEE RESPONSE

1. Why this course was chosen

1.1 What made people decide to train?
Several people had realised through the development of their existing work with patients that they wanted to work at a deeper level and had been encouraged by their supervisors to undertake a psychotherapy training. Other reasons included developing a capacity to work with more disturbed patients, and developing a greater sense of curiosity about self and other.

1.2 What were the aspects of this course that were most attractive?
The broad psychoanalytic theory base was an important element in the choice of training for many trainees and the Fairy Tale essay had also appealed to many. Several people chose this training because of the weekly analytic group throughout the first three years as well as the more experiential day groups that happen twice termly. The fact that the training was evening based was a practical consideration for some people. There was general agreement about the importance of the fact that the training is open to people who do not necessarily have a 'core' professional background. Finally it was agreed amongst the trainees that AGIP itself as an organisation with its own particular ethos had drawn people to seek out this training.

1.3 What was your experience of the selection procedure?
About the selection procedure, comments ranged from 'exciting!' to 'Gruelling – especially the group interview.' It was agreed that the group interview felt exposing but that selection procedure as a whole seemed well organised and thorough.

1.4 Before the start of the course, how informed did you feel about each stage of the training?
Before the start of the course there was a sense that the trainees had thought they were well informed. Information was clear (for example in the Handbook) but the actual experience of training inevitably brought forth new questions and uncertainties, which were answered along the way.

2. The atmosphere of the course

2.1 How do you feel about the way in which information is communicated?
It was felt that information about seminars and reading lists was good both in quality and timing. The Association's internal Newsletter was also valued as a means of communication about general information. Some of the processes about moving towards beginning clinical work seemed less clear to some trainees, however, perhaps because this process is an individualised one. This issue is currently being addressed.

2.2 What do you find the most confusing aspect of the training?
Some members of the group had difficulty with learning how to move from counselling approaches and techniques towards those of psychoanalytic psycho-therapy. This, however, is part of the challenge of the work and as such, creates a necessary confusion for those who may have worked in different ways previously.

2.3 How much opportunity do you have to share thoughts and feelings with fellow trainees?
The whole group felt there was a great deal of opportunity for sharing experiences within the year groups, particularly because of the analytic group and the day group. It was felt that there was not enough organised contact between different year groups and between Training members and Professional members. In order to facilitate more communication between these different groups, meetings are being planned for the future.

2.4 What do you feel about the methods of teaching?
It was agreed that the methods of teaching were varied because of the variety of teachers and the different styles and approaches they used. In general, the use of clinical material to illustrate and link theoretical points was particularly valuable and the active involvement of the students in casework discussions and presenta-tions was appreciated.

2.5 What did you think about the way assessments were done to allow you to progress to the next stages of training
The issue of assessment is inevitably one which will raise difficult feelings, particu-larly where the assessment indicates a need for further work or development. Some trainees experienced the written work as challenging and felt that a requirement for more written work might be helpful, particularly in preparing for the long essay. This was not a uniform view, however.

2.6 Has the course met your expectations?
In terms of the course meeting expectations, there was general agreement within the group that this had been the case. In some cases it was felt that it had exceeded expectations, or that it was not as expected but different and new and had led to unexpected learning.

2.7 How do you feel about your future with the organisation?
There was agreement amongst the group that people wanted to be involved in the future of AGIP as an organisation and wanted to feel that they also had opportuni-ties for their own professional development within the organisation. At this point in time, however, the priority for trainees was the establishment or consolidation of their own practice as independent psychotherapists.

2.8 What plans do trainees have for future practice and possible balance of different sorts of work in their career?
About longer-term future plans, it was difficult to answer in anything but an abstract way since the immediate issue for most people was to set up a viable practice.

AUTHOR'S COMMENTS

Since its development out of the Association of Psychotherapists (Scarlett 1991), AGIP training has attracted trainees who have wanted a full-range of theories: Freudian, object relations, Jungian and a group orientation to learning.

The emphasis on the self-development of the trainee in the group setting has provided a broad base for anyone wanting to develop their own approach to understanding theory. The trainees' comments on the ethos of the teaching style and the weekend study days suggests a tradition of participative learning associated with humanistic approaches that often see group learning as an essential adjunct to individual therapy. AGIP states that these are not humanistic therapy groups, but experiential non-analytic groups 'for meeting peers in intensive, expressive situations'. This course does not aspire to offer a training in group psychotherapy however much group learning methods are used.

ASSOCIATION OF INDEPENDENT PSYCHOTHERAPISTS (AIP – UKCP/PPS)

PO Box 1194, London N6 5PW
Tel. 020 7700 1911
<http:// www.aip.org.uk>

1. HISTORY OF THE ORGANISATION

The AIP was founded in 1988 to provide a referral service for the public, support the continuing professional development of its members and offer training and supervision in psychoanalytic psychotherapy. The first intake of trainees was in October 1992.

The AIP is registered under the Industrial and Provident Societies Act with the Registrar of Friendly Societies.

2. THEORETICAL ORIENTATION AND CURRICULUM

The training aims to maintain a creative tension between analytical psychology and psychoanalysis. It is pluralistic and emphasises an historical perspective on analytic theory and practice. The practice of psychotherapy is felt to be a vocation. The focus throughout is on the development of a psychotherapeutic identity as demonstrated through clinical work. The curriculum follows the lifespan from life in the womb to death. Lectures and reading seminars reflect on each stage of life from developmental and archetypal perspectives. There are lectures on psychotic states and the history and theory of analytic technique, and clinical case discussions from the beginning of the second year until qualification. There are three years of weekly meetings for seminars, lectures and case discussions. From the fourth year students attend a monthly seminar group until qualification.

3. TRAINING STRUCTURE

3.1 Training committee
Two groups share the responsibility for the training: the Core Group and the Membership Group. Members of the Core Group serve as training coordinators and manage the training. The Membership Group has oversight of the training and interviews trainees for qualification at the end of the course.

3.2 Selection procedure and admission
Written application form and two individual interviews.

3.3 Time commitment per week and length of training
The training takes a minimum of four years, part-time. Qualification usually takes five or six years. In the first year one evening a week is required, plus time for personal therapy and reading. The second and third years are usually the most demanding in terms of time, with group and individual supervision, in addition to the Wednesday evening meetings. From the fourth year until qualification there are monthly seminars.

3.4 Financial cost of training at different stages
Currently £1,200 per year for the first three years and subsequently £300 per year, until qualification. Fees for individual supervision, group supervision and personal psychotherapy are by arrangement with the supervisors and therapist.

3.5 Interruptions in training
Interruptions in training are not normally accommodated.

3.6 Graduating and beginning a career
Upon qualification trainees become members of the AIP and may go on the UKCP register. The development of a practice is seen as part of the training process.

3.7 Number of students per intake
We can take up to twelve, but in practice the average has been six to eight.

4. CLINICAL AND ACADEMIC REQUIREMENTS

4.1 Personal therapy
Minimum twice a week throughout course until qualification. More frequent therapy is expected for some period of the training.

4.2 Clinical requirements
Trainees work with five to seven clients. The duration and frequency of the therapy depends on the needs of the clients; however, one must be seen for 18 months and one for 24 months. Some clients must be seen at least twice a week.

4.3 Supervision
Two years of individual supervision and two years of group supervision. Additional supervision may be required.

4.4 Written work and course attendance

Course journal, book reviews, self-assessments, case history and final paper. Regular attendance is necessary.

4.5 Assessment, standards and ethical requirements

There is continuous assessment by the training coordinators, as well as supervision reports. The final assessment is by interview with the Membership Group. All trainees must abide by the AIP code of ethics and code of practice. The AIP is a member of UKCP.

TRAINEE RESPONSE

1. Why this course was chosen

1.1 What made people decide to train?
It was a way of deepening existing work and for further self-exploration and the next logical step in our inner life journey. And there was the potential for a fulfilling and rewarding job that could be continued even after pensionable age.

1.2 What were the aspects of this course that were most attractive?
That it was practically feasible whilst simultaneously holding down a full-time job. It combined both Analytical Psychology (Jungian, mythological and developmental) and Psychoanalytical (Freud, Klein, Winnicott) theories giving it both breadth and depth. The emphasis was on the development of an individual identity as a psychotherapist and we were not being moulded into 'AIP psychotherapists'. It was possible to progress at one's own pace to suit the individual's needs. It appeared less hierarchical than most and emphasised the role of the trainees 'woundedness'.

Although the credentials of personal analysts were checked, there appeared to be tolerance and recognition of the individual trainees' needs. And there was no consultation with the trainee's analyst.

1.3 What was your experience of the selection procedure?
The two application interviews were thorough but not threatening.

1.4 Before the start of the course, how informed did you feel about each stage of the training?
The requirements for the first year were known but there was a lack of clarity about future requirements. This has now been addressed by the AIP.

2. The atmosphere of the course

2.1 How do you feel about the way in which information is communicated?
and 2.2 What do you find the most confusing aspect of the training?
Communication of information at first was felt to be unsatisfactory. It was usually at the beginning of the evening. Announcements were made or odd documents

handed out. This led to a lot of hearsay between trainees, confusion and anxiety. This aspect has improved considerably as the AIP has developed.

2.3 How much opportunity do you have to share thoughts and feelings with fellow trainees?
Formal exchanges with fellow trainees were possible in the experiential group sessions during the second part of the evening training in the first year. But trainees did get together informally one to one and in small groups as we got to know each other.

2.4 What do you feel about the methods of teaching?
Teaching methods were often excellent and occasionally poor. The AIP have responded to the feedback from trainees and have changed trainers and training methods. Some trainers were very formal, preparing detailed notes for handout and sticking to their script. Others were very informal allowing discussion to develop freely but keeping the group to the subject. The latter was mostly preferred but the detailed notes were very much appreciated. The alternate weeks when trainees led the discussion generally worked very well.

2.5 What did you think about the way assessments were done to allow you to progress to the next stages of training?
Formal assessments were arranged when trainees had experienced one year of individual supervision. Assessment interviews could be requested at any time. There was no feedback on book reviews and termly course journals. Some trainees were happy with this, seeing it as a reflection of the self-directedness of the training, but others felt uncontained. There was the occasional shock for one or two trainees when they were later told they were not progressing. This aspect is being addressed by the AIP and more routine assessments are being introduced. The three tutorials each year during the first three years with an independent psychotherapist who offered very practical help and advice were found very helpful and reassuring.

2.6 Has the course met your expectations?
There was a resounding 'yes' to this. It was felt that the right balance was being struck encompassing the individual's personal journey, the academic work and the clinical work. The AIP is seen as an organisation that listens to individuals and tries to be flexible enough to meet individual needs within a solid framework.

2.7 How do you feel about your future with the organisation?
Very few trainees have qualified yet, but most trainees hope to continue to belong to the AIP after they qualify and play a part in its development.

We see ourselves as both individual, independent psychotherapist but also members of an exciting and developing organisation in which we want to play a part.

2.8 What plans do trainees have for future practice and possible balance of different sorts of work in their career?
There is an interest in other areas like short-term psychoanalytical work, training as supervisors or being trainers for counsellors. However, most feel that to work long term with individuals is what we have been trained for and want to do well.

AUTHOR'S COMMENTS

The emphasis on personal philosophy, the poetic and the mythological in this course appears alongside the earthly, body-based experience of life-long development. This suggests that it is a course as much in analytical psychology as in the psychoanalytic psychotherapy that is suggested by the training committee's entry. This is confirmed by the unusual combination of taught authors: Freud, Klein, Winnicott, Guntrip, Ferenczi, Searles, Laing, Lacan, Jung, Jacoby, Von Franz, Fordham, Edinger, Stein, Eliade and Hillman. The developmental in Jung is mixed with the archetypal, the transference based with the expressive elaboration of mythology. All this makes for a very broad curriculum, which may limit the depth at which it is possible to understand and integrate all these concepts and ways of working.

The training itself is less demanding than most, with once-weekly seminars for the first three years, and only monthly in the last year. This perhaps emphasises the individual development encouraged by the course ethos. 'Independent' in the title suggests the approach encouraged by the trainee, not the school of psychoanalytic thought.

In the name of independence of choice, there are no strict standards or procedures for selecting training therapists and supervisors to be found in this training, and no required reports from training therapists. The trainees expressed satisfaction with the course as a whole despite the criticisms along the way of lack of clarity in administration, teaching methods and how to progress.

The different ethos of this course, and the much lighter demands upon trainees who are expected to cover a much broader range of theories with less teaching and seminar work, suggest a course that is very different from many of the courses described in this guide.

ASSOCIATION OF JUNGIAN ANALYSTS (AJA – UKCP/APS)

Flat 3, 7 Eton Avenue, London NW3 3EL
Tel. 020 7794 8711 Fax. 020 7794 8711
E-mail: aja@dircon.co.uk

1. HISTORY OF THE ORGANISATION

Founded in 1977, the Association's approach to Analytical Psychology aims to hold a balance between the developmental and archetypal aspects of the personality.

The Association was established by Dr Gerhard Adler, a close friend and associate of Prof. C.G. Jung, and a group of like-minded colleagues.

All member analysts of the Association register with the Analytical Psychology Section of UKCP and are internationally recognised by the International Association for Analytical Psychology (IAAP).

2. THEORETICAL ORIENTATION AND CURRICULUM

The Association of Jungian Analysts offers a training programme in the theory and practice of Analytical Psychology which has arisen from C.G. Jung's model of the psyche and his work. The programme is concerned with clinical, personal, social, intellectual and spiritual aspects of individual development.

The training, in the context of a sustained personal analysis, aims to provide a thorough analytic foundation. Within this, the development of sound therapeutic practice cultivates a respect for the healing potential of the unconscious.

The archetypal character of the unconscious forms the centre of clinical and theoretical work. Dream analysis is an integral part of the therapeutic approach as is analysis of transference and counter-transference.

3. TRAINING STRUCTURE

3.1 Training committee

The AJA Training Committee plans and administers the Training Programme which includes responsibility for the following:

(a) Seminar programme:
    – determining the syllabus
    – appointing seminar leaders
    – setting seminar dates
(b) Group Tutor:
    – appointing a Group Tutor for each training group, and
    – liaising with the Group Tutor
(c) Liaising with the Assessment Committee
(d) Monthly meetings:
    – determining topics and selecting speakers and dates
(e) Arranging workshops and conferences.

3.2 Selection procedure and admission

Procedure for application
The application form for admission to the training programme may be obtained from the secretary. Completed applications for the next training programme should be received before the closing date and accompanied by a letter addressed to the Chair of the Selection Committee.

All applications will be referred to the Selection Committee, which will, in the course of selection, take into account the personal and professional integrity of individuals, their aptitude for analytical work, their professional experience and evidence of the ability to benefit from training.

Pre-training requirements
An applicant to the training programme of the Association:

• shall have undergone a minimum of 150 hours consecutive personal analysis over a minimum period of two years conducted by a qualified IAAP Jungian Analyst acceptable to the Selection Committee
• shall normally be not less than 30 years of age

- shall possess a relevant degree or equivalent acceptable to the Selection Committee. In special cases, a request for training will be considered if evidence of other appropriate qualifications is presented
- shall have a minimum half-day weekly experience of an approved clinical placement in the psychiatric field lasting at least six months.
  This shall include therapeutic work under supervision with two patients seen individually for counselling or psychotherapy.

Equal opportunities
AJA's Equal Opportunities Policy is in accordance with the UKCP guidelines on Equal Opportunities. AJA is committed to a policy of equal opportunity and non-discrimination in relation to admission to the training programme of appropriately qualified individuals.

3.3 Time commitment per week and length of training
Regular attendance at seminars, held in term times two evenings per week during the first three years and once weekly in year four, is a requirement. Attendance at monthly meetings, scheduled in as part of the course, is also mandatory.

Seminars last for four years, the minimum length of training. Because of clinical work, training will probably extend beyond that time. Individuals will vary in the length of time they take to complete all their requirements.

3.4 Financial cost of training at different stages
Current seminar fees (for 1999/2000) are £720 per annum. Additional costs include personal analysis three-times weekly and supervision fees at £38 per week, £76 when candidates are seeing two clinic patients in the third stage of training.

3.5 Interruptions in training
Training will be prolonged when there is an interruption due to, for example, illness, pregnancy, and so on. Decisions will be made through discussions with the relevant committees and will depend on individual circumstances.

3.6 Graduating and beginning a career
After qualification, Associate and Professional Members contribute to furthering the Association's aims through participation in the training and educational programme, holding positions of office on the Council of Management, its committees and working parties and contributing to the collective well-being of the AJA community.

The monthly meeting and the Professional Development Seminar promote and encourage professional development for Analytical Psychologists.

Associate Members may apply for Professional Membership three years after qualifying and after having discharged their clinic patient responsibilities. They will have established a clinical practice, gained further experience through supervision, taken active part in the affairs of the Association and furthered their professional development through continued involvement in or attendance at lectures, courses and workshops.

3.7 Numbers of students per intake
AJA currently sets a maximum of twelve and a minimum of six students per intake.

4. CLINICAL AND ACADEMIC REQUIREMENTS

4.1 Personal therapy
Three-times weekly personal analysis with an AJA Training Analyst is required for the duration of the training, and usually beyond it.

4.2 Clinical requirements
The candidate is expected to see two clinic patients three-times weekly during the training. The first case shall be seen for a minimum of two years; the second case for a minimum of one year. They are to be supervised on a weekly basis, individually with AJA-approved supervisors for a minimum total of 120 hours. There should be one supervisor for each clinic patient, one male and one female.

The AJA Clinic Scheme expects to provide most Candidates with their clinic patients.

4.3 Supervision
Supervision continues from the time the candidate in Training enters Stage Two of the training to Final Qualification. When all the clinical requirements of the training have been completed and the Candidate in Training has had a successful Final Assessment, supervision of one of the clinic patients may be ended subject to agreement by both supervisors.

4.4 Written work and course attendance

Written work
A short written paper on a chosen theme, making use of Jungian, or alternatively of Jungian and other theoretical standpoints, is required before proceeding to Stage Two of the training.

The first case study is presented after working for at least twelve months with the first clinic patient. This paper should be regarded as preparation towards writing the final clinical paper and aims to integrate theory with clinical practice.

A second case study is required after working for at least nine months with the second clinic patient.

A final clinical paper is required before qualifying for Associate Membership.

Course attendance
Regular attendance at seminars and monthly meetings is a requirement.
Attendance at occasional weekend seminars is expected.

4.5 Assessment, standards and ethical requirements

AJA Code of Ethics
The Code of Ethics is intended for all Members and Candidates in Training of the Association of Jungian Analysts. This code has been approved by the Analytical Psychology Section of the UKCP, and is consistent with their Ethical Guidelines.

The headings covered by the AJA Code of Ethics are:

1. Guidelines for Ethics and Practice
   Responsibility to Self

Responsibilities to Patients
Responsibilities to Colleagues
2. Serious Misconduct
3. Composition and Functions of the Committee dealing with Matters of Ethics and Practice.

AJA assessment procedure

Stage One is the pre-clinical period of training lasting approximately a year, at the end of which the candidate will be interviewed. The Assessment Committee will then decide, on the basis of written work, seminar leaders' reports and the interview, if the candidate is ready to proceed to Stage Two.

Stage Two refers to the clinical aspect of the training, in which at least two clinic patients are analysed three-times weekly, the first for two years and the second for one year. Work with the second clinic patient commences about six months after beginning with the first and after a self-assessment has been written and approved. When the prescribed periods of time with each clinic patient have been completed, self-assessment and two case studies written and presented, the candidate may apply to enter Stage Three.

Stage Three comprises a further self-assessment and an interview following which the committee will decide whether the candidate is ready to write their final clinical paper. Following receipt of this a panel, comprised of members of the Assessment Committee, will interview the candidate and submit a report. The committee will then decide whether to offer Associate Membership of AJA or to ask the candidate to resubmit the final clinical paper after further work has been done on it.

Personal analysis and supervision of clinic patients shall continue until Associate Membership is granted.

5. TRAINEE RESPONSE

1. Why this course was chosen

'This training was chosen to further our knowledge and to build on existing trainings. For most, experiences of Jungian analysis had radically affected both personal and professional lives and this had encouraged us to apply for a training in analytical psychology. We were seeking personal and professional development and to gain clinical experience of working at further depth. We were attracted to the course because it offered a balance between the archetypal and developmental aspects of the personality. Professional experience of members of the Association had been good and the evening seminars made it accessible. The selection procedure was found to be thorough and thoughtful, providing a clear framework and time scales. Interviews were experienced as both challenging and helpful, and the whole process, although nerve racking at times, suggested an organisation which cared about the individual process of the trainees whilst also giving a taste of what one was letting oneself in for. Finally the selection day offered a chance to meet the other applicants and there are fond memories of the now traditional gathering relaxing in the pub afterwards! Before starting the course, the bare bones of the syllabus were made clear and the prospectus set out the different stages succinctly. We could have asked for more detail had we wanted it.'

2. The atmosphere of the course

'Information is usually given in written form, and is mostly excellent. To get the "feel" of the steps of the training process, trainees have found their own analysts very helpful. Confusions and difficulties mostly related to the challenges and changes resulting from our personal therapies and integrating these alongside academic study. This has made existing work and relationships difficult and confusing at times. The opportunity to share thoughts and feelings with fellow trainees has been varied. It was felt these opportunities had to be made by the group as there was no formal time given for this within the training itself. Nevertheless the Training Committee has responded where problems arose and sympathetic support given when requested and to good effect. Different seminar leaders for different topics had the potential for confusion, while also offering a rich variety of style and approach. There are opportunities for us all to feed back our experiences to seminar leaders via our group tutor. Earlier groups had complained of lack of notice to prepare for seminars, but the present group has not had this problem. All felt their most intense and rewarding teaching experience was through their two individual supervisors and their personal analysis. The assessment process is challenging and rigorous. There is a sense of always being taken seriously and thought about consistently. Each stage engenders energy and motivation with anxiety and exhaustion as well. There is a balance between academic and clinical, and between interviews and written pieces of work. Support from analysts and supervisors are invaluable at these times. No course can ever meet the idealistic expectations we started with, but trainees found the whole process very worthwhile. The financial costs were heavier than had been expected by some. All trainees anticipated playing a role in the organisation at a later date, but degrees of involvement varied, some being cautious, others enthusiastic. Most felt a time of recovery was needed first. Plans for future practice were again varied, but all hoped to consolidate their private practice. Some planned to maintain existing external commitments, others in full time practice, envisioned teaching and supervision as a way of balancing their work.'

AUTHOR'S COMMENTS

The AJA course offers interaction between the developmental and the archetypal approaches to Analytical Psychology including the mythological elaboration along with transference/counter-transference interaction. This suggests a heavy range of learning across a broad field of writers and disciplines. The trainee response seems to confirm this by referring to heavier demands than expected. Clinical expectations are high with two thrice-weekly patients for two and one years and a personal analysis at the same intensity.

   The course is run by a small organisation founded by Dr Gerhard Adler whose style of passing on the Jungian tradition insisted on analysis with one of the founders of the organisation. This restrictiveness was one of the factors in the setting up of the Independent Group of Analytical Psychologists (IGAP, see p. 136f.). The course offers an ethos that is committed to the spiritual and mythological elaboration of analysands material and to that extent reflects the disatisfaction of its founders with the strong focus on the developmental approach and the rapprochement with psychoanalysis favoured by the Society of Analytical Psychology.

The course description is drawn partly from the AJA handbook which is one of the most thorough and coherent of all the trainings, covering not just training matters but the functioning and policies of the whole organisation. This confirms the trainee response that systems of communication, information and expectation have been improved in recent years. Their comments also suggest that this is one of the courses that give little or no opportunity for the group life of the trainees who have to seek time for it themselves.

BRITISH ASSOCIATION OF PSYCHOTHERAPISTS (BAP – BCP)

37 Mapesbury Road, London NW2 4HJ
Tel. 020 8452 9823 Fax. 020 8452 5182
Web site <www.bap-psychotherapy.org> E-mail: mail@bap-psychotherapy.org

1. HISTORY OF THE ORGANISATION AND GENERAL INFORMATION

The British Association of Psychotherapists (BAP) was founded in 1951. The aim of the Association is to promote the knowledge and application of psychotherapy and the training and competence of psychotherapists. From its inception, it has sought to bring together psychotherapists with varying theoretical viewpoints who share a psychoanalytic orientation to psychotherapy. The Association became a limited company in 1977 and charitable status was granted two years later. In 1990, the BAP became a founder member of the British Confederation of Psychotherapists (BCP).

The BAP is unique in offering four distinct and well established professional trainings through its Psychoanalytic, Jungian Analytic and Child Sections. Separate parallel training programmes, following a Psychoanalytic and a Jungian Analytic theoretical basis respectively, were first established in 1963. In 1982, the International Association of Analytical Psychology (IAAP) approved the Jungian Section for Full Membership and its members were able to call themselves Jungian Analysts. In the same year, the Child and Adolescent Psychotherapy Training was founded by senior members of the profession, who had been trained at the Anna Freud Centre and the Tavistock Clinic, who wished to establish a Child and Adolescent Training in the Independent Psychoanalytic tradition. The Child and Adolescent Training was granted full accreditation by the Association of Child Psychotherapists (ACP) in 1986 and recognised for work in the NHS. A Modified Training in Adult Psychoanalytic Psychotherapy for Child Psychotherapists was introduced in 1989 to meet the needs of Child Psychotherapists for an additional qualification for work with adults.

The BAP welcomes applications to train from every sector of the population and makes no discrimination on grounds of ethnicity, religion, gender or sexual orientation. Successful applicants become Trainee Members of the BAP and will have many opportunities to join in the intellectual life of the BAP, through its Scientific Meetings, clinical forums, Members' Meetings, and through receipt of the Association's Journal and Newsletter. The BAP headquarters in North London has an extensive library, photocopying facilities, consulting rooms, seminar rooms, and a student common room. Overnight accommodation is available for out of London members. A Student Organisation is open to all Trainees.

As the cumulative costs of training (outlined below) are considerable, it is most important that applicants consider carefully how they will make financial provision before undertaking the training. The Victor Kantor Memorial Fund is administered by the BAP to offer a limited amount of financial assistance to trainees who experience difficulties as a result of changed financial circumstances.

Upon qualification, Trainees receive Associate Membership of the BAP and are automatically eligible for registration with the British Confederation of Psycho-therapists and/or the Association of Child Psychotherapists and the International Association of Analytical Psychologists. As Associate Members they will be encouraged to join fully in the busy scientific and organisational life of the BAP, and it is hoped that, around five years after qualifying, many will be considering applying to take Full Membership of the BAP. Full Membership is a requirement for any Member who wishes to become a Training Therapist or Supervisor for the BAP, as well as for some senior appointments within the Organisation, including eligibility for election to Council, the Executive body of the BAP, which is ultimately responsible for overseeing the policies, trainings and professional life of the Association.

The BAP offers a wide range of External Courses for members of the helping professions, and since 1997, has run a two-year MSc/one-year Diploma course in the Psychodynamics of Human Development, in association with the Department of Psychology at Birkbeck College, London University. The course, which is part time, may be a suitable introduction for individuals thinking of applying for a BAP Training. Candidates can choose a Psychoanalytic or a Jungian Analytic MSc course. Discussions are in progress with Birkbeck College about a possible Clinical Doctorate.

Members of the BAP contribute regularly to the published literature. Recent books by BAP Members include: *Psychoanalytic Psychotherapy in the Independent Tradition* and *Psychoanalytic Psychotherapy in the Kleinian Tradition*, edited by Sue Johnson and Stanley Ruszczynski (Karnac Books, 1999); *Jungian Thought in the Modern World* by Elphis Christopher and Hester Solomon (Free Association Books, 1999); and *The Handbook of Child and Adolescent Psychotherapy: Psychoanalytic Approaches*, edited by Monica Lanyado and Ann Horne (Routledge, 1999).

Code of ethics

All Members of the BAP, including Trainee Members, must abide by the Associa-tion's Code of Ethics, a copy of which is available on request. A Standing Ethics Committee continuously updates the Association's Code of Ethics and Guide to Pro-fessional Conduct, and investigates complaints regarding matters of professional misconduct. Any serious breach of the Ethical Code would lead to careful reappraisal of the Trainee's potential to work as a psychotherapist.

PSYCHOANALYTIC PSYCHOTHERAPY SECTION (BAP-P-A – BCP)

2. THEORETICAL ORIENTATION AND CURRICULUM

The theoretical training is founded on the central tenets of psychoanalytic thought, as originally expounded by Sigmund Freud. Accordingly the theoretical seminar programme during the first year is mainly devoted to the study of seminal papers by Freud, taught as four series of seminars, each series led by a different tutor. These are followed by a short series on the work of Karl Abraham. The aims of the first-year programme are to familiarise Trainees with the psychoanalytic model, its origins, core ideas and language, through the reading of these classic texts, studied in the context of trainees' accumulating experience in personal psychoanalytic therapy, and as practitioners in a variety of clinical settings.

After the first year, the theoretical curriculum turns to the varied and sometimes conflicting strands of contemporary psychoanalysis, looking in turn at the contributions of Klein and the post-Kleinians, Contemporary Freudians and the Independent British School. Understanding these differing theoretical view points is developed further throughout the remainder of the four-year programme of theoretical seminars, during which time trainees go on to study, amongst other topics, infant and child development, psychopathology, and key clinical concepts, such as transference and counter-transference.

Theoretical seminars take place once weekly in the evening (8.30–10p.m.) and are led by Members of the British Psycho-Analytical Society or Full Members of the BAP, invited on the basis of their expertise in the topics presented. The seminars usually begin with a brief presentation by one trainee, based on the weekly reading, followed by informal discussion in which all the Trainee group is encouraged to take part. Most, but not all, seminars are held at the BAP house at 37 Mapesbury Road, London.

Summary of the theoretical programme

Year 1:   S. Freud; K. Abraham
Year 2:   M. Klein; D.W. Winnicott; Infant and Child Development; Kohut; Comparative Clinical Concepts; W.D. Fairbairn; S. Ferenczi; M. Balint; Topics on Clinical Management (as preparation for work with Training patients).
Year 3:   Psychoneurosis and Character Disorders; Depression; Narcissistic Disorders; Psychosomatic Disorders; Perversions; Comparative Clinical Concepts Revisited.
Year 4:   Assessment; Research; W.R. Bion; Post-Kleinians; Current Themes in Sexuality; The Analytic Attitude.

3. TRAINING STRUCTURE

3.1 Training committee
The Training Committee is responsible for all decisions relating to the training. There are at least twelve members. They include the Chair, an Honorary Secretary, and a Finance Officer; Theoretical Seminar Organiser, Clinical Seminar Organiser, Reduced Fee Scheme Organiser and Reading-In Coordinator, and a Training Advisor for each year group in the Training. The Training Advisor is a key link between the Training Committee and the Trainee, offering feedback on all matters relevant to Trainee progress. The Training Advisor generally serves on the Training Committee for at least five years, and save in exceptional circumstances, will remain the Advisor

to the year group until all the trainees have qualified, meeting with the group once a term, and with individual trainees at least annually. All trainees are invited to an annual meeting with the Training Committee.

3.2 Selection procedure and admission
Applicants are required to hold a degree. Those with a degree equivalent, and working experience in a core profession, may be considered, but their acceptance onto the training is subject to ratification by the BAP Council. Applicants are usually aged 30–50. All are expected to have been in personal psychoanalytic psychother-apy/analysis with a BAP-approved Training Therapist for a minimum of three times a week for at least a year before beginning the training. Selection involves two, sometimes three, interviews with a senior member of the Psychoanalytic Section of the BAP. The main criterion for acceptance onto the Training is personal and emotional suitability for working as a psychoanalytic psychotherapist. Applicants without psychiatric experience will be required to attend a placement at a relevant psychiatric setting, as arranged by the Training Committee before beginning the course, which starts in September.

3.3 Time commitment per week and length of training
Qualifying generally takes five to six years; four years is the minimum. The design of the training allows most trainees to continue their full time work, but trainees must be prepared to devote about 15–20 hours per week to fulfilling all the various requirements of the training.

3.4 Financial cost of training at different stages
Currently, fees range from £1,218 in Year 1 to £624 in Year 5 and £564 in subsequent years. The costs for personal analysis and supervision are additional. Trainees also pay a student subscription of £165 and must purchase insurance for malpractice.

3.5 Interruptions in training
Only in exceptional circumstances (for example, life events, such as pregnancy or illness) may a Trainee take time away, up to a maximum of one to two years, from the Training. The Training Committee will consider in each instance how the time is to be made up.

3.6 Numbers of students per intake
The number varies, but can be between four and twelve trainees per year.

4. CLINICAL AND ACADEMIC REQUIREMENTS

4.1 Personal psychoanalytic psychotherapy/analysis
The trainee's personal psychoanalytic psychotherapy/analysis is central to their development as a psychoanalytic psychotherapist, and all trainees must continue in individual psychotherapy for a minimum of three times a week throughout their training and until election to Associate Membership.

4.2 Clinical requirements

The clinical requirements for the Psychoanalytic Psychotherapy Training are as follows.

In Year 1, weekly observation of a mother and infant and attendance at Infant Observation seminars, culminating in the writing of a short paper.

Beginning in Year 2, treatment at least three times weekly of two patients (one male, one female), with accompanying weekly supervision for each. One patient must be treated for at least two years, and one for at least eighteen months. The BAP runs its own Reduced Fee Scheme for the assessment of prospective patients.

From the second year until the completion of training, fortnightly clinical seminars, for the presentation and small group discussion of work with training patients; in addition, a seminar is held once each term for the discussion of trainees' six-monthly reports on their patients.

Once the course requirements have been fulfilled, the trainee can apply to Read-In and, if accepted, is required to write a Reading-In paper.

4.3 Supervision

Trainees are required to have two supervisors, one for each patient, and each is seen weekly for the duration of the training.

4.4 Written work and course attendance

Trainees are expected to attend all seminars offered.

The Infant Observation Paper (about 4,000–6,000 words), must be written during the first summer term and passed before taking a training patient.

A short report is required on each training patient every six months.

The Reading-In paper (about 6,000–7,000 words) is an essential part of the final assessment of each trainee's readiness to practise independently as a psychoanalytic psychotherapist. The trainee is allocated a tutor for the writing of the paper, which is then read and discussed with the trainee by two Readers appointed by the Training Committee.

4.5 Assessment, standards and ethical requirements

The trainee's progress and development is continuously assessed at each stage of the training. The process of assessment is closely monitored by the Training Advisor on behalf of the Training Committee. The trainee's Analyst or Psychotherapist will be asked to comment at each key stage on the trainee's readiness to proceed to the next stage of training. Reports are requested every six months from both supervisors. Theoretical and clinical seminar leaders, and six-monthly report tutors are also asked to comment on the trainee's progress, and all of the above will be asked to comment on the trainee's readiness to practise independently before the trainee can Read-In. The final decision on Reading-In, as on all matters of trainee progress, lies with the Training Committee.

If after presentation of the Reading-In paper, the two appointed Readers are satisfied with the paper and its discussion, the trainee is recommended for Associate Membership. Following final decision by the Training Committee, the recommendation goes to the Council of the BAP for ratification and election to Associate Membership.

The training standards set out are in line with those laid down by The British Confederation of Psychotherapists (BCP).

5. TRAINEE RESPONSE

1. Why this course was chosen

1.1 What made people decide to train?
Some trainees had previously studied psychoanalytic therapy in a less intensive way (seminars at the Tavistock, for example) – and most came with some prior clinical experience. Their interest in psychoanalysis led them to want to improve their theoretical understanding and clinical skills so as to be able to work with patients in greater depth.

1.2 What were the aspects of this course that were most attractive?
People were attracted by the well-established reputation of the BAP as a highly professional organisation with rigorous standards of excellence, and they valued the opportunity of undertaking an advanced course with a high level of theoretical teaching as well as intensive focus on clinical work. Many were also keen to gain BCP registration.

1.3 What was your experience of the selection procedure?
Most people found the application and selection process very positive and some compared it favourably with equivalent experiences elsewhere. The interviews were remembered as being generally challenging without being persecutory, and some trainees who had not been accepted at their first application recognised that this decision had been in their own interests.

1.4 Before the start of the course, how informed did you feel about each stage of the training?
The overall requirements and structure of the course were generally adequately explained and are set out in detail in a training manual. Some people felt that it was not made sufficiently clear that seminars might be held in other parts of London. It was also felt that trainees were not made realistically aware of the possible length of the training.

2. The atmosphere of the course

2.1 How do you feel about the way information is communicated?
Although there can be hitches, on the whole information is communicated efficiently via post, newsletters and contact with the Year Advisor. The Student Organisation holds regular committee meetings after which minutes are circulated via year representatives.

2.2 What do you find the most confusing aspect of the training?
Trainees did not find any aspects of the course itself particularly confusing. There was some concern about the nature of the relationship with the Year Advisor, who has an allegiance both to the trainee and to the Training Committee.

2.3 How much opportunity do you have to share thoughts and feelings with fellow trainees?
The Student Organisation is valued as a forum for meeting with trainees from different years and from the other streams within the BAP. Within individual year

groups it is sometimes difficult to find time for meeting except at seminars, but some make efforts to arrange social events. There is much more opportunity for discussion when seminars are held at the BAP house, where there is a kitchen which serves as a meeting place for trainees.

2.4 What do you feel about the methods of teaching?
Theoretical teaching takes place in year groups, which may be sub-divided for clinical seminars. Theoretical seminars are generally lead by experienced psycho-analysts, often with a specialist interest in the particular subject, and this was greatly valued. On the whole, trainees were very satisfied with the standard of teaching, although they occasionally found seminar leaders too inclined to lecture rather than encouraging a sharing of ideas. Some felt it might be useful if there were some way of addressing issues of group dynamics.

2.5 What did you think about the way assessments were done to allow you to progress to the next stages of training?
On the whole this was felt to be well managed and unobtrusive. Some felt that more feedback would be helpful and that it would be more effective if it came directly from the seminar leaders instead of via the Training Advisor. Hold-ups in individual progress were most commonly caused by the non-availability of training patients, but it is recognised that this is increasingly a problem common to all the intensive psychotherapy trainings.

2.6 Has the course met your expectations?
It was generally felt that the course had met or exceeded expectations.

2.7 How do you feel about your future with the organisation?
Although trainees who had attended BAP meetings and events had felt welcomed, it was thought that more could be done to encourage students to feel part of the wider organisation. There was, however, an appreciation of the opportunities for further development available after qualification.

2.8 What plans do trainees have for future practice and balance of different sorts of work in their career?
Most trainees plan to combine private practice with psychotherapeutic work in the NHS and in other settings. Some expect to continue working within their previous professions, hoping to apply the psychoanalytical experience they have gained. Many are interested in expanding their experience through writing, teaching and supervising.

BAP JUNGIAN ANALYTIC SECTION (BAP-J BCP)

2. THEORETICAL ORIENTATION AND CURRICULUM

The Jungian Analytic Training aims to train and qualify competent Jungian Analysts who will be able to work with individuals in depth in the analytic setting, and continue their development through a range of learning and experience after qualification. It aims to enable trainees to learn (from their own analysis, and from practice and theory) to use 'themselves' via the processes of introjection and projection, transference and counter-transference, in the service of the psycho-therapeutic relationship and their patients' processes of individuation, and to develop a professional and ethical attitude to their work.

There is no formal Introductory Course. A two-year Infant Observation is a requirement of the training, and may be undertaken either before the course begins or concurrently with the first two years.

Summary of the theoretical curriculum

Year 1   Jung in Context; History of Jungian thought; models of the mind; Internal worlds and object relations; classical Freud and post-Freudians; Fairbairn, Klein and post-Kleinians; Winnicott and Bowlby; Jung and post-Jungians; the normal individuating Self; Transcendent Function; Psyche–Soma.

Year 2   Vicissitudes, disorders and defences of the Self; epistemology; unconscious communication; how the psyche speaks; map of the defences; ego defences; concretisations; Self care systems; primitive defences; emptying out of the Self; enactments; core complex; sexualisation; perversions; eating disorders; cutting; psychiatric view; narcissism; borderline personalities; psychosis; overwhelming nature of the archetypes.

Year 3   Jungian concepts in depth; the alchemical metaphor in the making of meaning; dreams; myth and fairy tale; the individual, the group and the culture; spirituality and religion; endings; looking ahead and further study.

Year 4   A guided exploration of a topic or topics, based on interest and need and to link with epistemology.

3. TRAINING STRUCTURE

3.1. Training committee

The Training Committee has at least twelve members, all of whom have trained with the BAP. They include the Chair, a Training Adviser for each year, the Honorary Secretary and the Honorary Treasurer, Theoretical Seminar Organiser, Infant Observation Co Ordinator and Clinical Seminar Organiser, Reading-In Coordinator and Reduced Fee Scheme Organiser. The Training Advisor is the main link between the trainee and the Training Committee and meets with trainees once a term and individually at least once a year. The Training Committee meets once a month. A representative of the student body attends one meeting each term.

3.2 Selection procedure and admission

Applicants are advised to have an informal interview before applying, in order to discuss the prerequisites. Clinical experience is essential, and should include some psychiatric experience, obtained if necessary before the course begins or during the first year. Application will involve two interviews. Applicants should have a degree, preferably in medicine, psychology, social sciences or an allied subject. Applicants with a degree equivalent and work experience in a core profession may, however, be considered, and if suitable, their acceptance has to be ratified by the BAP Council. There is no provision for joining midway through the course.

The number of trainees in each year does not usually exceed ten; there is no upper age limit. Suitability depends on personality in general, ability to think and work analytically, and practical circumstances such as whether the applicant will be able to commit the time and finance needed for the training, and is within reach of London. Applicants who are pregnant or have a child under one year old are not accepted on the grounds that the demands of the Infant Observation, and the pressures on time generally, can be very stressful.

3.3 Time commitment and length of training
It generally takes five years to qualify but may take less. The design of the training allows most trainees to continue to work full-time, but they should be prepared to set aside 15 hours each week to pursue all the requirements of the training, including reading and preparation for seminars, Infant Observations, the treatment of patients and supervision. Theoretical seminars are held on Tuesday evenings throughout the training. Infant Observation seminars take place once weekly throughout the first two years, and clinical seminars once fortnightly from the second year until qualification.

3.4 Financial cost of training at different stages
The cost of training at 1999/2000 rates totals £4,777 over four years. This includes the costs of tuition, initial application fee and student membership. The costs of personal analysis, supervision and malpractice insurance are additional.

3.5 Interruptions in training
It is unusual for trainees to take time out from the training. Consideration may be given in exceptional circumstances, such as a family crisis or pregnancy, when the maximum time out would be one year.

4. CLINICAL AND ACADEMIC REQUIREMENTS

4.1 Personal therapy
Trainees must have been in therapy for a minimum of three times a week for at least six months before applying. Potential applicants who need to find a Training Analyst will be guided, through informal interview, to select a suitable and approved person.

The Training therapist or analyst is consulted by the Training Committee, four times during the training: first, at commencement, to verify the suitability of the applicant; second, to ascertain the trainee's readiness to take on a first training patient; third, to check readiness to take on a second training patient; and fourth, to ensure readiness to read-in and practice independently. Beyond this verification, a fuller report is not requested, so confidentiality between the Training analyst/ therapist and the trainee is maintained.

4.2 Clinical requirements
A trainee may start seeing their first training patient after the first year of seminars, provided their training therapist agrees. The Training Advisor may assist the trainee

in finding an approved training supervisor. Medical cover must be arranged and malpractice insurance is mandatory. The Reduced Fee Scheme provides some training patients but trainees are increasingly needing to find their own patients. Trainees are expected to attend a Six Monthly Report Workshop once a term. Before qualification each trainee must have seen two training patients, one male and one female, one for two years and one for eighteen months, each for a minimum of three times a week.

4.3 Supervision
A trainee must have a different supervisor (one male and one female) for each training patient, and must attend both supervisors once a week.

4.4 Written work and course assessment
The trainee is required to write an Infant Observation paper, covering at least 14 months, towards the end of the observation. A six-monthly report is required on each training patient until qualification. The final Reading-In paper (about 7,000 words) is assessed by two readers at a viva, attended by the Training Advisor. The Assessors are chosen by the Training Committee. Following qualification a Reading-In ceremony and celebration is held with colleagues where the report on the viva is presented to the trainee.

4.5 Assessment, standards and ethical requirements
The different strands of the Jungian Analytic Training (Infant Observation Seminars, Theoretical Seminars, Clinical Seminars, and Supervision of Training Patients) are closely linked and, for each part, assessment is continuous. Assessment is based on clearly agreed procedures and criteria, with explicit objectives. Seminar leaders (Infant Observation, Theoretical and Clinical Seminars) base their written report on the trainee's contribution in the group, verbal presentations (at least one per term), ability to retain and use knowledge, and, for the Infant Observation module, the completion of a satisfactory Infant Observation paper. Trainees themselves are asked to make a self-assessment at the end of each term or seminar module.

Supervision of individual clinical work is through written six-monthly reports including a comprehensive feedback form, completed by both the Supervisor and the trainee.

The Training Committee receives copies of all assessments, which are channelled through, and discussed with, the Training Advisor.

The assessment procedures accord with the general and specific aims that inform the training as a whole. Thus, it is intended that, by qualification, trainees will have gained competency in therapeutic technique, and will have demonstrated a capacity and desire to continue learning, and to work intensively and independently with patients. They should be able to assess patients and judge how and when to work in different ways, such as once weekly or in a different setting, and should be able to understand and use clinical and technical analytic terms appropriately and comfortably. They should have a good appreciation of theoretical differences and be able to cope with the tensions and conflicts within the different constructs, and should have begun to evolve a model or discourse which fits their way of working, thinking and feeling. During their training, they should have experienced and appreciated that the therapeutic relationship is one of mutual transformation, and understood Jung's statement that the therapist can exercise no influence unless he/she is open to the influence of the patient.

5. TRAINEE RESPONSE

1. Why this course was chosen

1.1 What made people decide to train?
Trainees with experience in a related field wish to work in more depth than their previous skills allowed, and they viewed the course as providing a good grounding for the rest of their careers. For others, psychotherapy training represented a career change. They had usually been interested in the analytic world for some time and had seen the middle years of life as an appropriate time to retrain for this work, often with a view to self-employment.

1.2 What were the aspects of this course that were most attractive?
Viewed the BAP as a long-established organisation with a good reputation, unique in offering in-depth clinical trainings that brought Psychoanalytic, Jungian and Child Psychotherapy together. They were looking for the intensity of three times per week therapy as a training requirement, and for the prospect of being qualified to work to that level.

Supervision of two intensive training patients would encourage development of therapeutic skills and of the trainees' professional identity.

A Jungian perspective that also included the psychoanalytic perspective.

They valued the idea of being taught by senior clinicians as part of an experienced peer-group.

Enjoyed the other courses at the BAP.

1.3 What was your experience of the selection procedure?
The application and selection procedures were experienced as efficient, straightforward and clear. It was felt that the approach was rigorous and ethical – a real attempt to help suitable candidates to train at an appropriate time for them.

Interview style was fair and courteous, relating to each person in a humane way and considering people on their own merits. The standards and procedures were strongly established but allowed for flexibility.

1.4 Before the start of the course, how informed did you feel about each stage of the training?
The prospectus was clearly written and details were amplified at the pre-course induction day. Students therefore felt reasonably well informed. However, some elements of the workload were not explained sufficiently clearly, and some trainees were not made aware of the difficulties of working full-time during the course.

2. The atmosphere of the course

2.1 How do you feel about the way in which information is communicated?
Communication is generally good. Information is disseminated in various ways: via individual and group meetings with the Training Advisor for the year group, an

annual meeting for all students with the Training Committee and a newsletter. The Student Organisation includes representatives from each training group and holds regular committee meetings. It also organises three lectures during the year and an AGM in the summer term.

2.2 What do you find the most confusing aspect of the training?
Trainees are exposed to different aspects of Jungian thinking and experience, and this can cause confusion as to what it really means to be a Jungian. It can be a struggle to combine technique, theory and practice of psychotherapy. However, these difficulties are an important aspect of the training in that they enable each person to struggle with the tension of becoming a psychotherapist in their own right, and to their own level and understanding.

Some conflict is experienced between the expectations of the BAP and those of individual supervisors; rules can sometimes seem arbitrary and open to debate. There is also a certain tension between supervision and clinical seminars when conflicting views are expressed.

2.3 How much opportunity do you have to share thoughts and feelings with fellow trainees?
Training Advisor and Training Committee meetings provide a useful opportunity for this, and there is plenty of time to meet fellow trainees when seminars and informal meetings are held in the BAP house.

Some students feel that it would be useful to have a group facilitator.

The Student Organisation provides an excellent forum for meeting trainees from the other streams and from different year groups. Trainees feel it would be useful to have more collaboration with the Freudian-stream psychoanalytic trainees as part of the course.

2.4 What do you feel about the methods of teaching?
The standard of teaching varies. Analysts who are expert clinicians are not necessarily good facilitators of group learning, but on the whole trainees are well satisfied with the teaching they receive, especially when attention is paid to the dynamics of the group. Much responsibility is placed on the trainees themselves to read, think and contribute to the seminars.

2.5 What did you think about the way assessments were done to allow you to progress to the next stages of training?
Some trainees feel that the assessment procedures are thorough, accurate and fair; others that there is sometimes insufficient openness and clarity. Most feel that the feedback is useful and non-persecutory, with the emphasis on supporting the trainee in progressing to the next stage. The assessment procedures are being made more open, so the students will find out more directly how they are perceived. We are also being encouraged to assess our own progress.

2.6 Has the course met your expectations?
It is generally felt that the course fulfils its promise to help the individual develop towards becoming a psychotherapist. A few disappointments were expressed:

training patients not always immediately available when the trainee is ready; a wish for group discussions to be more lively and less inhibited.

2.7 How do you feel about your future with the organisation?
The BAP is a large organisation which offers many activities and opportunities for development following qualification.

2.8 What plans do trainees have for future practice and possible balance of different sorts of work in their career?
The BAP is generally well known and well respected and students therefore feel they have good prospects for the future. A thorough Analytic training provides an opportunity for working within institutional settings, both inside and outside the NHS, and for establishing a private practice. Some trainees are also interested in writing and teaching in the field of Analytic Psychology.

PSYCHOANALYTIC PSYCHOTHERAPY WITH ADULTS FOR CHILD
PSYCHOTHERAPISTS (BAP-CONV – BCP)

2. THEORETICAL ORIENTATION AND CURRICULUM

This training, in common with the Psychoanalytic Psychotherapy training, is designed for trainees who want a firm grounding in each of the three main psycho-analytic schools, Kleinian, Independent and Contemporary Freudian. An attempt is made to offer a balance of theoretical and clinical seminars, and trainees are taught by experts from each of the three schools.

Because all trainees have already completed an extensive training in Child Psychotherapy, theoretical seminars cover more advanced aspects of psychoanalytic theory, such as Comparative Psychoanalytic Concepts: Transference and Counter-transference, Transference and Counter-transference in Perverse States of Mind, Psychosis, Thinking and Linking, and Narcissism. The theoretical seminars constitute a rolling programme, enabling trainees to join at different points. Trainees are obliged to attend two years of theoretical seminars (five per term). Because the trainee group is relatively small, there is scope to programme seminars requested by trainees, whilst also ensuring coverage of essential topics.

Trainees attend five clinical seminars per term; each block of seminars is led by a senior Psychotherapist or Psychoanalyst, again with a balance of input from each of the three schools.

3. TRAINING STRUCTURE

3.1 Training committee
At present the Training Committee comprises a Chair, Finance Officer, Seminar Organiser, Student Advisor and Six-Monthly Report Tutor. The committee meets approximately monthly. The Chair, or a representative of the Chair, attends meetings of the BAP's Professional Trainings Division to ensure coordination and cross-fertilisation of the different trainings within the BAP.

3.2 Selection procedure and admission

All applicants must be qualified Child Psychotherapists and members of the Association of Child Psychotherapists. If they are not already members of the Child Section of the BAP, then they are required to become members of this section.

3.3 Time commitment per week and length of training

The maximum time commitment per week for a trainee attending all seminars and with two current training patients would be:

Evening seminar (8.30–10p.m.)	1.5 hours
Patient contact time	6 hours
Supervision	<u>2 hours</u>
	9.5 hours

Further time is needed for writing up sessions (approximately three hours), probable personal therapy or analysis (one to five hours), reading time, time spent writing six-monthly reports and travelling time. The total may add up to 15–20 hours.

Trainees have the option of ceasing theoretical seminars after two years (although many choose to continue), but are required to continue in clinical seminars and supervision until the completion of training.

If the training extends beyond two years, this is usually because of a delay starting with one or both training patients; if a patient drops out early in treatment the trainee will be required to recommence with another patient; occasionally there will be concern about an aspect of the trainee's work and they will be asked to undertake further work under supervision.

3.4 Financial cost of training at different stages

All trainees pay membership fees of the BAP as members of the Child Section; these fees are reviewed annually. Because this is a rolling programme seminar fees are paid termly according to attendance. For a trainee attending theoretical and clinical seminars throughout the academic year, the annual course fee is currently £1,290. In addition, all trainees are required to have appropriate indemnity insurance.

The total cost of training will vary considerably according to the amount paid for supervision, the amount paid and frequency of personal therapy, and the time taken for a particular trainee to complete all the requirements. Trainees must expect to incur costs of over £5,000, and the total cost may exceed £20,000.

3.5 Interruptions in training

Realistically some trainees are bound to experience life events during the course of training which may disrupt their work. No one would be permanently excluded from the training for such a reason, unless their ability to practise clinically was permanently compromised. Each individual's case would be considered separately, but the importance of providing continuity and professional treatment for patients would be a prime consideration when agreeing arrangements.

3.6 Graduating and beginning a career

People completing this training become Associate Members of the Adult Section of the BAP. Those wishing to do so may subsequently go on to obtain Full Membership of the Adult Section of the BAP, although there is no obligation to do so. Newly qualified therapists are expected to develop their own private practice and public sector work, but may register with Clinical Services to obtain referrals through the BAP.

3.7 Numbers of students per intake
This is a small course and can comfortably accommodate twelve trainees (two clinical seminars of six). A minimum of three or four trainees is needed for the course to be viable.

4. CLINICAL AND ACADEMIC REQUIREMENTS

4.1 Personal therapy
It is normally expected that trainees will be in personal psychoanalytic psycho-therapy, but the frequency of this is not specified, and reports are not solicited from personal therapists or analysts. All trainees will have had extensive personal therapy or analysis during their Child Psychotherapy training, prior to commencing this course.

4.2 Clinical requirements
Trainees see two three-times-weekly training patients, one woman and one man, for a minimum of two years and eighteen months. Because trainees are already experienced clinicians, they may take on training patients from the start of the training.

Trainees may obtain patients through the BAP Reduced Fee Scheme, but they have the option of taking patients paying a full fee if they can secure appropriate referrals themselves.

4.3 Supervision
Trainees have weekly supervision on each case; trainees arrange supervision themselves, with Psychotherapists and Psychoanalysts taken from a list of approved supervisors and training therapists.

4.4 Written work and course attendance
There is no written work of a purely theoretical nature. Trainees are required to write reports summarising each six months of treatment (up to 1,500 words) which are discussed in regular Six-Monthly Report Seminars.

When the trainee has fulfilled the course requirements, in terms of seminar attendance, treatment of both training patients, completion of six-monthly reports, and feedback from supervisors, they prepare a Reading-In paper, describing the treatment of one of their training cases (up to 8,000 words). This is primarily a clinical paper, but appropriate reference to psychoanalytic theory and literature is included. The paper is tutored, and two 'readers' are then appointed who ensure that an adequate standard has been reached in the written presentation of clinical material. The trainee then has a ceremonial 'reading' of their paper to their peer group and members of the Training Committee.

Registers are kept of those attending seminars. Excessive absences would be a cause for concern.

4.5 Assessment and standards

In general, assessment is qualitative rather than quantitative. Supervisors provide reports on the trainee's clinical work every six months, the Six-Monthly Report Tutor monitors the quality of written work, and seminar leaders provide feedback to the training committee on group and individual contributions to the seminars.

The culture of the training is to foster development and address difficulties, rather than to exclude trainees who fail to meet specified targets. However, if a trainee consistently functions poorly in a particular area, they might be asked to repeat a particular piece of work, or to withdraw from the training. Standard procedures and an appeals procedure exist for trainees in difficulty.

5. TRAINEE RESPONSE

1. Why this course was chosen

1.1 What made people decide to train?
Although all students had worked with parents during their careers as Child Psychotherapists, and some had already treated adults in psychotherapy, all wanted further training in work with adults and official recognition as adult psychotherapists. The BAP 'modified' training was chosen specifically because of the large colleague group in the organisation, a group comprised of professionals practising with a diversity of theoretical orientations.

1.2 What were the aspects of this course that were most attractive?
The recognition of previous professional training in psychotherapy, leading to a modification of requirements during the training compared with standard adult psychotherapy trainings, was most attractive. Trainees also welcomed the opportunity to revisit known theory, and to explore additional viewpoints. The possibility of being active within the BAP as a whole added to the appeal of the training.

1.3 What was your experience of the selection procedure?
All those trainees consulted experienced the selection procedures as 'reasonable' and 'interesting'.

1.4 Before the start of the course, how informed did you feel about each stage of the training?
Information about the stages of training was clearly set out in a manual, and there was also a chance to discuss aspects of the training with the Training Committee. There have subsequently been some procedural changes, and some trainees felt it had not been made clear enough initially that this could be the case.

2. The atmosphere of the course

2.1 How do you feel about the way in which information is communicated?
Between regular meetings with the Training Advisor and letters, it was felt that, for the most part, information was communicated sufficiently clearly.

2.2 What do you find the most confusing aspect of the training?
There was no main aspect of the course that was felt to be confusing, although some minor confusion has ensued over procedural changes.

2.3 How much opportunity do you have to share thoughts and feelings with fellow trainees?
There was felt to be much opportunity to share thoughts and feelings with fellow students.

2.4 What do you feel about the methods of teaching?
Clinical seminars and individual supervision were generally felt to be excellent. Trainees felt the quality of theoretical seminars varied, with some seminar leaders cognisant that all trainees had had a previous psychotherapy training and pitching the seminars accordingly, while others did not.

2.5 What did you think about the way assessments were done to allow you to progress to the next stages of training?
A system of individual annual reviews has recently been introduced, which should ensure that feedback to trainees is more formal and explicit than previously.

2.6 Has the course met your expectations?
It was generally felt that the course had met expectations, with trainees emerging from the course confident in their ability to treat adults. In the past few years there have been changes in the membership of the Training Committee. Trainees are appreciative that there has been much effort on the part of trainers to minimise any disruption that a change of personnel can cause. Additionally, trainees feel that their views on the training and ideas for change have been carefully considered, and incorporated into new policies as appropriate.

2.7 How do you feel about your future with the organisation?
Most trainees felt that they would like to become active within the organisation.

2.8 What plans do trainees have for future practice and possible balance of different sorts of work in their career?
It is important to stress that all trainees are already fully trained in Child and Adolescent Psychotherapy as well as work with parents, and thus have long-established careers working privately, within the NHS, or in a combination of these settings. Qualification as Adult Psychotherapists will open the possibility of working as Adult Psychotherapists in the health service if desired, but most trainees will use the training both to enhance their current work and to shift the balance to working more with adults than previously.

AUTHOR'S COMMENTS

As one of the longest-standing private psychotherapy training organisations, the BAP has earned a solid and well-founded reputation, based on well-resourced, tried and tested methods over decades. It has drawn most of its teachers and trainers from the British Psycho-Analytic Society for the Freudian stream and from the Society for Analytical Psychology for the Jungian stream, suggesting a hierarchy of loyalties beyond the boundaries of the organisation. As the trainee responses indicate this provides rich teaching from the most experienced sources in the field. In the light of this it is worth asking what changes there have been to make this more than a classically traditional training. Clearly, the theoretical and clinical teaching is up to date. There appears to be a lively and autonomous student organisation able to challenge the training committees. All twelve of the Jungian Training Committee are BAP-trained. The new books authored by BAP-trained members suggest ongoing development among BAP graduates.

As in the last edition of this guide, the trainees reported a lack of attention to group dynamics and to using group discussion to enhance the learning experience (see discussion on educational models, p. 50f.). The same critique is mentioned in the comments by two of the three BAP student groups.

It was not clear if there was any assessment of staff by trainees in place. It was interesting to note that the Jungian training is one of the few trainings in this guide to be specific about its educational objectives stating clearly what was expected of trainees before qualification.

Now that there are other courses in psychotherapy taught largely by analysts it will be interesting to see if the BAP approach to training continues to thrive. The psychoanalytic course was thought at the last edition of this guide to have a more Independent emphasis and lacking in Klein. It seems as if both Kleinian and post-Kleinian thinking are now included. The thoroughness and depth of the training is likely to make its graduates effective ambassadors for those who want a psycho-therapy training taught at depth mainly by analysts.

Modified Conversion training in Adult psychotherapy for child psychotherapists: there are few opportunities for the accreditation of prior learning in analytic training. This is one of them. The depth of training and analysis of practising child therapists is the recognised base for a training that offers to the considerable experience of child psychotherapists, the chance to train in intensive adult psychotherapy. It also offers the chance of belonging to a rich and diverse analytic organisation with many oppor-tunities for professional development and contribution.

Description of the BAP child and adolescent psychotherapy course is in the section on child trainings (p. 250).

CAMBRIDGE SOCIETY FOR PSYCHOTHERAPY (CSP – UKCP/PPS)

41 Beaulands Close, Cambridge CB4 1JA
Tel. 01223 510229
E-mail: info@cambridge-psychotherapy.org.uk

1. HISTORY OF THE ORGANISATION

The Society started in 1980 and arose from discussions about how best to educate people for the work of psychotherapy. These conversations put the notion of training itself into question:

- What are the qualities needed in a psychotherapist and how are they best developed?
- Why do people often feel that it is only after training that their real development begins?
- If training relies on the transmission of received knowledge and assured technique, what happens to qualities such as imagination, courage, curiosity and individual responsiveness?
- How can training provide genuine access to knowledge and experience without encouraging passivity, anxiety or grandiosity?

The Society does not offer a course in the ordinary sense of the word and does not have the usual demarcations of teachers and taught. We see ourselves as a learning community with people at different stages of development: 'ordinary members' (those qualified) and 'student members' (those moving towards qualification.) Our focus is on understanding the complexities and difficulties of relationships rather than on acquiring technique. We value the capacity to *be* rather than the ability to *do* and emphasise the growth of imagination and responsibility. We encourage a personal, critical and independent response to all aspects of the work.

Initially, minimal structures fostered these aims. Individual therapy, access to people with experience, discussions of psychotherapy, suggestions for intellectual and personal exploration of the literature and ideas, help with finding patients and supervision were what was considered necessary. Within this, people created their own path, arriving at a point of transition from student to ordinary member through work and discussion with others. These principles remain true but as the Society has grown, more formal structures have emerged, although many of these remain unconventional.

In 1992 we became a member organisation of UKCP and we have continued to grow, now having 54 members.

The Society continues to offer an unusual way of becoming a psychotherapist. It is not an easy path. It eschews certainty, demands a deep commitment and requires a particular kind of strength. Those who undertake this, value it and feel it offers a uniquely appropriate preparation for the work.

2. THEORETICAL ORIENTATION AND CURRICULUM

The ordinary vocabulary of training organisations, such as 'theoretical orientation', 'curriculum' and 'training committee', sits uncomfortably with our approach and practice. Essentially, students in the Society create their own encounter with the field, exploring a range of possible inspiration and knowledge and developing their own way through it. General themes are planned collectively by the student group in consultation with ordinary members and the student group meets weekly for discussions, sometimes alone, sometimes with ordinary members and sometimes with outside speakers. This structured work provides a helpful and containing background for the more individual work and involves sharing responsibility for others' learning. All students engage with the psychoanalytic inheritance that forms such a powerful background to all psychotherapeutic work but they also read widely beyond this and we value the quality of the engagement people have with their reading as much as the content. Ordinary members are always available for suggestions and advice.

When this approach to learning works it produces feelings of ownership, confidence, breadth and appreciation of complexity, in which there are genuine transformations of understanding. It doesn't suit everyone, however, and applicants must think carefully about whether they feel able to undertake it.

3. TRAINING STRUCTURE

3.1. Training committee

Responsibility for the general organisation of the Society, for clinical and academic work and for student learning, is carried by both students and ordinary members in a variety of ways.

The Governing Body of the Society is the General Meeting, called at least four times a year. All ordinary and student members may attend and vote. Much of its day to day work is delegated to sub-groups which have a mixed ordinary/student membership and are responsible for: admissions, graduation, student planning, the library, publicity, the Newsletter, the Journal, the Ethics Panel, referrals, UKCP Support and outside speakers. Elected officers (Secretary, Treasurer) are usually student members.

It is the responsibility of each student, with the support of other students and ordinary members, to develop the most appropriate way for themselves to learn. A key structure in this is the student group which meets weekly and is the focus for clinical and academic discussion and for practical and emotional support. The supervisor's role is also central. Other key structures include:

- The Planning Group which meets at least twice a year to plan the student programme
- Pairings with another student, and with an ordinary member for periods of six months, providing opportunities for information, support, mutual development and exploration
- Interest groups on various themes with mixed student and ordinary membership. Currently there are a number of reading groups, a group exploring Shakespeare, a group studying eating disorders and a peer supervision group
- Ordinary members are always available to respond to students, either individually or as a group.

3.2 Selection procedure and admission

We look for people who are curious, imaginative, sensitive, intelligent and enthusiastic, who think deeply and have that notoriously difficult-to-define 'something' that suggests that they might become good at this kind of work. We are aware that this spark comes in different guises and may have different cultural, gender and age-specific forms. We try to be accessible to the widest possible range of people. Serious commitments – in time, emotion, intellect and money – are required but no specific educational qualifications are demanded. Compatibility between applicant and current students is also taken into account.

The application process consists of an informal meeting with a current student, a written application, two meetings with the student group and two individual interviews. All members of the Society may be involved in this process. The final decisions are taken at a meeting of the whole Society.

3.3 Time commitment per week and length of training
A whole-hearted contribution is required from all student members, both to their own and to others' learning, and to running the Society. The type and extent of contributions varies with personal preferences and talents.

Each student needs time for seeing clients, supervision, personal therapy, reading, writing, thinking and meetings. All students attend the weekly student meeting and the quarterly Business Meetings. Pairings meet at mutual convenience and frequency. Most students belong to one or more sub-group and interest group.

Length of time as a student varies with individual needs but tends to take longer than with conventional trainings. The minimum is four years. Most important is each person's developing understanding of what is involved in psychotherapy, and how long *they* need to stay in the group.

3.4 Financial cost of the training at different stages
For students, the annual contribution to running costs is currently £140. Although the absence of fees makes the Society more accessible to those with limited means, students need to budget adequately for their own therapy and supervision, the purchase of books and journals, and renting a consulting room if necessary.

3.5 Interruptions in training
The structure and organisation of the Society allows for flexibility. Any period of 'time-out' has to be fully discussed and agreed.

3.6 Graduating and beginning a career
Graduation is seen as a gradual transition and involves much discussion with other members. After graduation, students continue as members, working out their own level of responsibility and contribution. The nature of the Society means that there are many opportunities for continued learning. Generally, people wish to give back the kind of support they themselves received as students.

Most graduates combine private practice with work in the public sector or voluntary agencies.

3.7 Numbers of students per intake
Recently, students have been admitted in alternate years, with a staggered entry and no set quota. The criterion is the healthy maintenance of an effective student group. There are currently eleven student members.

4. CLINICAL AND ACADEMIC REQUIREMENTS

4.1 Personal therapy
Personal therapy is fundamental to people's learning. Students are expected to be in therapy for a year before joining and throughout their time as students. The therapist should be in sympathy with the Society's ethos and aims.

4.2 Clinical requirements

Acquiring a variety and depth of clinical experience is extremely important. Students usually need to work for a reduced fee in order to get experience of long-term intensive work. Some people like to get experience of working in mental health services, if this has not yet featured in their working life. The Society's referral scheme helps students find suitable clients.

4.3 Supervision

Supervision comes in many forms – individual, group, peer – and some variety is encouraged. The Society asks that all student members are in a minimum of once-weekly individual supervision and that at least one supervisor is chosen from among the Society's ordinary members.

4.4 Written work and course attendance

We encourage a diversity of both private and public writing: for self-expression, exploration of ideas, and communication with others. Written work can be presented at student group meetings and published in the Newsletter and Journal. In addition, many people write something for circulation at the time of graduation.

The emphasis on self-responsibility is the only attendance requirement. Students who do not make the necessary commitment may find it hard to graduate.

4.5 Assessment, standards and ethical requirements

We rely on the responsibility, maturity and integrity of all our members, both ordinary and student, in maintaining standards through continuous reflection, discussion, criticism and challenge. Students must be prepared to be confronted with other people's views of their work and to meet these challenges creatively and constructively.

Graduation is approached very seriously during a sharply focused period of about nine months. Its exact form is defined individually by each student in negotiation with others but they will be expected to discuss their work openly and frankly and they will meet close examination of what they have done. Many students form a small graduation group to guide them through this phase. There is usually some written communication and an external consultant is also involved. The graduation process culminates in the student being welcomed as an ordinary member at a Business Meeting of the whole Society.

We believe that the best guarantee of ethical practice comes from the integrity and responsibility of each individual psychotherapist. Our ethical beliefs are based on respect for the client's autonomy and for the integrity and confidentiality of the therapeutic relationship. These principles are reflected in a written Code of Ethics and Practice.

5. TRAINEE RESPONSE

1. Why this course was chosen

1.1 What made people decide to train?
There are as many answers to this as there are students. However, a recurring theme was a wish to take existing training further, to enable work at a deeper level and get

to grips with major theoretical issues from a variety of viewpoints. There was also a shared interest in furthering personal growth and development.

1.2 What were the aspects of this course that were most attractive?
The course attracted people because 'nobody tells you what you ought to think'. Thanks to its student-led, non-hierarchical structure and the opportunity of working cooperatively, previous experience is valued, and we do not feel infantilised. Opportunities for personal discovery and the emphasis on personal therapy and supervision are welcomed. The self-managed nature of the training eliminates expensive administrative superstructures, allows freedom and flexibility, and keeps costs low. UKCP recognition, the local nature of the course, and the connection to a Cambridge-based psychotherapy network are all valued.

1.3 What was your experience of the selection procedure?
We felt it to be thorough and searching. Joining a discussion group with existing students was a challenging 'taster' for the training itself. People felt that the process of finding out and being found out about was a genuinely two-way one, and that we came away with an accurate picture of the Society.

1.4 Before the start of the course, how informed did you feel about each stage of the training?
The training is not designed in stages. This lack of structure did initially feel difficult but the challenge of making your own structure is a welcome opportunity to develop self-motivation, discernment and self-containment. Personal development is organic, not chronological, and the design of the course reflects the model of therapy: you can't know what's coming next. The *Information for New Members* folder gives new students a clear introduction to the Society. There are also plenty of opportunities to ask for information and feedback.

2. The atmosphere of the course

2.1 How do you feel about the way in which information is communicated?
This takes some getting used to. The Society is a network, and it can be difficult to know where information is located, and whom to ask.

2.2 What do you find the most confusing aspect of the training?
As above. Because the Society is a network, there is no single Society 'voice'. The training evolves as you mature.

2.3 How much opportunity do you have to share thoughts and feelings with fellow trainees?
There are many opportunities through weekly meetings and pairings, and additional opportunities can be created as and when needed. There is also the opportunity to share with ordinary members at monthly discussions, business meetings, pairings and interest groups.

2.4 What do you feel about the methods of teaching?
We are responsible for choosing and creating our own methods of learning, which can sometimes be hard work. We are constantly reviewing our learning needs and

take advice from ordinary members when planning our reading and study. We invite internal and external speakers on a regular basis.

2.5 What do you think about the way assessments were done to allow you to progress to the next stage of training?
At present this happens most intensively during the graduation process. We prefer the term evaluation, and feel that self-evaluation, using feedback from peers and others is the best model. We have the opportunity for using our pairings with peers and ordinary members for this purpose.

2.6 Has the course met your expectations?
This question is difficult to answer, as expectations varied widely. By and large, we feel that our expectations have been met, challenged and broadened, and our expectations of ourselves continue to rise.

2.7 How do you feel about your future with the organisation?
We welcome the prospect of continuing involvement. Because of the nature of the group, we expect this to be easy, natural and accessible.

2.8 What plans do trainees have for future practice and possible balance of different sorts of work in their career?
Many of us also work in other settings, both therapeutic and non-therapeutic. There are felt to be real difficulties of integrating clinical practice with the need to make a living, especially in Cambridge where there is a plentiful supply of psychotherapists.

Note: A fuller version of this entry can be found on our web site:
<www. Cambridge-psychotherapy.org.uk>

AUTHOR'S COMMENTS

This is the only training that is managed by the collective group of trainees who are the training committee. Many trainings aspire to involve trainees in shaping their learning or by being invited to assess teaching methods of staff. Only this course is designed and managed by the trainees themselves. This facilitative and collaborative approach is shaped by the participative and egalitarian values of 'the outfit' as they call themselves, where not-knowing is a valued resource in the service of learning and development. It may be argued that trainees cannot teach themselves; however, the selection procedure is thorough, offering plenty of opportunity for applicant and the outfit to get to know each other in order to ensure that there is sufficient ability and motivation of the prospective trainee to be able to use the structure and to contribute to the learning group. In fact, the membership of the outfit also provide support and facilitation for the trainee group in their role as the training committee and there is an ongoing culture of practice inherited down the years.

As the comments indicate this still places the burden of course design, negotiation and implementation upon the trainees, who call upon facilitators and teachers as they need to. This suits those who wish to control their own dealings with authority. No doubt the outfit does not avoid having to deal with issues of authority, but less of the authority that belongs to organisational power and experience. Some believe that struggling with authority is a vital element in analytic education, in evoking and having to deal with transferences shaped by a steeper hierarchy.

Some of the vision for this training stems from the work of Peter Lomas, formerly an Independent group psychoanalyst before he resigned from the British Psycho-Analytic Society. He was also involved in setting up the Guild. He has written an article, 'The Setting Up of a Psychotherapy Training' (Lomas 1990).

CENTRE FOR ATTACHMENT-BASED PSYCHOANALYTIC PSYCHOTHERAPY (CAPP–UKCP/PPS)

LVS Resource Centre
356 Holloway Road
London N7 6PA
Tel. 020 7794 4306 Fax. 01435 866216
E-mail: capp@dial.pipex.com

1. HISTORY OF THE ORGANISATION

Since 1976 CAPP has developed as an organisation for service and training committed to the practice of Attachment-based Psychoanalytic Psychotherapy. It provides a four-year part-time psychotherapy training. It is accredited by the UKCP. In 1999 there were 43 Registered Members and 63 students. CAPP offers a referral service for the public and a consultation and outreach service for individuals and organisations.

2. THEORETICAL ORIENTATION AND CURRICULUM

Attachment-based Psychoanalytic Psychotherapy has developed on the basis of the growing understanding of the importance of attachment relationships to human growth and development throughout life. This approach to psychotherapy, developing from the relational tradition of psychoanalysis, draws upon a broad range of psychoanalytic insights and the rapidly growing field of attachment theory.

Understanding psychotherapy within the context of attachment relationships leads to an approach to psychotherapy as a cooperative venture between therapist and clients. The aim is to develop a secure base from which to explore the unconscious and the experience of loss and trauma in the course of development. These are not confined to a private world or to early life. Attachment relationships formed by individuals are shaped by groups and society as a whole. The experience of loss and abuse as a result of structures and pressures within the wider society cannot be split off and left as a separate problem to those with which therapy concerns itself. The social structures, pressures and everyday experiences concerning race, sex, sexuality, gender, class and disability, together with the complexity of the individual's response, can be worked with in a profound way through Attachment-based Psychoanalytic Psychotherapy.

Mourning is vital to the acknowledgement and understanding of the effects of abandonment, loss and abuse, whether emotional, sexual, or physical. The support of an authentic process of mourning forms a central part of the therapeutic work. This is crucial to the development of a sense of self and the capacity to form and sustain intimate relationships. Both a strong sense of self and good attachment relationships are essential to managing stressful experiences.

John Bowlby's original development of attachment theory was prompted primarily by his concern to ensure social recognition for the central importance of attachment and the experience of loss in early development. He was also concerned to strengthen the scientific foundations of psychoanalysis. Since his original work attachment theory has come to occupy a key position in this fast developing scientific field, providing a link between psychoanalysis, developmental psychology, neurobiology, and the behavioural sciences.

Curriculum

To prepare trainees to practise Attachment-based Psychoanalytic Psychotherapy in a skilled, safe and ethical manner. CAPP is committed to diminishing all forms of discrimination – where there is an abuse of power either individually, in the therapeutic situation or as an institution.

1. Personal training therapy
Therapy commences at least a year before starting the Course and continues at least until Registration. Students must undertake twice weekly therapy no later than the beginning of their second year. It is recommended that this be increased towards the end of the Course.

2. Group work
Each Intake group meets weekly with a facilitator throughout the Course for one and a quarter hours. The purpose of this is to reflect on the impact of the Course.

3. Theoretical seminars
These commence in the first term of the first year.

Year 1: Freud and psychoanalysis are studied in parallel with seminars on attachment theory.

Year 2: The development of the self-concepts of the self, its relationship to others, its application to clinical practice. Introduction to object relations theory and its interface with attachment theory.

Year 3: Object relations theory and its application to clinical work. Trauma and its links with disrupted attachments. Disturbances of the self and attachment relationships – and ways people communicate anxieties/ trauma – such as relational difficulties, dissociative states, depression, phobias, eating difficulties, violence against the self, somatisation, addictions, and others.

Year 4: Disturbances of the self and communication of anxieties and/or trauma, including the interface with psychiatry.

4. Infant observation and Life Cycle Studies
In years 1 and 2 students observe an infant from birth until 18 months. The seminar meets weekly and integrates theory, observation and subjective experience and their

link with adult clinical work. These emphasise the centrality of attachment to the development of a healthy sense of self. In years 3 and 4, child and adolescent development, adulthood, ageing and death are studied.

5. Clinical seminars

These meet weekly from the start of year 2 until the end of year 4. The goal is to discuss practical themes, and techniques, such as working with transference and counter-transference; defences against anxiety, unconscious communications, dreams, and so on, and clinical work problems.

6. Supervision

Weekly supervision begins when students start to work with clients.

7. Tutorials

Matters concerning the course can be discussed with the Course Tutor who is appointed to take a group of students through the course to registration.

3. TRAINING STRUCTURE

3.1 Training/organisational structure

The Trustees form the Board of Directors, concerned with overall policy. The Executive committee is responsible for finances, administration, and public relations.

The Clinical Training Committee (CTC) is responsible for setting and upholding training standards for all aspects of the Course.

The Education Committee is responsible for the development, design and review of the curriculum.

The Ethics Committee oversees the implementation of the Code of Ethics of CAPP.

3.2 Selection procedure and admission

The Course is postgraduate. Competencies should include: experience in the helping professions; evidence of a capacity to work with people who have suffered trauma; demonstrable readiness to sustain the commitments required by the Course; experience of therapy is essential for at least a year before the course. The therapist of a candidate must meet CAPP's criteria for training therapists.

On receipt of a completed Application Form, available from the CAPP Administrator, suitable candidates will be offered an interview with two members of the Training Committee, which will give final approval. Applications are welcomed from all sectors of the community.

3.3 Time commitment per week and length of training

The taught part of the Course is part-time for four years on two evenings a week. There are three terms of nine weeks; 12–14 hours per week should be identified. This will increase when clinical training begins. Clinical Forums are on the second Saturday of each month in term time.

3.4 Financial cost of the training

Personal therapy: on average two to three times weekly for six years, sliding scales are offered by most training therapists ranging from £20 upwards.

Tuition fees: approximately £2,000+ per annum.

Supervision fees: £35 per session. Two Supervisors are required before Registration but do not have to be simultaneous.

Insurance.

Book, photocopying, journals, and conferences: approx £200–500.

3.5 Interruptions in training

Students are recommended to complete years 1 and 2 without interruption. If students then need a break they can rejoin another year group in year 3. In unforeseen circumstances, up to 15 weeks may be missed with the agreement of the Course Tutor and the CTC.

3.6 Graduating and beginning a career

CAPP encourages its graduates to be involved in the organisation and welcomes participation in the organisational structure, teaching, tutoring, and so on.

4. CLINICAL AND ACADEMIC REQUIREMENTS

4.1 Personal therapy

Students must undertake a personal therapy with a therapist who fulfils CAPP's criteria for training therapists and stay in therapy at least until Registration, having begun a year or more before starting the Course. They should be in therapy twice a week from year 2, increasing to three times a week.

4.2 Clinical requirements

Students must work with clients one to three times weekly. Their training client must have been seen at least twice a week for at least two years. Students cannot qualify without having seen a minimum of six patients as well as their training client. CAPP refers suitable clients to trainees as well as to CAPP Registered Members. CAPP undertakes to try to refer at least two clients to trainees.

4.3 Supervision

Weekly supervision is required from the beginning of clinical work until Registration. The student must work with two supervisors, not necessarily simultaneously.

4.4 Written work and course attendance

Students must attend 80 per cent of each seminar. Written presentations, an Infant Observation paper, and a Clinical Paper on work with a long-term patient are part of the final required written work.

4.5 Assessment, standards and ethical requirements

All CAPP members are required to abide by CAPP's Code of Ethics and Code of Practice. Modern adult education methods are employed.

Annual assessment meeting
Progress is considered at these meetings, which are informed by the teaching staff's assessments and reported to the CTC.

Term staff meetings
Once a term the teaching staff of each Year Group meets with the Course Tutor.

Interview for the clinical part of the training
After the fifth term, a student may apply to begin clinical work. Two members of the CTC interview the student and with the Course Tutor refer to the CTC for ratification.

Portfolio
The Portfolio is a compilation of essays, presentations, Learning Contract, Infant Observation paper, and report of long-term work with a client. It is presented with the Course Tutor's approval to two interviewers at the Registration Interview.

Interview for Registration
Two members of the CTC conduct the Registration Interview, discuss it with the Course Tutor and make recommendations to the CTC, which takes the final decision.

Supervisors' reports
Supervisors submit an Annual report to the Clinical Training Committee on students' clinical work.

Assessment Criteria
For Registration students are required to demonstrate:

- clear understanding of attachment-based psychoanalytic psychotherapy and its application
- evidence of a theoretical understanding of attachment theory and psycho-analysis acceptable clinical experience over a minimum of two years
- the use of supervision
- continuing professional development
- an understanding of the ethical requirements for practice.

5. TRAINEE RESPONSE

1. Why this course was chosen

1.1 What made people decide to train?
Students come to CAPP from many different occupations. Some are looking for an occupation that is as challenging, valuable and rewarding as their current one (teaching, social work, and so on) used to be before the human dimension gave way before crude target setting. A smaller number see a CAPP training as adding another dimension to what they are already doing – as counsellors, managers or academics.

1.2 What were the aspects of this course that were most attractive?
Many were attracted to CAPP by meeting someone involved in the organisation whose personal spontaneity convinced them that the CAPP course would give them

the freedom to 'think their own thoughts'. A focus on the writings of Bowlby, Winnicott and Alice Miller is attractive to many, as is a clearly stated commitment to recognise social causes of distress. Also appealing is a commitment to understanding issues around abuse and trauma, and an openness to students who are gay, lesbian or from ethnic minorities. CAPP students come from diverse backgrounds, and the course gives space for their differences to be explored.

1.3 What was your experience of the selection procedure?
This is generally experienced as a non-threatening and relatively informal opportunity to reflect on why students want to train, and what attributes they can bring to the profession. Those used to corporate selection procedures sometimes feel that they process could be more stringent.

1.4 Before the start of the course, how informed did you feel about each stage of the training?
Most students attend an Open Day before deciding to apply. This gives then an opportunity to meet students and teachers. A Handbook is distributed to new students, which provides a full outline of the course and lays out general principles. The specifics of the programme for any year are only available in the preceding summer, since the course is continuously being reshaped in response to feedback from students.

2. The atmosphere of the course

2.1 How do you feel about the way in which information is communicated?
The management of the organisation is felt to have a strong commitment to improving communication with students through a monthly newsletter and sessions with course tutors. Detailed information is provided about course content at the beginning of each term. Student requests for more information about particular areas – such as referrals and supervision arrangements – are listened to.

2.2 What do you find the most confusing aspect of the training?
Teachers at CAPP come from a wide variety of theoretical positions, and exposure to their outlooks is generally experienced as both stimulating and challenging. It also has the potential to provoke perplexity in those who want something more 'definite'. All students are given a strong grounding in Attachment Theory and Freud from an attachment perspective to help them navigate their way through the diversity of psychoanalytic theorising. Another potential source of difficulty is the experiential group, which brings up issues that are sometimes difficult to contain. This has led to discussions about introducing more input on the theory of groups, so that students have a clearer conceptual understanding of what might be going on between them.

2.3 How much opportunity do you have to share thoughts and feelings with fellow trainees?
Although the experiential group provides a weekly opportunity for students to share thoughts and feelings, there are some people in each year who do not experience this as a safe context in which to do this. There are also occasions in the structured

seminars to reflect upon experience and share ideas. There has traditionally been a requirement for students to attend Saturday workshops, which provide an opportunities for small-group exercises and bonding over a communal lunch. Students are also encouraged to participate in monthly clinical seminars, which bring together the whole organisation.

2.4 What do you feel about the methods of teaching?
The variation in teaching styles allows for the individual learning styles of different students to be accommodated. The balance of the teaching is facilitative rather than directive, allowing students to be creative in how they direct their learning. Although such an approach is experienced as challenging and stimulating, some students would like more straight teaching.

2.5 What do you think about the way assessments were done to allow you to progress to the next stage of training?
The tutorial process gives students opportunities to share in the discussion about their progress, identifying strengths and exploring those areas which need more focus. Some argue that they would feel more confident about taking their first clients if they had been subjected to more probing questions at this stage.

2.6 Has the course met your expectations?
The course is generally experienced as challenging, thought-provoking and offering a significant opportunity for self-development. It enables students to develop their own approach to the practice of psychotherapy by challenging and discussing in a relaxed way even those tenets held passionately by some within the organisation – around multiple personality disorder, for example. Some with an experience of postgraduate courses say they would prefer a more intellectual approach.

2.7 How do you feel about your future with the organisation?
All the students involved in the discussions for this book expressed a desire to be involved in the future development of CAPP after registration. They are able to do so by participating on one of the various committees set up to run the organisation and evolve new initiatives, and through an annual Open Forum.

2.8 What plans do trainees have for future practice and possible balance of different sorts of work in their career?
Most students have an ambition to combine private practice with work in less isolated working environments – such as teaching, working for voluntary agencies or within the NHS.

AUTHOR'S COMMENTS

A variety of training and experience has contributed to the teachers on this course, which has clearly developed its standards and approach over the years. This course has assembled an approach to psychoanalytic psychotherapy that is unique among the trainings in this book, for its adherence to attachment theory as a unifying theme throughout the course. In reading this entry there is a strong thread that explores the external world as a source for understanding difficulties in attachment, including an understanding of equal opportunities, social prejudice and cultural difference that shape psychological experience.

Although many other courses include Bowlby's theories, none takes them as a unifying theme exploring Freud, object relations theory and other approaches to psychoanalysis through the lens of attachment theory. This is also the only course that develops the work of Alice Miller with her particular focus on the trauma of abuse and analysis of the 'gifted child'.

Applicants interested in attachment theory might need to explore how much this course makes use of research methodology and findings associated with the work of Bowlby and colleagues at the Tavistock. The course appears to offer a training as thorough as any of the others in its clinical and personal therapy demands. However, it might be important for applicants to ask how Bowlby's 'concern to ensure social recognition for the central importance of attachment and the experience of loss in early development' is mixed with theories that emphasise intrapsychic issues.

THE CENTRE FOR FREUDIAN ANALYSIS AND RESEARCH (CFAR – UKCP/PPS)

76 Haverstock Hill, London, NW3 2BE
Tel. 020 7267 3003

1. HISTORY OF THE ORGANISATION

The Centre for Freudian Analysis and Research (CFAR) was founded in 1985 by a group of four founder members who had met as a result of their research and clinical interests in the work of Jacques Lacan. CFAR initially started out under the name of the Cultural Centre for Freudian Studies and Research as a research organisation, but it rapidly became clear that the work proceeding around Lacan's writing required a clinical orientation and in 1988 the training was established and the name changed. It is the only training in Britain orientated by Lacan's work. From being an organisation run by the four founder members CFAR has grown and is now an organisation with a formal structure, which includes an elected Management Committee and Training Committee, both of whom are answerable to the Members' Council. Any full member of CFAR is eligible for election to these committees. There are other committees, however, which trainees are encouraged to join. CFAR places a high value on student contribution to the organisation so that it is possible for trainees to have considerable influence in the life of CFAR.

2. THEORETICAL ORIENTATION AND CURRICULUM

Our aims are: (1) to transmit the teachings and clinical practice of the work of Jacques Lacan with an emphasis on Lacan's interpretation of Freud, and (2) to engage and engender debates about the nature and practice of psychoanalysis. We are an affiliate of a Lacanian network stretching across the world – the Freudian Field. This organisation runs under the auspices of Judith Miller, Lacan's daughter.

Its brief is to develop and transmit the work of Jacques Lacan *within* the milieu of a particular country. To this end the groupings within the Freudian Field are free to organise themselves, as they think fit.

CFAR runs a clinical training, a yearly series of public lectures and seminars, and an introduction programme to the work of Jacques Lacan. The clinical training is composed of closed seminars for the trainees only, together with the public lecture and seminar programmes. The clinical seminars are organised around the central concepts of Lacan. Throughout the training there is also a study and critique of international developments in psychoanalysis since Freud.

Those interested in following the training but who have little experience in the work of Lacan are asked to attend the Introduction Programme prior to their application being considered. The Introduction Programme is open to anyone with an interest in Lacan, whether or not he or she intends to apply to the training.

The training programme aims at combining the traditional model of training in the United Kingdom together with a Lacanian orientation. The latter is much more focused on creating a psychoanalytic environment which trainees can use in their own way and at their own pace.

The Training Programme is held on Saturdays (see section 3.3). On approximately nine Saturdays in the year the day is given over to a series entitled the Freudian Field seminars – a senior analyst of the Association Mondiale de Psychanalyse comes from Europe and gives a commentary on a chosen text of Lacan's. The morning session is followed in the afternoon by a clinical presentation upon which the visiting analyst will then comment. CFAR organises a yearly conference where speakers from a number of different orientations are invited to speak. Trainees and members are also encouraged, where possible, to attend International Conferences organised by the Freudian Field and the Associate Mondiale de Psychanalyse.

Trainees must also participate in small study groups named by Lacan as Cartels. These have a specific structure intended to counteract the stickiness, which usually emerges in group work. Their number is restricted to four or five, organised around a specific topic of interest rather than friendship. Each Cartel appoints another person named as a Plus-One whose main task is also to neutralise such stickiness. The cartels meet approximately monthly and run for a maximum of two years. Within this period each individual tries to produce a piece of work, using the other members for support and constructive criticism. Lacan found this format maximised the productive potential of group work.

3. TRAINING STRUCTURE

3.1 Training committee

The Training Committee comprises six Members of the organisation who have extensive clinical experience. It is elected by CFAR's Members' Council and sits for two years.

3.2 Selection procedure and admission

Candidates to the training should have either a first degree or equivalent. Our applicants come from diverse backgrounds, both in work experience and training, as well as from diverse cultures. It is expected that candidates, unless they have some familiarity with Lacan's work, will have attended the introduction to Lacan's programme. Each applicant undertakes two interviews: one is conducted by an individual member, and the other by two members of the Training Committee. The Training Committee takes the final decision. We ask for three references, and each applicant must apply by Application Form in the first instance and pay a fee of £70 to contribute to the costs. There is no age limit. CFAR actively promotes an equal opportunities policy.

3.3 Time commitment per week and length of training
The Training Programme runs on Saturdays from 1.15p.m. to 6.30p.m., and, therefore, it is possible for people who live out of London to attend. There are three terms each consisting of 11 weeks. The minimum length of the training is four years (see section 2, paragraph 3). In addition, trainees, as a condition of completion, must also see two analysands under once weekly supervision (see section 4.3); meet with their tutor termly and participate in at least two cartels (see section 2, final paragraph).

3.4 Financial cost of training at different stages
The Introduction to Lacan Programme costs £400 for the course of three terms. The Full Training Programme costs around £1,300 per year for three years: the fees are then reduced to around £600 per year (fees in 2000).

3.5 Interruptions in training
Each case is taken on its own individual merits and discussion takes place with the tutor who makes recommendations to the Training Committee on the trainee's behalf.

3.6 Graduating and beginning a career
New members are invited to participate in a monthly Members' Forum. We very much encourage our new members to actively participate in the organisation, including further research, teaching, committee work, and so on.

3.7 Numbers of students per intake
The number of trainees accepted for the training varies from year to year. The maximum usually is ten to twelve.

4. CLINICAL AND ACADEMIC REQUIREMENTS

4.1 Personal therapy
Trainees must be in analysis for a period of twelve months prior to starting the Full Training Programme, and this must continue throughout the training. It is strongly recommended that the trainee engage in analysis with a Lacanian psychoanalyst wherever possible. In some circumstances an analysis with a non-Lacanian analyst, which has began prior to the application and is well established, may be accepted by the Training Committee.

4.2 Clinical requirements
Trainees are not required to have clinical experience prior to being accepted for the training. Those with no clinical experience are strongly recommended to obtain some as soon as possible. The trainee makes the decision to undertake the clinical work for the course in conjunction with their tutor.

4.3 Supervision
Supervised analysis of two analysands for a period of *at least* 18 months each, once weekly, is a condition of qualification.

4.4 Written work and course attendance
Trainees are required to attend and participate in all aspects of the Clinical Training which runs on Saturdays (see section 3.3). The trainee is expected to present papers to the clinical seminars from time to time, and to participate in two cartels (see section 2). During the training, the trainees must write four essays of approximately 5,000 words of which at least two should be clinical. The first of these assessment papers often focuses on some aspect of Freud's work. The four papers are presented to the Training Committee as a support for the trainee's application for Full Membership, together with tutor and supervisor reports. Cartels meet approximately once a month.

4.5 Assessment, standards and ethical requirements
There is continuous assessment of the work of the trainees by the tutor and supervisor who make regular reports to the Training Committee. The function of the tutor is to monitor the progress of the trainee: it is strongly recommended that the trainee have the support of their tutor and supervisor when applying for membership.

CFAR has a Code of Ethics as required by the UKCP, the purpose of which is to protect clients from professional malpractice and/or negligence. This code is distinct from the questions Lacan raised around the problem of how to formulate an ethical practice – a critical question for him and for CFAR since it bears on questions of what is understood to constitute psychoanalysis as a practice.

5. TRAINEE RESPONSE

1. Why this course was chosen
One of the questions asked by the editor was: How informed did you feel about each stage of the training? This question produced gales of laughter from the group each time it was raised! Why? We think it was because it tapped into one of the most uncomfortable but important elements of training at CFAR. There are formal years 1, 2, 3, and a continuation year, and specific things to do (write papers, see people, be in analysis, and so on), but the stages are made by each of us as we make our way through the process.

This has produced anxiety in most of us at some point and many had expressed a demand to the institution to tell us what to do, what is expected, and when. But in the end we have been glad that it always became a question to be negotiated on our own. We each have a tutor with whom we can discuss our particular situations.

The questions, What is a psychoanalyst? And how is one made?, are very important in the Lacanian school of thought, and have implications for the form of institution and for understanding the end of analysis. One of Lacan's innovations in response to these questions is The Pass, which is only now becoming available to English-speaking people. These questions and their relation to analytic theory provide a lively source of debate in CFAR, but we have found that this has been an important dynamic, and has provided an avenue into discussions about Lacanian analytic practice world-wide. How did we hear of CFAR? Some of us had already completed a different training and had been practising for a number of years, others had come via academic study, hearing about Lacan through MAs in psychoanalysis, or from film studies and feminism, many of us had been working in mental health care: nursing and social work. Everyone was very positive about the way that Lacan's theory could be used when working with people in these various practices. Especially important was the emphasis on the unconscious as structured like a language. Other key points were the emphasis on Freud's work; the way out from an ego-centred analysis; a place for the father in the theory; and a tolerance for not knowing.

2. The atmosphere of the course

CFAR runs weekly public lectures, and a year-long preliminary programme which many of us had appreciated as a way to find out more about the place before joining the training. The accessibility of the training to a wide range of people was an especially appealing point. Everyone found that the cartels were a useful mechanism for maintaining a focus on questions of theory and practice and avoiding personality and politics. The regular clinical presentations and seminars were also highly valued as a place to speak about the reality of working with people to alleviate suffering.

The way lectures and seminars are organised allows opportunity for all trainees and members to meet and mix regularly. Each term there is a timetabled meeting for trainees and a regular meeting between trainees and members. We also help organise the annual public conference and publish a news bulletin once a term. There are usually two parties each year and an art exhibition. We have regular lectures from analysts practising in different parts of the world and a monthly lecture programme run jointly with the London Circle of the European School of Psychoanalysis. Access to the World Association of Psychoanalysis is also supported by CFAR's membership of the Freudian Field and connections to other Europeans working with Lacanian ideas is becoming more and more possible via the new English-Speaking Diagonal of the European School. Trainees felt that these links made CFAR a very productive place to learn in.

Thoughts on futures? Most of us thought we would combine private practice with other things like work with NHS, the voluntary sector, charitable institutions, or together with teaching, family, academic research, nursing or social work.

AUTHOR'S COMMENTS

As the comments from the trainees on this course suggest, there is considerable appeal to those who are academic and who wish to apply Lacanian thinking in a variety of fields. These include film studies, cultural studies, philosophy and organisational studies, as well as clinical work. That this continues to be the only Lacanian training in the UK suggests how little Lacan's teaching has been accepted in this country compared with the rest of the world.

Lacan's work is only just being made available in this country in a form where it becomes more accessible to the average reader. The use of and fascination with language are distinctive requirements for applicants to CFAR. Significant is the profound commitment to the ethic of not binding patient or student with alienating language, and yet many find Lacanian thinking difficult to access. There is a risk that such a course will be inevitably over-intellectual in the way some teaching methods try to avoid issues of 'personality and politics'. Students of Lacan will have to deal with their feelings about the outrageous stories about Lacan's behaviour in contrast to what many have found in the usefulness of his ideas. There is also the risk of mystifying by idealising the experience of 'not knowing'. It is not surprising that Lacan is misunderstood, and yet many attest to the practical and clinical value of his thinking.

In its policy of allowing analysand and analyst to determine frequency without the interference of the training, and in a similar clinical ethic, there is the risk that the course will not be as in-depth a training as some others.

Trainees clearly feel themselves stimulated and challenged by this training and feel that it can be applied in many settings. Teaching methods seem to provide peer learning. Most helpfully there is the opportunity to have a foretaste of CFAR's work through day workshops and the introductory course.

Graduates from this course have claimed the title 'Psychoanalyst'. The dispute about this claim is explored elsewhere in this guide (p. 24f.). In some measure the fact of this dispute is a sign that Lacan's ideas are having impact, and yet impact is very different from debate and understanding, so that the dispute about title risks detracting from key issues about differences in approach, theory and clinical practice. Clearly, interest in French psychoanalysis is growing in this country and not just in CFAR. A number of members of the British Psycho-Analytic Society refer to Lacanian and post-Lacanian thinking.

THE CENTRE FOR PSYCHOANALYTICAL PSYCHOTHERAPY (CPP – UKCP/PPS)

538 Finchley Road, London NW11 8DD
Tel. 020 8922 8551

1. HISTORY OF THE ORGANISATION

The Centre for Psychoanalytical Psychotherapy (CPP) was founded in 1979 as the Centre for Analytical Psychotherapy (CAP) by a group of psychotherapists and psychoanalysts who wanted to contribute to the growing need for training in psychoanalytic psychotherapy and to provide as wide a theoretical input as possible within the framework of attention to the development of sound practice.

CAP was the brainchild of Goldi Romm-Bartfeld, a psychotherapist working in the NHS and private practice. She was inspired by the psychoanalyst Dr John Klauber. Other founding members and the initial training staff included Dr Alex Holder, Dr Klaus Fink, Dr S. Lieberman and Dr W. Falkowski.

From 1991 under the chairmanship of Dr Alberta Hahn, a senior member of the British Psycho-Analytic Society, the Training Committee focused on sharpening the Centre's training philosophy as one clearly rooted in psychoanalysis and its recent post-Kleinian developments.

Changes and developments were introduced, designed to improve the structure of the training and its content. Notably, these changes included the change of name to CPP – the Centre for Psychoanalytical Psychotherapy. The frequency of personal psychotherapy/psychoanalysis during training was increased from twice to a minimum of three times weekly. These developments went hand in hand with the consolidation of the identity of the CPP as an organisation firmly rooted in British Psychoanalysis, and anchoring its training on the importance of 'learning from experience'.

The current Chair is Dr A. Hyatt Williams, psychoanalyst and former Director of the London Clinic of Psychoanalysis and the Adolescent Department at the Tavistock Centre. The members of the Training Committee are psychoanalysts and psychoanalytic psychotherapists committed to the development of sound practice of psychoanalytic psychotherapy in various settings in the community. They aim to provide a learning environment that fosters each individual's capacity to learn and develop and maintain the psychoanalytic attitude.

2. THEORETICAL ORIENTATION AND CURRICULUM

The orientation of the course is based on the British School of Psychoanalysis. It introduces the ideas and practices which have evolved from Freud's early discoveries, the particular emphasis being on the development of psychoanalytic modes of observation and thinking. To this end, students are exposed to a wide range of psychoanalytic writings and the seminars are inspired by the writings of Freud, Abraham, Klein, Winnicott, Bion and the post-Kleinian developments.

The Training Course is modular in structure and consists of two distinct stages namely, the Pre-Clinical Stage and the Clinical Stage.

Pre-Clinical Modules:
Work Discussion Groups
Infant Observation Seminars
Introductory Theoretical Seminars
Twice termly Individual Tutorials
Psychiatric Placement
Student Review and Reflection Groups.

Upon successful completion of this stage trainees can proceed to the Clinical Stage of training. Successful completion entails the Training Committee receiving satisfactory reports from seminar leaders, personal tutors, the satisfactory report on the psychiatric placement and the acceptance of the Infant Observation paper.

Clinical-Stage Modules:
Clinical Seminars
Seminars on Theory and Technique
Twice termly Individual Tutorials
Student Review and Reflection Groups.

Training Patients and supervision: trainees are required to treat two patients, preferably one of each gender, seen three times weekly under weekly supervision with a different supervisor for each case. The first patient has to be seen for a minimum of two years and the second for a minimum of eighteen months beginning at the earliest after the first year of treatment of the first training patient.

3. TRAINING STRUCTURE

3.1 Training committee – see section 1 above.

3.2 Selection procedure and admission
Candidates should be graduates or professionals in health, education or social services, and should preferably have had some experience in working with people.

Suitable candidates are offered two interviews with different members of the Training Committee. References are taken up before the interviews. The Training Committee subsequently discusses each applicant in detail and informs candidates in writing whether they are accepted or not.

3.3 Time commitment per week and length of training
There are two seminars per week comprising three hours. The seminars take place on Tuesdays, 7p.m.–10p.m. The length of training varies for different candidates. Generally, it can take between four and five years to complete all components of the course. Some trainees take longer to qualify. Trainees are encouraged to attend the Scientific Meetings that CPP holds once a term on Tuesday evenings. Clinical trainees should also allow time for two hours of clinical supervision with different supervisors per week.

3.4 Financial cost of training at different stages

- Pre-Clinical and Clinical Stage – £1,395 per annum
- Post-third-year Clinical: £885
- Post-fifth-year Clinical: £570

The fees are adjusted periodically.

3.5 Interruptions in training
Trainees are allowed under certain circumstances to take a sabbatical or suspend their training. The personal tutors assist in considering such circumstances in which an interruption is commendable. The tutor remains available for consultation. A student membership fee is charged whilst the training is interrupted.

3.6 Graduating and beginning a career
Once elected to associate membership, a graduate is eligible for voting at the AGM to help shape the future of the organisation. The clinical service will refer patients who are suitable for treatment to its members. Members are invited to the Scientific Meetings and can present papers at these meetings. Full members can be invited to join the Training Committee. Associate members can apply for full membership after four years post-qualification. They must be in clinical practice and have contributed

to the field of psychoanalytic psychotherapy; for example, publication of clinical work or research, and so on. Suitable members can be involved in the teaching programme of the CPP.

3.7 Numbers of students per intake

As stated, we have a modular system of training and candidates can apply at any time in the academic year. We believe that learning is best done in small groups to allow for careful attention to providing a setting where trainees have the opportunity to learn from a genuine experience of themselves in close contact with others. To this end, there is a limit of twelve to each learning group.

4. CLINICAL AND ACADEMIC REQUIREMENTS

Trainees must give a clear demonstration of their clinical abilities. Particular attention is paid to their ability to maintain a transference/counter-transference relationship in a clinical setting. Understanding of the complex relationship between intrapsychic and interpersonal issues as they arise in the transference/counter-transference revealing the ability to make use of the self as object is given careful consideration.

Communication, ability to think and written projects must be of a comparable standard to at least MA level.

4.1 Personal therapy

Minimum of three times weekly until qualification with CPP approved psychoanalysts or psychoanalytic psychotherapists. The criteria for training therapists conform to the BCP criteria for training psychotherapists (see p. 60).

4.2/4.3 Clinical requirements/supervision

See above, section 2. Supervision: Approved CPP supervisors.

4.4 Written work and course attendance

Trainees are expected to attend seminars regularly. Reading lists are circulated to cover required readings for each seminar. Additional readings are discussed in the individual tutorials. A short to medium essay is submitted each term to the tutor for discussion. The essays are written on topics that emerge from the discussions in the tutorials. They can cover a particular area of interest that the trainee wants to explore.

4.5 Assessment, standards and ethical requirements

Headings:

- Requirement of conformity with Code of Ethics by members, including trainee members
- Interest of the patients is paramount
- Disclosure of terms of treatment, including fees and payment of fees, frequency and breaks
- Non-abusive therapist–patient relationship
- Confidentiality
- Self-monitoring of therapeutic competence and responsibility to seek further supervision and/or analysis

- Conduct unbecoming of a psychoanalytic psychotherapist
- Maintenance of professional boundaries
- Members shall not act in a way as to bring the organisation into disrepute.

CPP has a Complaints Procedure Document.

Standards and assessments are inextricably linked. CPP maintains standards through the continuing monitoring of trainees' progress reports from seminar leaders, tutors, six-monthly supervisors' reports, and placement reports.

Lecturers are selected on the basis of their experience and expertise relevant to the subject that they teach. Lecturers and students submit a report to the training committee on the completion of each series of seminars. Trainees' progress is discussed at monthly Training Committee meetings and all trainees are reviewed once a term. Standards and assessments is hence a continuing process throughout the year.

The Training Committee is continuously assessing its own activities and functioning. Regular contact with the student representatives and students' feedback on the courses is used in the periodic reviewing of the teaching activities.

5. TRAINEE RESPONSE

1. Why this course was chosen

1.1 What made people decide to train?
Varies widely between individuals.

1.2 What were the aspects of this course that were most attractive?
CPP is a very small organisation, which permits a lot of individual attention, close relationships between teaching staff and students, and personal monitoring of students' progress and needs.

The course is flexible enough to accommodate people coming from outside London, for example, seminars are once-weekly; the Training Committee are willing to consider students having their training analysis, their supervision and training patients in their home town/outside London.

CPP's orientation is British object relations with a distinct leaning towards Klein and Bion. The course is rigorous and non-eclectic. It is an aim of the training for students to be able to apply psychoanalytic concepts and theories in their own work environment. This aspect of the training is facilitated by regular work experience seminars.

There is no requirement to report back from students' training analyses.

CPP has a non-dogmatic approach to training and entrance requirements; individual applicants are considered on their merits, past experience and ability to reflect.

1.3 What was your experience of the selection procedure?
An introductory interview followed by separate interviews with two members of the Training Committee is the standard procedure. The experience was reported to be thorough, thoughtful, focused on the individuals' motivation, experience and ability

to work psychoanalytically, but also sometimes stressful. The interviews are conducted with a seriousness which contrasts with some students' experiences in other training organisations.

1.4 Before the start of the course, how informed did you feel about each stage of the training?
Previously, students felt inadequately informed about the details of the course. However, the Training Committee is currently producing new course documents and is reissuing a handbook which will be more detailed and accurate.

2. The atmosphere of the course

2.1 How do you feel about the way in which information is communicated?
Information flows between the Training Committee and the student body through (a) termly attendance by student representatives at Training Committee meetings; (b) twice-termly meetings with personal tutors; (c) induction meetings at the start of each academic year, and (d) CPP is considering a newsletter and web site. Although experience varies, most students feel that their concerns are being heard and addressed.

2.2 What do you find the most confusing aspect of the training?
Some people have felt confused in themselves about whether they have made sufficient progress at key transitions in the training, for example, from the pre-clinical to the clinical phase of the training, or at the point of writing up their qualifying paper. This may be because students' training is monitored individually and does not follow a strict chronological progression.

2.3 How much opportunity do you have to share thoughts and feelings with fellow trainees?
Formally: there is a termly review meeting presided over by two psychotherapists. This is an important container for students' anxieties and provides a space for reflection on the experience of being a CPP student. However, the therapists' perceived lack of independence from the Training Committee sometimes provokes a split reaction in the student body.

Since the student body is small, there is plenty of opportunity for regular, semi-social communication.

We are in the process of setting up a student association, which will facilitate communication with fellow students, past and present.

2.4 What do you feel about the methods of teaching?
The main teaching method is seminars, clinical and theoretical. These are usually of a high standard. The theoretical seminars are organised thematically, not chronologically. This facilitates an interactive approach to learning; there is very little didactic teaching and theory is well related to practice. Tutorials incorporate a personalised academic element, following students' individual interests. Termly scientific evenings provide additional opportunity to discuss clinical papers.

2.5 What do you think about the way assessments were done to allow you to progress to the next stages of training?
A clinical paper on baby observation and tutors' reports are the basis of predominantly verbal assessments. Brief individual feedback is given to each student at the end of the term.

2.6 Has the course met your expectations?
The smallness of the organisation has its pros and cons. Most students are happy with the learning experience. It is a drawback that the organisation doesn't own its own premises.

2.7 How do you feel about your future with the organisation?
The future is what you make it! The referral system needs to become more active. Once this is achieved and the student association is formed, people will be able to have a better sense of a link between present and future within CPP.

2.8 What plans do trainees have for future practice and possible balance of different sorts of work in their career?
A balance of NHS work and private practice.

AUTHOR'S COMMENTS

The smallness and accessibility of the CPP course will attract some applicants, as will its espoused devotion to individual growth of understanding. What the trainees report about the person-focused teaching methods will be significant for some. The object relations approach with a post-Kleinian flavour and emphasis testifies to the huge shift within the organisation from its early days as an eclectic training. It would appear that the tension between the course aiming to train for NHS work versus private practice, reported on in the first edition of this guide has been resolved by a shift towards private work, even if that is not the exclusive focus. The training for thrice-weekly therapy indicates this. Many of its teachers are psychoanalysts. The course is currently exploring the possibility of moving from UKCP to BCP.

THE GUILD OF PSYCHOTHERAPISTS (GUILD – UKCP/PPS)

47 Nelson Square, London SE1 0QA
Administrative Office: 149 Faraday Road, London SW19 BPA
Tel. and Fax. 020 8540 4454

1. HISTORY OF THE GUILD

The Guild was founded in 1974 by a group of Freudian, Jungian and Phenomenological psychotherapists. Despite their different conceptual backgrounds they were
all agreed on the central importance of the nature of the relationship between
therapist and patient. Thus, they were less interested in conforming rigidly to theory
and technique than addressing the experience of the patient. Consequently they
saw psychotherapy as a craft, and the learning of the craft as an apprenticeship, the
aims of which remain:

1. To value and regard as central the relationship between therapist and patient
2. To expose trainees to the contributions made by a wide range of psychoanalytic
    traditions and schools
3. To encourage trainees to find their own voice through adopting a critical attitude
    to theory and practice.

2. THEORETICAL ORIENTATION AND CURRICULUM

The training is pluralistic and offers a broad-based psychoanalytic framework,
encouraging comparison and critique of different theories. The core curriculum
covers theories of Freud, Jung, Klein and British object relations, and basic concepts
of these theories are offered in the first year. In addition, trainees meet each member
of the current Training Committee for a series of seminars on clinical issues, at which
they are introduced to the variety of views within the committee.

In subsequent years, a closer look is taken at basic psychoanalytic concepts from
these and other different theoretical perspectives, including those of Lacan, phenomenology, ego and self-psychology.

The training syllabus is not fixed and changes every year to accommodate the
needs of trainees with the interests of the teachers.

In addition to theoretical input, there are clinical seminars in the second and third
years, in which trainees present their work for clinical and theoretical discussion.

3. TRAINING STRUCTURE

3.1 Training committee
The Training Committee is a standing committee, with a maximum capacity of
twelve members, dealing with admission, assessment and graduation of all trainees,
for which purpose it meets regularly during term time. It also meets annually to

consider the contents of the syllabus and appointment of teachers, part of which meeting is with student representatives.

3.2 Selection procedure and admission

Any two members of the training committee interview candidates. All interviewed applicants are then discussed at a selection meeting of the Training Committee and the decision is taken by the whole committee based on the application form, interviews and references.

Although the formal criterion for admission is normally education to degree level or equivalent, when the Guild was founded, it was agreed that the personal suitability and life experience of candidates should have precedence over academic qualifications. This guideline is still important in the selection of students.

Thus, we seek personal qualities, such as:

- An ability to listen carefully to others
- A capacity to think about different ways of viewing issues or phenomena
- An ability to reflect upon themselves and their life experience which will enable understanding of another's distress or psychic pain
- An interest in the project of psychoanalysis and its variety of application and expression
- General maturity of personality and attitude.

The Guild operates an equal opportunities policy in respect of age, gender, race and sexual orientation.

3.3 Time commitment per week and length of training

In line with UKCP requirements, the curriculum covers four years although individual trainees may take longer to fulfil all requirements. Seminars take place one evening per week during term time; there are three ten-week terms in the academic year, which runs from October to June/July. Time is also needed for weekly supervision, reading and any required written work.

3.4 Financial cost of training at different stages

Course fees for the four years of seminars are, at present, £930 per annum, inclusive of *British Journal of Psychotherapy* subscription. In addition, there are the following:

Library subscription: £8.50
Studentship Trust subscription: £5.00
Insurance premium: £45.00

Post-curricular fees for students until they are elected to membership are £313 per annum.

3.5 Interruptions in training

We are dealing with mature students, who have differing real-life experiences and events during the course of training, and the Training Committee recognises this. A request to take time out of the course is always a matter of careful discussion between student and his/her personal tutor, who will then make a recommendation to the Training Committee. Each case is taken on its own merits, but events such as pregnancy and childbirth, or illness, would be the most common reasons for wanting to take time out.

3.6 Graduating and beginning a career

Upon graduation the Council awards full membership of the organisation. Guild members are kept in touch with the organisation through a circulated noticeboard, and new members are encouraged to join one of the many thriving and active committees of the Guild. With the exception of the Ethics Committee, they may stand for any office at that time.

The Guild mounts two professional conferences – one in winter, the other in summer – as well as the Annual General Meeting. All members and trainees are encouraged to attend these events. In addition, members and trainees are kept informed about other professional events.

A few years after graduation we would expect that our members are settled professionally either in private or public practice – or a mixture of both, perhaps. They may be involved in committees of the Guild, and/or be teaching for other organisations or ourselves. More Guild-trained therapists are now becoming involved at a senior level, and there is plenty of opportunity for this. Those who are not directly involved in the Guild have usually become involved with local groups for professional development.

3.7 Numbers of students per intake

A minimum of ten, and a maximum of thirteen.

4. CLINICAL AND ACADEMIC REQUIREMENTS

4.1 Personal therapy

Trainees are required to be in psychoanalytic psychotherapy with an approved analyst for as many sessions per week as necessary, but not less than twice weekly throughout the training, and until they have been elected to membership.

4.2 Clinical requirements

There is a requirement that each trainee works with two training patients, who should be seen as frequently as necessary, but not less than twice weekly, for a minimum of 18 months. In addition trainees are expected to develop their experience of working with as wide a range of patients as they can manage. The Guild runs a referral service and low-cost referral system, and there are opportunities to work for the Guild low-cost clinic. Trainees are also encouraged to develop their own referral networks, and may discuss this with their tutors.

Trainees who have had no psychiatric experience are expected to complete a placement for at least six months in a psychiatric department, or equivalent.

4.3 Supervision

Each training patient must have a different supervisor, one of whom must be a member of the training committee. The other may be any suitable analyst of the trainee's choice providing it has been agreed with the tutor. The trainee must stay in supervision with one of the supervisors until he/she is elected to membership.

4.4 Written work and course attendance

Trainees are expected to attend the weekly seminar programme.
Basic requirements of written work are:

- Self-assessment at the end of the second year
- Theoretical essay in the third year
- Six-monthly reports for the tutor on training patients
- The final clinical case for membership.

Tutors or seminar leaders may require further written work if this is deemed to be appropriate.

4.5 Assessment, standards and ethical requirements

Assessment is continuous throughout the course. There is an assessment meeting at the end of each term and the tutor keeps in contact with both supervisors, usually requesting a supervision report every six months.

Day-to-day issues arising with students are also discussed at agenda meetings of the Training Committee.

Detailed criteria are given to the trainees about the assessment of written work. The criteria for assessment of supervised work with patients, seminar participation and other work, are the satisfactory reports from teachers and supervisors.

In the spirit of conducting an apprenticeship, each trainee is assessed in terms of their own unique development, and is encouraged to find their own style and competency as a therapist. However, within this flexibility of assessment and evaluation, there are standards that form the basis for competent psychoanalytic practice. For instance, students must show a developing ability to understand ideas of the unconscious, conceptualise and appropriately use transference, relate theory to practice, conduct an ethical and facilitating encounter with patients.

All teachers and trainees are accountable to the Guild Code of Ethics and Code of Practice for training organisations.
These include:

- Mandatory standards of conduct
- Functions and powers of the Ethics Panel
- Procedures for complaints against members/trainees
- Disciplinary action and appeals procedures
- Special provisions relating solely to trainees and post-curricular students.

The Guild is a member of the Psychodynamic and Psychoanalytic Psychotherapy Section of UKCP, which carries out a review of the Guild's training every five years. Graduation from the Guild leads to registration with UKCP.

5. TRAINEE RESPONSE

Twenty-two trainees were approached and eleven responded covering the four years of training.

1. Why this course was chosen

1.1 What made people decide to train?
The main reason was that the Guild offers an in-depth pluralistic training, leading to UKCP registration. It was a second training for several respondents who wanted 'continuing professional development' in terms of theory and supervision. Several people said that it had been positively recommended by practitioners who had trained there and had a good reputation in the psychotherapy world.

1.2 What were the aspects of this course that were most attractive?
The pluralism and practical considerations were cited most often. The time commitment of one evening a week and the twice-weekly (minimum) personal therapy requirement were attractive to trainees with already heavy work commitments and made it more manageable for those living outside London. It does not discriminate against age, colour, class or sexuality, and several people appreciated that their therapist is not consulted. Trainees could, if necessary, withdraw from the course and re-enter at a later date. This was viewed as enabling and realistic.

1.3 What was your experience of the selection procedure?
Although each year the procedure seemed to change – one year all successful applicants had had three interviews, whilst other years only two – the replies were fairly similar. It was mostly experienced as thorough, fair and well-handled and confirmed the interviewees choice. Some found it rigorous but less traumatic than interviews with other psychotherapy organisations, while one or two felt it was less demanding and not as efficient as expected.

1.4 Before the start of the course, how informed did you feel about each stage of the training?
Most felt reasonably informed, but a number thought that the information could be more clear and consistent and some said that not enough detail was available.

2. The atmosphere of the course

2.1 How do you feel about the way in which information is communicated?
Information is mainly communicated through the tutors and is dependent on tutor/trainee communication. There is also a Handbook, a regular newsletter and memos, but because of the flexibility of the training, some changes occur from year to year that are not always reflected in the Handbook. Some trainees have had to be more proactive than others – some have experienced confusion, possibly related to the Guild moving to new premises. Others commented on the general openness of the organisation which encourages communication. Annual day and residential conferences are another arena where this openness was experienced and several people commented on the high quality of thought that was in evidence on these occasions.

2.2 What do you find the most confusing aspect of training?
Respondents felt that the pluralism of the course, although a strength, makes it more difficult to have a clear theoretical ease. A criticism resulting from this aspect is that there is sometimes not enough in-depth examination of subjects.

2.3 How much opportunity do you have to share thoughts and feelings with fellow trainees?
Most trainees felt that this was satisfactorily achieved either informally or as part of the course. Although currently there is no experiential group, a few thought it would be a valuable addition. Others felt that with the move to the new premises there would be more opportunity to interact with other trainees. Conferences also add to the sense of community.

2.4 What do you feel about the methods of teaching?
One of the main teaching methods is to explore papers which encourages trainees to think for themselves. There are only a few formal or didactic lectures and some felt the need for more in order to cover the basic theory, which can be overlooked in such a pluralistic course. A greater use of external lecturers as requested and some trainees also said that having the same teachers for clinical seminars every year was not sufficiently stimulating.

2.5 What did you think about the way assessments were done to allow you to progress to the next stages of training?
These consist of self-assessment at the end of the second year, a theoretical essay at the end of the third, continuous assessment throughout the course, and a final clinical paper, which has to be presented for membership. Whilst the essay in particular was experienced as testing and rigorous, some trainees thought assessment was relaxed and haphazard. Feedback lacked uniformity because the method and timing varied with the individual tutors and several suggested it might be beneficial to change tutors more often (rather than have the same one for the whole course).

2.6 Has the course met your expectations?
The responses were mostly positive, stressing the importance of the non-hierarchical and non-infantilising approach of the organisation. A number said they would recommend the Guild and would select this training again. Several felt that pluralism is difficult and would have liked the option to specialise in the last year.

2.7 How do you feel about your future with the organisation?
Almost all the trainees felt welcomed into the Guild and that participation is encouraged. Everybody felt that they had a future with the organisation and wanted to make an active contribution.

2.8 What plans do trainees have for future practice and possible balance of different sorts of work in their career?
Most respondents already work in various settings and want this to continue. Particular emphasis was placed on financial security and the desire to combine and balance private practice with either working in a team environment, for example, a GP surgery, or in supervising and teaching.

AUTHOR'S COMMENTS

The commitment of the staff of the Guild to a pluralistic approach will attract many. Not only are Freud, object relations, Klein and Jung taught, but also phenomenology and Lacan. For trainees this is a rich mix, which some perceive to be too wide to give them a secure enough base in developing their clinical work, while others may enjoy the freedom to find their own way of working. This raises the issue faced by the aims of academic freedom espoused in some university courses concerning whether a pluralistic course maintains a depth of learning needed to support clinical work. In contrast with other less wide courses, this is all done in a one evening's seminar per week which places greater responsibility for theoretical development on the trainee's depth of reading.

The trainee response suggests that this might not be sufficient for those seeking an understanding of some of the basics (for example, Freud) as well as not enough time to integrate and differentiate such a wide canvas of theoretical approaches. It may also make it difficult for those who select to specialise in one approach, counter to the Guild's pluralistic philosophy. Perhaps the opportunity to choose and be critical of different approaches to analytic material is useful; perhaps not.

The commitment to equal opportunities expresses these values. In its early years the Guild tried to enable the trainees to shape the course as in Cambridge, but reverted to a taught course. This illustrates the commitment to searching for effective non-infantilising practice. This may be undermined by the insistence on one supervisor coming from the training committee, where, because of limited choice, the trainee is supervised by someone whose style and orientation is very different to their own. It could mean that the committee knows trainees better. However, they may feel constrained by the lack of choice and the strong views of committee members deciding about their qualification.

THE INDEPENDENT GROUP OF ANALYTICAL PSYCHOLOGISTS (IGAP – UKCP/APS)

PO Box 1175, London W3 6DS
Tel. 020 8993 3996

1. HISTORY OF THE ORGANISATION

IGAP came into being as a professional group in the early 1980s. It began offering its Programme of Studies (an annually published programme of seminars and lectures) in 1984, and its Programme of Preparation for Becoming an Analyst commenced in 1985. It is a member of the Analytical Psychology Section of the UKCP and fulfils the training standards requirements of the Section.

2. THEORETICAL ORIENTATION AND CURRICULUM

The IGAP programme, in the spirit of the work of C.G. Jung, is based on the view that becoming an analyst, like analysis itself, is a highly individual process and cannot be taught. It is therefore not a course, but a framework within which the candidate proceeds at his/her own pace, selecting seminars and lectures and requesting tutorials as appropriate, supported by and accountable to a panel of three members known as the Review Committee (RC). The Programme of Studies, much of which is also open to registered students other than candidates, offers a broad range of courses in which the historical context and development of analytical psychology and the cultural expression of archetypal patterns are represented alongside and in relation to clinical issues. Myths, fairy tales and alchemy are studied for their relevance to unconscious processes in the individual and in the transference situation. Those considering applying for candidacy are able to get a sense of IGAP's approach by attending some of these lectures and seminars.

The process is divided into candidacy and advanced candidacy, throughout both of which personal analysis and study continue. During the first phase candidates prepare themselves for theoretical examinations and for working with clients. As advanced candidates they begin analytic practice under supervision, attend case colloquia, write a thesis, and prepare for the final assessment procedures.

3. TRAINING STRUCTURE

3.1 Training committee
The preparation committee produces and updates a procedural document, which details the requirements of the different stages. Individual coordinators are responsible for different stages and aspects of the process, such as candidacy, advanced candidacy, examinations, clinical experience.

3.2 Selection procedure and admission
Applicants with a degree or equivalent, who have completed a minimum of 150 hours of analysis with a member of the IAAP, obtain from the IGAP office a form, which they complete and return, together with a short autobiographical review. Applications must arrive by 1 November for admission the following spring. Applicants are then interviewed separately by the three members who will form, if the application is successful, their RC, and one external analyst. The individual reports and recommendations are collated and presented to a selection committee for decision. We have a policy of non-discrimination in relation to applicants/candidates on grounds of religion, age, race, ethnic origin, sex or sexual orientation.

3.3 Time commitment per week and length of training
The Programme of Studies offers on average two to three seminars or lectures per week, in evenings or at weekends. Case colloquia are arranged for advanced candidates who are working with patients. Time must, of course, also be found for personal analysis, supervision and study. Frequency of attendance may vary, as does the number of years taken to qualify. Deadlines are not normally imposed.

3.4 Financial cost of training at different stages
Again this varies a great deal. Basic costs are as follows. Application fee of £100; preparation fee (currently £100 per term); all-in fee for the studies programme (£120 per term) – advanced candidates and others exceptionally may opt to pay instead for individual courses attended (currently £11 per session). Interviews with RC members (average c. £150 per year); fees for the first set of exams (£400); fees for any tutorials arranged. In advanced candidacy, the more financially demanding

period, there are additionally fees for case colloquia (£10 per session), for consultation with the thesis advisor, and for supervision. Throughout the process analysis must also be paid for. Fees to analysts, supervisors and other advisors are negotiated individually. A substantial amount of reading will be required, and candidates need to build up their book collections, but many books can be borrowed; for example, from the library of the C.G. Jung Analytical Psychology Club.

3.5 Interruptions in training
Candidates may, with the agreement of their RC, obtain a leave of absence for one year, renewable for a second year.

3.6 Graduating and beginning a career
Graduates are welcome to participate in the running of the organisation, and may eventually offer to teach on the programme of studies. Successful conclusion of the preparation process leads to a diploma, membership of IGAP and of the International Association of Analytical Psychologists and the right to be listed in the UKCP register. Five years after qualification members may become senior members and as such may act as analysts or supervisors to candidates. What activities individual members develop beyond their private practices is again very varied.

3.7 Numbers of students per intake
The number of students per intake is variable. It is possible that in some years the Group might decide to take no new candidates.

4. CLINICAL AND ACADEMIC REQUIREMENTS

4.1 Personal therapy
A minimum of 150 hours of analysis with a member of the IAAP must be completed before applying. Throughout the process of preparation personal analysis continues as training analysis with an IGAP analyst; a frequency of three times a week is required.

4.2 Clinical requirements
A suitable experience of patients with psychological illness in a psychiatric setting – normally of at least six months – must be completed before work with patients begins. This can be discussed with the appropriate member of the preparation committee, but must be arranged by the candidate. Advanced candidates are required to take on a minimum of three cases, which should include a male and a female analysand. One analysand must complete at least two years of analysis; the other two must complete at least one year. A frequency of three times a week is required. IGAP has recently started a clinic to help candidates find patients.

4.3 Supervision
Each case must be supervised by a senior IGAP analyst, normally with a ratio of one session of supervision to three of analysis. A male and a female supervisor must be consulted.

4.4 Written work and course attendance
Candidates are required to keep a record of attendance at courses and to discuss this with their RC.

At the end of initial candidacy and before commencing work with analysands there is a set of examinations: a written paper must be presented on the History of Neurosis; an interpretation of a Myth, Dream or Fairy Tale is written under examination conditions; oral examinations must be taken on Fundamental Concepts of Analytical Psychology; Psychological Illness and Pathology in a Jungian Context; the Psychology of Dreams; Psychology and Religion.

At the end of the stage of advanced candidacy the following must be presented: a thesis on a relevant topic, agreed with a member who acts as thesis advisor, and normally consisting of between 15,000 and 20,000 words; a paper on alchemy; written reports on each training patient, one of which must be of 5,000 words (the others may be shorter). There is also a final oral examination on Individuation and its Symbols. One case is presented orally to examiners and the thesis is presented orally to the Group.

4.5 Assessment, standards and ethical requirements
Our code of ethics covers responsibilities to analysands; relationship with colleagues; serious misconduct; composition, functions and procedures of the ethics committee; appeals; monitoring of complaints.

Assessment is partly by examination, partly by the continuous monitoring of the RC, partly by observation by seminar leaders and supervisors, and finally by an assessment committee made up of members who have not been closely associated with the candidate, who consider reports from the RC, from readers and examiners, supervisors, seminar leaders and coordinators of preparation. The main criteria for assessment are candidates' grasp of and individual relationship to theory, the development of their particular skills in the analytic encounter and evidence of their continuing personal development.

5. TRAINEE RESPONSE

This is a summary of the views expressed by a small group of candidates on the Programme of Preparation for Becoming an Analyst. There were five candidates at the meeting on different stages of the Programme.

1. Why this course was chosen

1.1 What made people decide to train?
For some candidates the decision to train came out of their experience of personal analysis. For others, who were already working in the therapeutic field, the decision grew from a desire to deepen their understanding of a Jungian approach to the depth psychological work.

1.2 What were the aspects of this course that were most attractive?
'IGAP's approach to psyche which encompasses and amplifies Jung's work, combining the clinical with the imaginal.' 'IGAP's unique self-directed Programme

under guidance and scrutiny from Senior Analysts.' It is a UKCP registered training conducted as a part-time Programme allowing earning to continue at the same time.

1. 3 What was your experience of the selection procedure?
'Thorough and searching.' The initial written work which accompanied the preliminary application 'stimulated self-reflection'. The interviews were experienced as 'deeply personal dialogues', sometimes 'challenging', occasionally 'even, gruelling' and also, sometimes 'enjoyable'.

1.4 Before the start of the course, how informed did you feel about each stage of the training?
The course literature adequately covered each stage of the Programme. However, IGAP's Programme of Preparation 'focuses as much on personal evolution as on academic and clinical development and hence the training operates more within the framework of a spiral than a pyramid'. It is therefore very difficult to appreciate fully at the beginning of the course the implications of future stages.

2. The atmosphere of the course

2.1 How did you feel about the way in which information was communicated?
Formal communication has improved over the years as IGAP's structure has developed. The self-directed nature of the Programme requires active participation from the candidates. One consequence of part-time office staff is that there are inevitable delays sometimes in receiving answers to administrative questions which can be experienced as 'frustrating'.

2.2 What did you find the most confusing aspect of the training?
'The nature and complexity of the work itself'; 'The overall tone and feel of the Programme is not confusing once you have accepted appropriate responsibility for its self-directed orientation.'

2.3 How much opportunity do you have to share thoughts and feelings with fellow trainees?
This is not a course organised formally into, for example, Year 1, Year 2, and so on, and as IGAP has, to date, no permanent central meeting place, it can take time for students to establish regular personal contact with each other.
    On an individual basis 'there is valuable interaction'. Students organise their own informal ongoing study sessions and the system of Student Representatives has developed for more formal collection and presentation of candidates' views to Senior Analysts.
    In the latter stages of the Programme, the case colloquia are experienced 'as an important place to share thoughts and feelings with fellow candidates'.

2.4 What do you feel about the methods of teaching?
The candidates felt that it was important to emphasise that the 'teacher–pupil' model of learning does not really apply. IGAP's Programme offers education and guidance from Senior Analysts in a variety of settings, for example, text study, discussion

seminars, participatory workshops and lectures. Some parts of the Studies Programme are open to non-trainees, which the candidates felt was 'ultimately enriching', although some at first, would have preferred 'exclusivity'. Advanced candidates particularly valued the clinical work (closed to non-trainees) which focuses on small-group case colloquia and the individual supervision of their work by Senior Analysts.

They agreed that 'the most profound learning experience is felt to be within the personal Analysis'.

2.5 What did you think about the way assessments were done to allow you to progress to the next stages of training?
Assessments were experienced as 'intensive and insightful, demanding high standards of work'. Students felt 'held and supported by the structure, while being tested in a very challenging way'.

2.6 Has the course met your expectations?
In general, 'yes indeed'. This course requires 'staying power'. The surprise for most is still the extent to which students are expected to organise their own path through the Programme.

2.7 How do you feel about your future with the organisation?
'If you wish to be involved, this organisation has a lot to offer.'

2.8 What plans do trainees have for future practice and possible balance of different sorts of work in their career?
This is very much up to the individual. Some plan working within the Health Service and/or in private practice. In addition, others include plans to write and/or lecture at university or on different therapy programmes which have a Jungian input.

AUTHOR'S COMMENTS

This course will attract candidates looking for deep foundation in classical Jungian thinking and practice. It is the one Jungian course that is devoted mainly to teaching theories of Jung rooted in the Zurich school. It has been shaped historically by former members of the Analytical Psychology Club, Zurich trained Jungian analysts who have moved to this country and those who did not want the Society of Analytical Psychology (SAP) Jungian line so dominated by the developmental school and psychoanalytical influences.

The emphasis is therefore upon Jung's teaching on the collective unconscious, archetypes and the use of mythology and fairy tale to expound upon and understand developments within the individual human psyche. That is not to say that the transference and counter-transference are neglected, nor are developmental perspectives, however these do not lead the way as they do in the SAP. This offers a different approach to technique that focuses on the transference as an indicator of complexes and collective imagery unindividuated, rather than as a means of understanding individual relating.

The course is divided clearly into the preliminary pre-candidacy stage and the later post-candidacy stage when clinical work with patients is undertaken. The course appears to be thorough, demanding, both intellectually and clinically and produces Jungian analysts recognised nationally and internationally who have a familiarity of thrice-weekly intensive analysis. The candidates emphasise the individualised nature of the experience with a focus on their personal understanding and development. There is some suggestion that the lack of year divisions helps individual development but makes it hard to understand the organisation's policies on progress in the training.

THE INSTITUTE OF PSYCHO-ANALYSIS AND BRITISH PSYCHO-ANALYTICAL SOCIETY (INSTP-A, BP-AS – BCP)

Byron House, 114 Shirland Road, London W9 2EQ
Tel. 020 7563 5000 Fax. 020 7563 5001
E-mail: info@psychoanalysis.org.uk
Web site: <www.psychoanalysis.org.uk>

1. HISTORY OF THE ORGANISATION

The International Psychoanalytical Association was founded in 1910 to promote the development of psychoanalysis and maintain the professional and training standards of its member organisations throughout the world. In 1919 Ernest Jones, the leading figure in British psychoanalysis for many years and the first biographer of Sigmund Freud, founded the British Psycho-Analytical Society as one of those member organisations. In 1924 the British Society established the Institute of Psycho-Analysis, to be responsible for the financial and administrative aspects of the Society's work. The London Clinic of Psycho-Analysis was set up in 1926, to make psychoanalytic treatment available to those who would not otherwise be able to afford an analysis.

The Institute of Psycho-Analysis is the only organisation in the United Kingdom authorised by the International Psychoanalytical Association to train and qualify psychoanalysts to work with adults, adolescents and children.

2. THEORETICAL ORIENTATION AND CURRICULUM

The training is based on the theoretical principles and clinical practice of psycho-analysis, as discovered by Sigmund Freud and further developed by later generations of analysts. The theory and practice of psychoanalysis continue to evolve, down to the present day. Notable former members of the British Society include Michael Balint, Wilfred Bion, John Bowlby, Anna Freud, Ernest Jones, Melanie Klein and Donald Winnicott.

The curriculum, based on this theoretical orientation, is described below.

3. TRAINING STRUCTURE

3.1 Training committee
The training is organised by the Institute's Education Committee, which administers with the same criteria for acceptance and qualification the training of (1) London-based students, (2) those living at a distance from London, and (3) overseas students who move to London for their training.

3.2 Selection procedure and admission
The Institute of Psycho-Analysis is committed to an equal opportunities policy regarding applicants for training.
  Applicants are eligible for consideration if they have:

(a) a medical qualification or are undergoing medical training, or a university degree, or its equivalent;
(b) a background of clinical experience, or other relevant professional work;
(c) a suitable personality, aptitude to work analytically, and an anticipated ability to support themselves financially throughout the training.

  All prospective applicants who fulfil these prerequisites are offered a preliminary interview. Following this, permission to proceed with an application is at the discretion of the Admissions Committee. Applicants are asked to fill out an application form and give the names of two referees. Each applicant is interviewed by two, or occasionally three, senior analysts whose confidential findings are considered in the Admissions Committee where decisions on applications are made.

3.3 Time commitment per week and length of training
The course is part-time and organised so that trainees are able to continue working during the training. The number of hours per week involved varies from stage to stage of the training. Although the length of the training varies among individuals, it is not less than four years.

3.4 Financial cost of the training at different stages
The largest element in this is the cost of the trainee's own psychoanalysis (see below). This is by personal agreement between the student and training analyst. The usual range of fees is currently £25–50 per session, varying according to individual circumstances. Fees for supervision of training cases are by agreement between the student and supervisor, often at the same amount as the student's analytic fee.
  There is an application fee and, later, a registration fee, currently of £100 each. Course fees for seminars are currently £130 per term.
  Financial assistance is available, in cases of need, to students permanently resident in the UK. The amount loaned varies with the availability of funds and the financial needs of the applicant.

3.5 Interruptions in training
These are dealt with according to individual circumstances.

3.6 Graduating and beginning a career

The training leads to qualification as a psychoanalyst and Associate Membership of the British Psycho-Analytical Society. The British Society has a busy scientific life, with several meetings a month, and Associate Members also play a part in the organisational structure of the Society.

Associate Membership brings membership of the International Psycho-Analytical Association, and the British Society is a member organisation of the British Confederation of Psychotherapists. On completing the training, therefore, a student becomes part of a strong, active national and international professional community.

There is a Post-Qualification Course leading to Full Membership of the Society.

Analysts pursue their careers in many different ways. Some work wholly or mainly in private practice, others work in institutions such as psychotherapy or child guidance clinics, or hospital psychiatry departments. There are increasing opportunities to do psychoanalytic research.

The Society is also particularly concerned to help students who live outside London to train and establish themselves professionally.

3.7 Numbers of students per intake

There is no quota system. All students who are considered suitable following the admission procedure are accepted at the time of their application.

4. CLINICAL AND ACADEMIC REQUIREMENTS

4.1 Personal therapy

Students are required to have a personal training analysis with a Training Analyst approved by the Education Committee. This involves 50-minute sessions five days a week (Monday to Friday) and lasts throughout the training, from acceptance as a student until qualification as a psychoanalyst. It may continue for longer; the training requirement is that it must not be stopped before qualification. Students are generally able to make their own arrangements, subject to the Education Committee's approval, in finding an analyst from among those recognised as Training Analysts.

4.2 Clinical requirements

Students treat two patients in five-times-weekly psychoanalysis. One patient must be treated for at least two years and the other for a minimum of one year before qualification. For students training in London, patients are drawn from the waiting list of the London Clinic of Psycho-Analysis, which is run by the Institute of Psycho-Analysis to offer low-cost analysis by students in training. For those training elsewhere, other arrangements may be made.

4.3. Supervision

For each training case, a student has weekly supervision with an analyst approved for this by the Education Committee.

4.4 Written work and course attendance

In the London-based training, theoretical and clinical seminars are usually held on three evenings a week, over a minimum of three years, but there is flexibility so that from the second year onwards students may need to attend only one or two seminars a week. The first year is devoted to introductory seminars, the study of Freud's writings and psychoanalytic theories of personality development. Thereafter a variety of topics is covered, including different psychoanalytic schools of thought and the theoretical understanding and clinical treatment of various types of disturbance.

During the first year students also observe a mother and baby in their home, once a week, and one of the seminars is an Infant Observation Seminar at which the students' observations during these visits are discussed.

Weekly clinical seminars begin in the second year and continue until qualification.

There is no compulsory written work, but there is an optional seminar for students who are interested in writing a paper.

Training for students outside London takes account of the particular circumstances of individual students. A course for regional students might typically comprise lectures and seminars by local and visiting analysts, with other students in the area if applicable; participation in training events in London by audio-visual linkup, and in person when possible; and monthly attendance at weekend workshops in London.

4.5 Assessment, standards and ethical requirements

The Society's Code of Ethics obliges members and students to observe correct professional behaviour in the best interests of patients, to maintain confidentiality, and to behave with due consideration to all those with whom they are professionally involved.

The progress of students is assessed throughout the training. The Student Progress Committee monitors the reports of seminar leaders and supervisors, and students each have an individual Progress Advisor, with whom to discuss their choice of seminars, potential supervisors, and any issues, which may come up during the training.

When students have had their training cases in analysis for the required time, and have also completed the necessary number of seminars, they become eligible to complete the training course. This depends on an overall assessment of their progress on the training, and recommendations from their analyst and from both supervisors that they are ready to work independently as psychoanalysts.

5. TRAINEE RESPONSE

1. Why this course was chosen

1.1 What made people decide to train?
Present students agree that they believe the Institute of Psycho-analysis offers the most in-depth training in the field. Some candidates have long experience in psycho-therapy and others have come from other disciplines; all, however, share a belief in and interest in the fundamental ideas of psychoanalysis and think that training as psychoanalysts is the only way to develop these ideas fully. The Institute training is the only training in the UK that offers membership in the International Psycho-Analytic Association, i.e. that is recognised throughout the world.

1.2 What were the aspects of this course that were most attractive?
The Institute training offers the best opportunity to be taught academically and trained clinically by analysts currently developing psychoanalytic ideas. It offers teaching from analysts from the three main schools of thought in British psycho-analysis (Contemporary Freudian, Independent, Kleinian) in one institution. Many senior members who teach on the training have additional fields of interest including psychiatry and other branches of medicine, literature, the arts, literary and arts criticism, philosophy, and the relationship between psychoanalysis and the history of ideas. There is the opportunity to hear papers on these subjects as well as important clinical papers discussed at Scientific Meetings from the beginning of the training. Importantly, there is the experience of learning on the basis of seeing five-times-weekly patients in an open-ended way, and emphasis given to clinical training and skills.

1.3 What was your experience of the selection procedure?
Applicants can expect a lengthy and thorough selection process. In the first instance the Institute should be contacted for a training prospectus. There is a preliminary interview to ascertain whether the applicant has the relevant qualifications to proceed. Following this a detailed questionnaire has to be completed, and then two further in-depth interviews. Current students described the questionnaire as 'thought provoking', and the experience of interviews as 'interesting and illumi-nating'. Some 'felt in good hands throughout', and that the process had been an enriching experience. Others found that the selection procedure could be fallible and that occasionally suitable people are left out. All agree that the applicant needs to be prepared for a testing procedure, which provides an opportunity to think and reflect about motivation and interests, giving a flavour of how complex and demanding the training itself is.

1.4 Before the start of the course, how informed did you feel about each stage of the training?
The training prospectus is informative but quite succinct. Once the student has become eligible to begin the formal part of the training, however, the student's Progress Advisor is available to help clarify the requirements and stages of training.

2. The atmosphere of the course

2.1 How do you feel about the way in which information is communicated?
We are regularly communicated with in person and in writing by those responsible for our training.

2.2 What do you find the most confusing aspect of the training?
There was no perceived confusion amongst the students: there is plenty of opportunity to clarify any problems that might arise, either in clinical or theoretical seminars or with advisors.

2.3 How much opportunity do you have to share thoughts and feelings with fellow trainees?
There are frequent opportunities to meet colleagues in seminars and for informal contact at the Institute's common room. There is an active Students' Organisation

(affiliated to the International Psycho-Analytic Association) which meets regularly for discussion and for social events.

2.4 What do you feel about the methods of teaching?
The quality of teaching is very high. Methods of teaching include lectures, seminars, and group discussions. The teaching faculty is drawn from qualified Members of the British Psycho-Analytical Society, many of whom have wide interests outside psychoanalysis. There is an opportunity for student feedback at the end of every seminar.

2.5 What do you think about the way assessments were done to allow you to progress to the next stages of training?
Students are subjected to continuous assessment from all seminar leaders and supervisors. There is personal tutorship from the individual Progress Advisor who is available at any time for discussion of difficulties in the training.

2.6 Has the course met your expectations?
There is general agreement amongst the students that the course is intellectually demanding, emotionally challenging and ultimately very satisfying. Prospective applicants should be aware that the training is a major commitment of both time and money.

2.7 How do you feel about your future with the organisation?
We look forward to becoming first Associate Members and then full Members of the British Psycho-Analytical Society and hope to contribute to the future clinical and intellectual development of psychoanalysis. Students and Members of the Society are fully aware of current controversies surrounding the theory and practice of psychoanalysis and there is ongoing debate about how best to modernise the profession while retaining its core values and standards. The challenge we face as future psychoanalysts is stimulating discussion, thinking and research initiatives.

2.8 What plans do trainees have for future practice and possible balance of different sorts of work in their career?
Most qualified analysts work in a diverse range of contexts and organisations including the NHS in the application of psychoanalytic knowledge. Primarily we hope to use our hard-earned skills in clinical practice. The practice of intensive, five-times-weekly treatment also functions as research into the mind, so the clinical and research functions are intimately related to each other. Psychoanalysts are in demand to train and teach in other psychotherapy institutions. There is a wide variety of opportunities for analysts reflecting the different backgrounds and interests of the membership, including academic work, the NHS, private practice and research.

AUTHOR'S COMMENTS

This training is the longest established in this guide and has resources available from the best of the BP-AS teaching. It is significant to notice that all trainees at the

Institute are taught across the range of psychoanalytic schools which are part of the curriculum and which are appreciated by trainees who write about their involvement in the psychoanalytic debate. However, there is little from Lacan and the French schools of psychoanalysis, nor from the American schools, and there is no Jung. As in other trainings, trainees are shaped by their choice of analyst and supervisors.

The fact that trainees have a means of commenting on the quality of the teachers is also of interest to other trainings. Is it just that the teachers are well selected from a very experienced group of committed teachers and clinicians, or does the practice of feedback to the teacher after each course shift the quality of teaching and thereby learning? The trainees comment on the issue of maintaining rigour, standards and values while modernising the profession. This suggests that they feel they have a hand in shaping the training they receive as well as in the future clinical and intellectual development of psychoanalysis. All this is borne out by the comments on the active student organisation with its international dimension through international student conferences.

This course is the most demanding in this guide in terms of time, money and rigour, mainly for analysis and supervision within a five-times-weekly session psychoanalytic framework. However, trainees are well supported. Their teachers gift their work, making the taught aspects of the course the least expensive amongst all the trainings. There are also excellent supports in the shape of a library, book grants and interest-free loans.

For the benefit of the wider analytic community the BP-AS has come into the twenty-first century with an excellent web site and access through the *International Journal of Psycho-Analysis* (see appendix for addresses) to a stimulating on-line discussion where analysts and others can participate in open debate on psychoanalytic disputes and discussions. The Society (BP-AS) is well known for the liveliness of debate, its Scientific meetings open to students and its conferences open to all practitioners and trainees in the profession.

INSTITUTE OF PSYCHOTHERAPY AND SOCIAL STUDIES (IPSS – UKCP/PPS)

West Hill House, 6 Swains Lane, London N6 6QU
Tel. 020 7284 4762

1. HISTORY OF THE ORGANISATION

The Institute of Psychotherapy and Social Studies was founded in 1978 as a means of addressing the perceived need to offer a sound Psychoanalytical Psychotherapy training which also considered the socio-political context which may affect our self-awareness and our understanding of others.

The course is designed to give students the practical and theoretical experience needed to develop their own understanding of psychoanalytical practice. It is based on the MA and Doctoral level psychotherapy training programmes at the University of Goteborg in Sweden developed in the late 1960s by Dr Giora Doron, one of the founders of IPSS. He was a psychoanalytic psychotherapist and group analyst whose theory and practice was informed by Freud and the Frankfurt school critique of Freud in the European tradition, coming to England via Hungary, Israel and Sweden. In the early days of the IPSS Humanistic Psychology and its psychotherapies was an influence as a critique of psychoanalysis. Since then, for the last 15 years, the critique comes from philosophy and sociology.

An important part of our ethos is to make psychotherapy available to the widest spectrum of potential clients many of whom are not usually able to avail themselves of a therapist, particularly those with low incomes. To this end most IPSS-trained psychotherapists offer 'sliding scale' fees, and we are also able to offer low-cost therapy through our trainee therapists. Some members also offer low-cost therapy. IPSS is committed to equality of access in the provision of psychotherapy and training in psychotherapy and seeks to avoid discrimination on grounds of age, class, educational qualifications, ethnic or national origin, gender, physical disability or sexuality. It welcomes and encourages applications from all sections of society.

2. THEORETICAL ORIENTATION AND CURRICULUM

The Diploma, which also has MA status through the University of London, is a training in both the theory and practice of psychoanalytic psychotherapy incorporating both interpersonal and object relations theory and leads to UKCP registration through the Psychoanalytic and Psychodynamic Psychotherapy section. The training accords with the flag statement of the section and integral to the training, both theoretical and clinical, is an awareness of the social, cultural and political context within which psychotherapy takes place.

The theoretical location of the course is broadly within the Independent tradition of the British School of object relations with classical Freudian theory and Self-Psychology from the US.

There is a one-year pre-training course, 'Exploring Psychotherapy', that is encouraged but not mandatory, which is also of interest to people in other fields as a discrete course.

3. TRAINING STRUCTURE

3.1 Training committe
Composed of Chair, Clinical Director, Senior Tutor and up to five other members, it is responsible for (a) selection and admission; (b) the supervisor's committee and the clinical work; (c) the theoretical programme and its teaching; (d) graduate and post-graduate programmes that come under CPD (Continuous Professional Development), and (e) has an input into other committees regarding Ethics, Equal Opportunities, CPD, recruitment and finance.

3.2 Selection procedure and admission
The course and qualification is usually a second career and is aimed at those in the core professions of social work, health/psychiatry, nursing, medicine, community work both in the voluntary and statutory sectors, teaching, as well as those falling

outside these fields who have had relevant experience or who can demonstrate an interest and competency.

The admission policy is broadly to recruit people who have appropriate professional and personal experience and qualities, which allow for the reasonable expectation that they will complete the course.

The IPSS also has an explicit Equal Opportunities Policy concerning admission, staffing and syllabus.

The criteria for acceptance on the course are as follows:

1. A university degree of equivalent qualification. This would include the DipSW (CQSW) or RMN in appropriate cases.
2. Experience in the core professions. This may include education, health, welfare or youth work. We would also consider applicants with appropriate and relevant experience from other fields. Those without experience may be asked to complete a period of clinical work experience with a voluntary agency.
3. A prerequisite of a minimum of one year in individual psychoanalytic psychotherapy prior to the commencement of the course.
4. Ability to demonstrate a prior interest in the field of psychotherapy. Demonstration of the personal maturity, stability and flexibility required for the rigours of a psychotherapeutic training.

These requirements may be interpreted flexibly, so that if a candidate is considered suitable in other respects, one of the requirements might be slightly amended. As a general principle candidates will be considered for training from the age of 30+ and there is no formal upper age limit.

Applicants who meet these criteria and are considered to be potential candidates for training will be invited to two interviews with members of the Training Committee, whose decision is final. Two further criteria for successful applicants are the candidates' acceptance of the Institute's code of ethical principles and practice and the candidates' acceptance of the terms and conditions of the course as detailed in the Course Requirement Document. On occasion a small bursary may be given and in certain circumstances the fees may be spread over a longer term than the four-year training period at the discretion of the Executive and Training Committees to help with financial hardship.

3.3 Time commitment per week and length of training
Two afternoon into early evening sessions per week across three ten-week terms per year for three years, to one such session in year four. CPD is encouraged from then on. The award of Diploma and MA degree is at the point of the successful completion of the dissertation.

3.4 Financial cost of training at different stages
Supervision costs for the first two years of clinical work and training are borne by the IPSS. The total and inclusive fee is £2,424 p.a., and in year four when the trainee pays supervision fees the cost nets down to some £500 p.a.

3.5 Interruptions in training
The IPSS is now bound by the University of North London (applicable to all universities in England and Wales) rules and regulations, which cover every case, put to

the Faculty Committee with the IPSS Training Committee on grounds of health or other circumstance and find serious and permissible.

3.6 Graduating and beginning a career
Diploma of Psychoanalytic Psychotherapy and MA degree in Psychoanalytic Psychotherapy and Social Studies from University of North London and inclusion in the Register of the UK Council for Psychotherapy.

The Membership Committee organises bimonthly scientific meetings and annual conference and the Training Committee organises termly day meetings with another psychoanalytic training organisation.

Many of our members five years on from training have a mixed clinical practice of private work and sessions within the statutory (NHS) and voluntary sectors of Mental Health.

3.7 Numbers of students per intake
The upper limit to each year is usually 15.

4. CLINICAL AND ACADEMIC REQUIREMENTS

4.1 Personal therapy
Each trainee is in individual psychoanalytic psychotherapy (UKCP PP section registered or BCP – minimum of five years post-qualification) for a minimum of one year, prior to training a minimum of twice weekly until achieving diploma.

4.2 Clinical requirements
A minimum of work with two cases twice weekly, one must be eighteen months or longer. The Clinical Director, together with the Referrals Coordinator, sets out to make a minimum of two referrals to each trainee.

4.3 Supervision
Trainees must continue in weekly supervision until the successful completion of the dissertation with a supervisor appointed by the IPSS on the basis of qualification, experience and reputation, have a minimum of five years' post-qualification experience and be UKCP PP section or BCP registered.

4.4 Written work and attendance
Minimum attendance rate is 88 per cent – tutorials may be taken to compensate absence with approval of the Training Committee.

For the combined Diploma and MA six essays are required over three years and a fully written-up and presented case study and dissertation.

4.5 Assessment, standards and ethical requirements
Assessment at section 4.4 above is by teacher, one peer and the two external examiners appointed by the University and IPSS. Standards and assessment are moderated by IPSS, the University Faculty and Monitoring Unit, as well as by Sunset Review by our section in the UKCP. The required standard is of MA/MPhil degree.

The rationale, approach, procedures and criteria are set out in our Articles of Association with the University and in our Student Handbook.

5. TRAINEE RESPONSE

1. Why this course was chosen

1.1 What made people decide to train?
The choice to train was made largely to extend existing qualifications and improve career prospects. A social worker wanted to work more deeply with clients. A psychodynamic art therapist wanted to increase his skills as psychotherapist. A psychodynamic counsellor in private practice wanted to be able to practice also as a psychotherapist. An integrative therapist found her own approach was shifting toward a psychoanalytic orientation. Gaining UKCP recognition was a definite advantage. Although most of us came from the caring or paramedical professions, other backgrounds included historian, lawyer, businessman, academic. Their interest grew from reading, contact with colleagues, having had therapy themselves, or an introductory course.

1.2 What were the aspects of this course that were most attractive?
The inclusion of a social and political critique of psychoanalytic ideas and a questioning approach drew many. Of major importance was a focus on the 'Independents', and 'pluralism', which offered freedom to compare different schools and choose preferred practice. The written equal opportunities commitment was important, to be inclusive of existing students, gay and lesbian, the over-fifties and from ethnic minorities. The modular course structure allowed for accreditation of prior learning, helping those who had made 'sideways moves' from other trainings. The link with the University of North London and the attainment of a Diploma and an MA was an added inducement particularly to those who might want to practise abroad.

1.3 What was your experience of the selection procedure?
The selection procedure was seen as open and unthreatening. Candidates felt empowered to present themselves well.

1.4 Before the start of the course, how informed did you feel about each stage of the training?
Information given was generally thought to be adequate. Some felt more clarification should have been made about clinical requirements and the difference between the MA and Diploma routes. These were clarified as the course progressed.

2. The atmosphere of the course
The atmosphere has been open and exciting. Students feel free to question and challenge apparently accepted viewpoints. We felt treated as intellectual adults, able to think for ourselves and not forced to conform to ideas we disagree with. Quote: 'the sense that one is not being fitted into a rigid theoretical mould, the sense of respect for our individual development as therapists is good'. We find our ideas changing and developing as we progress. This is fostered by open debate rather than by pressure to conform.

The content of the academic part of the course has inevitably not satisfied everybody. Some would have liked more first-year seminar readings of original Freud and Klein papers and later more readings from Bion and Lacan. Some liked, others did not, the stress on American theorists such as Kernberg, Kohut and Stern. We have been able to feed these opinions back to the Training Committee via our year representatives and some accommodations have been made. For example, we have been able to design one term's seminars for ourselves and have chosen 'Post-Kleinian Perspectives'.

Teaching and assessment methods were generally thought to be good. 'There is a good mix of seminars, presentations and small group learning, and a mix of in-house and visiting tutors.' Some thought the quality of teaching was 'variable' – sometimes excellent, at other times poor. The open and informal atmosphere in seminars and group, some liked, but others felt lacked rigour and organisation. Theory and practice is well integrated by weekly presentations of case material by senior students, which all years attend, question and discuss.

Assessment procedures which include self, peer and staff assessment were generally seen as good, though some felt that assessment by staff could be more rigorous, and feedback more comprehensive.

The transmission of information from staff to students was generally seen as good, but sometimes contradictory. The organisation itself is undergoing development: some administrative methods are changing though basic principles remain the same. For example, there have been changing criteria for the acceptance of training patients which may have led to confusion. There is a formal representation of student representatives on termly council meetings with teaching staff and IPSS practitioners. Sometimes individual student queries to staff take some time to be answered.

Communication with fellow trainees: there is a termly community meeting for all years, conducted by the students, at which ideas and concerns about the course are collected and sent to the IPSS council via student representatives. Weekly experiential groups also provide an opportunity to air thoughts and feelings about the course. At more informal levels regular visits to the local pub are a great aid to communication, but some students would like a coffee room to be available.

Expectations and future plans

Students on the whole seemed to feel their expectations of the course had been met. Students reported: greater confidence, challenge, enjoyment and changing preconceptions in the work. Almost all wanted to continue their association with IPSS after the end of training, and a few wanted to play an active part.

Most wanted to combine their public sector work in the NHS, Social Services or Education with a private practice. A few want to concentrate on private work but are aware of the difficulties of setting up a practice. The possibility of setting up group practices with other IPSS members has been mooted.

AUTHOR'S COMMENTS

The IPSS course combines a variety of elements. It is pluralist, includes a tradition of social and philosophical critique of analysis as well as offering a master's degree as part of the course. Originally the course offered a humanistic stream as well as a psychodynamic stream. It has come a way from its more humanistic leanings, but has not abandoned its social critical stance. The course believes firmly in the importance of the training therapy and clinical supervision while offering a social studies seminar alongside psychoanalytic theory. It should also be noticed that this is one of the few courses to teach American psychoanalytic thinkers, including those from the interactionist school. These commitments appear to be echoed in the way the trainees report on their experience of being taught and treated.

There is some suggestion that the range of theories and approaches being taught as well as the openness of the teaching methods does not suit all and that it deprives trainees of opportunities to understand more rigorously the teachings of primary figures in the field and getting to grips with an authority that does not reside in the group.

LINCOLN CLINIC AND CENTRE FOR PSYCHOTHERAPY (LINC – BCP)

19 Abbeville Mews, 88 Clapham Park Road, London SW4 7BX
Tel. 020 7978 1545 Fax. 020 7720 4721
Web site: <http://www.lincoln-psychotherapy.org.uk/development>
E-mail: info@lincoln-psychotherapy.org.uk
**   training@lincoln-psychotherapy.org.uk**

Registered Charity and founding member of British Confederation of Psychotherapists.

1. HISTORY OF THE ORGANISATION

The Lincoln was founded in Lambeth in 1967 and moved to Clapham in 1989. We provide patient treatment and offer a thorough training in psychoanalytic psycho-therapy to people from a variety of professions with opportunities to acquire a range of sound clinical skills.

2. THEORETICAL ORIENTATION AND CURRICULUM

Our orientation is psychoanalytic and includes the work of the Contemporary Freudian, Independent and Kleinian schools.

The Pre-Clinical Programme comprises:

- personal therapy
- infant observation and seminars; with a final paper
- work discussion seminars laying foundations for later clinical seminars
- theoretical seminars: a thorough introduction to Freud's work, and to clinical concepts; personality development.

Applicants not yet accepted for training may be able to join prior work discussion seminars. We also offer a Psychoanalytical Observational Studies Course with the

Tavistock Centre and the University of East London, which may lead to full training in child or adult psychotherapy. Those joining the Associate Membership Course (AMC) from observational studies may move directly to the Clinical Programme, as may qualified child psychotherapists.

The Clinical Programme comprises:

- personal therapy
- clinical seminars
- theory seminars including Contemporary Freudian and Independent thought, work of Abraham, Ferenczi and Klein, borderline states, depression, psychosis, perversion, thinking and symbol formation, dreams, psychopathology, sexuality, advanced study of clinical concepts, techniques of interpretation, assessment and analysability, psychiatric diagnosis and topics of choice; also on writing a paper and psychotherapy research
- training patients and reports
- supervision.

To ensure appropriately wide theoretical and clinical perspectives we rotate seminar leaders of the different theoretical orientations.

3. TRAINING STRUCTURE

3.1 Training committee
The AMC Committee comprises seven elected psychoanalysts and senior psychotherapists, responsible to the Professional Committee for all aspects of training.

3.2 Selection procedure and admission

Individual therapy
We expect applicants to have been in individual psychoanalytic psychotherapy for at least one year prior to beginning training for a minimum three times weekly with a Lincoln approved therapist (at present a Lincoln-approved training therapist or an approved Member or Associate Member of the British Psycho-Analytic Society).

Academic and clinical experience

- a degree, preferably in a relevant subject, or, exceptionally, an appropriate qualification or equivalent academic status
- relevant work experience
- some knowledge through experience, study or research of the mental health field.

Applicants without relevant psychiatric experience/knowledge will be helped to find an honorary psychiatric placement.

Potential applicants not fulfilling these requirements may arrange a preliminary interview with us to discuss training.

Selection
Applicants complete a form and, references received, complete a questionnaire. Two interviews follow (a third if necessary). We offer successful applicants either a full or provisional place.

Equal opportunities policy
As in other areas of its institutional practice, the Lincoln Centre's selection criteria for each of its courses are made in line with Equal Opportunities Legislation. The Lincoln aims to foster the principle of non-discrimination on grounds of gender, sexual orientation, age, disability, religion and ethnic origin. Selection procedures vary according to the requirements of particular courses and we consider applicants in the context of experience and personal readiness for the specific course to which application is made. All those serving on selection panels and training programmes on behalf of the Lincoln adhere to this policy.

3.3 Time commitment per week and length of training
The course, which takes four to five years, is designed to enable full-time work to continue. For students from far outside London, we allow some flexibility. Time in the Pre-clinical period depends on work experience and on readiness in personal therapy. Progression to the Clinical Programme is not automatic and progress is monitored.   .

Clinical Programme: (Year 2 onwards)

- personal therapy throughout, as above
- clinical seminar, weekly to qualification
- theoretical seminar, weekly for three years, then reduced
- two training patients, three times weekly each
- two supervision sessions, each once weekly
- six-monthly report writing
- tutorials (30–60 minutes each)
- preparation and writing of qualifying paper.

Seminar days, times and places Monday and Thursday evenings, 90 minutes per seminar; venues in both north and south London.
   Post-curricular period: usually clinical seminars continue until qualification. However, if the required time with training patients is complete, attendance may not be required while preparing the qualifying paper.

3.4 Financial cost of training at different stages
As a registered charity, we endeavour to keep fees within reasonable limits. Personal therapy fees are arranged between the therapist and student, as are supervision fees. Fees are subject to change. For 2000:

Application fee	£140
Year 1	£1,365
Years 2, 3	£1,095
Year 4	£945
Annual student subscription	£132
Insurance cover	£22

3.5 Interruptions in training
Generally we only agree to interruptions for reasons such as illness, pregnancy or bereavement.

3.6 Graduating and beginning a career

Qualification
When all seminars and supervised work are complete a paper on one training patient is submitted. To assist the Committee, an external examiner comments on the strengths and weaknesses shown in the presented work. The therapist's consent and opinions from the clinical supervisors as to the student's ability to work independently are sought. The Committee reviews the required components and decides whether overall the student is ready to qualify.

Associate membership
On qualification, students become Associate Members of the Lincoln and are registered with the British Confederation of Psychotherapists. After two years, they are eligible to take the Lincoln's Full Membership Course. As Associate Members they may participate in all election procedures and serve on certain committees, and in running the Newsletter, the Annual Lecture, the Scientific Programme of lectures and meetings, workshops, and other activities. They have full access to and may participate in running the Lincoln's Clinical Services which refer work to Lincoln therapists.

We expect that five years after qualification therapists will be firmly established in their private practice. Some may also work part-time in the public health services. They may be playing a full part in the Lincoln organisation.

3.7 Numbers of students per intake
Up to ten students per year.

4. CLINICAL AND ACADEMIC REQUIREMENTS

4.1 Personal therapy
Students remain in individual psychoanalytic psychotherapy at least three times weekly with an approved training analyst/therapist (see section 3.2) throughout training until qualification.

4.2 Clinical requirements
Training patients: Two training patients – one male, one female – each three times weekly.

Referrals Service: The Lincoln's Referrals Psychotherapist, as part of the Lincoln's Clinical Services, administers the Low-Fee Scheme and arranges training patients. Some students, particularly from outside London, may need to seek patients locally. Students may elect to treat one training patient within a NHS or other approved institutional setting.

4.3 Supervision

A different approved psychoanalyst/training therapist (one male, one female) supervises the two training patients weekly, each.

4.4 Written work and course attendance

Pre-Clinical Programme written work:

- detailed notes on infant observations
- detailed session notes for work discussion seminars when presenting
- an infant observation final paper of 7,000–8,000 words (the best paper is awarded the Kelnar Prize).

Clinical Programme written work:

- patient session notes for supervision
- a six-monthly report of 400 words on each patient (the first on each may be 600 words)
- qualifying paper (see section 3.5) of 7,000–8,000 words on the work with one patient.

Course attendance: twice-weekly seminars over three ten-week terms annually (see section 3.3 for variations).

Assessment, standards and ethical requirements

Ethical code
The Lincoln's Ethical Code complies with that of the British Confederation of Psychotherapists covering all aspects of Professional Boundaries and Patient Care and Confidentiality.

Approach to standards and ethical requirements
The Lincoln seeks to ensure the highest standards in its training as well as furthering professional standards throughout the profession. Members and students adhere to the ethical standards outlined in the Code.

Assessment
We monitor each student's progress throughout training. We make fuller assessments before progress to the Clinical Programme, before taking first and second training patients and before qualification.

Tutors see all reports and discuss them with each student. Supervisors report twice yearly, seminar leaders after each series of seminars. The Committee reviews each student at meetings six times annually.

Criteria for assessment
We assess each student's readiness to work professionally and independently as a psychoanalytic psychotherapist. The criteria include the following: he/she has shown a good level of understanding of psychopathology and of how to work effectively in the transference. The student will also have demonstrated an ability to hold professional boundaries and be able to work within the ethical guidelines.

Other activities for students
An open meeting of students and AMC Committee members is held annually. We arrange special events including workshops on infant observation, and to discuss in detail particular clinical concepts. Students receive and contribute to the Lincoln Newsletter, attend and contribute to Scientific Meetings. The active Student Committee also arranges social events.

5. TRAINEE RESPONSE

1. Why this course was chosen
The rigorous and professional reputation of the Lincoln's training programme was one of the main factors attracting trainees.

The training is seen to be exacting, fair and thoughtful, with a consistently high standard of teaching. It offers the opportunity to integrate psychoanalytic thinking within clinical work in the NHS and other statutory settings.

The trainees feel that the training has considerably improved in recent years. The current prospectus is clear and comprehensive.

There is a perception among some trainees that the course has a Kleinian emphasis; but this is not at the expense of covering Contemporary Freudian and Independent ideas within the syllabus.

The Lincoln's South London location was an attraction, though in reality nearly all of the seminars are in North London.

2. The atmosphere of the course
The seminar leaders and teachers are excellent. Most are members of the BP-AS, but not all. It is felt important that the rigour for which the course is valued does not turn into inflexibility. An enquiring attitude to the academic papers under discussion is encouraged.

At the end of each series of seminars, students complete an evaluation form, commenting on content of seminar (particularly the reading), style of seminar leader and overall enjoyment of seminar.

Progress through the training goes smoothly for most students, however some experience difficulty in progressing through the course. This can be due to a shortage of training patients in their geographical area or due to personal reasons. Each student has a personal tutor who they meet two or three times a year to discuss their progress.

The training administrator is the backbone of the administrative side and is extremely helpful, friendly and accessible. She is particularly helpful in finding papers that are assigned for theory seminars, which can sometimes be difficult to get hold of.

Year groups vary in size from three to ten. It is felt that seven should be the maximum, while three is too small.

There is an active Student Committee that maintains links between year groups and the training committee. The Student Committee also initiates social activities. There is a newsletter to which students are invited and encouraged to contribute. A new addition is a bulletin published between newsletters, offering a further chance to reply to articles within the newsletter. This provides an opportunity to raise controversial issues.

There are monthly Scientific meetings.

Communication is felt to be clear and defined, although it is thought that when there is a change in rule or expectation, it takes some time to come down through the hierarchy to the trainees.

In general, trainees feel that the training more than meets their expectations and they are satisfied with the curriculum and the support they feel is available for them. The exception to this can be when a training patient has left just before the required time limit. This is a situation where the flexibility of a particular training is tested.

AUTHOR'S COMMENTS

The Lincoln course aims for rigourous standards and a firm commitment by the training committee to applying psychoanalytic ideas and practice to psychotherapy using BP-AS psychoanalysts as the main teachers, supervisors and training analysts. A Jungian analyst would not be acceptable as a training analyst. The restriction on using this institution exclusively creates dependence upon an outside organisation and makes it almost impossible for graduates to contribute as teachers, analysts or supervisors on this course. It is not clear why this is as many Lincoln graduates have analysis and clinical experience equivalent to many psychoanalysts. There has also been some suggestion that the room for debate about membership of the BCP and UKCP was not as open as it might have been at the Lincoln and that there is pressure upon trainees to adopt a school of thought loyalty that might feel restricting to some while enabling others to feel underpinned clinically in a way that is crucial for their analytic education.

The training has developed intellectually and clinically from its commitment to low-fee psychotherapy and counselling south of the river set up in 1982 by Gil Parker and Prophecy Coles, and its religious inspiration and liberal ideals inspired by Abraham Lincoln, after whom it was named.

As the last edition of this guide suggested, Judith Jackson's tenure as Dean of Studies has made the course popular with those who seek a Kleinian approach, although, as at the Institute of Psycho-Analysis, other schools of psychoanalysis are taught. As at the Institute, there is no French or American psychoanalysis taught, and no Jung.

Particularly worth noting were the trainee's comments on the efficiency and friendliness of the administrator – gold for any training, but a presence and an ethos that makes clarity and immediacy of communication a hallmark noticed by all who have contact with a training organisation.

For psychotherapists with less stringent clinical and personal therapy experience, the Lincoln membership course offers an accessible route to training at a higher standard without having to return to basic training.

One of the issues raised by the trainees is about the course's perceived Kleinian bias. They point out that this does not restrict independent and contemporary Freudian teaching, but it might suggest the main emphasis and encouragement from the core teaching staff who interview and assess applicants. What is clear is that trainees will get a thorough grounding in Kleinian and post-Kleinian understanding.

LONDON CENTRE FOR PSYCHOTHERAPY (LCP – BCP)

32 Leighton Road, Kentish Town, London NW5 2QE
Tel. 020 7482 2002/2282 Fax. 020 7482 4222
E-mail: lcp@talk.com

1. HISTORY OF THE ORGANISATION

The London Centre for Psychotherapy had its origins in the Association of Psycho-therapists, which was founded in 1951 by a group of pioneering practitioners who shared an ambition to make psychotherapy more widely available. The Clinic (known as the Well Walk Centre) was placed at the heart of the organisation, and the Association always included both Freudians and Jungians.

In 1973, a small group with divergent views about the running of the Clinic broke away from what had become known as the British Association of Psychotherapists and formed the London Centre for Psychotherapy. The LCP began its own training programme and clinic, under the directorship of Ilse Seglow, operating from Fitzjohn's Avenue, Hampstead, for 23 years.

The LCP now owns spacious premises in Kentish Town, North London, where the clinic, trainings, scientific meetings, cultural and social events are held and where consulting rooms are available.

The building also houses the John Padel Library, named to honour John Padel who donated his comprehensive library of books and journals to the LCP before he died.

The Centre currently provides an association for around 200 practising psycho-therapists.

The LCP became a member institution of the British Confederation of Psycho-therapists in 1998.

2. THEORETICAL ORIENTATION AND CURRICULUM

The Four-Year Qualifying Course (4YQC) provides an intensive professional training in adult individual psychoanalytic psychotherapy (including analytical psychology). The LCP is one of the few psychoanalytically based trainings to offer analytical psychology as an integral part of the curriculum.

The first (pre-clinical) year of the training studies the major psychoanalytic theorists of all schools initially, by way of an historical survey.

Year II completes the historical survey and also begins clinically orientated seminars in practice and technique.

In years III and IV the focus is essentially clinical with theoretical formulations underpinning the work.

Teachers are drawn from Kleinian, Independent, Contemporary Freudian and Jungian orientations to give the course as wide a theoretical base as possible.

A weekly Infant Observation seminar takes place over two years, where the development of observed infants is studied, along with theories of infant and child development. Interested professionals who are not enrolled in the 4YQC may join a two-year Infant Observation Seminar.

One-year introductory course
An introduction to Analytical Psychotherapy offers a foundation in psychoanalytic thinking and practice to professionals from varied backgrounds and includes an experiential group. It can also provide a foundation for prospective applicants who have not had a relevant preliminary training.

Masters degree and professional doctorate
The LCP plans to offer the above degrees in conjunction with a university. Students will have the option of combining the Introductory Course with the first (non-clinical) year of the 4YQC, to obtain a Masters Degree. Trainees completing the clinical training will have the option of gaining a Professional Doctorate.

3. TRAINING STRUCTURE

3.1 Training committee
The Training Committee consists of the Chair of Training, and the Chair of each year sub-committee. The sub-committees are made up of the personal tutors who coordinate supervisors and seminar leaders reports, discuss progress and meet regularly with trainees until qualification.

The Training Forum meets twice a year, and includes the Training Committee, plus the tutors from all the year sub-committees, and student representatives. Here policy is discussed and recommendations can be made to the Training Committee. The Training Committee will refer policy change to an elected Council, which carries ultimate responsibility for the LCP's work and policy.

3.2 Selection procedure and admission
Trainees are expected to have a degree or equivalent.

Applicants who are not working in a clinical setting will need to have completed a minimum of six months continuous supervised clinical experience before taking on the first training patient and usually before application.

The application form requires details of academic qualifications, professional and personal history. References will be taken up, and there will be two, or occasionally three, interviews.

The Membership Committee selects candidates for training on the basis of personal integrity, analysability, motivation, emotional resourcefulness, maturity and academic capacity.

There are no age restrictions. To date we have not been able to provide bursaries for trainees who are finding funding difficult. However, we do stagger course fees if requested and a small travel bursary is available for trainees from outside London.

3.3 Time commitment per week and length of training
The academic training takes place over two evenings per week for four years.

Trainees will also attend a once weekly clinical seminar after the four-year course ends, until qualification.

There is no official time limit for duration of training, although there is a deadline for completion of clinical papers. Most trainees should expect to complete the training in under five years.

Taking into account all aspects of the training, it would be realistic to allow for 20 hours per week, particularly in the later stages of training.

3.4 Financial cost of training different stages
Fees are approximately £ 1,300 p.a.

3.5 Interruptions in training
Requests for sabbaticals are considered sympathetically.

3.6 Graduating and beginning a career
Qualified graduates may apply for Associate Membership immediately on qualification, and three years after that for full membership. Further clinical requirements must be met before an application for full membership can be considered.

Alternatively, after two years of Associate Membership, the Full Membership Course may be undertaken, which is a two-year course of once-weekly clinical seminars, involving two intensive cases, with two supervisors.

The Membership Course includes one year of Advanced Clinical Seminars, which are also offered as a separate course.

Appropriately qualified members of other trainings are welcome to apply for membership.

To further professional development, the LCP organises a full and well-attended programme of professional activities, including two scientific meetings a month, one of which is open to the public, Papers by members and invited speakers are presented, including the 'Reading-In' of qualifying papers of recent graduates.

Reflections, an in-house journal, is published termly.

A high proportion of associate and full members participate in the committees, which run the LCP. Many suitably qualified LCP graduates teach on the training, and are encouraged to do so.

Five years after graduation, members would typically be in full-time private practice, or in part-time private practice with work, for example, in the NHS.

3.7 Numbers of students per intake
There is no upper limit to the number of trainees accepted for each year. Six or seven is the average intake of trainees at present.

4. CLINICAL AND ACADEMIC REQUIREMENTS

4.1 Personal therapy
Trainees are required to be in a minimum of three-times-a-week psychotherapy with an approved training therapist or analyst for one year prior to starting the 4YQC, and thereafter until training is completed.

The training therapist is asked to verify that the potential trainee is ready to start a training, and then towards the end of the first year, that the trainee is now ready to take on a training patient.

It has always been a matter of principle that LCP members are eligible to apply for training therapist status.

4.2 Clinical requirements
Training patients are usually referred by the Clinic, following a diagnostic assessment. An experienced assessor will endeavour to find suitable training patients who will be able to commit to the therapy over the period of time required. Out-of-London trainees may have to find their own referrals, although an LCP assessor would normally undertake assessment. The first and second training patients are seen three times weekly, for a minimum of two years and eighteen months respectively.

4.3 Supervision
Trainees must select two LCP-approved training supervisors for once-weekly individual supervision for each of their two training patients, which will continue until qualification.

4.4 Written work and course attendance
Four written papers are required, of approximately 5,000 words each, although the clinical papers are usually considerably longer: Theoretical Paper, Infant Observation Paper, Clinical Paper I, Clinical Paper II. Trainees also write six-monthly reports on training patients.

Trainees are expected to attend all seminars.

4.5 Assessment, standards and ethical requirements

Code of ethics
Members and trainees are bound by all sections of the LCP Code of Ethics.
Essentially, members must act in the way that they reasonably believe to be in the best interests of the patient, taking full responsibility for maintaining the professional relationship in all respects, and for ensuring that professional competence is maintained.

The Professional Practice Committee deals with any breach of the Code of Ethics when a complaint is formally made in writing. Individual matters of concern may also be taken to this committee for informal consideration, and support.

Standards and assessments
Standards are set by the Training Committee, and are always determined by consideration of the welfare of the patient.

Tutors' yearly reports provide a summary of all the reports and must be signed by the trainee, who will have opportunities to discuss progress throughout the year.

The tutor will inform the Training Committee of the trainee's development, and will fully inform the trainee if there is cause for concern.

The clinical papers are assessed by the Training Committee, who consider the trainee's ability to think clearly, with empathy and compassion, and with an evident integration of theory and practice.

The final clinical paper will be sent to the External Assessor, provided it has been demonstrated that the trainee is ready to practice independently. The External

Assessor's report is considered very carefully but the final decision as to qualification rests with the Training Committee.

5. TRAINEE RESPONSE

1. Why this course was chosen

1.2 What were the aspects of this course that were most attractive?
Candidates who chose to train at the LCP were attracted by the pluralistic approach and for some the inclusion of Analytical Psychology was essential. The infant observation was considered to be important, as was the experiential group (which may in fact now be on its way out). It was felt that the LCP laid great emphasis on the clinical aspects of training and this was felt to be desirable. The LCP's reputation of welcoming applicants from a wide variety of professional backgrounds, as well as the lack of age discrimination, were also considered positive factors when choosing a training. Some had been encouraged to pursue training at the LCP after attending and enjoying the introductory course.

1.3 What was your experience of the selection procedure?
The selection procedure was felt to be rigorous and thorough and most felt the interviews to be containing and well organised. Some had found their interviews, while challenging, to be appropriate, benign and even enjoyable. However, a few felt that certain aspects of their interviews were inappropriate as a selection process.

1.4 Before the start of the course, how informed did you feel about each stage of the training?
Many people felt that they were insufficiently informed about the training before the start of the course. It was agreed, however, that this has been and is continuing to improve. The lack of clear communication was felt to be the result of some years of upheaval when the LCP was in transition between premises and between the UKCP and the BCP. An improved handbook has been brought up to date and it is hoped that it will be updated regularly.

2. The atmosphere of the course

2.1. How do you feel about the way in which information is communicated?
The Student Association (SA) has taken on the task of trying, where necessary, to clarify and circulate information. As a result, communication between candidates and committees staffed by volunteer members, which had sometimes previously been hampered by misunderstanding, has improved considerably. Student representatives from each year group as well as representatives from the Student Association are invited to attend some committees and can then report back to the student body. The opportunity at the start of training for new candidates to meet the outgoing student group was felt to be useful. Administrative office staff are helpful.

2.2 What do you find the most confusing aspect of the training?
There have been improvements in the procedure concerned with the processing of qualifying papers, which was overlong and unclear. Some procedures, however,

still need to be streamlined. The organisation of timetabling has at times been erratic. The curriculum is in the process of being modified, it remains to be seen if this will be for the better.

2.3 How much opportunity do you have to share thoughts and feelings with fellow trainees?
The LCP has a thriving Student Association. Formed in 1996, the SA's aim is to support the interests of students throughout their training and to provide a forum for the exchange of information and ideas. The SA's objectives are:

- To provide information and clarification for the student body
- To offer support and representation in the case of difficulties arising during the course of training
- To work with the LCP to initiate and develop aspects of the training
- To represent the views and perspectives of trainees with regards to current issues in the profession.

The SA has an Annual General Meeting with speakers and a social event at which all trainees can meet together.

Post-curricular students meet twice yearly together with the chair of training.

2.4 What do you feel about the methods of teaching?
The heterogeneous nature of the student group and the pluralistic nature of the course engender lively exchanges of ideas in academic and clinical seminars, although some people found the teaching at times sectarian. The quality of teaching is varied, from the occasional inadequate seminar leader to the truly excellent. Students are encouraged to fill in termly feedback forms on each seminar leader. The experiential group was felt by some to be valuable; others found it painful and unhelpful.

2.5 What did you think about the way assessments were done to allow you to progress to the next stages of training?
The policy of open reporting, which has been recently instituted, has meant that students are more involved in the process of assessment and this has been appreciated. There are regular meetings with year tutors where comments from supervisors and seminar leaders are reviewed and the student's progression through the different stages of training are discussed. Some were comfortable with this process but others found it at times punitive.

2.6 Has the course met your expectations?
While some years had felt that overall the course had met their expectations, others had not felt so positive. Over the last few years there have been a few changes in policy leading to some restructuring which has fostered a certain amount of insecurity adding to the inevitable anxieties and difficulties inherent in training.

2.7 How do you feel about your future with the organisation?
Students have mixed plans for future work. While some were enthusiastic about taking part in and contributing to the life of the LCP once qualified, others were somewhat tentative and ambivalent as to their future involvement.

AUTHOR'S COMMENTS

In the early days of the LCP the commitment was to a training for those wishing to work in the public services as much as privately. The emphasis now is on preparing for private practice. Once the course contained elements of group and family therapy and trained people for once- or twice-weekly work. It is now very different.

However, the course is still characterised by its pluralism, with teachers from the three Freudian groups as well as London Jungians who work in transference and counter-transference. There is openness to build on a breadth of analytic thinking, but what has become a hallmark of its graduates is the depth at which thinking has been understood and applied in a clinical context. This is due in some measure to increasing standards over the years as former graduates have deepened their training, supervision and personal therapy in a way that has insisted on those standards being applied to the LCP course resulting in eventually joining the BCP. The breadth of approaches means that there is no dependence upon external organisations for its teaching and training roles and that there is encouragement for LCP graduates to contribute to these roles as their clinical experience and analytic education develops. Having said that, a significant proportion of teachers, supervisors and training therapists are analysts.

The LCP is the only organisational member of the BCP that offers a course that covers Jung as well as psychoanalysis (apart from the Jungian trainings). In some measure the depth and width of the course comes from the fact that there are two evenings of seminars throughout the four years. This is a heavier demand on the resources of trainees than many trainings, and yet one that bears fruit for those who want a thorough grounding in the field. The consequences of this broader course are that some may value the place Jung has in the curriculum, as the trainee response suggests, while some may find in it a distraction from their wish to concentrate more deeply on contemporary Freudian, Independent and post-Kleinian developments.

Those who want to get to know what the LCP has to offer can do the one-year introductory course, but many who apply come from equivalent experience of training in other contexts. There is also a membership course for those who may wish to deepen their analytic education and join this organisation.

NORTHERN IRELAND ASSOCIATION FOR THE STUDY OF PSYCHOANALYSIS (NIASP – BCP)

Honorary Secretary NIASP, 136 Groomsport Road, Bangor, Co. Down BT20 5PE
Tel./Fax. 028 91 472523
E-mail: anne.anderson29571@btinternet.com

1. HISTORY of the ORGANISATION

The NIASP was formally constituted in 1989 by a number of individuals from different disciplines – psychiatry, sociology, dentistry, psychology and literature – with a serious interest in psychoanalysis.

At its outset NIASP had to rely on the only one accredited Psychoanalyst in the Province, Dr Thomas Freeman. This difficulty was circumvented by devoting one session of the personal analysis to the supervision of clinical work. The process of training included the completion of a M.Med.Sc. in Psychotherapy (QUB). We were greatly assisted at first by attendance at monthly Saturday meetings of individual senior members of the British Psycho-Analytical Society and later by the Society itself. Up to the present day, the day-long Saturday meetings with visiting analysts have remained a central feature as have our monthly Tuesday theoretical meetings.

Over time the visits of the London analysts led several individual therapists to travel to London for supervision of their own work. These same individuals then took up the British Psycho-Analytical Society's scheme for training psychoanalysts outside London. Four members of NIASP completed this further training and are now associate members of the British Psycho-Analytical Society. Two further NIASP members are currently training with the British Society.

When the British Confederation of Psychotherapists (BCP) was established to monitor rigorous standards in psychoanalytic psychotherapy, NIASP, in 1995, applied for membership of the BCP and was accepted. NIASP is a Study Group of the IPA.

2. THEORETICAL ORIENTATION AND CURRRICULUM

The theoretical orientation of NIASP is psychoanalytic and the educational curriculum includes the leading theoretical schools within psychoanalysis.

3. TRAINING STRUCTURE

3.1 Training committee

Training is overseen in all respects by the Training Committee.

There are two categories of membership in NIASP: Full and Associate membership. Full members are registered with the British Confederation of Psychotherapists (BCP).

3.2 Selection procedure and admission

(a) Candidates should already possess a degree *or* a qualification to practise in one of the caring professions.

(b) A candidate should have completed a minimum of one year of four- or five-times-a-week personal analysis with a recognised training analyst at the time of consideration of the application.

Application and admission for student membership

(a) With the approval of the training analyst, the candidate writes to the Honorary Secretary of NIASP for an application form is which is submitted with a curriculum vitae. This may be done after nine months in analysis to allow time for the Training Committee to arrange two selection interviews. Two selection interviews are conducted by full members of NIASP approved by the Training Committee, one of whom must be a training analyst.

(b) When accepted for training, the student is allocated a progress advisor, who receives six-monthly reports on supervised clinical work from the student and the supervisor. These reports, together with the student's report on theoretical education, form the basis of the six-month progress interview.

4. CLINICAL AND ACADEMIC REQUIREMENTS

For Full Membership:

(a) Personal analysis: candidates must have completed a minimum of four years of four- or five-times-weekly personal analysis with a recognised training analyst. The analysis must continue until the completion of training.

(b) Clinical experience: the student must have experience of clinical contact in a variety of settings and be acquainted with a full range of mental disturbance before starting supervised training cases. If the student has had no previous experience, this may be arranged during the initial stage of training. A minimum of 140 hours of clinical experience in a psychiatric unit must include interviewing and assessing patients under the supervision of a consultant psychiatrist.

(c) Educational requirements: theoretical and clinical seminars must be attended over three years,totalling a minimum of 250 hours. The course leading to the MA in Psychoanalytic Studies (QUB) provides the most appropriate means of satisfying the main theoretical requirements. Approval must be granted by the Training Committee for any alternative course of study. The MA course will be supplemented by clinical seminars conducted by members of NIASP. Students may attend specified meetings of NIASP after at least one year in analysis, when recommended by their training analyst.

(d) Supervised training cases: two training cases must be supervised weekly. The assessment of each case as suitable must be endorsed by the supervisor. The two cases shall normally be one female and one male. Each case must be treated three to five times weekly in psychoanalytic psychotherapy. One case must be in treatment for a minimum of two years and a second for a minimum of one year. The two cases must be supervised by different approved supervisors. Six-monthly reports on each case, approved by the supervisor, shall be submitted to the progress advisor.

(e) Reading-In paper: the Reading-In paper shall be a clinical presentation (with a reading time of not more than 45 minutes) of one of the training cases, presented at a meeting open to all full and associate. It should have been discussed before submission with the supervisor and approved for presentation by the progress advisor.

AUTHOR'S COMMENTS

NIASP illustrates the effectiveness of the BP-AS policy of developing training for psychoanalysts in the regions where a small number of psychoanalysts trained at a distance have developed an intensive psychoanalytical psychotherapy training. This training is partly the result of the pioneering work of Thomas Freeman, a member of the British Psycho-Analytical Society who represents a very classical approach to psychoanalysis using the work of both Sigmund Freud and Anna Freud.

The Belfast University course together with the resources of a handful of analysts and supervisors has developed a much needed focus for psychoanalytic work beyond London. At present the organisation felt it was too small and too new to warrant a more detailed entry from its training committee or its trainees. It will be interesting to see how far such a small organisation with high standards is able to develop in the years to come, and whether there is room in Northern Ireland for a less intensive psychotherapy training.

NORTH OF ENGLAND ASSOCIATION FOR TRAINING IN PSYCHOANALYTIC PSYCHOTHERAPY (NEATPP – BCP)

c/o Dept. of Psychotherapy – Claremont House, off Framlington Place, Newcastle Upon Tyne NE2 3NN
Tel. 0191 282 4547 Fax. 0191 282 4542

1. HISTORY OF THE ORGANISATION

The NEATPP was set up in 1993 to provide a substantial psychoanalytic psycho-therapy training for the North of England. Previously there had been no other trainings available outside Scotland and the South of England to equip trainees to practise independently and at a level equivalent to the standard of other major training organisations. There already existed considerable interest in such a training being provided as the Northern Region had developed a psychoanalytically orientated culture which lacked a locally based training focus for clinicians unable to travel further north or south. There was an established group of practising psychoanalytic psychotherapists and psychoanalysts working across the Northern Region who together created the structure for the course and became its first Training Committee. NEATPP is a registered charity and a company limited by guarantee. It is overseen by a committee of trustees and is managed by a Management Committee.

The first cohort of trainees began their training in 1994 with some graduating in 1999. There is a rolling yearly intake and the training is now recognised as an established high-quality venture, with applicants being drawn from the North West across to the North East and up as far as the Scottish Borders. The training itself is based in Newcastle. It achieved full membership of the British Confederation of Psychotherapists in 1999.

2. THEORETICAL ORIENTATION AND CURRICULUM

The aim of the course is to provide a core training in psychoanalytic psychotherapy to the standard required for independent specialist status, for senior and autonomous practice in the NHS and to a standard approved by the British Confederation of Psychotherapists.

There are four core components to the course:

- personal psychoanalytic psychotherapy with an approved training therapist
- supervised psychoanalytic psychotherapy treatment of three patients
- an academic course of theoretical seminars
- an infant observation course.

There is no introductory or pre-clinical course directly linked to NEATPP although an admission requirement is to have completed a basic or introductory course in psychoanalytic psychotherapy. The Regional Department of Psychotherapy in Newcastle provides such a course.

3. TRAINING STRUCTURE

3.1 Training committee

The Training Committee is comprised of 13 members, all fully trained psychoanalytic psychotherapists or psychoanalysts working in either the NHS or in private practice. There is an external assessor who is a senior training psychoanalyst with the British Psychoanalytical Society.

Of the 13 Training Committee members, 7 are approved training therapists for NEATPP providing training therapies in the north and the south of the Northern Region.

3.2 Selection procedure and admission

Applicants would normally be already experienced in psychotherapeutic work and be at a stage of their professional development which would allow uninterrupted training for a period of four years or more, and will usually have had experience of personal therapy.

Applicants should:

- hold a degree in medicine, psychology, social studies or equivalent, or hold a recognised professional qualification and demonstrate the ability to complete an intellectually demanding theoretical course
- have had several years of postgraduate professional practice including experience working with clients or patients with mental and psychological disturbance
- have completed a one-year basic or introductory course in psychoanalytical psychotherapy or its equivalent.

There is no formalised equal opportunities policy but NEATPP is a non-discriminatory organisation, assessing applicants and students on the basis of their aptitude regarding the training.

3.3 Time commitment per week and length of training

Each student will be committed to the following:

Year 1	10 hours a week on average
Years 2–4	20 hours a week on average
Year 5 and beyond, until graduation:	12 hours a week on average

In addition, there will be occasional Saturday morning seminars, each lasting three hours.

It is expected that the training will take a minimum of five years to complete.

3.4 Financial cost of training at different stages

Administration fee	£60	(at application)
Training therapy	@ £4,500p.a.	(one year before academic course to qualification)
Academic course	£4,350p.a.	(years 2, 3, 4)
Supervision	@ £1,500p.a.	(years 5+ to qualification)

The above costs are an average, as training therapy negotiated directly with the training therapist. The academic course fees are paid for three years and include the cost of the academic seminars, the infant observation module and supervision for the minimum training length for all three cases. Extra fees may be charged for additional supervision sessions/seminars after the fourth year until the trainee qualifies.

3.5 Interruptions in training

NEATPP has no policy on interruptions in training but the trainee's tutor and the Training Committee will consider any reasonable request.

3.6 Graduating and beginning a career

NEATPP has a postgraduate organisation to which graduates of the course are invited to join post qualification. They will join as Full Members, a category also open to all Training Committee members and clinical members. There are three other categories included in the Postgraduate Organisation:

- A student member – open to all NEATPP trainees
- Affiliate members – open, by application to BCP members from other trainings
- Honorary members – open, by invitation, to those who had made a substantial contribution to NEATPP.

It would be expected, five years' post-qualification, that course graduates would use their professional training and qualifications for both independent practice and to develop a career in the NHS to consultant or equivalent level of responsibility.

3.7 Numbers of students per intake

We would normally hope to take three students but we would take more or less depending on the quality of the applicants.

4. CLINICAL AND ACADEMIC REQUIREMENTS

Each student will be committed to the following:

Academic Syllabus

- First Year:
  – Infant Observation once a week
  – Infant Observation Seminar – three seminars a term.
- First Year to Third Year (inclusive):
  – Theoretical seminars – two a week, held on Tuesday evenings, each lasting 75 minutes.
  – Occasional Saturday seminars: visiting lecturers and guest speakers.
- Fourth Year onwards:
  – Additional Clinical Seminars on Saturday mornings.

4.1 Personal therapy
A minimum frequency of three sessions of training therapy through the training. The training therapy will begin at least one year before the academic course until qualification for clinical membership.

4.2 Clinical requirements
The Training Committee of NEATPP has an Advisory Sub-committee, which includes members from the north and south of the Northern Region. It has been set up to assist trainees to find appropriate training cases. Potential training cases are referred to the Advisory Committee from private and NHS sources.

4.3 Supervision
The trainee will be required to see three individual patients under supervision during the training as follows:

1. One case seen three times weekly for two years minimum
2. One case seen three times weekly for 18 months minimum
3. One case seen once weekly for one year minimum.

Each case will be supervised weekly and supervision will continue until qualification or until satisfactory ending of the case with the approval of the supervisor and the Training Committee.

4.4 Written work and course attendance
The trainees will be required to write a paper on their baby observation the first academic year and six-monthly reports on their two intensive training cases subsequently. At the completion of the training, each trainee will write a Reading-In paper, which will be assessed and then presented to the Training Committee. Each trainee will be required to attend a minimum of 75 per cent of the academic syllabus.

4.5 Assessment, standards and ethical requirements
The Code of Ethics includes the following headings:

1. The Ethics Committee
2. Code of Practice
3. Confidentiality
4. Record Keeping
5. Exploitation and Safety

6. Ethical Duties of Members of the Association
7. Notification
8. Insurance
9. Advertising

Trainees are continuously assessed throughout training by the Training Committee via reports from supervisors and from seminar leaders. Good communications between the Training Committee and trainees is facilitated by course tutors whose task is to inform trainees of progress and to listen to trainees' views about aspects of the training. The course tutor will usually meet each trainee once per term.

In addition, each cohort of trainees elects a student representative who meets with the Course Director each term to discuss items to do with the course that have come up during that term. In this way both individual and group issues can be addressed. The Training Committee meets every six weeks and it is at these meetings that trainees' progress is discussed. The Training Committee has access to supervisors and seminar leaders reports on which to base their discussions and the method of assessment is, where possible, by consensus. The External Assessor, appointed by the Training Committee, may mediate should disputes arise.

The External Assessor will meet each student at the beginning and approximately midway through the training for individual interview. The assessor will interview each student before qualification, having read the final case reports of each supervised case.

The External Assessor, with the Training Committee, will confirm that each student is capable, on qualification, of practising independently as a psychoanalytic psychotherapist.

5. TRAINEE RESPONSE

'The course is very popular with its current students, who place a high value on being able to train to BCP standards in the North of England. Students are drawn from a wide variety of caring professional backgrounds, for example Mental Health Nursing, Clinical Psychology, Psychiatry, Social Work and General Medical Practice. There is a mixture of NHS and private practitioners among the students, who also include people who pursue part-time careers in other spheres such as music. The training therefore, has a number of meanings for the students, partly reflecting a shared encounter with the course and partly as a result of distinct expectations and experiences.

The two student representatives are willing to respond to individual informal enquiries from prospective students. They would be able either to help personally, or direct people towards students who may be able to give more specific assistance. The student representatives change from time to time, so interested parties should contact the NEATPP administration in the first instance, to be given an up to date contact telephone number.'

AUTHOR'S COMMENTS

In 2000 this course was the latest new member of the BCP. It has a tradition of solid work training people to work within the NHS as well as privately. It is housed within a psychotherapy department of the NHS offering a clinical opportunity to trainees. It recruits from those in the helping professions, counselling, health work as well as from graduates of courses with lower standards such as the Leeds course.

It has a thorough psychoanalytic framework and is well respected as a vehicle for applying analytic practice outside the London area. It organised a conference with the BCP entitled 'From Training to Setting' (1996), suggesting its commitment to the NHS as well as private practice work.

One of the issues facing people training in the regions is the shortage of experienced and senior training therapists and supervisors, who may also be called upon to teach. Each course and trainee group has to sort out these issues in their own way, but all are affected by this feature that is different from training in London. Some people may choose to train in Edinburgh at the Scottish Institute for Human Relations (SIHR) for just this reason, so that they may be free to work in the region without having been trained, analysed and supervised by colleagues.

THE PHILADELPHIA ASSOCIATION (PA – UKCP/PPS)

4 Marty's Yard, 17 Hampstead High Street, London NW3 1QW
Tel. 020 7794 2652 Fax. 020 7794 2652
E-mail: paoffice@globalnet.co.uk

1. HISTORY OF THE ORGANISATION

The Philadelphia Association was set up in 1965 by a group of people having in common a concern with the accepted ways of understanding and treating 'mental illness' in general and in particular schizophrenia. They included the writer Clancy Sigal, the psychiatrists David Cooper and Aaron Esterson and the psychiatrist and psychoanalyst R.D. Laing. Their approach was influenced both by psychoanalytical theory and philosophy, in particular phenomenology and existentialism. In keeping with their phenomenological orientation, emphasis was placed on attending to the specificity of the individual's experience within a particular social context. One of the Association's first activities was to set up therapeutic community households where people in conditions of mental distress might live outside of psychiatric networks. The most famous of these communities was Kingsley Hall in London's East End.

By 1970 the Association had established its own training in psychoanalytic psychotherapy. It is now a member of the Psychoanalytic and Psychodynamic Psychotherapy Section of the UKCP. It has continued with the practice of therapeutic community households and has over the years fostered more than 20 such houses. It currently has three houses, all in London. The Association has also established its own Psychotherapy Referral Service and holds regular public lectures.

2. THEORETICAL ORIENTATION AND CURRICULUM

The PA's approach to psychotherapy is informed by an encounter with philosophy, particularly phenomenology, and the relation of philosophy to the theory and practice of psychotherapy. The training offers trainees a context for critical thinking and questioning. In addition to studying some of the principal thinkers in the psychoanalytic tradition, including Freud, Ferenczi, Klein, Winnicott, Bion and Lacan, the training also engages with the work of philosophers such as Nietzsche, Heidegger, Kierkegaard, Merleau-Ponty, Levinas and Derrida. Attention is also paid to feminist and post-feminist thinkers including Jessica Benjamin, Julia Kristeva and Luce Irigaray.

For the PA, the practice of psychoanalytic psychotherapy is one of attunement to the specific language of the patient, attempting to approach her or his experience without *a priori* assumptions or resort to universalising interpretative systems. The therapist's sensitivity and respect for complexity and difference are crucial in opening out new possibilities of speaking and being for the patient. This includes particular attention to transference and counter-transference within the patient–therapist relationship.

The PA training is regarded as an apprenticeship. Trainees are encouraged to develop an individual approach that is both thoughtful and rigorous. The training aims to prepare people to work as psychoanalytic psychotherapists in a variety of settings.

The PA runs a one-year introductory course. Each evening consists of a seminar followed by group discussion. In addition, students attend a weekly group in which the process of the group is explored. The introductory course is compulsory for anyone seeking to join the training programme, but acceptance for this year-long course does not necessarily imply suitability for training.

3. TRAINING STRUCTURE

3.1 Training committee
The PA training programme is the responsibility of the Training Committee, which comprises several senior members of the organisation. The Training Committee assesses the progress of each trainee at the end of each term through the reports of the personal tutors, supervisors and the theoretical and clinical seminar leaders.

3.2 Selection procedure and admission
There are no formal academic criteria for admission to the training. Applicants must have attended the one-year introductory course and are required to submit an application form, outlining their reasons for wishing to train as psychotherapists and to train with the PA. Applicants regarded as suitable at this stage are invited to meet with a panel of three people who make a recommendation to the Training Committee. Candidates are expected to demonstrate sensitivity, maturity, flexibility and a capacity for critical thought.

Applicants are required to have been in personal psychoanalytic psychotherapy not less than twice weekly for at least one year before they apply. They are also expected to have some relevant clinical experience.

The PA aims to ensure equal opportunities throughout its work and intends that its thought and practice demonstrate a respect for and offer a welcome to all people regardless of racial or ethnic background, gender, sexuality or physical disability.

3.3 Time commitment per week and length of training

The training programme is held on one evening, Thursday, each week, for three nine- or ten-week terms. There is usually also one study weekend each year. Trainees must also find time for clinical supervision, personal psychotherapy, clinical work and reading.

Trainees are also expected at some point in their training to spend a period of six months being involved with one of the Association's therapeutic community households. The trainee negotiates the exact nature and timing of this involvement with her or his tutor and the particular house in the light of her or his specific circumstances.

3.4 Financial cost of training at different stages

The fee for the one-year introductory course is £600, payable in advance at the start of the course. There is, in addition, an application fee of £20. The fee for the training programme is £750 per year, payable termly in advance. There is also an application fee of £70, refunded if the applicant is not invited for interview. These fees do not cover the cost of personal psychotherapy or clinical supervision. All fees are subject to periodic revision.

3.5 Interruptions in training

There is no formal policy on trainees taking time off during training. Each case is considered on its merits by the trainee's tutor and the Training Committee.

3.6 Graduating and beginning a career

Trainees are required to attend the training for a minimum of three years (not including the introductory year). The majority of trainees graduate after four or more years. A trainee's decision to present her or his case for qualifying is made after discussion with the supervisor, personal tutor and the student group. The final decision as to a trainee's readiness to present her or his qualifying paper rests with the Training Committee.

The trainee is required to present a paper showing her or his own thinking and ability to take up the position of the therapist. A panel of three people then meet with the trainee for a detailed discussion reads the paper. The panel then makes a recommendation to the Training Committee, either that the trainee pass or resubmit in a year.

3.7 Numbers of students per intake

The PA training group is generally a small one and only a few people are accepted each year. The PA is unusual in that it operates a 'slow open' training group, that is new trainees join the existing student group which will include trainees who have been on the course for a number of years. This diversity offers a more fruitful context for critical discussion.

4. CLINICAL AND ACADEMIC REQUIREMENTS

4.1 Personal psychotherapy

Trainees are required to be in individual psychotherapy with a qualified psychotherapist or psychoanalyst of several years' post-qualification experience, at least twice weekly throughout their training. This psychotherapist need not be a member of the Philadelphia Association. The PA respects the privacy of the trainee's personal therapy and does not ask for reports of any kind from the training therapist.

4.2 Clinical requirements

Trainees are required to begin clinical work by the beginning of their second term. They must show an ability to sustain long-term work and have experience of twice-weekly therapeutic work. Evaluation of the trainee's readiness to graduate is based on their casework as whole.

4.3 Supervision

Trainees are required to be in weekly supervision with an approved supervisor, a psychoanalytic psychotherapist of several years' post-qualification experience. Trainees in therapy with a psychotherapist outside the PA are expected to be in supervision with a senior member of the Association for one of the two required supervisions.

Each trainee is also allocated a personal tutor with whom she/he meets once each term. The tutor is a member of the Training Committee and is available for discussion regarding the trainee's progress, personal difficulties and anything else that is felt to be relevant to the trainee's development as a therapist.

4.4 Written work and course attendance

Trainees are expected to attend each seminar and other arranged events and to participate in discussions and presentations. Each trainee is required to present clinical work for discussion, usually once each term. In addition, each trainee is required to submit a written theoretical paper of about 8,000 words in length, by the end of the second term of the second year.

4.5 Assessment, standards and ethical requirements

The PA believes in the highest possible academic, clinical and ethical standards. All trainees are assessed frequently, regularly and rigorously. The first year of training is regarded as probationary. Assessment at each stage of the training is aimed at finding out whether the trainee in question has the necessary sensitivity, thoughtfulness, openness and self-reflectiveness necessary to take up the position of the therapist.

All trainees are required to abide by the PA's Code of Ethics.

5. TRAINEE RESPONSE

1. Why this course was chosen

Students were attracted to the course for a variety of reasons:

- The work of the PA Houses was important; the ideas of R.D. Laing
- Thinking about Psychoanalysis from a critical, philosophical perspective; for example, Heidegger, Wittgenstein, Levinas, Derrida
- The relevance of the social/historical text/context
- An analysis with a PA-trained therapist/supervision with a PA therapist.

1.1. What made people decide to train?

- To build on previous experience as counsellor
- Psychiatric work
- Other therapy training
- Personal development
- Own experience of analysis
- To think about a way of addressing mental suffering.

1.2 What were the aspects of this course that were most attractive?

- Small student groups
- The open group incorporates trainees from different Years
- Training and experience
- Four years is the minimum requirement
- Trainees felt it facilitates individual needs, personal and clinical development.

It was felt that the smaller group provided an environment in which often difficult and complex theories could be read and questioned. It also allowed potential space for concerns to be aired.

1.3 What was your experience of the selection procedure?
All students said their experience was robust, challenging and positive in a way that encouraged them to think earnestly about their reasons for applying and commitment.

1.4 Before the start of the course, how informed did you feel about each stage of the training?
On the whole it was felt to be good.

2. The atmosphere of the course

2.1. How do you feel about the way in which information is communicated?
Lively; good participation; welcoming; plenty of scope; there is a termly meeting with members of training committee, and a newsletter. Good administrative support was seen as an essential link between students and faculty. Regular meetings take place with tutors and supervisors. Suggestions for improvements were felt to be welcomed from the faculty (a student representative is currently under discussion).

2.2 What do you find the most confusing aspect of the training?
Some students cited patient referrals as problematic and reading lists as difficult to sort out.

2.3 How much opportunity do you have to share thoughts and feelings with fellow trainees?
Trainees can and do meet up prior to the seminars. Training weekends were seen as important in this respect. In the end it is pretty much left to the inclination of students.

2.4 What do you feel about the methods of teaching?
Students felt the variety of methods reflected individual tutors interests and concerns. Students thought they were expected to read widely and be able to discuss. Clinicals were experienced as positive and challenging.

2.5 What did you think about the way assessments were done to allow you to progress to the next stages of training?
Assessments are carried out each year – there is also a peer group assessment prior to applications for graduation. The second-year essay was experienced as 'tough'. Some students requested more feedback on some aspects of the assessments.

2.6 Has the course met your expectations?
Some students found the philosophy difficult – otherwise all students were happy with their choice of the PA.

2.7 How do you feel about your future with the organisation?
Students felt positive and optimistic about a future in the association and looked forward to contributing in various ways post-training.

2.8 What plans do trainees have for future practice and possible balance of different sorts of work in their career?
Some trainees were hoping to combine clinical work with teaching and writing; others working in the NHS or related services. Some wanted to maintain links with the work in the Philadelphia Association Houses.

Students with a prior academic background, for example, anthropology, clinical psychology, feminist philosophy, were hoping to combine this with psychoanalytic psychotherapy.

AUTHOR'S COMMENTS

The history and development of this course have a background in anti-psychiatry, phenomenology and the study of philosophy, on the one hand; and commitment to offer psychological care to people needing both treatment and a safe house when they near breakdown, on the other. The legacy of R.D. Laing and A. Esterson and the anti-psychiatry movement has left to successive generations the task of integrating these traditions, which can threaten to divide, and there has been a change in the organisation with senior members setting up another analytic organisation (see the Site, p. 192). The vast breadth of the field studied and the range of approaches to understanding analytic thinking may encourage a more academic approach than all trainees wish to take.

However, the PA continues with this dual focus of the clinical and the academic philosophical combined. It also has a unique approach to the individual trainee, encouraging each to progress at his or her own pace rather than belonging to a cohort year group. Some may miss the recognition of stages of progress in the course, and its ending is difficult to mark as a source of progress and identity.

SCOTTISH INSTITUTE OF HUMAN RELATIONS (SIHR – BCP)

56 Albany Street, Edinburgh EH1 3QR
Tel. 0131 556 0924 Fax. 0131 556 2612

1. HISTORY OF THE ORGANISATION

The Scottish Institute of Human Relations was founded in 1969 by Dr John Sutherland, who had worked for many years at the Tavistock Centre in London and was director there when he retired in 1968. The SIHR was modelled on that institution and, like the Tavistock, many courses and trainings are offered for professionals working in the field of mental health. In 1973 the training in psychoanalytic psychotherapy was set up by a group of psychoanalysts (mainly psychiatrists) led by Dr Sutherland. Since that time there have been nine intakes who have followed the four-year course, and by 2004 the tenth intake of trainees will have completed their training.

The aims and objectives of the course have remained unchanged and are set out in the brochure thus:

The course is intended to equip trainees to conduct analytical psychotherapy at a specialist level, to act as trainers within their own professional centres and to stimulate the development through which psychodynamic knowledge can be used more widely in meeting the needs of the community for help with psychological stress.

2. THEORETICAL ORIENTATION AND CURRICULUM

The training is psychoanalytical, following the Independent tradition within the British Psycho-Analytical Society.

There has recently been a trial run of a one-year Introductory Course, and it is hoped that such a course may be introduced every other year. Currently, SIHR offers yearly ten public lectures introducing psychoanalytic ideas.

Outline of curriculum
The first seminars outline Freud's key works and the tenets and propositions of psychoanalysis are studied. These seminars form an essential basis for understanding the development of contemporary psychoanalysis.

The central part of the course surveys in detail the emergence and influence upon psychoanalysis of the works of Klein, Fairbairn, Winnicott, Balint, Bowlby, Bion and others, and the development of psychoanalytic technique, human development and psychopathology. It concludes with seminars on research, ethics, culture and the arts, and in-depth reading of the major figures of British Psychoanalysis from a modern perspective, with a study of recent trends in psychoanalysis. In addition to the theoretical seminars, there are continuous clinical seminars.

Infant Observation seminars are not a part of the course, but the SIHR offers a course on Infant Observation which interested trainees are encouraged to join.

3. TRAINING STRUCTURE

3.1 Training committee
A Training Committee made up of senior psychoanalytic psychotherapists and psychoanalysts oversees the training. The Committee oversees all aspects of the training, and its members act as training psychotherapists and as supervisors. A member of the Training Committee, who acts as course tutor, plays a more practical role in organising the course, and acts on the interface between the trainees and the Training Committee, being available to consult with trainee representatives and individual trainees over areas of difficulty.

3.2 Selection procedure and admission
Applicants must have a degree either in medicine, psychology, the social sciences or an equivalent degree or professional qualification, although in exceptional circumstances, other trainings and experiences may be taken into consideration. There must be experience in one of the core caring professions and experience in working with psychiatric patients. If this last is lacking, it might be undertaken either before the training begins or concurrently with the early stages of the training.

Application is by CV, which is discussed by the Training Committee, with promising applicants then being offered two separate interviews by committee members. Applicants are assessed on the basis of their professional experience, work record, intellectual level, personality development and (where appropriate) response to personal analysis. There is no 'equal opportunities policy', although there is no policy whereby any specific group of people would be excluded.

3.3 Time commitment per week and length of training
Three hours a week of seminars (that is, two seminars each Tuesday evening), four hours weekly of personal therapy, and (at the most demanding period of training) six hours of clinical experience weekly, plus two hours of supervision. The training lasts for four years, although it can take longer.

3.4 Financial cost of training at different stages
Academic seminars – £900 per year. Personal psychotherapy – at least £5,000 per year. Supervision – at least £1,250 per year per supervision (two years with first supervisor and one year with second supervisor).

3.5 Interruptions in training
Interruptions for legitimate reasons are accommodated at the discretion of the Training Committee.

3.6 Graduating and beginning a career
When qualified, trainees are eligible for Membership of the Scottish Association of Psychoanalytical Psychotherapists (a Member of BCP). Five years after graduation, we imagine that our graduates will be occupying a substantial post within the public sector and also continuing to work as a psychoanalytic psychotherapist, either within the public sector or privately.

3.7 Numbers of students per intake

There is no policy on this, although we would not expect to start a new course with fewer than five or six trainees.

4. CLINICAL AND ACADEMIC REQUIREMENTS

4.1 Personal therapy

This must comprise four sessions weekly with a member of the Training Committee. It need not begin until the trainee starts the course.

4.2 Clinical requirements

During the training, the trainee is required to see two patients individually, one female and one male, each three times a week; one case for at least two years and the other case for at least one year.

Before commencing clinical work, the trainee must have been in therapy for at least a year and have regularly attended the seminars throughout the first year. The first training case can only be started with the agreement of the trainee's therapist and the second case only after the first patient has been treated for one year and with the consent of the first case supervisor. Trainees choose their own supervisor from membership of the Training Committee.

Trainees are responsible for finding their own training cases, but members of the Training Committee endeavour to help with this.

4.3 Supervision

Supervision on each case must continue until the trainee has qualified, once weekly for the required duration of clinical work (one year or two years) and thereafter at the discretion of the supervisor.

There is a process of continuous assessment of clinical work (see next section).

4.4 Written work and course attendance

The trainee is assessed at the end of each six-month period with each training case on the basis of the quality of his/her work. To facilitate this process, the trainee provides the supervisor with a brief monthly written case review, which is replaced by an 'overview' at the end of each six-month period. The supervisor gives informal feedback on the reviews and a formal assessment report every six months which must include a direct assessment of the standard reached for that stage in training, in terms of it being satisfactory, borderline, or unsatisfactory.

Trainees are expected to attend at least 80 per cent of seminars over each academic year.

4.5 Assessment, standards and ethical requirements

Trainees are assessed on the basis of their attendance at the seminar course, the quality of their clinical work with both training cases, and their having completed a final case study on each training case.

The Scottish Institute of Human Relations has a Code of Practice and a Complaints Procedure.

5. TRAINEE RESPONSE

1. Why this course was chosen

1.1. What made people decide to train?
The decision to train stemmed from a wish to have personal analytic therapy, a curiosity about the self in relation to others, and dissatisfaction with a narrow biological perspective of psychiatry.

1.2 What were the aspects of this course that were most attractive?
Trainees were attracted to the Scottish Institute because of its reputation as a well established centre for analytic work, grounded in object relations, with links to the NHS and accredited by the BCP. Practically, it is the only centre of analytic therapy in Scotland.

1.3 What was your experience of the selection procedure?
There were various opinions about the selection procedure, these varied from benign to stressful but humane, to criticisms levelled at the delay in learning of the outcome because the Training Committee meets infrequently. No feedback apparently occurs if the trainee is turned down.

1.4 Before the start of the course, how informed did you feel about each stage of the training?
Some trainees thought there was insufficient information on the training they were about to embark on, although this has been rectified in the most recent intake with a provision of a handbook which sets out clearly what is expected at each stage.

2. The atmosphere of the course

2.1 How do you feel about the way in which information is communicated? and
2.3.How much opportunity do you have to share thoughts and feelings with fellow trainees?
The group as a whole only meets for the seminars and has little opportunity to discuss matters before or after because of the long distance some trainees have to travel. This may partly account for a delay before the group coalesced sufficiently to open communication channels through the tutor to the training committee. There is no trainee representative on the training committee. However, despite giving contradictory information at times, on the whole the Training Committee has responded to trainees' needs.

2.2 What do you find the most confusing aspect of the training?
Trainees found the procedure around searching for training cases and submitting reports rather confusing and anxiety provoking. In this intake a continuous assessment through monthly reports was instituted. In addition, six-monthly reports to assessors other than the supervisor was also expected, but this was not made clear at the beginning. Normally the trainee takes on an opposite-sex patient into three-times-a week therapy for two years having sought the approval of the trainee's own therapist, and then after a further year a second same-sex case can be taken into

therapy three times a week for a year's work. There is a paucity of suitable training cases both in the NHS and private sector, particularly men. This has led the Training Committee to relax the gender rule, which caused a little confusion. Through no fault of the institute the dearth of training cases has meant that some trainees will have to prolong their training, incurring financial consequences and delaying career moves. Perhaps the anxiety not to lose a training case, coupled with the intense supervision and continuous assessment needed to maintain training standards, has led to a criticism that personal styles can be inhibited. However, many trainees thought that overall the level of support from supervisors and personal training therapists was exemplary.

2.4 What do you feel about the methods of teaching?
The seminars are on the whole not didactic. Trainees are encouraged to present and frequently there is a lively discussion, which often feels foreshortened by the limited time available. The reading list has been divided into essential, optional and background, which has helped towards not feeling too overwhelmed. Overall, trainees thought the seminars were very rewarding.

2.6 Has the course met your expectations?
Trainees thought that the course had met their expectations and some expressed a wish to maintain links with the institute actively supporting it in the future. In conclusion, trainees found the course very rewarding and thought that it had met their expectations, and some expressed a wish to maintain links with the institute, actively supporting it in the future.

2.8 What plans do trainees have for future practice and possible balance of different sorts of work in their career?
Half of the trainees were non-medical from a wide variety of backgrounds. Those who worked in the NHS were hoping for Consultant or senior posts. One expressed an interest in retaining and developing intensive work through private practice as well.

AUTHOR'S COMMENTS

As the trainee response makes clear, this is the only adult analytic therapy training in Scotland at present. Its Tavistock and Institute of Psycho-Analysis connections suggest that it is a thorough, supportive, enriching and demanding course clinically and theoretically. The trainee comments suggested that they appreciated the central impetus of the desire for an analysis.

Unlike the child psychotherapy training in the SIHR, it is mainly committed to the Independent group of psychoanalytical thinking.

It sounded as though the course is in the throes of having to become clearer about its policies and practices for trainees who are used to that in the NHS and other institutions. Trainees were also aware of the training committee's shortcomings in being slower that wished for in responding to trainees' concerns.

Its limitations may be in the lack of range of choice of analyst and orientation, although it will be interesting to see how much influence of the more Kleinian and neo-Kleinian child psychotherapy course at SIHR influences the adult course in the future (see comments from trainees and the Author, pp. 266–7).

Graduates of this course are eligible to apply to the British Psycho-Analytical Society for further training to become Associate members. This arrangement arose because the BP-AS wanted to ensure that there were more of its members in the provinces to develop psychoanalysis outside London.

THE SEVERNSIDE INSTITUTE FOR PSYCHOTHERAPY (SIP – UKCP/PPS)

11 Orchard Street, Bristol BS1 5EH
Tel. and Fax. 01275 333266
Web site: <www.sipsychotherapy.org.uk>

1. HISTORY OF THE ORGANISATION

The Severnside Institute for Psychotherapy was founded as a charity in 1985 by a small group of London-trained psychoanalytic psychotherapists who were working independently in the South West of England and Wales, in professionally isolated circumstances.

The first training began in 1986 with five students and since then there has been a biennial intake of between five and ten trainees.

Over the past 15 years, the organisation has grown into a membership of nearly 70, a third of whom are its own graduates and it is currently training 25 students in four-year groups. Membership is open to SIP graduates and to those who have undergone a comparable training elsewhere. In 1994, the SIP acquired new premises, leased from the Lark Trust, in the centre of Bristol, which provides teaching rooms, library and consulting rooms for students. SIP is a member of the Psychoanalytic and Psychodynamic Psychotherapy Section of UKCP and its delegates have played a part in the wider world of Psychotherapy.

2. THEORETICAL ORIENTATION AND CURRICULUM

The SIP runs a training programme, which provides a training in Psychoanalytic Psychotherapy with adult individuals leading to qualification as a Member of the Severnside Institute for Psychotherapy and Registration with UKCP.

The training course reflects in its core curriculum and in its clinical teaching the pluralistic base of the organisation. It covers the theories, clinical concepts and techniques of Freud, Jung, Klein and the British Independents, both classical and contemporary.

The academic course extends over five years. Students are required to have a training therapy at least three times weekly, with one of SIP's approved training therapists, throughout the duration of the training. Two patients are treated at least three times a week, one for a minimum of two years and the other for a minimum of eighteen months, each case being supervised weekly by an approved training supervisor.

The curriculum includes weekly theoretical and clinical seminars for four years, an infant observation course, a psychiatric placement and a two-year experiential group.

3. TRAINING STRUCTURE

3.1 Training committee

The Training Committee is responsible for all matters relating to the training. It is appointed by the Executive Committee, which is elected by the membership. It consists of seven members and a Chair who meet monthly. The Chairs of the Executive and Training Committees meet student representatives twice a year to hear the concerns and suggestions of the students regarding the training and the organisation.

3.2 Selection procedure and admission

Applicants will be aged 25 or over and will have had previous experience of personal psychoanalytic psychotherapy and previous clinical experience or will have carried out other responsibilities for the development or welfare of individuals. They must have a recognised academic or professional qualification of degree standard. Attendance at an Introductory Course in considered an advantage.

All enquirers are offered a preliminary interview either individually or in a group to explore the nature, the requirements, the costs and suitability of the training. Those who proceed to application will be offered two interviews: one with a member of the Training Committee and one with a senior member of the organisation.

The interviewers and members of the Training Committee are required to carry out their assessments, their recommendations and decisions with respect for the diversity of applicants and must not discriminate on grounds of difference arising from gender, age, race, culture, class, sexuality, religion and disability.

3.3 Time commitment per week and length of training

- Curricular training: five years
- Year 1: two hours per week for 30 weeks – infant observation seminars;
  one hour per week for one year observing an infant;
  three hours per week for minimum of six months in a psychiatric placement;
  one hour per week – experiential group
- Year 2: five hours per week in seminars
- Years 3–5: three hours per week in seminars.

In addition, time is necessary for reading, writing, personal therapy, supervision, seeing patients and travel.

The post-curricular training has no seminars but it continues until all the required elements of the training are completed.

3.4 Financial cost of training at different stages

- Year 1 fees: £500
- Years 2–5 fees: £1,200 p.a.
- Post-curricular fees: £180 p.a.

In addition, there is the cost of personal therapy and supervision, which ranges from £25 to £35 per session.

3.5 Interruptions in the training

SIP's policy is to accommodate interruptions at any stage of the training due to life events such as illness, bereavement, pregnancy, and financial and family difficulties. The limit of the interruption would depend on each individual case but would be treated with understanding and flexibility.

3.6 Graduating and beginning a career

Graduates become members of SIP and become registered with UKCP. They may work in private practice and/or other related professions.

The Institute provides a formal programme of continued professional development.

Members join reading and clinical groups, present and publish papers and can graduate to becoming teachers, supervisors and training therapists.

3.7 Numbers of students per intake

The optimum size of each intake is eight, with a maximum of ten and a minimum of six. Intake is biennially, or less frequently if there are insufficient applicants of a suitable calibre. An intake of less than six can be considered depending on the state of the training budget.

4. CLINICAL AND ACADEMIC REQUIREMENTS

4.1 Personal therapy

A minimum of three-times-per-week training therapy with an approved training therapist has to be maintained throughout the training until graduation.

The criteria for a training therapist are: a minimum of five years' post-qualification experience, practising at least eighteen hours per week and to include the intensive treatment of at least three patients; to have had at least two years' supervision on those patients since qualification; to have had at least three years' intensive training therapy. A Training Therapists' Committee is responsible for appointing training therapists. Each applicant is interviewed by two senior professionals from other equivalent organisations, which are registered with either the Psychoanalytic and Psychodynamic Psychotherapy Section of UKCP or with the BCP.

4.2 Clinical requirements

A trainee has two supervised training patients, one for a minimum of two years and one for at least eighteen months' treatment, both seen at least three times per week. Patients are assessed carefully for their suitability as training cases.

A trainee may apply to take on a first training patient at the end of the second year and application for a second patient after a minimum of six months' treatment of a first patient and the satisfactory completion of a six-month report of that treatment.

4.3 Supervision

The selection and approval of supervisors is the responsibility of the Training Therapists' Committee. The criteria and the process of approval are identical to those for training therapists.

All supervision is weekly and individual.

The trainee must continue to work with one supervisor through to graduation even after completing the required time with the training patients. Particular attention is paid to the supervisor's assessment of the trainee's work and supervisors are expected to attend all reviews of the students' progress. The first supervisor gives approval to the trainee to take on the second training case and the second supervisor gives approval to the trainee to proceed towards qualification.

4.4 Assessment, standards and ethical requirements

The Code of Ethics covers issues of confidentiality and the autonomy of the patient, the aim of all therapy being the patient's welfare. All treatment is maintained on a professional basis and the patient must not be exploited or discriminated against. The vulnerability of the patient and the imbalance of power in the therapeutic relationship must be respected. The patient's needs must be properly assessed and serious consideration must be given as to whether Psychoanalytic Psychotherapy is the most appropriate treatment.

Assessment is a continuous review of all clinical and written work.

Seminar leaders provide termly written reports on trainees commenting on the level of participation, grasp of theory and awareness and use of clinical concepts. They assess the work discussion, the theory and infant observation papers. Supervisors provide annual reports on the students' clinical work with particular reference to their sensitivity to unconscious meaning, use of interpretations, self-awareness, use of theory and grasp of process. The training therapists and experiential group leaders are not involved in the assessment of students but therapists are given an opportunity to present their concerns or reservations about the trainee proceeding with the training.

Personal and Year Tutors meet with students once a term and provide reports of their progress. The Training Committee meets termly to discuss the trainees' progress. All written reports on the students are collated and trainees are given written feedback once a year including a mention of the areas that need attention and improvement.

The Training Committee assesses the qualifying paper. If there is a disagreement, the opinion of an external moderator is sought.

There are appeal procedures in place for trainees to question the assessment of their work and to voice disagreements. If this is deemed unsatisfactory, the trainee may have recourse to a formal grievance procedure.

5. TRAINEE RESPONSE

1. Why this course was chosen

1.1. What made people decide to train? and
1.2 What were the aspects of this course that were most attractive?
The Severnside training remains the only psychoanalytic psychotherapy training in the South West of England and is therefore the obvious choice for people living in this area who wish to train as psychoanalytic psychotherapists and who, for family and working commitments, cannot travel or move to London.

The eclectic nature of the course was also regarded by many as a key attraction, together with the fact that it follows the same format and structure of the London based trainings.

1.3 What was your experience of the selection procedure?
Generally, trainees felt that this was a fair and efficient, though for some, also a gruelling experience. Trainees had expected this and realised that the procedure was concerned not only with assessing their suitability but also with their commitment and 'staying power'. The two-interview format allowed time for reflection and for trainees to feel that their anxieties and questions had been addressed.

1.4 Before the start of the course, how informed did you feel about each stage of the training?
Trainees felt very well informed about the criteria and the requirements of the training. The distribution of the recently updated 'Training Guidelines' at the beginning of training has been an extremely helpful aspect of this. The guidelines give a clear indication of each stage of the training and have helped trainees know what to expect and what is expected of them. However, to some extent trainees felt that it is not possible in advance to know just how demanding the experience of training will be.

2. The atmosphere of the course

2.1 How do you feel about the way in which information is communicated?
Generally trainees have found members to be open and responsive to their requests and initiatives. Over the last two to three years this has led to a greater openness across the organisation and to an increase in the information made available to trainees. This includes copies of the annual accounts and the reports of most of the Institute's various committees.

2.2 What do you find the most confusing aspect of the training?
Although generally welcomed by the trainees it has been the eclectic nature of the training which has presented the main source of confusion for trainees. At times it can be a struggle to assimilate and to integrate the different theories and approaches within the psychoanalytic movement. Many trainees would have liked the opportunity to directly compare and contrast the different schools and their differing understanding and use of theory and technique.

Some trainees thought that this could be achieved by incorporating a more in-depth historical overview at the beginning of the training. Also by the addition of more seminars or key concepts such as narcissism, transference and projective iden-tification, rather than the separate study blocks on different groups/schools as is presently the basis of the theory seminars. Trainees also felt that at times the eclectic nature of the organisation necessitated an emphasis on unity at the expense of critical debate of key concepts.

2.3 How much opportunity do you have to share thoughts and feelings with fellow trainees?
There are two formal student forum meetings each year where trainees can raise and discuss issues of concern about the training. Student representatives then meet with the Chairpersons of the Executive and the Training Committee to discuss these issues.

Generally year groups form bonds of support and friendship but trainees regretted that the heavy workload and tight structure of the timetable do not allow much opportunity for more informal socialising between groups. This can be a particular disadvantage to trainees living outside of Bristol. At present trainees come from as far afield as Penzance and Oxford.

2.4 What do you feel about the methods of teaching?
Trainees had different reactions to the methods of teaching. Theory is taught on the basis of discussion of set readings. Some seminar leaders gave a more structured presentation of their thoughts on the subjects under discussion whilst others encouraged more discussion amongst the trainees. Some trainees would have preferred more of the former, whilst others preferred the latter method.

The clinical seminars are based on trainees presenting their own work; this has provided a valued opportunity for free and stimulating discussion which all trainees found helpful (see also section 2.2).

2.5 What did you think about the way assessments were done to allow you to progress to the next stages of training?
Generally, trainees felt supported in their development throughout the training, particularly by their personal tutors. With regard to feedback for assessments, some trainees felt that there was still some room for improvement and would have like more detailed written feedback on their progress. It was felt that seminar leaders varied in the amount of feedback, both verbal and written, that they provided.

This has made it hard for some trainees to gauge their progress and their training needs.

2.6 Has the course met your expectations? and
2.7 How do you feel about your future with the organisation?
Trainees felt that the course had exceeded their expectations, both in terms of their personal and professional development. Within the Institute it has been noticeable that over recent years members who have actually trained with Severnside have begun to take on leading roles within the organisation: serving on committees (including the Executive and Training Committees), acting as Year Tutors and teaching on the one-year Introductory Course.

As Severnside is still a relatively young organisation that is still developing there is much scope for new members to become involved at all levels of the Institute.

2.8 What plans do trainees have for future practice and possible balance of different sorts of work in their career?
A number of trainees hope to continue working in their original professions of education, psychiatry, psychology and nursing.

Others have from the beginning intended to develop a private practice, and some combining the two. However given the lack of NHS psychotherapy provision in the South West region, trainees can feel forced into private practice.

AUTHOR'S COMMENTS

This course pioneered training in private psychotherapy outside London. It is interesting to read the account of one of its founder members about the difficulties of setting up a practice outside London (Hahn 1988). This particularly contrasts with the familiarity of a culture in North London that accepts the cost and time commitment of frequent therapy with its unfamiliarity in the provinces.

The comments by the trainees on the difficulties of eclectic theories which are hard to 'assimilate and integrate' might apply to many trainings. It was not clear if the issue was one of incompatibility where different theories suggested very different therapeutic procedures or interventions, or merely one of difficulties over many choices of theory.

It might also be of significance in a situation where the Training Committee come from a diversity of London trainings each with its own slant, which might leave the trainees with the task of integrating diversity not so much of views, but how they might be integrated into practice.

This is a course that trains therapists to work intensively three times per week with patients. It is interesting to consider why this course might not be applying to be a member of BCP. Is it to do with lack of experience in the available trainers or a political conviction about where it wishes to place itself in the umbrella organisations? It is providing a powerful psychotherapy resource for a large region which it has and can influence. The training committee and staff are an experienced group of practitioners providing a model for other regional trainings.

THE SITE FOR CONTEMPORARY PSYCHOANALYSIS (SITE – UKCP/PPS)

37c Cromwell Road, Highgate, London N6 5HN
Tel. 020 8374 5934
Web site: <www.the-site.org.uk>

1. HISTORY OF THE ORGANISATION

The Site for Contemporary Psychoanalysis was established in October 1997, with the aim of fostering critical, reflective and imaginative thinking about psycho-analysis and its contemporary practices.

The Site's current membership consists of psychotherapists who previously had been involved with the Philadelphia Association, members of other psychoanalytic organisations, as well as some non-psychotherapists who have made significant contributions to the field. From its initiation the Site has been strongly committed to open and democratic structures.

In January 1999, the Site was accepted for membership of the Psychoanalytic and Psychodynamic Section of UKCP as a training organisation. The Site is the registering body for many of its members.

2. THEORETICAL ORIENTATION AND CURRICULUM

Our aim is to think psychoanalysis differently. Psychoanalysis can be understood as a cultural term of reference connected to a multiplicity of disciplines. The Site's training is distinctive in its emphasis on developing a critical perspective towards the history and theories of psychoanalysis. This is seen as integral to clinical practice. The Site's readings of psychoanalytic writers, such as Freud, Klein, Winnicott and Lacan, are informed by aspects of contemporary European philosophy, including, for example, phenomenology, post-structuralism and deconstruction. The Site draws on the work of philosophers such as Merleau-Ponty, Foucault, Levinas and Derrida, and feminist theorists such as Butler and Grosz, in its approach to psychoanalysis.

The Site aims to address questions of subjectivity, language and experience, diversity and difference, within a framework of theorising and practice. This framework includes critical reflection on the socio-cultural specificity of individuals. We therefore emphasise the historical and political contexts of the development of psychoanalysis, as well as contemporary concerns about gender, race, class and sexuality. This involves, amongst other things, a critique of universalising theories and those that claim to have a monopoly on truth.

Another prevailing interest is the psychoanalytic understandings of psychosis and how such understandings inform the practice of attending to people in extreme states of distress. Some members of the Site have considerable experience of working in therapeutic communities and of teaching on the subject.

The training course is designed to enable trainees to situate themselves thought-fully in the psychoanalytic field and its practice. The syllabus is not static and is redesigned each year according to the needs of the training group, as well as the particular current interests of the teaching faculty, thus enhancing the freshness of the teaching. We recognise that thought about the unconscious cannot be circum-scribed or reduced to conscious formal procedures without a risk of losing its creativity and vitality.

Reading lists and the programme for the whole year's seminars are available before the beginning of each year. From 2000 the Site will offer an optional intro-ductory year.

3. TRAINING STRUCTURE

3.1 Training committee
The Training Committee is a standing committee of the Site, consisting of senior members appointed by the Site's Council of Management. The Training Committee meets twice a term. The Training Committee is responsible for the running and conduct of the training course, for the selection and assessment of trainees, and for the appointment and assessment of teaching faculty, drawn both from within and outside the Site.

3.2 Selection procedure and admission

Applicants are expected to have been in personal psychoanalytic psychotherapy, at least twice per week, not less than one year prior to application. Whilst the Site is eager to avoid the disruption of anyone's therapy, the psychotherapist has to be approved by the Training Committee. Any prospective applicant to the Site is advised to consult the Site prior to starting with a new psychotherapist.

Applicants are expected to have had relevant work experience in related fields.

The training is at graduate level and, although formal academic qualifications are not necessary, applicants must be able to demonstrate the capacity for studying at the level required, as well as having had some formal learning experience.

On receipt of the completed application form and payment of the application fee three interviews are arranged with members of the Training Committee, references are taken up and a decision on the applicant's suitability is made by the Training Committee. Applicants usually join the training group in the autumn term.

Equal opportunities policy

The Site has developed an equal opportunities policy that pays particular attention to implementation. Our policy (available on request) is based on the understanding of how the roots of psychoanalysis in white European culture has often lead to the pathologisation of difference.

3.3 Time commitment per week and length of training

The training consists of three key elements: personal therapy, theoretical and clinical seminars, and weekly individual supervised work with patients. The minimum time for training is four years part-time.

There are three terms per year. The seminars take place one evening a week (at present on a Thursday), and all trainees are currently in one seminar group. The evenings consist of two parts: first, a theoretical seminar on readings from psycho-analysis and other relevant disciplines; and second, a clinical discussion in which a trainee presents clinical material to be discussed by the teacher and one other member of the Site.

Once a year there is also a non-residential training weekend. Trainees prepare for this by working together in small groups.

In addition to the set course, we expect trainees to attend talks, workshops and conferences and other events organised by the Site.

Once a trainee has fulfilled all the training requirements, the Training Committee will decide if she/he is ready to present their final pass paper and an oral presenta-tion, the Pass, will be arranged (see below).

3.4 Financial cost of training at different stages

The cost of the course includes the course fee, at present £230 per term. The fees for therapy and supervision are payable separately, by private arrangement.

3.5 Interruptions in training

The Training Committee is aware of the pressures that can occur in trainees' lives, such as pregnancy, illness, and financial hardship. We consider each request for interruption of training on an individual basis.

3.6 Graduating and beginning a career
Graduation will lead to full membership of the Site as defined by the constitution.
We expect graduates to be continuously involved in their professional development.

3.7 Numbers of students per intake
We do not have a numbers policy.

4. CLINICAL AND ACADEMIC REQUIREMENTS

4.1 Personal therapy
All trainees are required to be in individual psychoanalytic psychotherapy for at
least a year prior to the training and for the duration of the training with an
approved and experienced therapist. The minimum criteria set by the Psychoanalytic and Psychodynamic Section of the UKCP stipulate that a training therapy of
less than twice weekly would not be acceptable. Whilst accepting this, the Site does
not subscribe to the position that the depth and intensity of someone's therapy can
be circumscribed by its frequency. The Site does not ask therapists for reports.

4.2 Clinical requirements
Each trainee is expected to see at least two long-term patients (that is for not less
than 18 months) for which they will be supervised on a weekly basis. Trainees are
also expected to build up a varied practice and gain as much relevant experience as
possible. The Site has a referral service. Trainees may be offered suitable patients
with the agreement of members of the Training Committee.

4.3 Supervision
During the course of training the trainee is required to have at least two approved
supervisors, one of whom must be an experienced member of the Site. The other
supervisor may be from another organisation. Trainees must remain in supervision
for the duration of the training.

4.4 Written work and course attendance
Trainees are expected to attend regularly throughout the course, and to inform the
current faculty of any absence. Trainees are obliged to remain on the course and in
the training until they have completed the final Pass. At the end of the second year,
each trainee submits a paper on an aspect of psychoanalytic theory. At the end of
the third year trainees are required to submit a clinical paper on some aspect of
psychoanalytic practice.

4.5 Assessment, standards and ethical requirements
The Site's ethics code is available on request.

Assessment is ongoing at every stage of the course. Trainees meet with their
personal tutors at least once a term, to discuss their progress in the light of reports
from their supervisors, and from other teaching faculty. The Tutor is responsible for
reporting to the Training Committee termly on the progress of trainees. The second-
and third-year written papers are read by two members of the Training Committee.

Standards, of both the teaching and the trainees' work, are continuously reviewed by the Training Committee. Such discussions reflect the ethos and values of members of the Site.

A final written paper on a subject of the trainee's choice is a necessary part of progress to qualification. Permission to proceed with this final paper is dependent on the Training Committee's assessment. The final paper is then assessed by two members of the Training Committee, which then decides whether the trainee is ready to present their case for membership to the organisation. This occurs as an oral presentation by the trainee to the membership of the Site, and constitutes the Pass.

Successful qualification occurs when all training requirements have been satisfactorily fulfilled and there is consensus amongst the attending members at the Pass that the trainee can hold their own and has made their case to pass. Thereupon they become full members of the Site and become eligible for registration with UKCP.

5. TRAINEE RESPONSE

1. Why this course was chosen

1.1 What made people decide to train?
Students had reached a point in their lives when they wanted a clinical training in psychoanalytic psychotherapy. Students were attracted to the way the course contextualises psychotherapy in terms of European philosophy and takes up cultural and political issues such as race, gender and sexuality.

1.2 What were the aspects of this course that were most attractive?
A small training group allows students a lot of contact with teachers. Weekly seminars on some aspects of psychoanalytic theory are followed by a clinical presentation. The culture is one of facilitating students' contributions in order that they should find their own voice and authority within the psychoanalytic tradition, rather than form an adherence to a political school. The commitment to an openness of enquiry in respect of the concepts used in psychoanalysis helps students to develop creatively in their clinical work.

There is an emphasis on close attention to patients' language. Homosexuality is not regarded as pathology and lesbians and gay men are welcome on the training. The demands of the course are realistic within the standard requirements regarding students' own analysis and supervision. The Site public lectures and in-house study days provide opportunities for students to meet other members. Teachers are established clinicians renowned for their independent contributions within the field.

1.3 What was your experience of the selection procedure?
It was conducted speedily and efficiently. There was an application form and three interviews over ten days with a reply soon afterwards as to acceptance. The form and interviews were detailed and searching. Interviews were formal friendly and respectful.

1.4 Before the start of the course, how informed did you feel about each stage of the training?
Expectations and requirements of the course are clear and laid out in a handbook given to each student. Regular meetings with a tutor assigned to each student for

the duration of the training ensure that concerns can be aired. The timing and protocol of the final paper (Pass) has been clarified after some initial confusion. The Site is a new course. Great care is taken to inform students of any modifications to the curriculum.

2. The atmosphere of the course

2.1 How do you feel about the way in which information is communicated?
There is general satisfaction with this. Seminars and reading lists are posted well in advance as well as information about general business. A student representative was elected to improve liaison with the organisation as a whole.

2.2 What do you find the most confusing aspect of the training?
No particularly confusing aspects.

2.3 How much opportunity do you have to share thoughts and feelings with fellow trainees?
Being a small group, trainees have plenty of opportunities to share thoughts and feelings about the course. We always meet for half an hour before seminars and again at talks and study days.

2.4 What do you feel about the methods of teaching?
Teaching is generally excellent. Styles vary and teachers bring a lot of enthusiasm related to their own current practice and research. The syllabus is laid down in advance of every academic year. Discussion is lively and uninhibited. In the current training group no one holds back for fear of not saying the right thing. Students are expected to be reasonably familiar with the texts prescribed for each seminar.

2.5 What did you think about the way assessments were done to allow you to progress to the next stages of training?
Termly meetings with tutors provide feedback from supervisors and seminar leaders. Assessment is continuous and students are well advised and prepared for written assignments (for example, the theoretical paper at the end of the second year.)

2.6 Has the course met your expectations?
Intellectually very challenging, the course is stimulating and raises students' expectations. There is a general feeling that more must be done to develop a low-cost clinic, which would be of particular benefit to trainees.

2.7 How do you feel about your future with the organisation?
Students are confident that the new organisation will remain open to new ideas and that as the first trainees we will be able to make a mark and get involved in the development of the Site, both in the vibrant debate around psychoanalysis and in the provision of high quality psychoanalytic psychotherapy.

2.8 What plans do trainees have for future practice and possible balance of different sorts of work in their career?
Most trainees want to set up in private practice. This is combined, for some, with work in the voluntary sector and GP surgeries. Trainees come from various

backgrounds including the visual arts, television, theatre and publishing, and some maintain a connection with these areas to the degree that it is compatible with the demands of a psychoanalytic psychotherapy practice.

AUTHOR'S COMMENT

This course developed partly as a result of a dispute within the Philadelphia Association (see p. 175f.). A small group of its teachers along with others have established a new course at the Site inspired by the philosophical approaches to analytic thinking to be found in the writings of European philosophy, equal opportunities and feminism. This appears to be particularly what draws trainees to this new training. The Site offers a clinical training in psychotherapy and the main thrust of the comments by the trainees is upon support for the intellectual critique of psychoanalysis from a socio-political and philosophical perspective. Applicants might want to know more about how the clinical and the critical marry up.

It will be interesting to see whether the Site is able to offer a clinical service as the trainees propose, and one that is able to implement its commitment to offering psychotherapy to under-resourced groups in society.

Although the course requires the UKCP PP section's minimum of twice-weekly therapy, the statement about frequency is ambiguous and there is a policy of not asking for reports from training therapists. It might be worth wondering what this might indicate, and applicants might want to ask about such an important matter. The trainee response is characterised by no critical comments, unlike a number of other trainings. Is this a sign of unanimity with perhaps some idealisation; a sign of the honeymoon period of a newly established course; or a sign that there is less expressed openness to debate than would appear?

This course is controversial in that it is one of the two courses that in 2000 agreed to allow its graduates to use the title 'psychoanalyst' despite having clinically less demanding training requirements. Like some Lacanians, there is a wish to enlarge the world of psychoanalytic practice beyond the confines of the International Psycho-Analytic Association, and to do so from a perspective that claims to criticise the prejudice and the power play in theories and practices that are perceived as demeaning of personal and social identity.

THE SOCIETY OF ANALYTICAL PSYCHOLOGY (SAP – BCP)

1 Daleham Gardens, London NW3 5BY
Tel. 020 7435 7696 Fax. 020 7431 1495
E-mail: sap@jungian-analysis.org

1. HISTORY OF THE ORGANISATION

The Society of Analytical Psychology was inaugurated in 1946 as the first training course in analytical psychology outside Zurich. Several of the founding members had consulted or worked with Jung. The Society was preceded by the Analytical

Psychology Club founded in 1922, comprising not only analysts but also others interested in Jung's theories.

The SAP training is an initiatory process with its series of thresholds and ordeals. Trainee analysts attend small group seminars and each one has its own particular dynamic. The emphasis is on individual growth and learning which furthers the student's individuation. Personal analysis has always been an essential condition for undertaking the training.

2. THEORETICAL ORIENTATION AND CURRICULUM

The theoretical basis of the training derives from Jung's work, especially his view of the interaction between the patient and the analyst, the transference, as well as his concepts of the collective unconscious, the archetypes, and the individuation process. Later 'post-Jungians' have developed his original ideas, for instance, Michael Fordham's study of childhood and the development of personality from the original self. There are four years of seminars, but qualification may need a longer period if analytic work with patients is delayed.

The pre-clinical year gives the introduction to Jung's theories in the context of other psychoanalytic theories and gives an orientation to the practice of analytical psychology. Included are seminars concerned with the early mother–infant and paternal relationships reflected in the transference of adult patients. The focus in the second year is on the approach to the patient, developed with attention to trans-ference and counter-transference issues. Concentrated work on archetypes and instincts is amplified with study of dreams, myths and fairy tales, as well as under-standing resistance, defences and the use of reconstruction and amplification. The third year is concerned with the self and individuation and also includes seminars on subjects such as adolescence and the psychology of religion. As the course is based on a spiral model, themes recur in different combinations from year to year. Seminars on ethics and research methods are included in the fourth year. At this stage trainees are consulted about the content of the seminars.

3. TRAINING STRUCTURE

3.1 Training committee
Conditions for the training are laid down by the Training Committee and approved by the Council of the Society. The Committee consists of twelve members, of whom three must be Training Analysts. The Director of Training, elected by the Council, advises the trainees and monitors their progress.

3.2 Selection procedure and admission
The basis of the training is the personal analysis with a Training Analyst or Profes-sional Member of the Society. Applicants must have completed at least 150 sessions before the date of application, attending four sessions per week. Personal analysis continues until the candidate is elected to membership of the Society. The Society makes no discrimination on the grounds of religion, ethnic origin, or sexual orientation.

Candidates for the training are asked to complete a searching application form which includes a brief essay about themselves and the influences which have brought them to the intention to become analysts. Each one is interviewed by two senior members and if approved, attends a group selection procedure. Great care is taken to arrive at a fair assessment. A number of variables are taken into account, including aptitude for the work and the mental health of the candidates.

3.3 Time commitment per week and length of training

The course is designed for people who are in employment. However, the time commitment increases to a maximum in the second and third years of the training.

First year: there are two seminars per week, 8.30–10p.m. on Tuesdays and Thursdays for three ten-week terms. In addition, a fortnightly case discussion period of one hour precedes the seminar on one of these evenings.

Second year: two seminars per week continue. Analysis with the first patient begins in the autumn term. This entails four sessions of 50 minutes per week and one session of supervision. Six months after beginning the first analysis, a trainee may apply to take a second patient, also for four sessions per week with a different supervisor.

Third year: seminars continue twice weekly. Each trainee analyst prepares and delivers a case discussion paper.

Fourth year: one seminar per week. If the condition of working with one patient for two years and another for 1 year has been fulfilled and both supervisors agree, candidates begin to write the clinical paper required for application for membership of the Society.

3.4 Financial cost of training at different stages

Analytic fees vary. A few trainees may be accepted for a reduced fee analysis through the C.G. Jung Clinic, although for most trainees, the major cost of the training lies in the cost of the analysis.

Fees for 1999–2000:

Application for the training	£207
1st year seminar fees, per term	£165
2nd and 3rd year term fees	£135
4th year term fees	£68
Supervision per session	£40

Loans are available towards the costs of supervision.

3.5 Interruptions in training

The need for time out due to illness, pregnancy or bereavement is considered sympathetically and negotiated individually. If analytic work has begun, the needs of the patient must be considered as well as the difficulties for the group.

3.6 Graduating and beginning a career

The application for membership of the Society is assessed by the Professional Development Committee. The written paper, reports from both supervisors and a report from the Director of Training are all considered. New members of the Society are encouraged to attend the scientific meetings, reading and case discussion groups. They are also invited to take part in the organisation of the Society. Application for Professional Membership can be made after five years.

3.7 Numbers of students per intake
Numbers have not been restricted. Ten has been the maximum to date, but this may be increased in the first year by candidates taking the training in child analysis.

4. CLINICAL AND ACADEMIC REQUIREMENTS

4.1 Personal therapy
Candidates must be established in analysis, attending four or five times per week with a Training Analyst or a Professional Member of the Society. This continues until the application for membership is accepted.

4.2 Clinical requirements
Trainees analyse two patients, one man and one woman, who attend four or five times per week for 50-minute sessions. Before applying for membership the analysis of one patient must have continued for at least two years and that of another for a minimum period of one year. Trainee analysts who wish to work at a distance from London may have to find their own patients, who are referred to the Clinic Director for assessment.

4.3 Supervision
The treatment of each patient is supervised by a Training Analyst in regular weekly sessions, with a separate supervisor for each patient. This continues until the application for membership is accepted. The Director of Training is responsible for allocating supervisors and the trainee's preference is taken into account.

4.4 Written work and course attendance
Reports on the work with each patient are expected every six months. The application for membership must be accompanied by a written paper of up to 8,000 words. This demonstrates clinical work and understanding of relevant theories.

4.5 Assessment, standards and ethical requirements
Candidates are expected to be familiar with the Society's Code of Ethics. The first section of the Code consists of general statements concerning the primacy of the patient's interests. This is followed by Guidelines for Working Practice, Composition and Functions of the Ethics Committee, and Complaints and Appeals Procedures.

There is a process of continuous assessment of the candidates' progress through reports from seminar leaders and supervisors, the trainees' own reports on seminars and on their clinical work. Problems regarding standards of work are discussed between the trainee and the supervisor then, if necessary, with the Director of Training and the Training Committee.

FUTURE PROSPECTS IN THE SOCIETY

Members may apply for Professional Membership after five years of practice and for appointment as a Training Analyst after a further five years. Members may take part in all the Society's activities.

References
The Society of Analytical Psychology, 'Outline of Training in Adult Analysis' and 'Outline of Training in Child Analysis'. Both are available from the Society at 1 Daleham Gardens, London NW3 5BY.
Fenton, R., Knight, J.F. and Addenbrooke, M. (1998) 'Training and Supervision' in *Contemporary Jungian Analysis*, eds Ian Alister and Christopher Hauke (Routledge, 1998).
Journal of Analytical Psychology (1961 and 1962) Symposium on Training.

5. TRAINEE RESPONSE

1. Why this course was chosen

1.1. What made people decide to train?
In many cases it was an attachment to an SAP analyst or supervisor that was cited as the reason for choosing this particular training. The high reputation of the organisation, its rigour and clinical standards, the output of written material from its members, and its syntheses of Jungian and developmental approaches were strong factors. The SAP was the place best known for a Jungian approach combined with object relations and child development; the place best known for Archetypal theory coexisting with the analysis of transferences.

1.2 What were the aspects of this course that were most attractive?
As above; trainees also felt pleased with the provision of low-cost analysis at the C.G. Jung Clinic to those who could not afford full rates. The moderate amount of writing requirements was another factor. Good connections with the NHS and other organisations was felt to be attractive. SAP speakers at conferences had impressed some trainees, and the friendliness of SAP members was important.

1.3 What was your experience of the selection procedure?
Some felt it had been an important life experience, and used words like 'elation', 'moving', and 'terrifying' to describe it. Generally it was thought to have been stressful and rigorous, but humane. It was reported that being rejected first time round and accepted second time round was painful. Sometimes this was a real test of determination.

1.4 Before the start of the course, how informed did you feel about each stage of the training?
Trainees had widely differing views on this, ranging from poor to very good. Two issues stood out as unsatisfactory. One was the procedures for choosing supervisors. The other was the relatively unpublicised requirement that, once qualified, members must contribute fees from one clinic patient to the SAP for 20 years.

2. The atmosphere of the course

2.1 How do you feel about the way in which information is communicated?
There is no trainee association to act as the organiser in two-way communication. In addition to this central point, it was felt by one trainee that the curriculum should be more clearly laid out.

2.2 How much opportunity do you have to share thoughts and feelings with fellow trainees?
Many trainees felt that this is minimal. There are two meetings per term for each separate year group, but no meetings for contact across the years. Again, an association of trainees is felt by some to be needed.

2.3 What do you feel about the methods of teaching?
Many of us feel positive about the freedom of thought that is encouraged, and the best seminar leaders are very good indeed, often presenting highly original work for our comments prior to publication. It is also true that we have to deal with a change in seminar leader every two weeks, necessitating constant making and breaking of the teaching relationship. There is an advantage in that we are 'exposed' to lots of variety in approach and style. Some would like more continuity in content; others, more modern teaching methods.

2.4 What did you think about the way assessments were done to allow you to progress to the next stages of training?
The end of the first year assessment is a one-to-one interview, which trainees felt was helpful and relaxed. Supervisors show us written feedback in years 2, 3 and 4 on our clinical work, which is considered useful and constructive. Tutors and seminar leaders do not allow us access to their assessments of us, and some trainees cited this as unsatisfactory.

2.5 Has the course met your expectations?
Trainees said 'yes and no'. Some felt the range of supervisors was too limited and that an influx of fresh supervisors would be a great improvement. Some felt there could be more 'cut and thrust' in discussions. One said the course had exceeded their expectations. We recognised the inevitability of a degree of disappointment. Generally we felt SAP as an organisation was supportive of trainees, and that the current Director of Training was in the process of addressing some of our issues.

2.6 How do you feel about your future with the organisation?
Most of us report feeling keen to become integrated into the organisation. The exceptions were people living at a geographical distance. Trainees envisaged joining SAP committees later on, giving papers in the society, setting up or joining SAP supervision groups and taking part in debate on policy issues.

2.7 What plans do trainees have for future practice and possible balance of different sorts of work in their career?
There was a variety of plans – NHS work, private practice, teaching, writing and publishing, new projects, supervision, international work using SAP links in the US, Japan, Poland, Russia, and so on. Some thought of further training in group work or family therapy.

AUTHOR'S COMMENTS

The course prepares graduates for intensive analytic work in a way that is both intel-lectually and emotionally demanding. The training is rooted in the rigour of four-or five-times-per-week analysis, close weekly supervision for each of two patients and the background of understanding both Jungian and psychoanalytic thinking. As the trainee response suggests, it is the fact that psychoanalysis and object relations appear alongside developments in Jung's approach that draw many to the course. There is no clue about how tensions are dealt with between the 'Klungians' (as the Klein–Jung hybrid has been coined) and those who draw more on the mytho-logical; Winnicottian ideas or Kohut's self-psychology (see section on Analytical Psychology in Part One, p. 12f.).

To the outsider there is such a bewildering array of interests that Jungian thought has developed into, that there seem to be as many kinds of Jungian as there are individual practitioners. Jung might have smiled and liked this idea as he always was sceptical about a Jungian school. So, no uniformity, a breadth of approach ranging from the psychoanalytic to the archetypal, from post-modern criticism to the mythological and religious – all that and an in-depth clinical preparation.

Readers should note the comments on the diversity of Jungian schools described above (p. 12f.). This suggests that within the SAP graduates are likely to work in a wide variety of ways depending upon their own personalities and their own choice of preferred theories; however, it is likely that SAP Jungians are likely to work with an approach informed by object relations and the transference–counter-transfer-ence interaction.

Jungian trainees attest to the importance of the group experience in the way some of their teachers enable learning (Addenbrooke 1998). These ideas have a ring of mutual respect within which differences can thrive.

Interestingly, the SAP has not yet developed a student organisation. The trainees who organised responses for this guide consulted almost every trainee and used the project to develop some issues for their internal journal. This sounds like work in progress. Clarity about information and demands, such as the post-qualifying requirement to treat a clinic patient free, sounds also like an area that trainees would like to have had addressed earlier.

TAVISTOCK ADULT PSYCHOANALYTIC PSYCHOTHERAPY TRAINING (TAVI-AD – BCP)

Tavistock & Portman NHS Trust, Academic Services Directorate
120 Belsize Lane, London NW3 5BA
Tel. 020 7447 3722
Web site: <www.nthames-health.tpmde.ac.uk/tavistock/>
E-mail: academic@tavi-port.org

1. HISTORY OF THE ORGANISATION

The Tavistock Clinic was founded in 1920 and the Portman Clinic in 1933. The two clinics became the Tavistock and Portman NHS Trust in 1994. The Tavistock and

Portman NHS Trust is the leading NHS mental health postgraduate training organisation. More than 120 professional staff – psychiatrists, psychologists, child psychotherapists, family therapists, social workers and nurses – provide training for 1,200 students a year. The training is rooted in the broad range of psychotherapeutic and consultative clinical services across the whole lifespan which we provide for our contracted purchasers in the North Thames region; some of our specialised services are also available more widely in the NHS. Each year around 3,000 patients are seen in the Clinics, with an annual average of around 47,000 attendances.

Alongside training and clinical services the Tavistock and Portman NHS Trust is a centre of scholarship and research. Many of the clinical trainees take higher degrees on the basis of their work here, awarded by one of several universities with whom we have close links: University College London, University of East London, Birkbeck College, Middlesex University and the University of Essex. There are also trainings outside London accredited by the Tavistock – in Birmingham, Oxford, Leeds, Nottingham, Liverpool and Bristol, as well as close links with trainings in two centres in Italy, in Zimbabwe, a possible new venture in South Africa, and courses set up by alumni in Spain, Australia, France, Brazil and India. There are former trainees in all continents of the world. Each year the Trust puts on several major conferences related to our work and also launches around half a dozen books by clinical and research staff.

The Dean of Postgraduate Studies, who is elected for a five-year period from among the senior staff of the Trust, has overall responsibility for academic leadership. The Director of Academic Services has overall responsibility for the administrative support of our academic activities. Both sit on the Training Committee, together with representatives of each of the clinical departments, and this committee approves, with representatives of each of the clinical departments, new courses and monitors existing trainings.

2. THEORETICAL ORIENTATION AND CURRICULUM

There are introductory level courses for both adult and child psychotherapy. The part-time Foundation Course in Psychoanalytic Psychotherapy is not a prerequisite for the adult psychotherapy training but may serve as an opportunity to explore the Tavistock approach. Completion of two-year part-time Psychoanalytic Observational Studies course (PGDip/M/A) is a requirement for applicants to the Child Psychotherapy training.

The clinical trainings are psychoanalytic in approach and provide an extensive study of psychoanalytic theory, together with supervised long and short-term clinical work, both intensive and non-intensive, and opportunities for supervised consultancy, which makes use of systemic theory and theories of organisational development and dynamics.

Interdisciplinary Programme of Training in Adult Psychotherapy

3. TRAINING STRUCTURE

3.1 Training committee
The Adult Psychotherapy Training is organised jointly by the four Disciplines of Psychiatry, Clinical Psychology, Social Work training and Nursing. Overall the

Organising Tutor, together with the Adult Department Training Committee, holds responsibility for the training. The External Assessor to the Training is Mrs Anne-Marie Sandler, Training Analyst, British Psychoanalytical Society. The British Psychological Society and the Joint Committee on Higher Psychiatric Training accredit the course.

3.2 Selection procedure and admission

The intention is to provide an in-depth training in psychoanalytic psychotherapy and its applications. The course aims to equip course members to function as clinical, training and consultative personnel within the health and social services wherever possible within their discipline of origin. Selection criteria include personal suitability and assessment of relevant past experience and the applicant's commitment to this wider intention of the training. The training has a good record of taking candidates from a variety of ethnic groups, and we are mindful of the importance of actively monitoring this aspect of intake.

3.3 Time commitment per week and length of training

The training is full-time over a period of four years. The majority of trainees are full-time staff appointments to the Tavistock Clinic and also St Ann's Hospital, Haringey and Forest Health Care, with which we have rotational training arrangements. These are all advertised by the discipline concerned in the usual professional journals.

Other trainees are based in other NHS or public sector institutions. These 'Option 2' course members hold a full-time staff appointment in their external sponsoring institution, where the clinical requirements of the training are carried out. They attend the Tavistock Clinic on a two-days a week basis for supervision, seminars and workshops.

There are also a limited number of vacancies from time to time for other full-time Course Associates, usually from abroad.

3.4 Financial cost of training at different stages

Those course members holding a staff appointment in the Tavistock Clinic or associated rotational training institutions do not pay course fees. Course fees are charged for Option 2 course members and also for a limited number of students (usually from abroad) appointed to a four-year Course Associateship. The course fees are currently £9,480 per annum for non-EC trainees and £4,740 for EC trainees. The fees remain the same at all stages of the training. In addition, all trainees, whether holding staff posts or not, are responsible for the costs of their own personal analysis.

3.5 Interruptions in training

We do our utmost to facilitate the continuation of training after breaks due to maternity leave or extended illness.

3.6 Graduating and beginning a career

Course members graduate from the training with the Tavistock Qualification in Adult Psychotherapy and are then eligible to belong as full members of the Adult Division of the Tavistock Society of Psychotherapists (TSP). The TSP puts on a variety of talks, discussions and seminars that contribute to postgraduate training. The graduates from our training are also eligible to become members of the British Confederation of Psychotherapists.

Five years after graduation, we hope and expect that our graduates will have substantive consultant-level posts in the Health Service or other public sectors.

3.7 Numbers of students per intake

All trainees holding posts and also all other appointments to the training have to be personally and professionally suitable for this extremely demanding course. All the posts in the training are highly competed for.

4. CLINICAL AND ACADEMIC REQUIREMENTS

4.1 Personal therapy

Each course member is required to undertake personal psychotherapy throughout the training at a minimum of three sessions weekly. The cost of personal therapy is borne by the course member unless subsidised by an external sponsoring institution. The course member's analyst will be a member or Associate Member of the British Psycho-analytic Society or the Society of Analytic Psychology of at least five years' standing. The course member's tutor will be available to discuss and help if necessary in the choice of personal analyst. The content of the analysis is confidential; the personal analyst is not asked to submit reports on the progress of the analysis. Wherever possible, allowance will be made for attending analytic sessions during the working day, but the timing of the sessions cannot be accepted as a reason for being unable to fulfil course requirements.

4.2 Clinical requirements

In order that the course member shall gain a secure understanding of the operation of unconscious processes, he/she will see two adult patients at least three times a week. These patients will be amongst those referred to the Clinic or associated rotational institution under the National Health Service. The trainee is also required to do extensive assessment work, lead a psychotherapy group, and undergo extensive other clinical experience. These again are patients referred to the Clinic under the National Health Service.

4.3 Supervision

A senior staff member individually supervises the two, three-times-a-week cases. Senior staff members in a group supervision setting also supervise the trainee's psychotherapy group, assessment work and other clinical work.

4.4 Written work and course attendance

The progress of a course member is monitored by means of regular assessment, including a formal annual assessment. The annual assessment consists of the course member presenting to the Organising Tutor and other members of the Department Training Committee, reports from his/her supervisors, and seminar and workshop leaders. Course members are required to attend two weekly theoretical seminars. The first of these is concerned with the historical development of psychoanalysis, for which the course member attends for the first two years of his/her training. The second seminar, exploring applications of psychoanalysis through a variety of settings and clinical categories, is attended throughout the training.

Each trainee is also required to submit a clinical/applied paper. It is preferred that this is presented towards the end of the training, but can be completed shortly after it.

4.5 Assessment, standards and ethical requirements

A trainee's assessment is based on an accumulation of knowledge put together over the time of their training. Clinical sensitivity, clinical judgement, evidence of theoretical understanding, capacity to work within a multidisciplinary team, understanding the requirements of a NHS psychotherapy service and awareness of organisational dynamics and process are among the criteria for the final assessment. A continuous assessment is made at the end of each year of training, but it is understood that these criteria are used flexibly, consistent with the level and progress of the training.

All trainees are required to adhere to the ethical code of the Tavistock Society of Psychotherapists, in addition to the ethical code of their own profession.

5. TRAINEE RESPONSE

1. Why this course was chosen

1.1. What made people decide to train?
Many wanted to practice psychotherapy within the National Health Service and be part of a long established course. This is the only course which enables trainees to be employed within their respective core profession notably, Medical, Clinical Psychology, Social Work, Nursing and Child Psychotherapy and undertake an intensive psychoanalytic training.

1.2 What were the aspects of this course that were most attractive?
As previously stated, working within the NHS and the opportunity for diverse experience within this public sector work drew trainees. The training has a great strength in the fact that it is a well-established in-service training where there is opportunity to work as part of a multidisciplinary group and retain an awareness of one's original discipline. The experience is varied with weekly individual and intensive, couple, group and Consultancy work.

There is the possibility of being employed, seconded or self-funding. The self-funding option makes the training available to overseas trainees and all trainees are able to train on a full-time or part-time basis. The different permutations of the training bring a variety, richness and mix to the training group.

1.3 What was your experience of the selection procedure?
This is a rigorous, intense and anxiety-provoking experience. This process slightly varies between disciplines but broadly involves personal and professional interviews and a presentation of some of your work.

1.4 Before the start of the course, how informed did you feel about each stage of the training?
On the whole trainees were fairly well informed about the requirements at each stage of their training.

2. The atmosphere of the course

2.1 How do you feel about the way in which information is communicated?
On the whole information is communicated well but there is at times clear distinction between trainee and substantive staff.

2.2 What do you find the most confusing aspect of the training?
Perhaps the initial stages of the training integrating both being a trainee and employed. The tension between training and service provision is an ongoing one.

2.3 How much opportunity do you have to share thoughts and feelings with fellow trainees?
There is plenty of opportunity to share thoughts and feelings with peers. This occurs through obvious informal opportunities and more formally via a regular trainee meeting.

2.4 What do you feel about the methods of teaching?
An analytic stance is taken were self-responsibility and discipline is required. There is a good range of workshops, seminars, supervision sessions and didactic teaching are available.

2.5 What did you think about the way assessments were done to allow you to progress to the next stages of training?
The process is becoming more transparent which is welcomed, but trainees mostly feel contained and informed about their progress and any difficulties. The medical trainees' assessment is linked to Calman and Royal College requirements.

2.6 Has the course met your expectations?
Trainees do feel this an excellent training, which provides varied experience, a lot of supervision and support.

2.7 How do you feel about your future with the organisation?
Posts are very limited within the organisation and there is an expectation that most trainees, once qualified, will seek employment outside.

2.8 What plans do trainees have for future practice and possible balance of different sorts of work in their career?
This is difficult to know but most trainees will seek employment within the NHS if possible and have some links with the organisation. Trainees are equipped for a combination of clinical, research and academic posts. Perhaps this is the most problematic aspect as many feel well trained but there is an awareness of few posts within the NHS.

AUTHOR'S COMMENTS

The Tavistock is without doubt the most prolific and influential training organisa-tion in training psychoanalytical psychotherapists in the field (see Part One, pp. 17–19). This multidisciplinary course is the result of decades of psychotherapy training for members of the key professions in psychiatry, psychology, social work and nursing. The course combines training for those in NHS posts as well as offering training for independent fee paying trainees from the UK and overseas. The trainee has therefore, the opportunity to be a part of a widespread learning community that applies psychoanalytic findings across the fields of individual work, groups, couples, families and organisations (see *Talking Cure*, ed. D. Taylor, 1999).

What is distinctive about this learning experience is that clinical work is conducted on-site or in partnering NHS settings, with patients assessed and referred by Tavistock staff within the NHS. This provides a much wider experience of social and cultural mix from most of the trainings that assess and refer training patients from within the private sector, who pay for themselves, albeit at a reduced fee.

As the trainee responses indicate, differences may be felt between those who support themselves and those who are funded by rare psychotherapy training posts, which may provide both burden and support through being at the vicissitude of changes within the NHS.

The Tavistock has attracted the reputation of being a stronghold of Kleinian and post-Kleinian thinking and clinical practice. There is some minimal influence of the Independent and Contemporary Freudians and the Jungians who work there. Without doubt it is the Kleinian influence that is the stongest. It should be noted that there is in addition a whole range of psychological theories that are also a crucial part of Tavistock life as the *Talking Cure* represents. These include the application of open systems theory to groups and organisations, the thorough research base and application of attachment theory and the understanding of the findings of develop-mental psychologists concerning infant, child and adolescent development.

WEST MIDLANDS INSTITUTE OF PSYCHOTHERAPY CONTEMPORARY FREUDIAN & INDEPENDENT TRAINING COURSE (WMIP-F – UKCP/PPS)

Rooms 123/124 First Floor, Gazette Buildings, 168 Corporation Street, Birmingham B4 6TF
Tel. 0121 248 4450 Fax. 0121 248 4451

1. HISTORY OF THE ORGANISATION

During the Second World War Birmingham was the seat of the 'Northfield Experiment'. A military hospital for servicemen suffering with neurosis saw work by Foulkes, Bion and Rickman. A psychoanalyst, Dr H. Haas, continued in Birmingham working at the Uffculme Clinic. In 1965 the Clinic was designated an NHS regional centre for psychotherapy. This facilitated the development of the West Midlands Institute of Psychotherapy, which was formed in 1981. The Contemporary Freudian and Independent Training began in 1988.

2. THEORETICAL ORIENTATION AND CURRICULUM

Students are trained to be psychoanalytic psychotherapists. The main theoretical orientation is psychoanalysis, with all theory studied in the British Psycho-Analytic society included.

3. TRAINING STRUCTURE

At the moment the course is under revision. What follows is a description of the existing state of affairs and not a commitment for the future.

3.1 Training committee
The training committee is comprised of practicing psychoanalytical psychotherapists. The committee meets regularly during term time. Members of the committee also act as course tutors.

3.2 Selection procedure and admission
Applicants are usually graduates, often professionals in their own right who have had experience of face to face work in one of the helping professions.

They must have had a minimum of one year's analytical psychotherapy twice weekly before being assessed by a trained analyst for their suitability for the course.

Applicants write in for an information sheet and application form. They are then interviewed by the Committee, who may accept them for assessment, or recommend further learning or experience. No discrimination is made on the grounds of gender, sexual orientation, religion or race. A competence in English is required.

The age limit for those applying is 55.

3.3 Time commitment per week and length of training
Someone in full-time work can complete the course. Usually, however, their work accommodates a proportion of the time needed for study and some of the clinical demands.

It is necessary for students without psychiatric experience to begin a psychiatric placement, usually for one half-day weekly for a year.

3.4 Financial cost of training at different stages
Fees for the course are £1,600 a year, reducing after four years. Students are responsible for meeting the cost of their own personal therapy and supervision.

On joining the course all students must become student members of the West Midlands Institute of Psychotherapy (WMIP) and obtain Professional Indemnity insurance.

3.5 Interruptions in training
The course can accommodate interruptions due to illness or life events at any stage of the training, though this is not usual. The period accommodated would depend on the student and their circumstances, and would be complicated if work with a training patient was in progress.

3.6 Graduating and beginning a career

Qualification entitles the graduate to seek 'Associate Professional Membership' of the WMIP. This carries with it the entitlement to seek registration as a psychoanalytic psychotherapist with the UKCP. After two years, and the completion of 1,600 hours of supervised clinical work, 'Professional Membership' can be sought.

The course is intended to equip graduates with the skill to work independently as psychoanalytic psychotherapists. A good proportion of graduates build successful private practices. Others use their skills in the NHS or academia.

Graduates are able to attend the course's open seminars free of charge following graduation. They will also be able to take advantage of the Institute's evening meetings, study days, conferences, and twice-yearly Journal.

3.7 Numbers of students per intake

Students can join the course at the beginning of any of the three terms. Intake per year has averaged four students.

4. CLINICAL AND ACADEMIC REQUIREMENTS

4.1 Personal therapy

Experience in personal twice-weekly therapy is required before assessment for the course, and then until qualification at least twice-weekly, with a therapist recognised by the course committee.

On application, the would-be student is advised on possible therapists. If she/he is already in therapy, the committee will make inquires to ascertain if the therapist is acceptable to the course.

4.2 Clinical requirements

Students are required to treat two patients, one of each sex, for two years: one at least twice-weekly, one at least weekly (the frequency to be that considered relevant to the patient's need).

Before a training case is started, the tutor will inquire from the student's therapist whether the student is ready to take a case. The student should establish treatment with one case before seeking permission to start a second.

Students will be expected to be working with other patients in addition to their training case.

Students will also be expected, once as a junior student and once as a senior, to present ongoing work with a patient (other than their training patient) to their peers and a visiting analyst.

4.3 Supervision

Students must arrange weekly individual supervision with a supervisor recognised by the course. A different supervisor is needed for each training patient.

The student's tutor will require a report from the supervisor every six months. A similar report will be sought from the facilitator of the case discussion groups (see below).

4.4 Written work and course attendance

Written work

Three essays are required during the course. Essays should be of about 4,000 words. The object of the essays is to facilitate the student's learning: they are not for 'passing' or 'failing' but do need to be of a satisfactory standard to show that learning has taken place.

Six-monthly reports are required on each training case, along with a final report at the end of treatment. These reports are expected to be as concise as possible.

The therapist's consent is required to allow the student to proceed to the final qualifying paper. Its content should be a detailed report of the treatment of a patient (a patient other than a training case), not longer than 10,000 words.

The student will also be required to prepare for the work groups, and clinical presentations.

Course attendance

An attendance rate of 100 per cent is expected of students on the course. Students must accumulate the full number of hours of the taught course. If a seminar or work group is missed the student will be expected to attend a latter one covering the same topic.

Students meet their tutors at least once a term.

Visiting analysts and other senior therapists lead small case discussion groups fortnightly in term time to which students bring cases other than their training cases. These groups are held in Birmingham on weekdays, currently Thursday or Friday.

There are sixty double seminars spread over four years. They are held on a Saturday. Work groups are held prior to the seminars. The day begins at 9.15a.m. and ends at 1.30p.m. A reading list for each seminar is distributed beforehand. Students should ensure that they leave enough time to do the reading in order to obtain maximum benefit from the seminar.

Once a year, during the Spring term, students will be required to attend the Institute conference.

4.5 Assessment, standards and ethical requirements

The assessment procedures are as follows:

- The student's tutor and one other training committee member read and comment on essays
- The student's tutor and supervisor read and comment on training patient reports
- Case discussion group leaders write a report also and discuss this with the student
- At some stage, one or more of the student's six-monthly reports will be sent to an external analytic advisor
- An overall view of the student's progress is undertaken at the biannual meetings which are attended by all the training committee members and analytic advisors

- A discussant, usually an analyst with whom the student has not worked, must be sought to help in the final preparation of the qualifying paper. When complete, the paper is read by the training committee and commented on. Should there be a disagreement as to the standard of the paper, it will be sent to an independent analytic advisor.

Criteria and requirements are as those specified in the Handbook at the time the student was accepted for training.

Student representation and feedback
Feedback meetings for students and committee members are held once a term. A written response from the committee to students follows addressing the issues raised. The student members of all the training courses elect one student to attend the meetings of WMIP Council.

Complaints procedure
Students can bring complaints via their tutor to the training committee, or via their student representative to Council.
WMIP Ltd also has a formal Complaints Procedure.

Code of ethics
The course adheres to the West Midlands Institute Code of Ethics and Practice, which applies, in addition to clinical practice, to supervisor–supervisee and teacher–student relationships.

5. TRAINEE RESPONSE

1. Why this course was chosen

1.1 What made people decide to train?
All trainees expressed their need to study psychotherapy in more depth and were attracted by the psychoanalytic aspect of the training and its emphasis on clinical work. This course was experienced as realistic in its expectations. For example:

'You can do the course and continue with some semblance of a life.'
'There is a practical streak in the course that I really like, they realise about real life and what is achievable.'

1.2 What were the aspects of this course that were most attractive?
Trainees on the course feel that there is an understanding that people begin from different backgrounds and are at different stages of development and that there is a degree of flexibility over how long any individual takes to complete the course.

'It is possible to go at your own pace.'

1.3 What was your experience of the selection procedure?
The selection procedure was felt to be a good experience.
'The process is quick.'
'The process is supportive.'
'I felt I was given something, not at all what I was expecting.'

Although there is a clear understanding that individual experiences of the assessment interview by an analyst varied depending on who the assessor was. There was some disagreement on how the trainees feel about the involvement of the therapist in the process.

1.4 Before the start of the course, how informed did you feel about each stage of the training?
The opportunity to start right away and not wait for the next intake is experienced as a very positive aspect of the course. However, the absence of a defined beginning and end can mean that there is a sense of loss when people go.

'There isn't a beginning which is good because you can start when you are ready, but it can feel as if there is no end either.'

This is now being addressed by the presentation of certificates and a post-graduation party.

2. The atmosphere of the course

2.1 How do you feel about the way in which information is communicated?
The course is experienced as an organisation, which works in a very flexible manner but where clarity can be sacrificed in order to achieve this flexibility. The areas of confusion tend to be connected to course regulations as they have developed over the life of the course.

'It's confusing about which regulations apply to which individuals.'
'You are told it depends on the version of the course handbook that you were given when you started.'
'All that anxiety about requirements ... and nothing to contain it.'

Not all trainees agreed with this point of view, however, and some felt strongly that these difficulties needed to be taken back to one's own personal work.

'Of all the trainings I felt that this was the training that was going to require me to be the most adult and therefore the most demanding of me.'
'I have to manage the anxiety in my therapy and my supervision and I find myself responding very positively to that.'

2.2 What do you find the most confusing aspect of the training?
There appeared to be most frustration about lack of a coherent structure for the sharing of information. Alongside this there is an acknowledgement that

'This is one of the most difficult things we *have* to experience in life.'
'There is something quite liberating in the realisation that the training committee is made up of individuals who are human and who make mistakes.'
'There is something very excluding about not knowing how decisions are made.'
'We want a nice firm daddy who knows everything and a lovely gentle mommy who anticipates all that we need.'

2.5 What did you think about the way assessments were done to allow you to progress to the next stages of training?
Another area of confusion tended to be connected with the diffuse nature of the assessment process and frustration about lack of coherence of standards for assessment.

'What *are* the assessment criteria? We are not there when they are discussed.'
'You are sometimes expected to be adult, sometimes infantilised – you just don't know which aspect is coming up next.'

2.3 How much opportunity do you have to share thoughts and feelings with fellow trainees?
The trainee group meets three times a year with the Training Committee to give feedback on issues as they arise on the course. However, some trainees feel that there could perhaps be more creative ways of providing trainees with channels to air their views and to take part in decision-making. Some trainees feel that a student representative on the Training Committee would address the communication problems.

2.4 What do you feel about the methods of teaching?
The experience on this course is that this is a rigorous, demanding training. There is a high expectation on individuals to take responsibility for their own learning.

'The freedom to be relatively self-directing, exploring issues and ways of working stimulated by particular patients at particular times, can be a liberating, creative experience.'

Some trainees mentioned that they would have welcomed more structure and more encouragement with the academic aspects of the course. The model of teaching is experienced as successful in most of its aspects but somewhat traditional. It was suggested that more space for discussion, both in the student work-groups and following the seminars, might address this.

2.6 Has the course met your expectations?
Many trainees referred to the need for more 'space'.

'There needs to be space in the course for the group to get together to be self-supportive and to discuss – psychoanalytic training is demanding emotionally but also intellectually, and the theory is difficult.'

Again, not all trainees agreed that this was necessarily a bad thing.

2.8 What plans do trainees have for future practice and possible balance of different sorts of work in their career?
There was some concern about the sources of referrals for building up a viable practice for those trainees who are not from clinical backgrounds. All trainees feel positive about practising in the future in a way that would not have been possible without the training.

AUTHOR'S COMMENTS

The WMIP Freudian course appears to be in transition as the entry clearly states. This means that interested applicants need to ask more detailed questions to discover the latest changes. What is not clear from the outline is what balance of Freudian and Independent thinking and clinical practice will be found on the course, and what relation these may have to the Kleinian influences that have shaped object relations in both these schools of thought.

Nevertheless it appears as a well thought out and flexible course considering that it can be joined at any point and requires 100 per cent attendance, which means catching up later on what is missed. The problems and advantages are well described in the trainee response. This in itself suggests that the course is robust enough to deal with the inevitable conflicts that will arise from the basic problem of identifying to which group a trainee feels they belong. It is more like a slow-open group from group analysis, yet it may be that trainees' comments suggest that the dynamics of comings and goings are not addressed as clearly as they might need to be.

The training sounds rewarding, challenging and pragmatic, which may well suit a regional training that has to be responsive to what need is there when it appears.

WMIP TRAINING IN JUNGIAN ANALYTICAL PSYCHOTHERAPY (WMIP-J – UKCP/PPS)

Address/Tel./Fax. as WMIP-F (p. 210)

1. HISTORY OF THE ORGANISATION

The Training in Jungian Analytical Psychotherapy is one of three qualifying trainings offered at the West Midlands Institute of Psychotherapy in Birmingham. The WMIP, founded in 1981, is a UKCP-Approved Training and Accrediting Institute. The Jungian Training was founded in 1990 by Jungian psychoanalytic psychotherapists who are Professional Members of the West Midlands Institute of Psychotherapy.

2. THEORETICAL ORIENTATION AND CURRICULUM

The curriculum reflects our orientation and is based on the teachings of C.G. Jung and the development of his ideas in relation to contemporary analytic practice.

Although there is no formal introductory or pre-clinical year, prospective applicants are encouraged to attend the annual series of Jungian Public Lectures hosted by the Jungian Training Committee.

Through personal therapy, attendance at seminars and lectures, supervision of clinical work, written work and infant observation the training provides a forum for the development of personal insight alongside intensive academic study and observation. The capacity to link insight, observation and theory is the kernel of good practice and its education is the purpose of the training.

The training consists of:

- Personal Jungian analytical psychotherapy
- Lectures and seminars
- Two year Infant Observation and Seminar
- Annual paper
- Annual assessment of learning by the trainee
- Supervised clinical experience
- Psychiatric placement.

3. TRAINING STRUCTURE

3.1 Training committee
The Training Committee meets monthly to administer the training. Members of the Training Committee act as tutors to students and are involved in teaching, supervision, and preparation of the syllabus.

3.2 Selection procedure and admission
Trainees are accepted on to the training at two-year intervals. The next intake is scheduled for October 2001. The Training Committee considers applications without prejudice to race, gender, sexual orientation, religion, disability or age, in accordance with the WMIP Statement of Equal Opportunities.

On application the candidate must:

- be established soundly and creatively in a profession or craft,
- have been in individual psychotherapy at least twice weekly, for a substantial period prior to application,
- show an ability to function at a post-graduate level of study, with evidence of sustained learning.

Selected applicants are invited to attend two interviews with experienced analysts who are not members of the Training Committee.

Upon receipt of the Interviewers' recommendations, the Training Committee assesses applications. Decisions of the Training Committee are final.

Application forms and the Prospectus are available from the Course Administrator at the above address.

3.3 Time commitment per week and length of training
The training is a four-year course, with three ten-week terms in each year. Teaching seminars and Public Lectures take place on Saturdays in central Birmingham in up to three one-and-a-half-hour sessions.

During years two and three of the course the teaching will also include a one-and-a-half-hour Infant Observation Seminar, which may occur during the week. Trainees must allocate time in these two years to conduct the observation of an infant.

Trainees must also consider time necessary for conducting three training cases and attending weekly supervision and three-times-weekly therapy for the duration of the course.

The course is rigorous in its academic requirements and trainees must allow time for reading and writing, both of which are integral to the training.

The Training Committee recognises that it will be appropriate for some trainees that completion of clinical or academic requirements extends beyond the formal four-year syllabus. These trainees continue to pay an appropriate fee to cover costs of tutorials and attendance at public lectures, and must remain in supervision and therapy until qualification.

3.4 Financial cost of training at different stages
The training is self-financed and non-profit-making. The trainee's therapy and supervision costs are negotiated with the therapist concerned and are over and above the costs of providing the training.

Application fee: £135. (£100 refund if not selected for interview.)

Course fees are payable termly in advance and are based on the cost of providing teaching and administration divided by the number of trainees. Fees for each subsequent year are announced not later than the beginning of the third term of the preceding year.

3.5 Interruptions in training
There is no official policy regarding interruptions in training. These situations would be handled individually in the context of the reason for the interruption, the trainee's position on the course (that is, what year), the trainee's standing on the course, and alternatives considered in consultation with the trainee, tutor and Training Committee.

3.6 Graduating and beginning a career
The aim of the course is to encourage expansion in the Midlands of a group of informed Jungian psychotherapists.

On completion of the requirements of the course, the Training Committee recommends to the Council of WMIP that a Qualifying Certificate in Analytical Psychotherapy be conferred. Because WMIP is a member of the Psychoanalytic and Psychodynamic section of UKCP as a Training Institute, qualification establishes the right to be included on the UKCP National Register of Psychotherapists.

The Training Committee also recommends at this time that Council award the graduate with Associate Professional Membership of the WMIP. On completion of a further two years (1,600 hours) of analytic psychotherapy practice, Associate Professional Members are entitled to apply to the WMIP for Professional Membership.

There are opportunities for graduates to make a contribution towards the growth and development of the profession and the Jungian culture in all its aspects.

3.7 Numbers of students per intake
Up to ten students per intake.

4. CLINICAL AND ACADEMIC REQUIREMENTS

4.1 Personal therapy
Three sessions per week with an Analytical Psychologist or a Jungian Analytical Psychotherapist, as defined in the Prospectus, until qualification.

4.2 Clinical requirements
Clinical work for the purposes of the training usually begins in the second year of the course. Approval for beginning clinical work under supervision is given by the Training Committee in consultation with the tutor.

Trainees are required to see one training patient three times weekly over eighteen months, one patient seen twice weekly over twelve months, and one patient seen once weekly over twelve months.

Theoretical and clinical issues concerning assessment of patients' suitability for analytical psychotherapy are included in the syllabus. Clinical assessments of patients for the purposes of training are carried out by the trainee, in consultation with supervisors and tutors.

4.3 Supervision
Trainees are required to have individual supervision on a weekly basis and the experience of two supervisors over the course of the training.

4.4 Written work and course attendance
Written work of the course consists of:

- preparation of material for seminars, clinical notes, and infant observation recordings
- annual essay
- infant observation essay (year 3)
- annual assessment of learning
- final clinical paper.

All essays are read and responded to in writing by two readers, both of whom are members of the Training Committee. An external reader appointed by the Training Committee also responds to the final clinical paper.

Regular attendance at all aspects of the course is required.

4.5 Assessment, standards and ethical requirements
All trainees are required, on admission, to become Student Members of the West Midlands Institute of Psychotherapy. As such they are required to abide by the WMIP Code of Ethics and the Code of Practice, which are consistent with the UKCP Ethical Guidelines.

While the Jungian Training Committee bears the responsibility to administer the course, and also to award a qualification that acknowledges that each graduate has completed the requirements of the course, it is the trainee who bears the responsibility for learning.

Each year, having received written feedback from essay readers, supervisors, and infant observation seminar leaders, the trainee is asked to write an assessment of his or her learning on the course during the previous year. The question to be addressed in this assessment is: 'What have I learned in the past year concerning my development as a psychotherapist?'

The trainee's own assessment, along with the tutor's written response to it, plus all the written reports about the work of the trainee is then considered by the

Training Committee at its Annual Assessment meeting. The Training Committee then makes one of three decisions: Pass, Referral, or Fail.

If disagreements between the trainee and the Training Committee cannot be resolved between them, the trainee has the right of appeal to the Chair of Council of WMIP.

5. TRAINEE RESPONSE

1. Why this course was chosen

1.1 What made people decide to train?
A prior encounter with Jungian thinking which stimulated the desire for a thorough Jungian training.

1.2 What were the aspects of this course that were most attractive?
The central locality of the course with easy access by road and rail. The ethos and organisation of the course and the high standard of theoretical and practical training leading to UKCP registration.

1.3 What was your experience of the selection procedure?
The selection procedure was felt to range from being a relaxing experience to a harrowing and anxious time. The initial application form and the two external interviews for psychological assessment were experienced as probing, searching, and objective, rigorous, but kind. The experience as a whole gave prospective trainees the confidence that a good overall picture of the applicant would be presented to the Training Committee for their final decision.

1.4 Before the start of the course, how informed did you feel about each stage of the training?
The information in the handbook and prospectus, plus the pre-course reading list and the first year timetable, meant that students felt generally very well informed. On reflection, one group felt that a more specific overview of how the different aspects of the course were to be scheduled during the four years would have been appreciated.

2. The atmosphere of the course

2.1 How do you feel about the way in which information is communicated?
Information was communicated very efficiently, in a confidential and personal manner with ample time to order books or relevant papers. Only rarely did anyone experience delay.

2.2 What do you find the most confusing aspect of the training?
There was only occasional confusion over the allocation of the room that is rented in the Birmingham Public Library and minor discrepancies in the timetable which had to be sorted out in consultation with the Training Committee.

2.3 How much opportunity do you have to share thoughts and feelings with fellow trainees?
Informally, all trainees exchange telephone numbers for individual contact. All group members can share their thoughts during the coffee and dinner breaks on the training days and at the public lectures. In the more formal setting of the seminars and baby observation groups, substantial time is given for discussing thoughts and feelings connected to the individual presentations.

2.4 What do you feel about the methods of teaching?
The benefit of having the teaching seminars led by practising therapists, who are acknowledged to be experts in their particular school or subject, added intensity and stimulation to the overall training. However, occasionally real effort was needed to connect these differing ideas coherently into the wider theoretical framework. Feedback on the teaching seminars, to the Training Committee, is requested of the trainees at the end of each year.

2.5 What did you think about the way assessments were done to allow you to progress to the next stages of training?
The overall feeling is that the process of self-assessment placing the onus for learning with the trainee, is a fair and rigorous system. It enables the trainee and key people involved in their training to demonstrate to the Training Committee, how they are progressing, learning and relating to their strengths and weaknesses each year and throughout the four years.

2.6 Has the course met your expectations?
The course has met and is still meeting the trainees' expectations.

2.7 How do you feel about your future with the organisation?
There is an expectation that there will be future participation at the public lectures and at the developing postgraduate group. This is based on two feelings, the wish to continue learning and developing and the attachments formed to the Jungian group.
    There is opportunity in the wider context for dialogue and for presenting papers at the Monday evening meetings arranged by the WMIP.

2.8 What plans do trainees have for future practice and possible balance of different sorts of work in their career?
The plans of most trainees are based around a private practice with present and future expansion expected in the areas of teaching, writing, supervising and possible research work.

AUTHOR'S COMMENTS

The WMIP Jungian course seems to offer a coherent sense of belonging. This may be because of the attachment to Jungian ideas or to the course group, or both. It is also a course that demands thrice-weekly work with the first patient and in personal therapy, which is more intensive than the Freudian course, suggesting a greater commitment to depth of work and acknowledgement that a psychotherapist has to see patients at varying frequencies.

The seminars described in the brochure are worth mentioning: Jung's theories, analytic theory (including psychoanalysis), fundamentals of practice, psychiatry, psychopathology, symbolic life, archetypes, the socio-cultural context for psychotherapy, management of practice, well-being of the therapist. This suggests both a wide but also pragmatic approach to the task of becoming a Jungian psychotherapist. What is not altogether clear is whether the approach to Jungian thinking has more of a developmental approach as the presence of infant observation suggests or how much Jung's archetypal researches are encouraged. Applicants may wish to ask about this.

This is the one Jungian training whose graduates belong to the PP section of UKCP, by virtue of WMIP's membership of that section. This suggests that graduates may be cut off from wider participation in Jungian debates and organisations on the UK-wide and international scene.

WMIP KLEINIAN ADULT TRAINING (WMIP-K – UKCP/PPS)

Run by the Birmingham Trust for Psychoanalytic Psychotherapy under the auspices of West Midlands Institute of Psychotherapy
Company Limited by Guarantee (No. 2883306) – Registered Charity (No. 1031001)
Address/Tel./Fax. as WMIP-F (p. 210)

1. HISTORY OF THE ORGANISATION

During the Second World War Birmingham was the seat of the 'Northfield Experiment'; a military hospital for servicemen suffering with neurosis, which saw work by Foulkes, Bion and Rickman. A psychoanalyst, Dr H Haas, continued in Birmingham working at the Uffculme Clinic. In 1965 the Clinic was designated a NHS regional centre for psychotherapy. This facilitated the development of the West Midlands Institute of Psychotherapy, which was formed in 1981. The Contemporary Freudian and Independent Training began in 1988.

BTPP was established in 1990 to further psychoanalytical thinking within the Region and to raise money to enable people to train within irrespective of their financial standing or resources. It is a Registered Charity and a limited Company. We have UKCP recognition for our Adult training, which is run under the auspices of the West Midlands Institute for Psychotherapy by KATC. (We also run a child psychotherapy training accredited by the Association of Child Psychotherapists and most of our trainees do both simultaneously; see entry below.)

2. THEORETICAL ORIENTATION AND CURRICULUM

The theoretical orientation is Kleinian. There is a two-year pre-clinical course, which has as its core components observational studies of infants and young children, work discussion and theory, which covers Freud, Abraham, Ferenczi, Segal, Klein and in the clinical years many other authors, such as Bion, Rosenfeld, Meltzer, Steiner, and so on.

3. TRAINING STRUCTURE

3.1 Training committee
The Training Committee comprises Senior Psychoanalysts and Child Psychotherapists, and includes a local management committee of Child and Adult Psychotherapists.

3.2 Selection procedure and admission

The Pre-clinical course
All candidates are interviewed personally to make sure that they know what they are letting themselves in for and this is what they really want. Sometimes people are advised to go to one of the other trainings in WMIP. We always try to get prospective students to attend one or two open lectures to make sure that they find the orientation and way of working attractive. This is a long and arduous course and it would be an appalling waste of time and energy to embark on it without thinking very carefully first. WMIP also runs a Contemporary Freudian and a Jungian adult training, so that making sure that the orientation fits the student seems to us a very important issue.

Selection for the clinical years is a protracted affair involving all the supervisors and teachers who the student had during the first two years. They are canvassed for their opinion, not only of where the student is currently in their thinking, but how he or she responds to new ideas and also to giving up old ones when they no longer fit and to facing not knowing, possibly the most important component in the training. We reserve the right to ask the student to see one or two senior members of staff for formal interview, should this seem necessary.

Clinical Training:

3.3 Time commitment per week and length of training
The training is usually undertaken on a Friday afternoon and up to fifteen Saturday's, 10.00a.m. to 1.00p.m. per year. Students also have to be in work, where they can have a range of appropriate once- or twice-weekly cases, as well as three intensive cases three or more times per week. The student will have one hour per week of line management supervision, that is, supervision on none intensive cases, plus an hour a week on each of the training cases (these will not normally run concurrently).

3.4 Financial cost of training at different stages
Pre-clinical: approximately £1,000 per year. The clinical training costs £6,000+ per year.

3.5 Interruptions in training
Training is geared to each individual and interruptions would be considered according to circumstance.

3.6 Graduating and beginning a career
Graduates are put forward by the Chairman of the Kleinian Adult Training Committee to the Council of the West Midlands Institute of Psychotherapy to be accepted as Associate Professional Members and are eligible to seek UKCP registration.

Students have an elected representative with whom they meet at regular intervals to feed in suggestions, positive and negative, about the running of the School. Because of the small numbers and because of the desire to spend a minimum of money on running costs and a maximum on needy students, the student body have always played an active part in the day-to-day running of the Trust.

So far all our trainees have already been working as Psychotherapists in the NHS or privately and so continue on as much as before upon graduation. We do seem to have a great many people approaching us for therapy, because they know of the calibre of the training and the orientation of the school, so there is no shortage of work for the moment.

4. CLINICAL AND ACADEMIC REQUIREMENTS

4.1 Personal therapy

Personal analysis/therapy must be with a KATC acceptable person. Therapy is a minimum of three times weekly.

4.2 Clinical requirements

Some patients are seen on the NHS and are usually assessed and chosen by or always in close discussion with the line management supervisor and the training school. Private patients are either assessed by a senior member and passed on; or if, after exploration, it seems that they should not be transferred, a senior trainee may assess and offer therapy under supervision.

4.3 Supervision

Throughout training, the following is obligatory:

- a weekly hour of general line management supervision.
- attending regular clinical seminars.
- three intensive training cases (usually not all concurrent) with a mix of sexes, one of which is of two years' duration, the others of a year. Each case is supervised for an hour a week by a senior therapist. Each case has a different supervisor.

   If a student is having particular difficulties, extra supervision is offered until this has been resolved.
- Students are expected to attend *all* events unless they have a good reason not too. This would be a matter for discussion between the course tutor and the student. We take reliability very seriously because of the nature of the work and the effect of irregularities on patients
- Experience of adult psychiatric illnesses and how these are treated
- Students are expected to produce a small portfolio of GP letters, case summaries etc, the kind of writing the job entails. They are also asked to write an extended and focused paper on a case before they qualify. Writing for publication is encouraged.

4.5 Assessment, standards and ethical requirements

Assessment is ongoing and done by all teachers and the student themselves. We ask them all to fill in a 'strengths and weaknesses' form each year, 'so we can consolidate on the strengths and work on the weaknesses'. These are discussed with the student by his/her personal tutor. But feedback, in terms of close supervision, is constant.

Qualifying papers are read by:

(a) the supervisor to see that it reflects the actuality of the patient and the work done
(b) an internal, senior member of the teaching team
(c) our external assessor.

Students may be asked to rewrite sections or to have supervision on areas discussed, but in the readers' opinion not understood. In fact, most students ask for help and much discussion, reference suggesting and reshaping occurs as part of the learning experience, *before* the paper is submitted.

Code of Professional Conduct and Ethics

All teachers and students abide by the West Midlands Institute of Psychotherapy Code of Conduct and Ethics.

The Code of Ethics spells out regulations aimed at preventing patients from being manipulated or exploited. It underlines the need for clear boundaries and conditions to the relationship, and makes a distinction between privacy and secrecy. Confidentiality may be broken to keep the patient and others safe.

5. TRAINEE RESPONSE

1. Why this course was chosen

1.1 What made people decide to train?
All of the trainees had had some exposure to Kleinian ideas either in their clinical work, on courses, or in analysis, and wanted more.

1.2 What were the aspects of this course that were most attractive?
'The course was very flexible, it was open to those who were interested but weren't necessarily sure at the outset that they wanted to pursue a full training as a Psychoanalytic Psychotherapist. You could start with modules such as the infant observation and work discussion seminars. These could be combined with young child observation seminars and theory seminars on Freud and Klein towards a Diploma in Psychoanalytic Observational Studies. You could then move on to doing an MA in Observational Studies and/or the clinical training. The clinical training leads to registration with the Psychoanalytic Psychotherapy Section of the UKCP.'

'The training is offered through the West Midlands Institute of Psychotherapy.'

'The course was aimed at those working in the NHS and I could do it in the West Midlands alongside my NHS post there.'

'The pre-clinical course in particular attracted a wide range of people from different disciplines with different outlooks.'

'There were bursaries available for those with the aptitude for the course but who were on low incomes.'

'I wanted something solid and coherent, not a mish-mash of different theories. This course felt coherent thinking about the experience of object relating from babyhood to adulthood and consolidating the theory with baby and young child observations and clinical work.'

1.3 What was your experience of the selection procedure?
All on the clinical training had initially been through a selection interview for the pre-clinical course. This felt informal. It involved discussion of a piece of recent work and an exploration of personal development hopes and aims, this was followed by some astute comments about what we might find difficult about the course.

1.4 Before the start of the course, how informed did you feel about each stage of the training?
After completing the pre-clinical course (Work Discussion, Baby Observation, Young Child Observation, Freudian Theory and Kleinian Theory Seminars), those who wished to proceed to the clinical training as Psychoanalytic Psychotherapists again met with their tutors to discuss this.

'Intellectually informed but in retrospect I hadn't taken on board what the emotional impact of the course would be.'

2. The atmosphere of the course

2.1 How do you feel about the way in which information is communicated?
Information is given to you on an informal, person to person basis, this can feel like information comes through the group in an uneven way.

2.2 What do you find the most confusing aspect of the training?
'Initially there were no formal exams to tell me how I was doing and I found it hard to know if I'd reached the required standard!'
'The emphasis on learning from experience!'

2.3 How much opportunity do you have to share thoughts and feelings with fellow trainees?
There is ample opportunity for this at seminars and trainee meetings. There is also a strong informal network amongst the trainees.

2.4 What do you feel about the methods of teaching?
'Initially it was both exciting and frustrating as the emphasis is on learning from experience. Gradually I felt that ideas started to become more firmly held inside me as the theory informed the clinical work and vice versa and it all seemed to make more and more sense.'

2.5 What did you think about the way assessments were done to allow you to progress to the next stages of training?
We have at least annual reviews by our course tutor but in reality meet more frequently. Our course tutor has feedback from other tutors and supervisors involved with our work.

'Despite this, initially I found this difficult there were no exams and I didn't know how I was doing.'

'I was raring to go on to the next clinical stage but was told I wasn't yet ready to progress ... in retrospect a wise decision as I was racing to meet external deadlines and wasn't ready internally to progress. It was frustrating at the time, though!'

2.6 Has the course met your expectations?
'It has met expectations I didn't know that I had!'

'You discover things you had no knowledge or only an inkling about and can help others to do the same'

2.7 How do you feel about your future with the organisation?
Trainees tend to stay linked as a postgraduate peer group both informally and for continuing professional development.

'The things that I have learnt from the training will always be a part of me, I'm grateful!'

2.8 What plans do trainees have for future practice and possible balance of different sorts of work in their career?
All trainees and those qualified from the course are currently working part or full time in the NHS. Some also have a private practice.

We feel we have learnt or are learning a method of thinking about object relations that can be applied in different ways to individuals, groups and organisations. Some plan to offer individual psychoanalytic psychotherapy, others a combination of this and other applications of the model, for example, in thinking with other NHS staff about patients who are difficult to contain.

AUTHOR'S COMMENTS

What is striking in both the course entry and the trainee response is the emphasis on openness of the trainee to learn from experience and reflection. Kleinian theory provides the framework for this emphasis and process that seems to make the course both enlivening and engaging. It suggests that the inspiration of Shirley and Brian Truckle and their colleagues have created a course based on years of Tavistock experience that enable deep thoughtfulness about the dynamic processes at work in psychotherapy and with families, groups and organisations within the NHS as well as in private practice. The theoretical base suggests an approach that is much narrower than any other course in this guide, with no opportunity to compare other theoretical approaches. This may have advantages, especially when it produces such a coherent focus on learning from experience. It may also have a draw back in limiting the psychoanalytic reading and education of trainees and later relating to the work of colleagues.

The trainees seemed to confirm that the course is flexible in offering introductory exposure to the ideas and observations used on the course so that professionals can decide what direction to take, adult or child training or both, and whether they wish to stop or intermit after the child observation and introductory seminars (see entry under BTPP child training, p. 244).

No doubt the organisational base, partly related to WMIP as an umbrella and accrediting organisation, with the independence of the Birmingham Trust for Psychoanalytic Psychotherapy create a framework within which this work can be protected, funded and thrive as well as survive.

WESTMINSTER PASTORAL FOUNDATION TRAINING IN COUNSELLING AND PSYCHOTHERAPY (WPF – UKCP/PPS)

Training in Individual Psychoanalytic Psychotherapy
23 Kensington Square, London W8 5HN
Tel. 020 7361 4800 Fax. 020 7361 4808
E-mail training@wpf.org.uk

1. HISTORY OF THE ORGANISATION

WPF Counselling and Psychotherapy, originally known as the Westminster Pastoral Foundation, was founded in 1969 and has developed into a counselling service for about 650 clients per week. WPF provides a training programme offering many different forms and levels of training. These include one day workshops, brief courses, foundation courses in counselling skills, followed by a ladder of training which enables those who are able to progress, to psychotherapy training even if they begin without initial qualifications in the field. People may also join the psychotherapy training without going through the initial stages at WPF.

All the training takes place on the Kensington campus: a centre shared with Heythrop College of the University of London, surrounding a peaceful seventeenth-century enclosed garden.

WPF is a charity and has retained the ethos set out in its original mission – that is, to offer therapy that is not free, but is affordable. There are also more than thirty affiliated centres around the country.

Advanced training in psychodynamic counselling or psychoanalytic psychotherapy at WPF leads to professional membership of the appropriate section of the Foundation for Psychotherapy and Counselling (FPC). All training up to the point of registration with the United Kingdom Council for Psychotherapy (UKCP) is the responsibility of WPF. When candidates are ready to graduate, FPC takes over and puts the names forward to the UKCP register. FPC is responsible for professional conduct and professional development and works closely with WPF so that each body is well aware of the other's needs and aims.

WPF has played a central role within the UKCP since the days of the Rugby Conference. We believe in the inclusive ideals of UKCP but are aware of the strength of the British Confederation for Psychotherapy (BCP) in contributing to psychoanalytic work.

2. THEORETICAL ORIENTATION AND CURRICULUM

Philosophy of individual psychoanalytic training
WPF individual psychotherapy training is based on a belief that there is no one truth yet available in psychoanalytic theory and that therapists must find the theory and

the way of working that brings out the best in them and in their patients. We expect our therapists to make up their own minds and we therefore present them with a broadly pluralistic training within the psychoanalytic area which does not allow for a comfortable assumption of being right.

Issues of difference and the needs and claims of minority groups are very important to us and discussion and debate is an integral part of the training. WPF pays particular attention to the spiritual in the seminar known as *ontology* which asks each individual to address his own sense of what is 'I' and what is 'other'. WPF aims to equip its graduates to work with the widest variety of people for whom individual psychological treatment is appropriate. Graduates will be expected to be able to work in depth at the once weekly or more intensive session frequency of psychotherapy and to set up open-ended or time-limited contracts as needed.

The training consists of three stages (credit may be awarded for the foundation course and the Graduate Diploma if the equivalent has been covered elsewhere):

1. Foundation course in basic listening and responding skills with emphasis on ethics and values (Certificate in Counselling Skills and Attitudes)
2. Graduate Diploma in Psychodynamic Counselling (Validated by the University of Surrey (Roehampton), leading to an MSc in Psychological Counselling or an MA in Psychodynamic Studies (to be confirmed) and accredited by British Association for Counselling)
3. Qualification in Individual Psychoanalytic Psychotherapy leading to an MA (to be confirmed)

Content of Graduate Diploma

The theoretical teaching in the Graduate Diploma involves the following graduate level modules: Human Development, Psychopathology, Clinical Concepts, Clinical Practice/Techniques, Advanced Theoretical Issues, Advanced Clinical Issues. There are also modules in ontology, groupwork theory, family and marital perspectives, psychiatry and a variety of workshops.

Content of psychotherapy training

*   There are two years of taught seminars, an infant observation seminar and a psychiatric placement.
*   During years 3 and 4 there are clinical seminars in which theory is to be integrated into the needs and demands of clinical work. Candidates are expected to see two training patients.

3. TRAINING STRUCTURE

3.1 Training committee

The Head of Training and the Chair of the Training Committee manage the psycho-analytic training.

3.2 Selection procedure and admission

Each stage of the training has a rigorous selection process, which assesses personal suitability at all stages. At the Graduate Diploma level, experience of counselling-type work is taken into account. For Psychoanalytic Psychotherapy candidates are expected to have been in approved therapy three times per week for at least one year before the course begins and have completed the WPF Graduate Diploma or equivalent.

Equal opportunities statement
WPF Counselling and Psychotherapy is positively committed to opposing discrimination. All departments have policy documents and seek to promote and monitor equality of opportunity in all its procedures.

3.3 Time commitment per week and length of training
Time for seeing clients or patients and one's personal therapy may need to be additional to the times mentioned below.

The Graduate Diploma as one route to admission to the psychoanalytic training can be taken over two, three or four years.

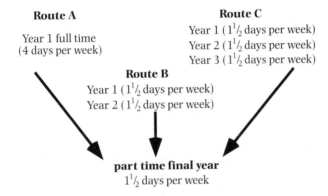

Route A
Year 1 full time
(4 days per week)

Route C
Year 1 ($1\frac{1}{2}$ days per week)
Year 2 ($1\frac{1}{2}$ days per week)
Year 3 ($1\frac{1}{2}$ days per week)

Route B
Year 1 ($1\frac{1}{2}$ days per week)
Year 2 ($1\frac{1}{2}$ days per week)

part time final year
$1\frac{1}{2}$ days per week

Figure 2.2.1 Routes to the Westminster Pastoral Foundation Graduate Diploma

The psychoanalytic psychotherapy training takes place on Thursdays and consists of three hours of teaching. Individual supervision on each of the training cases is additional to seminar time. This part of the training may be completed in three years but depends on casework and writing the final paper.

3.4 Financial cost of training at different stages (1999–2000)
Graduate Diploma per year (approximately):

Route A	£4,000 (Year 1)	£1,700 (Final Year)
Route B	£2,500 (Year 1 and 2)	£1,700 (Final Year)
Route C	£1,900 per year	

This includes the cost of supervision but not of personal therapy.
Psychotherapy per year:

Years 1 and 2	£1,700
Year 3 on	£450

This does not include the fees for individual supervision of each training patient nor the cost of personal therapy.

3.5 Interruptions in training

If a candidate needs to take time out of training we will do all we can to assist in managing the break with patients and in making up lost time.

3.6 Graduating and beginning a career

On qualification as a psychoanalytic psychotherapist, graduates become professional members of the psychoanalytic psychotherapy section of the Foundation for Psychotherapy and Counselling (FPC). The most recent FPC survey of its members showed that most psychotherapists were pleased with the amount of work that they were doing and that this is usually a mixture of private practice and salaried work in an agency such as the NHS or voluntary sector.

3.7 Numbers of students per intake

For the Graduate Diploma we accept approximately 40 students per year. For the psychoanalytic training we accept eight to twelve per year.

4. CLINICAL AND ACADEMIC REQUIREMENTS

4.1 Personal therapy

Personal therapy is required throughout training.

4.2 Clinical requirements

All students in the Graduate Diploma will see WPF clients on the premises during their training. For part-time courses, the caseload is usually three clients seen once per week each. In the final year this increases to six for most trainees. In the psychoanalytic training, patients are seen in the candidate's own consulting room. One patient must be seen three times per week for two years, and one must be seen twice or three times per week for at least eighteen months. All training patients must be assessed by WPF, which takes clinical responsibility.

4.3 Supervision

Supervision during the Graduate Diploma is weekly in groups for 42 weeks per year. For psychotherapy the requirement is for individual supervision for each of the two training patients and one supervisor for other work being carried out.

4.4 Written work and course attendance

Each module of the Graduate Diploma involves written work, which must be passed. A case must be written up as a final paper for graduation. In the psychotherapy training, permission will be given to write the final paper when the casework is completed.

4.5 Assessment, standards and ethical requirements

While working in the Graduate Diploma, trainees are accountable to the Code of Ethics and Complaints Procedure of the British Association for Counselling and the

Foundation for Psychotherapy and Counselling. While working in the psychotherapy trainings, candidates are accountable to the Foundation for Psychotherapy and Counselling Code of Ethics. This code emphasises the paramount values of the patient's welfare, confidentiality, therapist competence, and non-exploitative treatment. All trainees are subject to the WPF complaints procedure.

- The philosophy of our assessment process is based on the need to equip competent and creative practitioners with a clear theoretical rationale for their own practice as well as the ability to give a reasoned critique of theoretical concepts. For this reason we place great emphasis on supervisor's reports and self-assessment in addition to written work and academic performance.
- In the psychoanalytic psychotherapy training, assessment includes Supervisor's reports and self-assessment reports, and a final dissertation on one of the training cases.

All reports are available to trainees. Assessment Committees carry out assessment.

5. TRAINEE RESPONSE

1. Why this course was chosen

1.1 What made people decide to train?
To work at greater depth than psychodynamic counsellor level. For own personal development.

1.2 What were the aspects of this course that were most attractive?
Natural progression from WPF Diploma and satisfaction with previous quality. Course fully accessible to disabled. Excellent course without rigid academic entry requirement. Preference for a daytime course. Preference for an eclectic course. WPF's rigorous clinical requirements including three times weekly supervised training patient. WPF's deserved reputation for a socially responsible and ethical stance coupled with highly professional teaching. As the Diploma and Psychotherapy courses form a two-stage training, they suit trainees who may not be certain when they embark quite at what level they want to end up, and provide a good structure for this. The lovely gardens in which buildings are situated. As a second training, requiring a considerable minimum entry level of clinical experience and personal therapy, trainees on this course find a rich resource in each other; in that all trainees have already developed an ability to reflect on theory in the light of live clinical experience. This fosters self-aware and well-informed discussion in seminars and encourages individuals to think about the usefulness and limitations of the various theories in a way that is grounded in practice rather than purely academic.

1.3 What was your experience of the selection procedure?
Recognised as a good and well-organised procedure but a few trainees felt individual interviews could have been handled better and distress was caused when, for one intake, the original date when trainees were to be notified was overshot. Overall the

process was seen as quite rightly rigorous and searching, and trainees were impressed by the quality of selectors. Applicants who were not accepted initially felt encouraged to reapply after further work.

1.4 Before the start of the course, how informed did you feel about each stage of the training?
Variable feelings about this, although the consensus is that trainees were reasonably well informed, or that the information was available on further enquiry. A few felt they received some over-optimistic predictions about the availability of training patients. Some would have liked structured liaison with trainees in the years above. Current course organiser is accessible to trainees and feed back from trainees actively sought throughout the training.

2. The atmosphere of the course

2.1 How do you feel about the way in which information is communicated?
Fairly all right, but a bit chaotic at times. Channels are in place to access information, and a number of trainees felt that they have some responsibility to inform themselves. There is a consensus that things have definitely improved in this area and the clear information pack now available is very welcome. Generally, a more user-friendly approach is now in place.

2.2 What do you find the most confusing aspect of the training?
Not so much confusing, more bothered and stressed at times, especially over organising training patients and coordinating baby observation and psychiatric placement and juggling them with existing commitments. The main uncertainty, perhaps, comes particularly at the outset over what is expected of trainees. Making the transition from the Diploma to the psychotherapy course needs some adjustment to a more independent and self-motivated approach.

2.3 How much opportunity do you have to share thoughts and feelings with fellow trainees?
No timetabled format for this, but some opportunities in the short break between seminars and within the seminar discussions. Trainees were divided over whether they think more opportunity could or should be provided, or whether it is mainly up to trainees to organise this for themselves. All trainees seem to be informally in touch with others to a greater or lesser extent. All are made welcome to attend FPC Psychotherapy Section study days where they can mix with peers and future colleagues.

2.4 What do you feel about the methods of teaching?
Some highs and some lows with individual seminars. Overall, a good and positive experience, reflective rather than didactic. With such a huge volume of theoretical material, seminars are seen more as a springboard and pointer for further study rather than in-depth surveys. Trainees generally feel stirred up, made to think and encouraged to take a critical approach. Course organisers request feedback and there are trainee representatives on the Curriculum Working Party.

2.5 What did you think about the way assessments were done to allow you to progress to the next stages of training?
In general, satisfaction (with one initial bad experience reported). Members of staff accessible. Expectation based on experience of Diploma, that it will be fair and thorough. The final paper weighs on the spirit somewhat, but support is available on this through personal tutors. A few felt that more help would be welcome in grappling with clinical reports in discussion with supervisors, but others felt that individuals should negotiate this for themselves.

2.6 Has the course met your expectations?
In general, and overall, yes. A few individual gripes but, for some, expectations were exceeded. Some disappointment over availability of training patients. Supervision and clinical experience excellent.

2.7 How do you feel about your future with the organisation?
Opportunities to participate are perceived to be there, and some trainees are already involved, some not currently interested. There are apprehensions for the future in view of what appear to be very rapid changes and fierce competition within the psychotherapy world. Trainees felt that the referral network could be better marketed and that WPF and FPC better promoted to the general public.

2.8 What plans do trainees have for future practice and possible balance of different sorts of work in their career?
The main hope and expectation of all trainees is to expand their existing private practice with a move towards more two- and three-times-weekly work. Many expect to combine this with a balance of other related work, planning to take up or increase their existing commitments in teaching and supervision or administrative posts within the WPF and affiliate centres or elsewhere, clinical psychotherapy posts within the NHS and private medicine, GP practice work, time-limited agency counselling, and community-based work. Cross-fertilisation from the training is already felt to pay off in varied current part-time non-therapy work, from computer development to family mediation.

AUTHOR'S COMMENTS

Training with WPF involves working for a large and complex organisation. There are some advantages: variety of staff and trainees on a variety of trainings geared to their different availabilities and resources, policies designed to offer a good, open and fair counselling and psychotherapy service, an equal opportunities policy and an openness to spiritual and personal life-values. The disadvantages are having to deal with the complex and precise procedures and bureaucracy of such an organisation and work out from the variety of intensity of the different pathways to counsellor training which one to take en route to the psychotherapy training.

The course once attracted the perception that it was predominantly Jungian, inspired perhaps by its pastoral origins and title as well as from its core staff. In the past decade this has changed with a much stronger Freudian and object relations input and a focus for transference-based work within the counselling as well as the psychotherapy training. This means that the syllabus is broad, rather as the trainees suggest, with more pointers of ideas to follow after qualifying, than issues resolved during the course. There is therefore the issue of having to resolve contradicting theories as with any eclectic training.

The sense of containment is particular in a large servicing organisation where every hour at ten minutes to the hour clients and patients leave, therapists-in-training write notes and prepare for their supervision or the next patient/client. This suggests that an applicant needs to be open to the support and the burdens of such a framework. Those whose psychotherapy apprenticeship begins in WPF regional counselling agencies have the benefits of belonging to a smaller enterprise, but one which participates in WPF's policies and practices, less vulnerable to the changing personnel of a modular training.

The clinical training as a counsellor, prior to the psychotherapy training provides a range of low fee paying clients not encountered by other psychotherapists-in-training except perhaps at the Tavistock. This may help develop a wider social practice and the bridge from agency work into private practice that the psycho-therapy training provides.

Counselling trainees, hoping to be psychotherapy trainees have to go through many years of training carrying the uncertainty about whether they will be accepted on the psychotherapy training. This suits some, who want to see how their therapy and their clinical work unfolds. Others may wish to know of their suitability sooner.

In many ways the Graduate Advanced Diploma in Counselling course resembles the new psychotherapy trainings that were set up in the 1970s at AGIP or the LCP. These courses, like the present Counselling Diploma, are more like training for once-weekly psychotherapy than for supportive psychodynamic counselling that tends to use positive transference as an aid to the therapeutic alliance. The WPF is considering a training for once-weekly psychotherapy as an alternative choice to the more intensive existing course.

2.3 Child and Adolescent Trainings

INTRODUCTION

The AFC, BTPP, BAP-Ch, SIHR-Ch, SAP-Ch and TAVI-Ch described here form the six trainings accredited by the Association of Child Psychotherapists (ACP). The InstP-A-Ch training is the extension to the psychoanalytic training at the Institute for Psycho-Analysis, that provides training in child analysis. The FAETT training is in educational therapy, provided by the Forum for the Advancement of Analytic Educational Teaching and Therapy. The InstP-A-Ch and FAETT trainings are not members of ACP.

The Association of Child Psychotherapists
Requirements for the member training organisations of ACP are the same. For this reason they are set out here rather than under each training.

Personal analysis
The norm is four or five weekly sessions with an analyst or psychoanalytic psychotherapist. Sometimes thrice-weekly sessions are permitted where this is impossible. The training analyst has to be of five years post-qualification with the British Psycho-Analytic Society (BP-AS) or the Society for Analytical Psychology (SAP), or else specially approved by the ACP because of comparable training experience.

Clinical work under supervision

(a) Intensive psychotherapy with children should include both boys and girls, include a pre-latency child, a latency child and an adolescent. The work must involve at least three times weekly, with one, preferably four or five weekly sessions. One patient must be seen for two years, the rest for at least one year.
(b) Non-intensive psychotherapy, one or two weekly session, long-term work with at least six children or adolescents. Alternatives to one case can be a children's group, treating a mother and child, or longer-term family therapy.
(c) Other clinical experience should include work with parents whose child is in therapy, brief counselling or therapy with adolescents, young adults, parents of babies and young children, family work, assessments, work with other professions including statutory social service staff, possible consultation to these staff, experience of NHS management and structures, child protection issues and procedures including court work.

THE ANNA FREUD CENTRE (AFC – UKCP/PTCS)

21 Maresfield Gardens, London NW3 5SD
Tel. 020 7794 2313 Fax. 020 7794 6506
E-mail for training enquiries: cressida.stevens@annafreud.org

1. HISTORY OF THE ORGANISATION

The Anna Freud Centre began as the Hampstead War Nurseries, set up by Anna Freud in 1940 after fleeing from Vienna with her father, Sigmund.

After the war the nurseries evolved into the Hampstead Child Therapy Training Course and Clinic, offering free psychoanalysis to disturbed children. It was renamed the Anna Freud Centre upon the death of its founder in 1982.

The Centre is dedicated to improving the mental health of children, locally, nationally and internationally. At the heart of its work is a range of clinical services offering diagnostic therapeutic and educational services to the community, helping disturbed youngsters from all walks of life. Of equal importance is the pioneering research work which has done much to advance the scientific understanding of child development across the globe and a unique, in-depth training programme that attracts trainees from all over the world.

The Anna Freud Centre also holds regular specialist conferences, study days, short courses for clinical practitioners and allied professionals, and an annual International Scientific Conference.

The Anna Freud Centre is based in three houses in Maresfield Gardens, Hampstead. It is a registered charity and depends on grants and donations to fund its work.

2. THEORETICAL ORIENTATION AND CURRICULUM

The theoretical orientation is broad based but has a special emphasis on the developmental perspective pioneered by Anna Freud and the work of neo-Freudians.

The first (pre-clinical) year of the course provides a thorough grounding in psychoanalytic developmental psychology and can lead to an MSc offered by University College London. It is also possible to take this course without being registered for the clinical training.

Subsequent clinical years cover the following.

Observation
Systematic observation of babies, toddlers and nursery school children during the first two years of training is essential both as a means of further understanding of normal child development and of enhancing clinical observational skills.

Further observation will take place in other settings such as paediatric hospitals and units for disturbed adolescents and young adults. A series of seminars will help students integrate their observational data with their theoretical work, to develop sensitivity to the child/caregiver relationship and to reflect on their responses in a psychoanalytic way.

Seminars and workshops
The academic curriculum encompasses a wide-ranging number of seminars covering theories and research on child development, psychoanalytic concepts, childhood disturbances, the psychotherapeutic treatment of children, the application of psychoanalytic principles to child welfare, research techniques, case management, legal issues, education and working with parents.

Seminars span four years of the training, although the main theoretical content is in the first three years. Seminars are led by staff from the Centre and other experts in the field.

Clinical and theoretical seminars are taught in small groups offering plenty of opportunity for participation. Weekly clinical seminars based on presentation and discussion of case material are an important part of clinical work.

Clinical work
Trainees start their clinical case, under supervision, during their first clinical year, subject to satisfactory progress and their analysts' agreement. They will treat at least three analytic cases (four or five times weekly) from different age groups (under five, latency and adolescence) as well as several non-intensive and parent work cases. Trainees gain experience with treating children of both genders with a range of developmental difficulties.

Trainees can opt to undertake the Centre's clinical training combined with the clinical doctoral programme leading to a clinical doctorate degree (DPsych) awarded by the University of London. The Doctorate in Psychotherapy (Child and Adolescent Psychotherapy) is run in conjunction with University College London and is essentially the same as the clinical training programme with some additional components.

3. TRAINING STRUCTURE

3.1 Training committee
The Training Committee manages and oversees the whole course, monitors trainees' progress, conducts an annual review of trainees' progress and selects candidates for the clinical training.

3.2 Selection procedure and admission

Entrance requirements
Applicants for the Anna Freud Centre training course in psychoanalysis and psycho-therapy of children and adolescents are required by the Association of Child Psychotherapists to hold one of the following qualifications:

- an honours degree in psychology or some related subject, or
- an honours degree and postgraduate diploma or higher degree in another related subject which includes the study of human nature, or
- an equivalent degree from another country.

Previous experience
Applicants must have practical experience of working with children of different age groups. Ideally this will include work with both normal children and children with

developmental difficulties in settings provided by health, social or educational services. The Head of Training is able to offer advice on how to gain the necessary experience according to individual needs.

Admission procedures

Applicants who meet the entrance requirements will initially be offered a preliminary informal interview with the Head of Clinical Training followed by two further interviews with psychoanalysts associated with the Centre. Successful applicants will then be recommended to the Training Council of the Association of Child Psychotherapists for acceptance.

The Anna Freud Centre operates an Equal Opportunities Policy for employees. The Centre is in the process of developing a policy specifically for the training.

3.3 Time commitment per week and length of training

Pre-clinical year can be either taken one year full-time or two years part-time.

The clinical training takes three to four years and is intensive. Seminars are on two evenings a week to enable trainees to undertake training posts. Attendance at the Centre is required on two afternoons for clinical groups and the Wednesday conference meeting. The remaining time is for training cases, supervisions and personal analysis.

3.4 Financial cost of training at different stages

MSc (pre-clinical) course fees 1999/2000	EU	£2,675
	Overseas	£11,890
Clinical training course fees 1999/2000	1st year	£1,200
	2nd year	£1,000
	3rd year	£1,000
	4th year	£800
Doctorate (part-time)	EU	£1,305
	Overseas	£5,063

Personal analysis and supervisions are additional costs.

Trainees can compete for NHS training posts. These are salaried posts, which also cover the costs of training.

3.5 Interruptions in training

There is some flexibility according to individual circumstances.

3.6 Graduating and beginning a career

Upon graduating, trainees become members of the Association of Child Psycho-therapists. They can then apply for Child Psychotherapy posts in NHS hospitals and Child and Family Guidance. Graduates also work in the voluntary sector, often developing an area of specialism, for example, work with refugee children. A number of graduates also do sessional work at the Anna Freud Centre.

The Anna Freud Centre holds an annual Colloquium attended by analysts from all over world. In attention to clinical work, graduates also teach widely and publish their work.

3.7 Numbers of students per intake
Trainees are taught in small groups averaging in number from 4 – 6 per year. Trainees can expect a lot of individual attention.

4. CLINICAL AND ACADEMIC REQUIREMENTS

4.1 Personal therapy
All trainees are in five-times-weekly psychoanalysis throughout their training with an Anna Freud Centre-approved analyst.

4.2 Clinical requirements
Three analytic cases (four or five times weekly) from different age groups, six non-intensive cases and parent work cases. Trainees also undertake a number of social histories and diagnostic assessments.

Trainees not in NHS training posts take on cases at the Anna Freud Centre.

4.3 Supervision
Trainees have weekly supervision on intensive cases and weekly or fortnightly for non-intensive and parent work.

4.4 Written work and course attendance
Trainees are required to do a number of assessments. They also present infant and toddler observation papers.

Trainees taking the Doctorate are assessed on two further extended essays per year and a research paper over three years. A final Doctoral portfolio is submitted.

4.5 Assessment, standards and ethical requirements
We adhere to the Association of Child Psychotherapists code of ethics. Our internal standards are rigorous and we feedback seminars annual reports from supervisors and termly feedback from seminar leaders. Trainees also complete an end of year self-assessment form. There are yearly assessment procedures. Interim assessments are done as and when required.

Criteria for assessment are based on growth of the trainees understanding of child development, development of clinical sensitivity and an ability to work in the transference and counter-transference.

5. TRAINEE RESPONSE

1. Why this course was chosen

1.1 What made people decide to train?
Answers differed enormously, as they are highly personal – ranging from dissatisfaction in a prior (child) related career or training in, for example, psychology, teaching, social work or art therapy; or due to a personal belief in psychoanalysis through personal experience or theoretical knowledge/curiosity.

1.2 What were the aspects of this course that were most attractive?
The small size, 'welcoming'. The reputation.

Some valued the Freudian tradition, history and connection with Anna Freud.

Some felt the full-time pre-clinical year was an advantage too, over other courses that are part-time. Some were keen, as the training has been allied with a Clinical Doctorate at UCL.

1.3 What was your experience of the selection procedure?
Again, personal responses: 'stressful', 'demanding', 'fair', 'appropriate'. An application is filled out and a fee paid for interviews. One is then interviewed by a Psychiatrist who is usually a (child) psychoanalyst, as well as by a Child Psycho-therapist, usually on the Training Committee of the AFC. One comment was that the selection process was unlike any previous interview – extremely thought-provoking and moving and helped this particular trainee to decide it was the right training for them to do.

1.4 Before the start of the course, how informed did you feel about each stage of the training?
'Reasonable'; 'one learns more as one proceeds through each stage'. A handbook is given as to what the requirements are and what the seminars will cover for the four years. Most seemed to find this clear, but also felt talking to other trainees was essential for clarification of certain details. Many of these enquiries are dealt with informally by talking to trainees.

2. The atmosphere of the course

2.1 How do you feel about the way in which information is communicated?
Most felt this could be better. Some felt there was a lack of adequate administrative organisation, that one is left to find things out through other colleagues or by oneself.

2.2 What do you find the most confusing aspect of the training?
Trainees felt this was too personal or inappropriate to answer.

2.3 How much opportunity do you have to share thoughts and feelings with fellow trainees?
Some felt there was enough opportunity initially, but when work commitments become heavier there is little time for anything, especially by those who have training posts externally (at NHS clinics/hospitals). Alternatively, people responded that there were few opportunities, but that one can informally do this through colleagues/friendships, due to the small course size.

2.4 What do you feel about the methods of teaching?
Most felt the teaching is generally of high standard, with teachers of great experience and knowledge, although in some cases trainees felt unsatisfied by lack of coverage of topics of specific personal interest. Some felt these could be more interesting/challenging.

2.5. What did you think about the way assessments were done to allow you to progress to the next stages of training?
Most felt these were good, or fair. Although more specific feedback would be appreciated – that is, actual copies of supervisors' reports, and so on, as these are not always given. Most found them to be handled as sensitively as possible, although on occasion there were confusions and difficulties for some. One comment was that communication between the training school and one's personal analyst raises all kinds of (perhaps inevitable) complications.

2.6 Has the course met your expectations?
Mostly trainees said 'yes'. Some reported they had expected something different or were only just beginning.

2.7 How do you feel about your future with the organisation?
Most said 'positive'. Some were unsure yet whether they would like to remain connected or go elsewhere. Many will probably work in the NHS or, in the case of many non-UK students, will return to their countries.

2.8. What plans do trainees have for future practice and possible balance of different sorts of work in their career?
Quite a few of us would like to continue seeing patients in individual analytic work – possibly in private practice or in a clinic. Other interests are to combine this type of knowledge and work with applied or consultation-type work in hospitals, GP surgeries, children's homes, and so on. Also perhaps to work with Parent–Infant projects, Adoption–Fostering agencies, or children in care, or working with particular age ranges or disturbances. Some also feel with the Doctorate that they would be equipped to do research. Many will remain in the NHS, but possibly in combination with some of the above ideas.

AUTHOR'S COMMENTS

This course provides the longest established and only classical training in child analysis and child psychotherapy in the UK. The original inspiration of its founder, Anna Freud, established a commitment to training younger therapists who would have the energy for work with children. This, together with its international reputation, its intensive, nearly full-time training, its research base, with the possibility of a Doctorate degree, all supported by senior and experienced analysts, make it a unique opportunity to make a distinctive contribution to services for children. While the approach to psychoanalytic theory is Contemporary Freudian, current debate between the psychoanalytic schools and their common interest in object relations theory insists that all are known within this course. For an account of its history and current developments, see 'A Profile of the Anna Freud Centre' (Fabricius and Kennedy 1999). The breadth of the future career interests of current trainees is testimony to the enduring social commitment of the AFC and to its desire to apply psychoanalytic ideas and practice across a broad field.

As at other training organisations that involve trainees in full-time posts that support their training, there is a huge demand and pressure to fulfil all the obligations. There may also be a very different experience for those who are self-supporting with less pressure on them from paid work and the vicissitudes of the public services.

BIRMINGHAM TRUST FOR PSYCHOANALYTIC PSYCHOTHERAPY (BTPP – UKCP/PTCS)

Selly Oak Colleges, Elmfield House, 998 Bristol Road, Birmingham B29 6LQ Tel. 0121 472 4231 ext. 2630

1. HISTORY OF THE ORGANISATION

The BTPP was established in 1990 to further psychoanalytical thinking within the Region and to raise money to enable people to train with us irrespective of their financial standing or economic resources. It is a Registered Charity and a limited Company. Our Child Psychotherapy training has been accepted by the Association of Child Psychotherapists, and we have UKCP recognition for our Adult training (which is run under the auspices of the West Midlands Institute for Psychotherapy, see p. 210).

The Child Psychotherapy training school received NHS funding in 1999 allowing us to move from being a well run cottage industry of the 'let's make an opera' variety to a real institution with paid workers, pleasant facilities and an extensive specialist library.

2. THEORETICAL ORIENTATION AND CURRICULUM

The theoretical orientation is Kleinian, and the curriculum is based on the requirements of the ACP.

There is a two-year pre-clinical course, which has as its core components observational studies of infants and young children. The elements of this course can build into a postgraduate diploma and, if trainees do well enough, lead to an extra year and the submission of a thesis to obtain an MA.

3. TRAINING STRUCTURE

3.1 Training committee
The Training Committee comprises Senior Psychoanalysts and Child Psychotherapists, and includes a local management committee of Child and Adult Psychotherapists.

3.2 Selection procedure and admission

The pre-clinical course
Students must:

(a) work in the public sector (although in exceptional circumstances others may be considered)

(b) have some idea of the psychodynamic approach and accept it – that is, if a child has a hand around your throat and is squeezing, you accept that they are in all probability furious or frightened. We can argue until the cows come home about what the implications of the feelings are, but all should share the conviction that feelings relate to behaviour and experience

(c) have been interviewed and presented a piece of work and been supervised on it, have the flavour of how painful thinking about feelings can be, have had a chance to 'run like hell' and have decided against it. We also believe that we *all* have learning difficulties and invite the students to think about their potential difficulties in relation to this sort of work. If they do flounder, this should be viewed as pretty ordinary but needing attention

(d) be able to work at a postgraduate post-qualification level.

All comers have equal opportunity to run. Given our bursary system, all comers have equal opportunity to come.

The clinical training
Selection is over a two-year period as a range of teachers get to know a student, his/her intellectual ability and emotional capacity to learn. If a student has not done the pre-clinical training with us, we will ask permission to talk to their teachers informally. We would (geography permitting) usually ask if they would like to sit in on a few clinical seminars and speak to current students and only after this put in an application. There is then a formal interview for all students, presided over by an external assessor from ACP.

3.3 Time commitment per week and length of training
The pre-clinical course runs for two years on Friday afternoons, and includes eight full Saturdays.

The clinical training is an apprenticeship, including Friday afternoons and about fifteen Saturday mornings per year as training days.

We have not yet had anyone fail to complete the training in the four allotted years.

3.4 Financial cost of training at different stages
Pre-clinical: approximately £1,000 per year. The clinical training costs £6,000+ per year, but fully funded training posts give a salary currently in the region of £18,500 plus all expenses, including travel.

3.5 Interruptions in training
Training is geared to each individual and interruptions would be considered according to circumstance.

3.6 Graduating and beginning a career
Graduates are put forward for membership of the ACP and UKCP.

Students have an elected representative with whom they meet at regular intervals to feed in suggestions, positive and negative, about the running of the School. Because of the small numbers and because of the desire to spend a minimum of money on running costs and a maximum on needy students, the student body have always played an active part in the day to day running of the Trust.

We anticipate that our graduates will become respected members of Child and Adolescent Mental Health Teams (CAMHS teams). This involves, helping children and families with their skills, generating outcome studies to evaluate their work, and teaching others, through the school or on their home patches, the ideas and techniques that they have found useful when faced with hurt and troubled children. Most probably because ours is a pioneer training, our students seem to be a hardy, independent breed. Two have already moved far North, to Cumbria and Lancashire to start work on analytically virgin patches. We hope this trend will continue, so that all our children throughout the country will have access to child psychotherapists on the NHS.

3.7 Numbers of students per intake
The Child Psychotherapy training currently has fifteen trainees, and there is a proposed annual intake of five, with fully funded regional trainee posts.

4. CLINICAL AND ACADEMIC REQUIREMENTS

4.1 Personal analysis/therapy
This must be with an ACP acceptable person. It should ideally be five times weekly, but three or four times is accepted.

4.2 Clinical requirements
Patients are all seen on the NHS and are usually assessed and chosen by or always in close discussion with the line management supervisor and the training school. Three intensive training cases (usually not all concurrent) with a mix of sexes, aged under five, latency and adolescent, one of which is of two years' duration, the others of a year. Each case is supervised for an hour a week by a senior therapist. Each case has a different supervisor.

4.3 Supervision
Throughout training it is obligatory to have: (a) a weekly hour of general line management supervision; (b) membership of a group of five who have group supervision weekly in term time (30 weeks).

If a student is having particular difficulties, extra supervision is offered until this has been resolved.

4.4 Written work and course attendence
Students are expected to attend *all* events unless they have a good reason not too. This would be a matter for discussion between the course tutor and the student. *We* take reliability very seriously because of the nature of the work and the effect of irregularities on patients.

Students are expected to produce a small portfolio of GP letters, case summaries, and so on, the kind of writing the job entails. They are also asked to write an extended and focused paper on a case before they qualify. Writing for publication is encouraged.

4.5 Assessment, standards and ethical requirements

Assessment is ongoing and done by all teachers and the student themselves. We ask them all to fill in a 'strengths and weaknesses' form each year, 'so we can consolidate on the strengths and work on the weaknesses'. These are discussed with the student by his/her personal tutor. But feedback, in terms of close supervision, is constant.

Qualifying papers are read by:

(a) the supervisor to see that it reflects the actuality of the patient and the work done
(b) an internal, senior member of the teaching team
(c) our external assessor.

Students may be asked to rewrite sections or to have supervision on areas discussed, but in the readers' opinion not understood. In fact, most students ask for help and much discussion, reference suggesting and reshaping occurs as part of the learning experience, *before* the paper is submitted.

5. TRAINEE RESPONSE

1. Why this course was chosen

1.1 What made people decide to train?

• Ideas encountered in the pre-clinical training made sense and there was a wish to explore them in greater depth
• Professional and Clinical development.

1.2 What were the aspects of this course that were most attractive?

• Kleinian orientation
• Access to clinical supervision
• The locality of the training
• The small and intimate nature of the training
• Breadth of and detailed understanding gained, including work with children of all ages, parents and families
• Teaching offered by thoughtful and thought provoking and experienced child psychotherapists and analysts
• A cooperative and dynamic trainee group, with a shared awareness of the exacting nature of the training
• The level of honesty in the critical analysis of the work
• Qualification would mean membership of the ACP and eligibility for UKCP registration.

1.3 What was your experience of the selection procedure?

Selection for the pre-clinical training was through interview with one of the course tutors. This involved a discussion of a piece of recent work and a discussion of what the course involved and how it might impact on the applicant. On completion of the pre-clinical training a decision was made about moving on to the clinical training in discussion with the course tutor and ultimately the head of training.

1.4 Before the start of the course, how informed did you feel about each stage of the training?
There was a written course booklet on the pre-clinical training, which gave clear information on the modules needed to complete it. There was some muddle about the written work, which was required to complete this part of the course partly because the components of the pre-clinical training can also form part of a Diploma or a MA. There was a clear differentiation between the pre-clinical and the clinical training. There was a lack of clarity regarding the specific requirements for the clinical training. Knowing someone on the course was helpful in this respect.

2. The atmosphere of the course

2.1. How do you feel about the way in which information is communicated?
Up until last year there was not a funded training school or a building, which created some difficulties in the dissemination of information. With the establishment of a training school this aspect of the course is evolving. The use of the student representative to pass on important information has continued to be helpful.

2.2 What do you find the most confusing aspect of the training?

- Each trainee seems to progress though the training at different rates. It can feel difficult to assess specifically how far you have developed
- The complex and integral relationship between the training school, personal analyses, and the workplace is demanding and can feel contradictory at times.

2.3 How much opportunity do you have to share thoughts and feelings with fellow trainees?

- Breaks between seminars
- Trainee meetings
- Personal relationships formed during the training
- Interest group to informally discuss and explore specific aspects of psychoanalytic psychotherapy.

2.4 What do you feel about the methods of teaching?

- A balance between the technical and the theoretical
- Mainly seminar and interactive style teaching
- Some lectures on particular aspects of the work
- While it was understood that it was impossible to meet all needs given the variety of settings trainees are in, some students felt it would be helpful to develop more workshops on particular aspects of the work, for example, autism, self-harm
- A range of child psychotherapists and visiting analysts provide weekly supervision, case discussion and seminars.

'The analysts who participate in offering training are talented teachers and extremely sound in their provision of technical and theoretical knowledge.'

2.5 What did you think about the way assessments were done to allow you to progress to the next stages of training?
'It gets worked out somehow!' probably captured the response most accurately. There is an awareness that there is communication between training case supervisors, head of training, visiting analysts, and personal analysts. However, students aren't always clear how the information is assimilated and what aspects inform decisions which ultimately lead to progression through to different stages.

- There was an idea you had to be ready to progress to the next stage, although what 'ready' meant sometimes seemed intangible.
- The introduction of personal appraisals seems to help gauge development from the second year on. First-year students were only aware of these in passing, however.

2.6 Has the course met your expectations?

'It's essential to talk to other students on the course to be realistic about the rewards, challenges and implications of taking it on.'
'You can be prepared for the course on an academic level, but nobody can prepare you for the all consuming nature and the emotional investment.'

2.7 How do you feel about your future with the organisation?
The expectation is that the student will be supported through to the completion of the training any further links would be on more of an informal basis. Some previous students have become tutors on the pre-clinical training or provide supervision and management of trainees. There has been an interest group set up for students in the later stages of training and who are recently qualified.

2.8 What plans do trainees have for future practice and possible balance of different sorts of work in their career?
Funded trainees are not guaranteed jobs. However, there is hope as more clinical posts for qualified child psychotherapists become available within the Midlands and in the North. Most clinical posts are attached to CAMHS teams and tend to be general posts, concentrating on working directly with all ages of children. Again there is hope of further service developments within which child psychotherapists could be located.

AUTHOR'S COMMENTS

The BTTP course owes much to the energy and determination of Shirley and Brian Truckle (see p. 273f.) in establishing a training in child psychotherapy in the Midlands. The training has a Kleinian and post-Kleinian framework and applicants appear to be offered a valuable selection process of confronting whether they are suitable for the work and how much they might want it. The success in obtaining funded posts in the NHS outside London is a real achievement for BTTP and for child psychotherapy. The establishment of a school base is recent so this new course, the latest among the child trainings, is only just getting going. This is indicated in the way the trainee responses suggest the importance of using the experience of fellow trainees to find their way through a new and flexible system. This might be daunting for some who want a clearer pathway mapped out for them.

Readers should also refer to the sister WMIP Adult psychotherapy training and the author's comments made there (p. 229). They indicate the possible advantages and disadvantages of an exclusively Kleinian-based course.

As will be seen from both the course entry and the trainee response, the experience is lively, challenging and demanding. The course, although small, appears to offer an excellent basis for work in the Midlands and North West region of England in developing the toehold psychoanalytic ideas and practice have within Child and Adult Mental Health Services in the NHS.

BRITISH ASSOCIATION OF PSYCHOTHERAPISTS TRAINING IN CHILD AND ADOLESCENT PSYCHOTHERAPY (BAP-CH – UKCP/PTCS)
For address, see BAP adult training (p. 87).

1. HISTORY OF THE ORGANISATION

See history section of the BAP (p. 87).

2. THEORETICAL ORIENTATION AND CURRICULUM

The training represents the thinking of the Independent and Contemporary Freudian schools within the British Psychoanalytic movement, as well as contemporary thought. This wide span of psychoanalytic perspective has been particularly attractive to many of the trainees who find the breadth of theoretical understanding which this offers, stimulating and challenging.

Theoretical seminars (brief outline)
Year one: basic aspects of Freudian theory; mother–infant interaction; play and symbolic communication; the Oedipus complex and latency; race, culture and psychotherapy; attachment theory.

Year two: adolescence and its disturbances; further seminars on Freud; transference and counter-transference; defence; object relations theory (for example, Klein, Fairbairn, Winnicott); writing six monthly reports.

Year three: assessment; brief work and consultation; neuroses and psychoses; sexual deviation in childhood and adolescence; learning difficulties and behaviour problems; psychosomatic disorders; borderline, atypical, autistic and psychotic children.

Year four: sexuality, gender and delinquency; working with families; working with couples; writing reports in the public sector; child sexual abuse and abusive behaviour; children and the law; consultancy to institutions and professionals.

The curriculum is under constant review by the Training Committee and is responsive to trainees' views about the balance and content of the seminars as well as changing requirements from the ACP. The seminar leaders' come from a wide range of clinical experience and theoretical perspective, which is in keeping with the Independent Psychoanalytic tradition of the course.

In the first year there is a weekly work discussion seminar to bridge the gap between the trainees' current work and psychotherapeutic work with children. This is replaced by clinical seminars in the subsequent three years. Infant Observation takes place in years one and two of the training.

3. TRAINING STRUCTURE

3.1 Training committee
The Chair and members of the Child Training Committee, which currently has 15 members, are senior members of the profession. There is a Year Tutor for each trainee intake who is responsible for the organisation of the trainees' programme and is a member of the Training Committee. Each trainee has a Progress Advisor who is a member of the Training Committee, and meets with the trainee termly, or more frequently if required. The Progress Advisor liaises with the trainee's work place supervisor and manager, and is responsible for monitoring the trainee's progress throughout the training.

3.2 Selection procedure and admission
Training prerequisites are as laid down by the ACP. Suitable applicants have two interviews with members of the selection sub-committee, which reports to the Training Committee.

Since 1997 the BAP has run a joint two-year MSc course, 'Infancy to Adulthood', in conjunction with Birkbeck College, which is recognised as a pre-training qualification for applicants to the training.

3.3 Time commitment per week and length of training
Many current trainees have been successful in gaining fully funded training posts. Other trainees already hold posts within professions and in clinical settings where they can, with their employer's permission, see their training cases. Trainees spend between three and five hours weekly in training psychoanalysis, and for each intensive training case undertaken, three or four hours weekly, plus one hour in supervision. The amount of time spent by a trainee on the training per week varies considerably depending on the number of intensive training cases being seen at any time.

Lectures and seminars are held on Monday (first and second year only) and Tuesday evenings. In addition, trainees attend assessment and case discussion meetings at the BAP Child Consultation and Treatment Centre on Tuesday afternoons. The length of the training varies depending on the availability of training cases, but most trainees qualify within five years, although sometimes this may extend to six years.

Trainees who have not completed their clinical requirements by the end of the fourth year attend clinical seminars and continue their training analysis until they are formally qualified by the BAP.

3.4 Financial cost of training at different stages
At the time of going to press, trainees pay an annual subscription fee of £145; the cost of years one and two is £1,050, and £810 in years three and four; from year five

onwards it is £660. Analytic fees can vary from £30–40 per session and supervision fees from £15–35. Small bursaries are available on application through the Child Psychotherapy Trust and the BAP. Progress Advisors make every effort to help trainees find suitable settings in which to see patients and to advise trainees who are in financial difficulty.

3.5. Interruptions in training
If a trainee needs to interrupt Training for any reason, the matter would be discussed with the trainee's Progress Advisor and in the Training Committee. Appropriate arrangements can then be made to enable the trainee to recommence the training in due course.

3.6 Graduating and beginning a career
Graduates of the training usually continue to work within the Health Service and voluntary sector. They can offer a wide range of treatments and consultations and often supervise the work of colleagues from other professions who wish to work psychotherapeutically. Many graduates develop special interests – for example, work with physically ill children, consultation to social services departments and health visitors, parent–infant psychotherapy. A number of BAP graduates are now Heads of Service for their Health Trusts. Some graduates run private practices alongside their NHS or voluntary sector employment.

Within the BAP, graduates may undertake the two-year modified training for psychotherapy with adults (described under the BAP Adult Trainings, p. 87). Two years after qualification, some interested graduates may be invited to join the Training Committee. Some graduates are also invited to give clinical or theoretical seminars. Graduates also become active within the ACP.

Five years after graduation, we would expect graduates to be making significant contributions in their varied work settings and seeing the most problematic section of the child and adolescent patient community. Some graduates may be publishing papers in journals, or within books of collected papers.

3.7 Numbers of students per intake
There is a biennial intake of six to eight Trainees.

4. CLINICAL AND ACADEMIC REQUIREMENTS

The first year of the training is probationary.

4.1 Personal therapy
At least three times weekly (although many trainees attend four to five times weekly), with a BAP/ACP approved psychoanalyst or psychotherapist.

4.2 Clinical requirements
As required by the ACP (see p. 237).

4.3 Supervision

Each intensive training patient is supervised weekly by a different BAP approved supervisor. Weekly cases may be supervised by a senior child psychotherapist at the trainee's place of work.

4.4 Written work and course attendance

Trainees are expected to keep regular, detailed records of their baby observations and their clinical work. In addition the following reports and papers are required to be completed before a trainee can graduate: six-monthly reports on each intensive training case; a paper on infant observation; a paper (each) on one intensive training case, a non-intensive treatment case and work with parents. The paper on the intensive training case is presented at a 'Reading-In', which is attended by trainees and members of the Child Section of the BAP. These important occasions are followed by a lunch in the trainee's honour.

Attendance at all seminars is expected, and absence notified in advance.

4.5 Assessment, standards and ethical requirements

These are as for the ACP and BAP. Close attention is paid to the standard and ethics of the work carried out by the trainee throughout the Training. In some circumstances trainees may not be allowed to progress beyond their probationary year – or may have to have a further probationary year. Trainees' progress is discussed at least once a term by the Training Committee with the Progress Advisor, and any concerns fed back to the trainee, if necessary in a formal letter. In some rare circumstances trainees may regrettably, after lengthy and careful discussion in the Training Committee, be asked to leave the training if their work consistently falls below an acceptable standard.

5. TRAINEE RESPONSE

1. Why this course was chosen

1.1 What made people decide to train?
The BAP tends to attract people with diverse experience of working professionally with children who are in the main within the public sector. Trainees share a wish for professional development; to have a deeper understanding of the inner world and work in a child-centred way.

1.2 What were the aspects of this course that were most attractive?
BAP applicants value the broad theoretical perspective offered within an atmosphere of a small training school. Overnight accommodation was seen to be an additional feature for students outside of London.

1.3 What was your experience of the selection procedure?
Trainees viewed the selection procedure as balanced, fair, searching and rigorous.

1.4 Before the start of the course, how informed did you feel about each stage of the training?
The introductory day and training prospectus were seen as helpful in providing information prior to training. Some trainees found the financial implications and time commitments could have been clearer.

2. The atmosphere of the course

2.1 How do you feel about the way in which information is communicated?
On the whole, trainees considered communication to be personalised but sometimes variable.

2.2 What do you find the most confusing aspect of the training?
In the early stages, the most confusing aspects were felt to be around time commitment and duration of the course. Some trainees felt that clearer guidance was needed about clinical placements.

2.3 How much opportunity do you have to share thoughts and feelings with fellow trainees?
Opportunities for sharing thoughts and feelings varies according to the motivation of the different year groups. Year tutors may facilitate this process.

2.4 What do you feel about the methods of teaching?
The mixture of diverse theoretical teachings, taught by visiting seminar leaders from the various training schools, and linked to clinical material provides a strong education in the independent tradition.

2.5 What did you think about the way assessments were done to allow you to progress to the next stages of training?
Some trainees felt that the overall assessment procedure for progression within the course could have been clearer.

2.6 Has the course met your expectations?
The course was considered exciting and dynamic with opportunities to contribute to a small training school.

2.7 How do you feel about your future with the organisation?
Generally, trainees felt positive and committed to the BAP and to its future developments.

2.8 What plans do trainees have for future practice and possible balance of different sorts of work in their career?
Trainees in the main, plan to work predominantly within the state sector with a view to specialist areas within child development and research.

AUTHOR'S COMMENTS

This training in child psychotherapy is unique in being the only child training inspired by the Independent and Contemporary Freudian schools, which responds to a lack of such an approach in the other child trainings. It is newer than many of the child trainings and yet it is set within a well established training organisation. It is dedicated to prepare trainees for future work in the public services in which it has been very successful. The small size of the training is an appealing factor to some in providing a secure base and a facilitating environment.

Graduates of this course have the advantage of belonging to a scientific community alongside adult-trained psychotherapists of different viewpoints, as well as the possibility of joining the modified adult training within the same organisation in order to train for work with adults (see entry, p. 99).

FORUM FOR THE ADVANCEMENT OF EDUCATIONAL THERAPY AND THERAPEUTIC TEACHING (FAETT – UKCP/PTCS)

Caspari House, 1 Noel Road, London N1 8HQ
Tel. 020 7704 1977

1. HISTORY OF THE ORGANISATION

The Forum for the Advancement of Educational Therapy and Therapeutic Teaching was established in 1991. It represents the amalgamation of two organisations, the Forum for the Advancement of Educational Therapy and the National Association for Therapeutic Teaching. Both of these organisations grew out of the work of the late Irene Caspari, Principal Psychologist at the Tavistock Clinic, London, Department for Children and Parents, and her courses on the psychological aspects of learning difficulties.

2. THEORETICAL ORIENTATION AND CURRICULUM

The programme introduces experienced teachers to a psychodynamic way of thinking about and addressing the emotional and social factors, which affect learning. The programme concentrates on the development of observational skills and psychodynamic understanding and their application to the processes of teaching and learning.

The programme of study comprises courses on the following:

- Attachment Theory
- A Psychodynamic Approach to the Assessment of Learning Difficulties
- The Inner World and Creative Expression
- Group and Family Dynamics
- Conscious and Unconscious Processes in Mental Functioning
- Baby and Nursery Observation involving detailed observational studies of infants and young children
- Work Discussion – relating theory to daily practice
- Educational Therapy Practice in Placement (including supervised practice)
- Educational Therapy Case Study.

A one-year course is run which introduces students to educational therapy thinking and practice. It is not a prerequisite for the training but is a useful introduction for those who have not previously encountered this way of thinking.

3. TRAINING STRUCTURE

3.1 Training committee
A Programme Board of five, including the Programme Convener, runs the Diploma Course.

3.2 Selection procedure and admission
Applicants are asked to complete an application form and those fulfilling the entry criteria are interviewed. The entry requirements are:

- qualified teacher status
- minimum of two years' teaching experience
- appropriate references
- relevant experience.

Factors considered in the interview include:

- evidence of the candidate's ability to observe and reflect on a child's functioning and to appreciate that social and emotional factors affect the child
- candidate's capacity to communicate thoughts coherently
- candidate's capacity to contain strong emotion
- evidence that the candidate has thought about the practicalities of the course in terms of time, finances and personal psychotherapy. The trainee should be well established (usually at least six months) in personal psychoanalytic psychotherapy at least once weekly before seeing children in educational therapy. The course requires personal psychotherapy to continue for the duration of the course
- Capacity to be flexible in attitudes, to tolerate uncertainty and to be a learner.

The programme policies involve a commitment to the provision of equal opportunities in recruitment of students, from advertisement to selection, and equitable treatment throughout the programme, of all students regardless of, for example, age, ethnic background, marital status, religion, sex or social class. The programme policies respect the needs and rights of minority groups and applications from minority groups are welcomed.

3.3 Time commitment per week and length of training
The course lasts for four years. Seminars are held on one evening per week for three ten-week terms each year. On alternate years, one hour is required each week for baby observation or for the observation of a nursery child. Additional time is required for writing up this observation. Reading time is also required. From the second year onward, time is needed for the clinic placement of preferably one day per week with one hour weekly for supervision of clinical work in the placement.

Consideration is given to deferment for those students who have not completed clinical or written work by the end of the four years, but this need has to be established before the due completion date and an alternative date established.

3.4 Financial cost of training at different stages
Currently (1999) the course costs £400 per term, including supervision fees. Students are required to pay for their own personal psychoanalytic psychotherapy.

3.5 Interruptions in training
Consideration is given to the need to interrupt the training on an individual basis, but since the Diploma follows a rolling programme it has to be recognised that it may take several years to complete the training after an interruption.

3.6 Graduating and beginning a career
We hope that graduates will continue to be involved in the organisation and will endeavour to promote educational therapy.

They have often taken posts, which offered promotion, particularly within special education. Some have begun to work privately as educational therapists or are employed as educational therapists by Local Education Authorities or the Health Authority.

3.7 Numbers of students per intake
We are able to take up to twenty students in total – this being on average five per year.

4. CLINICAL AND ACADEMIC REQUIREMENTS

4.1 Personal therapy
(See above.)

4.2 Clinical requirements
Placement in a Child Guidance/Child and Family Therapy Service is arranged for the student.

4.3 Supervision
Weekly supervision is arranged throughout the clinical placement.

4.4 Written work and course attendance
There are eight courses of seminars within the four-year programme. The work related to each course is separately assessed by a marked written assignment. A ninth piece of written work is a case study based on the work with one of the educational therapy cases.

An attendance rate of 80 per cent at seminars is a course requirement.

4.5 Assessment, standards and ethical requirements
The code of ethics is not organised under headings but covers issues under numbered points relating to the relationship with the client, ways of working and technique,

relationships with other professionals and advertisement of their service, issues of confidentiality and consent regarding audio-visual recording, publication and research; issues relating to physical contact with children, avoidance of exploitation, therapists' physical and mental fitness to practise, criminal behaviour, responsibility regarding colleagues and the profession.

Complaints and Appeals Procedures are also set down.

There is also a Code of Practice for training in line with UKCP Guidelines.

Standards and assessment procedures are validated by the Roehampton Institute, and include:

- monitoring of students' progress throughout the course by means of termly meetings of main course tutors, supervisors and seminar leaders who take the work discussion and observation seminars
- course written work is marked by one tutor and second-marked by a different tutor. The External Examiner monitors a sample of written work to ensure consistent marking
- the Internal Assessment Panel receives the marking of each student's work and this will determine whether the student has passed and at what level
- the Moderator also monitors assessment standards on behalf of the Roehampton Institute.

The assessment of Educational Therapy Practice in Placement is on a pass/fail basis and takes account of the extent to which the student has demonstrated, to the satisfaction of his/her supervisor and link person in the placement:

- the capacity to provide a facilitating environment for the child's learning and self expression
- observational skills, including self-observation, a capacity for objectivity and the ability to understand the part played by his/her own actions and reactions
- teaching skills; the management of learning tasks in educational therapy, the appropriate use of learning materials and the ability to adapt to the needs of the child
- the capacity to be receptive to the child's expression of feelings, either directly, or indirectly through educational tasks, play, games, or other activities which lend themselves to self-expression
- the capacity to set limits
- the ability to work as part of a team and liaise with parents and other professionals about children with whom he/she has worked in the placement
- the ability to use and learn from supervision
- the capacity for personal and professional development, in terms of awareness and style of work, during the course of the placement.

Additionally, students are required to produce a written assignment, which is an Educational Therapy Case Study. Assessment of this work takes into account the degree to which the student:

- gives a clear and detailed account of the content and process of educational therapy with one child

- demonstrates the ability to reflect on the interaction between him/herself and the child and between the child and the educational task or expression work; gives meaning to the feelings expressed
- shows an implicit understanding of the theoretical basis of the therapy, thus demonstrating the capacity to integrate theoretical concepts taught on the course with his/her own experience of the child in educational therapy
- makes explicit links with theory, if and when these links contribute significantly to the understanding of the content and process of the educational therapy as described in the case study.

The Examination Board, including the Moderator, the Programme Convenor and permanent teaching staff and the External Examiner receive the results and recommend to the Roehampton Institute candidates for the award, or otherwise, of the Diploma.

UKCP Registration of Educational Therapists
The Diploma in Educational Therapy, or equivalent theoretical and practical training and experience recognised by FAETT is a prerequisite for Registration. A Registration Panel meets to make decisions on recommendations for registration. The majority of candidates who have qualified for the Diploma will be recommended for registration but some of those who have qualified for the Diploma, and whose supervised clinical work has been satisfactory in most respects, still show limited awareness, at the point of qualification, of certain inhibited areas of conflict in their clients. Where it is considered necessary that a candidate further develop clinical awareness, the Registration Panel will stipulate a period of further supervised practice, followed by the presentation of an account of work with an educational therapy case to a group of three assessors. The assessors and supervisor will report back to the Registration Panel, which will then make a decision about whether to recommend registration.

5. TRAINEE RESPONSES
This year there are five students in Year Two, three in Year Three and four in Year Four, making twelve altogether. Most of us met together during a session of the course, with the five first years attending also.

1. Why this course was chosen

1.1 What made people decide to train?
As we are all teachers most wanted the opportunity for greater understanding of a child's emotional life when there is so little of this in school.

The course was seen as a natural extension of the skills already gained as a teacher to find ways to support the learning of emotionally disturbed children.

A combination of teaching and a therapeutic approach is often suited to a child's needs, especially for those who fail to progress or reject support.

1.2 What were the aspects of this course that were most attractive?
The part-time nature of the course offers the opportunity to work and train at the same time.

The theoretical breadth of the course encompasses a range of pertinent theories.

The time demands are not too onerous initially, that is, one evening session per week.

The course is validated by the Roehampton Institute and accredited by the UKCP.

1.3 What was your experience of the selection procedure?
Most felt it to be a thorough but fair and intense interview, but good.

1.4 Before the start of the course, how informed did you feel about each stage of the training?
Members were aware but often found that the time commitment was more than they had anticipated. It is necessary to negotiate time for supervision and other aspects of the course.

2. The atmosphere of the course

2.1 How do you feel about the way in which information is communicated?
The annual course books are very good. Some felt that an overview of the whole course would be helpful.

2.2 What do you find the most confusing aspect of the training?
Mixed views. Some felt that the mixture of teaching and therapeutic aspects lacked coherence. Some felt that mixed-year groups meant lack of continuity, but others felt it was an advantage.

There is an annual review of the course and a termly programme evaluation for students.

Clarification was needed between therapeutic teaching in schools and educational therapy in a clinic.

2.3 How much opportunity do you have to share thoughts and feelings with fellow trainees?
Formally, at the end of year session, and informally, at tea breaks in between the two evening sessions each week.

2.4 What do you feel about the methods of teaching?
Overall agreement about the worth of the mix of lectures and seminars. There is no experiential work as a group.

2.5 What did you think about the way assessments were done to allow you to progress to the next stages of training?
Written feedback in assignments is currently being negotiated.

2.6 Has the course met your expectations?
Mostly 'yes'. One added that personal therapy had also helped in understanding the problems of the children.

2.7 How do you feel about your future with the organisation?
Mostly hopeful, particularly with regard to the expansion through the establishment of new premises. Many felt that more publicity and networking would be good.

2.8 What plans do trainees have for future practice and possible balance of different sorts of work in their career?
Many were very keen to become Educational Therapists. Most felt that the issues of working in schools involved groundbreaking work. All were hopeful that they could integrate it into their present work.

AUTHOR'S COMMENTS

Educational therapy provides an unusual and important vehicle for the application of psychoanalytic ideas to children who struggle with all-important learning experiences at school. This course provides a unique opportunity for teachers to train as educational therapists and to use their new skills in a familiar context for the benefit of both children and of their colleagues in the settings where they work. In this sense it is not like a psychodynamic counselling or psychotherapy course, but something quite distinctive addressing the psychological difficulties in learning experienced by children and adolescents.

For this course, years of thoughtfulness have gone into applying clinical psychoanalytical psychotherapy ideas and methods to the learning difficulties of children. These are applied in this course to the experience of learning a new profession. Modelling how to assist with learning difficulties, which all have, is the hallmark of this course. It is in the light of this that comments by trainees about the course that are both appreciative and critical suggest how effective the course is at creating a robust learning community. Depth of understanding and engagement in the work are assured by the insistence on personal therapy.

The Forum is an organisational member of the Psychoanalytically-based Therapy with Children Section along with the Association of Child Psychotherapists of which it is not a member because it is not a training in child psychotherapy, but focused on applying psychoanalytic ideas to children's learning difficulties of many sorts.

INSTITUTE OF PSYCHO-ANALYSIS AND BRITISH PSYCHO-ANALYTICAL SOCIETY TRAINING IN THE PSYCHO-ANALYSIS OF CHILDREN AND ADOLESCENTS (INSTP-A-CH – BCP)

Address under adult training, p. 142.

Qualified psychoanalysts and students who are working with their second adult training case are eligible to apply for the Institute's training in the psychoanalysis of children and adolescents.

These trainees attend theoretical and clinical seminars in child and adolescent analysis and undertake, with supervision, the psychoanalysis of two children and one adolescent seen five times weekly. One of these patients should be in each of three age groups: 2–5 years, 6–12 years and 13–17 years old. They should not all be of the same sex.

Ordinarily, a minimum of one year's five-times-weekly analysis of each of the three cases must be completed before qualification as a child and adolescent analyst. Some exceptions to the requirements for clinical work and seminars are made in the case of trainees who have already completed a course in child and adolescent psychotherapy. There is considerable flexibility about the duration of the course to accommodate the varying needs of post-qualification psychoanalysts.

There are two separate and collaborating programmes for this training under the auspices of the Education Committee: a course organised by the Child and Adolescent Analysis Committee of the Institute of Psycho-Analysis, and another course run by the Anna Freud Centre.

AUTHOR'S COMMENTS

The advantage of training as a child psychoanalyst within the Institute as a post-qualification experience is that further training can be pursued within the same institution, organised by a separate committee, at a pace that suits the candidate. If an analyst wishes to become more involved in research or the world of child psychotherapy then the Anna Freud training might be more appropriate, as it is also recognised as training in child analysis by the Institute.

This training is not registered with the Association for Child Psychotherapists. It does not contain the rigourous demands of extensive work in the public services. It is designed for candidates and psychoanalysts wishing to work with children in private practice as well as the Anna Freud Centre.

THE SCOTTISH INSTITUTE OF HUMAN RELATIONS CHILD PSYCHOTHERAPY TRAINING (SIHR-Ch – UKCP/PTCS)

13 Park Terrace, Glasgow G3 6BY
Tel. 0131 556 0924 Fax. 0131 556 2612

1. HISTORY OF THE ORGANISATION

Over the past 25 years the Scottish Institute of Human Relations has provided training with the aim of increasing therapeutic services within the caring professions in Scotland. Dr 'Jock' Sutherland put theory into practice when he said in his paper, the 'Psychodynamic Image of Man', 'What supports the carer is not encouragement in the conventional sense ... It is to be part of a learning system greater than himself.' The Scottish Institute of Human Relations programme has evolved through responding to the demands of the caring professions for further training.

2. THEORETICAL ORIENTATION AND CURRICULUM

Theoretical strands influencing the course are Kleinian and post-Kleinian Theory, Object Relations Theory and Attachment Theory. Within the Institute two training programmes for work with children and young people are on offer.

Therapeutic Skills with Children and Young People

This modular course aims to provide professionals working with children and adolescents the opportunity to explore and deepen their understanding of personality development from a psychoanalytic perspective, and to use this to consider the nature and value of a therapeutic relationship in work with children and young people. A central part of the course focuses on the development of detailed observational skills on which psychotherapeutic work depends.

The modules available are:

- Baby Observation (2 modules)
- Young Child Observation
- Introduction to Psychoanalytic Theory and its application to work with children
- Introduction to Personality Development from a psychoanalytical perspective
- Detailed discussion of individual work (2 modules) with children and young people
- Institutional Processes/Application Group Seminar
- Child Development Research

The modular structure of the course permits students to progress at the pace of their choice, but the full course can be completed in a minimum of two years part-time study. Negotiations are being undertaken to link this course to a post-graduate degree, which would involve a further year's study and submission of a dissertation.

This course also forms the foundation for those who may later undertake a professional training in child and adolescent psychotherapy.

Training in Child and Adolescent Psychotherapy

This four-year course provides a thorough training in the clinical practice of child and adolescent psychotherapy, and is fully accredited by the ACP. (See section 4.2.)

3. TRAINING STRUCTURE

3.1 Training committee

Trainings are operated under the aegis of the Child and Adolescent Training Committee, which is responsible through its chairperson to the Council of the SIHR. Course content and delivery is the responsibility of the Organising Tutor.

3.2 Selection procedure and admission for the Clinical Training in Child and Adolescent Psychotherapy

The prerequisite for the training is an Honours Degree in Psychology or a related subject, prior experience in work with children and adolescents, and a foundation course in Therapeutic Skills (see section 2) or a recognised Observational Studies Course.

3.3 Time commitment per week and length of training

This is considered a full-time training and, on occasions, funded training posts may be available within the NHS. Seminars on clinical practice and theory involve attendance at the Scottish Institute one day a week. Sufficient time should be allocated within work settings to undertake a wide range of clinical work, for service supervision, to record detailed process notes, and to liase with colleagues working jointly with ongoing cases.

3.4 Financial cost of training at different stages

For the Clinical Training personal analysis is approximately £4,000–5,000 per annum. Course costs average £2,500–3,000, which includes two supervisions of intensive cases. Supervision of the third intensive case is expected to be undertaken with a supervisor external to the course. Following completion of the formal elements of the training, and prior to completion of the clinical work, group supervision and discussion may be arranged at a reduced cost of £750 per year.

3.5 Interruptions in training

It is not unusual for students to take an extended break between the Therapeutic Skills Course and the Clinical Training, but students are encouraged to complete the Clinical Training without interruption. Occasionally interruptions are inevitable and can be accommodated by discussion with the Organising Tutor.

3.6 Graduating and beginning a career

Graduates of the Clinical Training are eligible for membership of the ACP and the Scottish Association of Psychoanalytic Psychotherapists (SAPP). As a Department of Health recognised profession, graduates are eligible to apply for qualified child psychotherapy posts in the UK and Europe. Candidates are also eligible for registration with the UKCP and the BCP through SAPP and the ACP.

Postgraduate education and research is encouraged by the profession and some students may want to go on to complete a Masters or a Doctorate in Psychoanalytic Psychotherapy.

3.7 Numbers of students per intake

On the Clinical Training we would expect an intake of six students every two years.

4. CLINICAL AND ACADEMIC REQUIREMENTS

4.1 Personal therapy

Personal analysis with a qualified practitioner recognised by the SIHR and by the ACP is a requirement of the course, and must begin at least one year before undertaking work with an intensive training case. It is expected that personal analysis would continue four times a week throughout the training.

Personal therapy is encouraged but is not a requirement of the foundation course.

4.2 Clinical requirements

The training includes:

- personal analysis (see section 4.1)
- the intensive treatment of three children – one pre-school, one latency and one adolescent. Two of these children will be seen at least three times weekly

under individual supervision for a minimum of one year, and the third case for two years
- additional experience of less frequent treatments with children of varying ages, with parents and families, and with other treatment modalities.

4.3 Supervision

(a) Individual supervision – each intensive case is individually supervised on a once weekly basis. The task of the supervisor is to help the trainee to understand the patient's communications and to discuss the management and setting of the psychotherapy.
(b) Group supervision – within the context of the training, group supervision provides an opportunity to share clinical material and to gain an understanding of a wide range of work undertaken in different settings.
(c) Service supervision – the training structure requires the employing authority to provide service supervision from an experienced child psychotherapist or, where that is not possible, from an experienced clinician with a closely related training background. It is the responsibility of the service supervisor to monitor the trainee's caseload in order to ensure the training needs are being met. The service supervisor liaises between the training school and the trainee's line management system, alerting both parties to potential conflicts between training needs and service needs.

4.4 Written work and course attendance

In order to ensure that all training requirements are met, trainees and their tutors should keep a training log, which is updated throughout the training.

In discussion with supervisors, students should write six-month summaries of clinical work.

In addition, each student is required to present, for examination, a portfolio of written work built up over the period of training. This should include a qualifying paper of 10,000 words, based on work with an intensive training case.

Other written assignments should include a theory essay of 5,000 words, an assessment for psychotherapy and an account of one of the following:

- a brief psychotherapeutic intervention,
- an account of group or family work or work with a parent.

Reports written in the course of clinical work should present overall clinical competence, including a closing summary of a case and reports written for external professionals (for example, Court Report or Report to Social Services or the Education Department).

4.5 Assessment, standards and ethical requirements

Code of ethics
We adhere to the Code of Ethics of the ACP and the SIHR.

Assessment process
Student progress throughout the clinical training is monitored and supported in the following ways:

- regular (minimum two per term) meetings with personal tutor
- regular (minimum four per term) meetings with service supervisor
- weekly individual supervisions on three intensive training cases.

The written work assignments are designed to demonstrate the trainee's professional competence and are evaluated by senior members of the Training Staff Group. Written assessment reports from each of the supervisors of the three individual training cases, the service supervisor and personal tutor should be signed by the trainee and the supervisor or tutor and submitted as part of the final assessment.

A recommendation from the Assessment Board will be conveyed to the Child and Adolescent Training Committee by the Organising Tutor regarding the qualification of the trainee. If the trainee has successfully completed the training requirements, the Training Committee will recommend the student for membership of SAPP and the ACP.

Appeals procedure
An appeals procedure has been drawn up with the SIHR.

Code of Professional Conduct and Ethics
All teachers and students abide by the Association of Child Psychotherapists Code of Conduct and Ethics. This can be divided into three main areas:

1. The patient's welfare and interests are 'paramount'.
2. A member shall only practice within the bounds of his training and will get psychiatric advice when needed.
3. This large section is about confidentiality, spelling out when it is permissible to break confidentiality and suggesting that if in doubt, the Chair of the association should be consulted.

Graduation
When all the course requirements have been fulfilled to the supervisor/teacher/seminar leader's satisfaction, and the candidate has written an acceptable qualifying paper, they are put forward by the school for membership of the ACP.

5. TRAINEE RESPONSE

These were written in consultation with the whole third-year intake and the majority of previous trainees.

This training which began in 1989, admits six trainees per intake. These occur every three to four years. Consequently, the present group is only the third intake. Members of this group, all of whom live and work in Scotland, were not able to move or commute to a London training; thus the choice of training school was a pragmatic one. For most, the decision to train was a natural progression from their previous areas of work, whether Music Therapists, Social Workers or Occupational Therapists.

All the trainings that take place under the auspices of the Scottish Institute have separate and distinct identities. The reasons for this are numerous, but the distinctiveness of the Child Psychotherapy training is highlighted by currently being post-Kleinian in orientation, even though the Institute is usually seen as lying within the broad Independent tradition. This range of perspectives could prove confusing for trainees if their analyst's practice differs markedly from that of the course. Some of the trainees who have been in this situation have described it in various ways, including 'useful, but difficult', and 'ultimately enriching'. Therefore, discussion with a course tutor about the orientation of the course and the range of training analysts available, prior to beginning an analysis, is recommended.

All current trainees feel: that the positive experience of becoming part of a small, loyal and enthusiastic group of child psychotherapists, who are developing psychoanalytic work with children in Scotland, is enormously stimulating; that despite administrative shortcomings, travelling long distances and financial worries, the course has in general met expectations. In our view, teaching methods are sound and the most positive experiences have been the course content and the excellent supervision of intensive cases.

However, as with many new ventures, its very newness contains the seeds of its various weaknesses: to date, clear procedures for communicating between staff and trainees, the training school and workplaces, the Training Committee and trainees' analysts, have yet to be developed. Likewise, a students' handbook with a detailed course outline is still awaited. Nevertheless, staff are aware of these shortcomings and intend to rectify them before the next intake in Autumn 2000.

AUTHOR'S COMMENTS

This course represents a dynamic innovation for the influence of psychoanalytic psychotherapy in Scotland. With a first training with a Glasgow base, this course has developed a focus for child psychotherapy training north of the border in the last three years. This is an important development for the region as well as for the Scottish Institute for Human Relations under whose auspices it is organised.

Like many courses described in this guide, both new and old, there are complex issues to address and the trainee response indicates some of them, particularly a prospective trainee's need to sort out their own orientation and that of prospective analysts and supervisors. This inevitable issue is discussed in the guide to do with difficulties with diversity and loyalties when there are different orientations within the same training. These sound like issues that this training is in the throes of sorting out. Many longer-established trainings find themselves confronted with similar issues. Like other regional trainings, it would seem as if there are fewer training analysts and supervisors upon whom to draw, which is inevitable in a pioneering analytic community, but is one aspect that may impose a limitation on this training.

SOCIETY OF ANALYTICAL PSYCHOLOGY-CHILD PSYCHOTHERAPY TRAINING (SAP-CH – UKCP/PTCS)

1 Daleham Gardens, London NW3 5BY
Tel. 020 7435 7696 Fax. 020 7431 1495

1. HISTORY OF THE ORGANISATION

The training was founded in 1973 by Dr Michael Fordham. He was the heart and inspiration of the child training and the Society for many years until his death in 1995. It is recognised by the Association of Child Psychotherapists as an accredited training. The training is a small, privately funded training.

2. THEORETICAL ORIENTATION AND CURRICULUM

The curriculum broadly follows that laid down by the ACP (see ACP training standards document). Dr Fordham developed Jung's ideas and created a model of child development at the centre of which was his concept of a primary self (for further information read James Astor, *Michael Fordham: Innovations in Analytical Psychology*, Routledge, 1995). The course includes study of other models and theories, Freud, Klein and Bion. The training places particular emphasis on detailed study of clinical data.

Prospective applicants are expected to have completed at least two years of analysis at four or five sessions per week. They must also have successfully completed the Society's infant observation course.

Infant observation consists of domiciliary observation of a mother and baby for a period of two years. The candidate will be required to write a paper on his observations showing evidence of his ability to integrate theory and observation. One-and-a-half-hour seminars are held weekly by arrangement with the leader. In addition some sustained observation of young children is required for six months to a year.

3. TRAINING STRUCTURE

3.1 Training committee
The training is run and administered by the members of the Child Analytic Training committee.

3.2 Selection procedure and admission
Prospective applicants must have satisfied the criteria for selection as laid down by the ACP (see ACP training standards). After the application has been received, two analysts on behalf of the Committee will interview the applicant. A fee is charged for the application. The decision of the Committee will be made known to the applicant as soon as possible. In the event of an applicant not being selected they may request a meeting with the Chairman of the Committee to discuss their

application. Applications must reach the Chairman of the Child Analytical Training Committee by 1 February.

Anyone who has satisfied the entry requirements may apply for the training.

3.3 Time commitment per week and length of training

(a) Seminars: twice weekly for four years.
(b) Analysis: students must be in analysis throughout the training. The number of sessions per week to be decided by the student and their analyst.
(c) Supervisions: four intensive cases have weekly individual supervision.
(d) Students are expected to attend the monthly Children's Section meeting.

The training takes four or five years.

The student has to write a qualifying paper, which is presented at the Children's Section meeting at the end of the training.

3.4 Financial cost of training at different stages

The student will incur the following costs:

* Analysis (fees depend on student and analyst)
* Supervision (fees variable 1999 £37 per supervision)
* Seminars. 1999 fees:

1st year	£171
2nd year	£141
3rd year	£141
4th year	£74

(All fees include subscription to the *Journal of Analytical Psychology*.)

Costs of training can be partly offset by grants and loans made available by the Society. Students apply to the Committee for these grants and loans.

Trainees are expected to apply for Traineeships (trainee posts at clinics). If successful the authority employing the student will pay for much of the training. (Approximately £350 per month towards analysis, all supervision fees, all seminar fees.)

3.5 Interruptions in training

It is possible to interrupt the training. Any interruptions in the training would be discussed by the Committee in consultation with the student.

3.6 Graduating and beginning a career

On graduating, a member will be given the title 'Associate Professional Member' and can become involved in almost all aspects of the Society's life.

They can work towards becoming professional members (procedures available from the Professional Development Committee). The training involves the analysis of a mother, and as such this will count as part of the clinical requirement should a member wish to train as a adult analyst, as does the first year of seminars. It is hoped that graduates will involve themselves in the life of the Society and especially the Child training. This might involve teaching and supervision.

3.7 Numbers of students per intake

There is no policy on numbers of students per intake, but in practice there are usually no more than four or five per intake.

4. CLINICAL AND ACADEMIC REQUIREMENTS

4.1 Personal therapy

It is expected that prospective applicants are well established in their analysis. Candidates should approach the Chairman of the Committee for advice on choosing an analyst. The candidate is required to be in analysis prior to applying for two years at four or five sessions per week. Students must remain in analysis throughout their training. Frequency to be decided by student and analyst.

4.2 Clinical requirements

The Association of Child Psychotherapists lays down the clinical requirements for the trainees. In addition to those requirements the SAP expect a student to analyse a mother intensively four times per week It is expected that students will undertake their clinical work within a trainee child psychotherapy post. The student's clinic supervisor will be responsible for referring patients.

4.3 Supervision

Students are expected to be in weekly individual supervision for each of their intensive cases. The Committee will decide the supervisor.

4.4 Written work and course attendance

Students are expected to attend all the seminars and supervisions. They are expected to keep detailed process notes to present at supervision. At the end of the training they are expected to write a qualifying paper.

4.5 Assessment, standards and ethical requirements

The SAP and the ACP both produce their own code of ethics which students are expected to sign.

The training is a small one, therefore it is possible to continually assess student development throughout the training. There are termly meetings for students to discuss issues of concern. Each year group is allocated a year tutor to monitor student concerns about the training. The student's clinical supervisor, usually the senior Child psychotherapist at the Clinic, monitors the student's work with the patients and with other members of the Clinic. There are twice-yearly meetings involving the clinic supervisor, the student and a member of the committee to discuss the student's progress.

5. TRAINEE RESPONSE

1. Why this course was chosen

1.1 What made people decide to train?

- Interest in learning more about the human psyche and thinking creatively about people.

- Interest in developing further skills in regard to theoretical knowledge and clinical practise with professional recognition at the end.
- A combination of interests with practical demands that enabled individuals to consider a professional training.

1.2 What were the aspects of this course that were most attractive?
The integration of all the different ideas held by both Psychoanalysis and Analytical Psychology, which could be seen as integrating different aspects of human nature. The Jungian contribution was important in allowing a broad framework from which to develop.

The Child Analytical training encompasses work with children, adolescents and adults.

The training body and particular individuals who undertook much of the teaching was important for one individual.

1.3 What was your experience of the selection procedure?
We all felt it had been a fair procedure. We had interviews with two different analysts, sometimes returning for a second meeting with one person. The process was felt to be serious and thoughtful but also human. The Chair of the Training Committee informed us by telephone on the same day as the decision was made, which felt welcoming and considerate.

1.4 Before the start of the course, how informed did you feel about each stage of the training?
We all felt that the current outline of training is lacking in detail, although we believe this will be addressed in the near future.

The first year of seminars is shared with the adult training and there is more information available about this course.

One person felt uninformed about the stages of training, and another felt that the details had been communicated by word of mouth from past trainees.

2. The atmosphere of the course

2.1. How do you feel about the way in which information is communicated?
Some information is posted and usually received. Sometimes information is shared in a rather more random method, which leaves some of us feeling in the dark. Hopefully this will be addressed in the near future as someone has recently been appointed to take on responsibility for trainees in Child Analysis.

2.2 What do you find the most confusing aspect of the training?
There is an organic quality about the training in that it develops gradually. This can be confusing at times, but is also a positive aspect as it allows flexibility and creativity.

Planning the future practically with regard to analysis, supervision and clinical placements can feel overwhelming when one has to have enough time and energy to work in order to finance oneself.

2.3 How much opportunity do you have to share thoughts and feelings with fellow trainees?
Formally, we meet twice a term. Informally, we meet before seminars, but there is a shortage of rooms for an informal meeting.

2.4 What do you feel about the methods of teaching?
In the first year the seminars are shared with those trainees undertaking the Adult Analytic training. The quality of teaching is dependent on the individual leading each set of seminars and this changes every two weeks. This brings richness to the course but also continual change, which can be difficult. The seminars are clinically orientated which is a valuable way of thinking about theoretical ideas, and this is also true of our work discussion group, which is for those doing the Child Analytic training.

2.5 What did you think about the way assessments were done to allow you to progress to the next stages of training?
This is unknown to us.

2.6 Has the course met your expectations?
So far, yes, but it is too early to tell. However, the indications are that the rest of the course will be good.

2.7 How do you feel about your future with the organisation?
Positive. There is a welcoming and valuing of different views and ideas that gives freedom to develop in ways most appropriate to each individual. We look forward to being part of the Society if accepted for membership. We are aware of historical difficulties and appreciate being treated as equals in that respect.

2.8 What plans do trainees have for future practice and possible balance of different sorts of work in their career?
We would like to work in the NHS with children, but are aware of possibilities in private practice and other institutions such as industry.

We would all like to consider training to work as an analyst with adult patients at some later date after consolidating this training.

AUTHOR'S COMMENTS

The Child Psychotherapy training at the SAP is rooted in a society that combines psychoanalytic thinking with analytical psychology (see comments on the SAP training, p. 204 and the section in Part One that deals with different Jungian approaches, p. 12f.). This course appears to be rooted in Fordham's developmental Jungian approach. It provides a thorough training within the standards laid down by the ACP and there is the opportunity of a modified training at a later stage in order to include training in adult Jungian analysis, which all the trainees said interested them.

Like all the child and adolescent trainings described in this guide, the work is demanding. There are a lot of patients to see as well as completing the academic demands of the course.

Being a small course exposes the group to each other; however, there appeared to be some protective dependency with the chair of training informing applicants on the day of interview and the lack of awareness of any assessment process. This was also suggested by the way that supervisors are chosen by the training committee. The comment that there was appreciation for individuals on the Training Committee as well as finding the regular turnover of teachers a demanding change suggests the character of the bonds on the course, heavily focused on the Committee.

TAVISTOCK CLINIC PSYCHOANALYTIC PSYCHOTHERAPY WITH CHILDREN, PARENTS AND YOUNG PEOPLE (TAVI-CH – UKCP/PTCS)

For address, history, theoretical orientation and curriculum, see entry under Tavistock Adult Training (p. 204).

3. TRAINING STRUCTURE

3.1 Training committee
Overall, organising tutor Margaret Rustin with assistant organising tutor Jennifer Kenrick hold the responsibility for the training. They are supported by the Training Advisory Group: Trudy Klauber, Lisa Miller, Sue Reid, Margot Waddell and Gianna Williams. The course is accredited by the Association of Child Psychotherapists, and recognised by the Department of Health.

3.2 Selection procedure and admission
Equal opportunities policies apply to the application criteria for admission to the training. The following are prerequisites for the course.

Work experience
Applicants are required to have substantial experience of work with children and adolescents of varying ages, preferably including children under five.

Pre-clinical studies
Applicants are expected to have satisfactorily completed the pre-clinical course in Psychoanalytic Observational Studies, including required written work. Occasionally those who have already qualified as child psychotherapists overseas or have other relevant professional qualifications may be considered for exemption from some events of the observation course.

Personal suitability
Applicants will have had opportunity during the observation course to reflect on their personal suitability for the training.

Academic requirements
The academic requirements are a degree of honours standard in Psychology or some related subject, or an honours degree in another subject followed by a course which includes the scientific study of human nature. The observation course is one such course. The observation course can also lead to a degree at MA level. However, it is not necessary for those who already possess an honours degree to continue to the dissertation component of that course.

Personal analysis
Although personal analysis is optional for those taking the observation course, those intending to apply for the clinical course should have commenced a personal analysis at least six months before making an application.

Selection is made on the basis of an applicant satisfying the above prerequisites. A member of the Training Advisory Group interviews applicants, and this Group decides whether an applicant will be offered a place on the course.

3.3 Time commitment per week and length of training
The programme for the clinical training in Child psychotherapy is based on a course of four years full-time clinical work and study. It is possible to take the main training events on a basis of attendance on either one whole day or two half days with additional time required for personal analysis and individual supervision. The clinical component of 15–25 hours per week is undertaken in local NHS clinics; there is a limited number of regional trainee posts, or there are sessions, which can be held at the Tavistock Clinic. For those who are unable to undertake a full-time programme, the course may be taken on a part-time basis over an extended period.

3.4 Financial cost of training at different stages (2000–2001)
The course fees for the 2000–2001 academic year are £1,100 for self-funded EC trainees and £2,200 for non-EC trainees. Trainees are responsible for the cost of their own personal analysis unless they are in a regionally funded post.

3.5 Interruptions in training
Trainees may have breaks during the course of the training because of illness or for maternity leave and are encouraged to continue their studies whenever this is possible.

3.6 Graduating and beginning a career
The Tavistock Clinic course for child psychotherapists is one of six recognised by the training council of the Association of Child Psychotherapists. Students offered a place on the clinical training are recommended to the Training Council of the ACP and are eligible for student membership of the association, and on satisfactorily completing the course, for full membership.

Successful completion of the course leads to the Masters in Psychoanalytic Psychotherapy award of the Tavistock/University of East London. Students may then apply to proceed for the award of Doctor of Psychoanalytic Psychotherapy, which is based on clinical research work and the writing of a dissertation.

Students accepted for training are eligible for employment within the NHS as trainee child psychotherapists. Those who successfully complete the training are eligible for full membership of the Association of Child Psychotherapists and for employment as qualified child psychotherapists on an agreed national salary scale in the NHS. The Tavistock Society of Psychotherapists (TSP) offers student membership to students on the course and full membership to graduates of the child psychotherapy training. TSP supports further professional development and provides an ongoing scientific programme. Graduates of the training are eligible for registration with both the BCP and UKCP.

Five years after completing the training our graduates will be expected to be holding posts of responsibility and seniority, often at consultant ('B' Grade) level within the NHS.

3.7 Numbers of students per intake

Annual intake varies from twelve to twenty. All students have to be personally and professionally suitable for the very intensive training in child psychotherapy.

4. CLINICAL AND ACADEMIC REQUIREMENTS

4.1 Personal therapy

While in clinical training students are expected to have a minimum of four and where possible five weekly sessions of personal psychoanalysis. For students travelling from long distances it may be agreed that they attend three sessions per week. Students are required to have at least one year's personal analysis before embarking upon the intensive treatment of a child, as part of the clinical course. Students are normally required to be in analysis for the whole course of their training.

Personal analysis is kept as separate from the training as possible and analysts are not as a rule consulted about a student's progress. They are asked initially whether there is any contra-indication to the analysand undertaking clinical training and beginning an intensive case under supervision and finally if they have any objection to the analysand being recommended for qualification and membership of the ACP.

4.2 Clinical requirements

Students are required to have three cases attending for intensive psychoanalytic therapy between three and five times weekly. Cases must include a pre-latency child, a latency child and an adolescent. One case is expected to have been in supervised treatment for two years and two cases for a minimum of one year in supervised treatment. Students are also required to treat a variety of children and adolescents on a less intensive basis and to gain experience of psychotherapy with a family, or with a group of children or adolescents. Students are also required to have experience of working with one or more parents whose children may or may not be in treatment. Students are expected to undertake assessment work and to have experience of brief work and consultation with children, young people and families, normally as a member of a multidisciplinary team within the NHS. Consultation to and work with community organisations are encouraged and research work is encouraged both during and after the training. Patients are referred from among those in the NHS clinical setting in which the student is working.

4.3 Supervision

Students receive individual weekly supervision on each of their intensive therapy training cases from a different supervisor. They will also be a member of a small supervision group meeting weekly and are offered a range of clinical seminars including year based clinical seminars, work with parents, and a number of specialised seminars, for example, on assessment work, brief counselling, family therapy. There are also opportunities for attending specialist workshops, for example, eating disorders, autism, adoption and fostering, groups. Students are expected to attend a number of departmental and clinic events. Students are required to attend a weekly theoretical seminar for four years. Each student has a personal tutor who is available for consultation about all aspects of the work, discussion of any problems that may arise, and to help students in finding suitable employment opportunities at the point of qualification.

4.4 Written work and course attendance

In order to qualify, each student is required to produce a substantial clinical paper, together with a record of clinical experience and training events attended. In addition, since 1996, the course has provided an academic as well as professional qualification with registration for the postgraduate degree of Masters in Psychoanalytic Psychotherapy at the University of East London. For this, each student has to provide a portfolio of written work and a clinical paper of between 8,000 and 12,000 words.

4.5 Assessment, standards and ethical requirements

Students are now required to sign an agreement to abide by the ACP Code of Ethics.

The training standards of the course are monitored by visits of accreditation of the training from the ACP at approximately three-yearly intervals. These visits examine all aspects of the training and include interviews with current and past trainees of the course. The course as a whole is required to meet the criteria of the ACP's Outline of Training and Quality Standards, including the professional Code of Ethics.

5. TRAINEE RESPONSE

1. Why this course was chosen

1.1 What made people decide to train?
The Tavistock has the reputation of being a centre of excellence, which is the reason why many people chose this particular training. Many professionals develop an interest in psychodynamic thinking through their previous work, which has introduced them to literature or part time courses and conferences at the Tavistock and provided contact with those teaching on this course. This has influenced their choice when deciding where to train; they chose the Tavistock in order to work with and be supervised by those they know and respect.

Some people chose this course in order to gain a qualification recognised by the NHS, and which is also the first stage towards achieving a Doctorate, through its association with the University of East London.

1.2 What were the aspects of this course that were most attractive?
People were drawn to the apprentice/experience style of teaching and learning. There are close, regular levels of supervision in clinical practice provided at the Tavistock with a wide choice of specialist workshops to attend. Combined with a major theoretical input, an attractive balance is provided.

Some trainees were influenced by the mandatory intensive personal analysis, which plays a crucial role in personal development.

1.3 What was your experience of the selection procedure?
Completion of the M7 (infant and toddler observation) course or equivalent is necessary in order to proceed to this course (M8).

Application to the M8 course is felt by some to be rigorous, and the selection procedure is regarded by many as mysterious and somewhat intimidating, although the support and advice provided by personal tutors was found by many to be invaluable. The interview procedure, whilst intimidating beforehand, was generally experienced as non-threatening and satisfying.

1.4 Before the start of the course, how informed did you feel about each stage of the training?
There are mixed feelings about how well informed people feel they are. There are not 'stages' as such, but a lot of information about the course is given at the beginning of the training. Most relevant information is available from both tutors and distributed literature, but there is so much that it is difficult to absorb everything at the beginning.

2. The atmosphere of the course
Some trainees do all their training and clinical work within the Tavistock but the majority are employed by clinics both in London and spread across the UK. Some trainees hold posts split between two clinics. Seminars and workshops take place during the week, but are concentrated on one day for those trainees who attend the Tavistock on one day only.

2.1 How do you feel about the way in which information is communicated?
On the whole it is felt that information is communicated well, if occasionally inconsistently, and that this is continually being improved. Some 'out of London' trainees feel that the communication between their clinics and the training school could be improved.

2.2 What do you find the most confusing aspect of the training?
One of the most confusing aspects of the training, which may be the same with any training is how to manage oneself whilst in analysis and working as a clinician; possible identification with the patient, the parent of the patient, and so on.

Some find difficulty in balancing their training needs for the course with the specific work demands of the clinics that employ them.

2.3 How much opportunity do you have to share thoughts and feelings with fellow trainees?
During the first year trainees attend more seminars as a year than in other years and this is felt as a loss during the second year. It seems that as they progress,

trainees feel there are sufficient opportunities to talk to colleagues, both informally or during seminars. For some, finding this time can be difficult, as timetables are so full. Sharing thoughts and feelings with fellow trainees is considered extremely valuable.

2.4 What do you feel about the methods of teaching?
The methods of teaching are felt to be very good. Some of the seminars are rather large, due to popular demand and these are felt to be less satisfactory. Some trainees who only attend the Tavistock for one day during the week find the necessary long and tight schedule of the day rather demanding.

2.5 What did you think about the way assessments were done to allow you to progress to the next stages of training?
The lack of clear awareness of how one is progressing has been voiced by several as confusing, at some time or other during the course, maybe due to the absence of formal assessment stages and reviews. Some trainees would like more ongoing feedback on their individual strengths and weaknesses.

There is a very clear definition between M7 and M8; however, the progress assessment stages during the four or five years of M8 have been unclear in the past. A new mandatory annual tutorial for the trainee with both personal tutor and service supervisor is being introduced in order for formal feedback to take place.

2.6 Has the course met your expectations?
The general feeling is that expectations are unclear at the beginning of the training but as they become more real they are met. There are difficulties for some in finding the appropriate training case at the right time and in the right place, especially for those in separate clinics. One trainee voiced an opinion held by many: 'This training has changed me more than I could have expected and taught me more, and on a deeper level than I could have known.'

2.7 How do you feel about your future with the organisation?
Most trainees wish to maintain contact with the Tavistock; either through attending conferences and workshops, or more directly by supervising or teaching.

2.8 What plans do trainees have for future practice and possible balance of different sorts of work in their career?
The common desire is to work within the NHS, maybe with some private work, and there is a growing interest in research. Some are interested in teaching or consultation to other professions or becoming involved in the political/organisational side of the profession.

AUTHOR'S COMMENTS

The advantages of training at the Tavistock in child psychotherapy are considerable: the quality and range of staff and facilities, some funded posts, access to research facilities and academic degrees on top of clinical training and the breadth of international experience of fellow trainees.

Some may find the Kleinian approach in the majority of teachers and supervisors dominates theoretical and technical matters to the point where other views are excluded. For some this will be an attraction; others may be put off.

The occasional difficulties reported in the trainee response suggests that at times, knowing where you are in this big enterprise can be daunting. This appears to be the case particularly between the course and the clinical settings outside where trainees may be working. Attempts to improve feedback and ongoing assessment appear to be well received.

Like other trainings where there are people divided between being self-supporting and funded, there are possible conflicts in demands and support. The Tavistock is also committed to understanding the management and creative use of group dynamics through its group relations training programme, which might help participants in learning from as well as dealing with these and other complexities.

2.4   Couple and Group Trainings

THE TAVISTOCK MARITAL STUDIES INSTITUTE (TMSI – UKCP/PPS)

120 Belsize Lane, London NW3 5BA
Tel. 020 7447 2367 Fax. 020 7435 1080
E-mail: tmsi@tmsi.org.uk

The Tavistock Marital Studies Institute (TMSI) training is for practitioners with post-qualifying experience in couple or individual work. It will appeal to psychotherapists, counsellors, psychologists, social workers, doctors, psychiatrists, nurses and others who wish to work as a psychoanalytical psychotherapist with couples.

Couple psychotherapy provides a unique opportunity to observe and understand the way that intrapsychic conflicts of one partner impact on those of the other and lead to enactments within the couple relationship. For some, often those who would not seek individual help, couple psychotherapy can be a powerful vehicle for intrapsychic and interpersonal change. Couples are offered long-term open-ended psychotherapy. A unique aspect of this training is that the structure of couple psychotherapy often involves a co-working pair of psychotherapists. For the trainee, this opportunity to work alongside a senior member of staff is a challenging learning experience. The co-therapy relationship is a valuable tool for exploring projections and counter-transference to a couple, as well as to each therapist individually.

1. HISTORY OF ORGANISATION

Founded in 1948 as The Family Discussion Bureau, TMSI has developed within an ethos that is characteristic of the work of the Tavistock and Portman Clinics Trust with whom it shares a building and has strong professional links.

In 1999 the TMSI was granted academic recognition by the University of East London for its clinical training, to become a practice-based research degree. The Professional Doctorate in Couple Psychoanalytic Psychotherapy is the first in the UK.

2. THEORETICAL ORIENTATION AND CURRICULUM

The TMSI has developed in the psychoanalytic tradition and its work is focused into three main activities, which support and inform each other:

- Training
- Practice-based research
- Psychoanalytic psychotherapy for couples.

Clinical trainings
The TMSI offers:

- Clinical Training in Couple Psychoanalytic Psychotherapy
- Doctorate which incorporates the Clinical Training and research into couple relationships
- Conversion Training (can also be undertaken as the Professional Doctorate).

Pre-Clinical Course
The TMSI offers a two-year part-time MA in the Psychoanalytic Study of the Couple Relationship, which is not a prerequisite for the Clinical Training, but may be an appropriate pathway for those whose professional and academic work needs further development prior to training.

Clinical Training in Couple Psychoanalytic Psychotherapy
This is a part-time intensive training over a minimum of four years, leading to a professional qualification as a Couple Psychoanalytical Psychotherapist, and eligibility for full membership of the Society of Psychoanalytical Marital Psychotherapists (SPMP) – see section 3.6. Graduates are eligible for registration with the United Kingdom Council of Psychotherapy (UKCP).

Curriculum

Weekly events
Infant observation: (to observe a baby in his/her own home) and seminar (1 year).
Psychoanalytic theory: a reading seminar, which takes a historical and thematic approach, linking to an understanding of unconscious couple interaction (3 years).
The development of psychoanalytic thought: a lecture series run by the Tavistock Clinic (1 year).
Research Methodology and Writing Seminar: commencing in Year 3.
Supervision: (see section 4.3).
Clinical Seminar: clinical work is presented and technique discussed (minimum of three years).

Other events
Psychiatric placement: fortnightly, for a minimum of six months, for those students with insufficient experience of working with psychiatric illness.
Group relations event: for five days, at the Tavistock Centre.

The professional doctorate in couple psychoanalytic psychotherapy
Five years. Combines an intensive clinical training with advanced academic research.

Graduates are eligible for the same professional registration as specified under section 3.1.

Curriculum
Part One: The first three years comprise the same elements as those listed under section 3.1 above, but with a higher expectation of students' written work for the

research components. During Part One most of the clinical requirements will be completed, and the first stage of the research programme commenced.

Part Two spans Years 4 and 5. In Year 4 students will complete their clinical requirements and start the fieldwork for their research. In Year 5 students can expect to be completing their research and writing up their final thesis.

Part Two includes the following elements: Research Supervision; Advanced Research Seminars; Research Project Workshops, of varying frequency.

Conversion Training in both the Clinical Training in Couple Psychoanalytic Psychotherapy and the Professional Doctorate in Couple Psychoanalytic Psychotherapy (see section 3.2 for admission requirements).

3. TRAINING STRUCTURE

3.1 Training committee
Joanna Rosenthall (Organising Tutor), MSc, BSc, CQSW, SPMP (FM) Dorothy Judd, PhD, BA, Dip. Art. Th., PGCE, MACP, TSP, SPMP (FM) Mary Morgan, BA, MSc, CQSW, Dip. Marital Psychotherapy, SPMP (FM).

3.2 Selection procedure and admission
Selected students undergo two interviews. Applications for training have to be received by the end of April each year.

Admission requirements
- Several years post-qualifying experience in couple or individual work.
- Personal psychoanalysis or psychotherapy (see section 4.1).
- Relevant academic and/or professional qualifications, to MA or equivalent level. This can include counselling trainings.
- For Conversion Trainings: successful completion of a previous training in psychoanalytic psychotherapy (subject to approval by the Training Committee).

Applicants with lesser degrees may apply for admission with 'advanced standing' where they can produce evidence of prior learning, which is equivalent to identified components within Part One of the programme. Details upon request.

3.3 Time commitment per week and length of training
Clinical Training in Couple Psychoanalytic Psychotherapy and Professional Doctorate in Couple Psychoanalytic Psychotherapy
See above (Curriculum), sections 4.2 and 4.3.
- Years 1–3: approx. 6½ hours seminars/supervision (minimum) per week.
- Years 4–5: approx. 3½ hours per week seminars/supervision per week.

3.4 Financial cost of training at different stages

(i) Clinical Training		£3,000 p.a.
(ii) Professional Doctorate	Years 1 & 2	£3,000 p.a.
	Years 3 & 4	£4,500 p.a.
	Year 5	£1,500 p.a.

(iii) Conversion Training   £2,600 p.a.
(iv) Conversion Training leading to
    Professional Doctorate   Years 1 & 2   £4,100 p.a.
                                        Year 3   £1,500 p.a.

These fees cover all training costs including supervision and use of the Tavistock Centre library, but not personal psychotherapy. They are relevant for 1999/2000. Subject to annual review.

3.5 Interruptions in training
The Training Committee would discuss circumstances around each situation of prolonged absence, and, where appropriate, students would be facilitated in completing their training.

3.6 Graduating and beginning a career
All graduates of the TMSI Clinical trainings are eligible to become Full Members of the professional body, the Society of Psychoanalytical Marital Psychotherapists (SPMP). Student Members are welcome to take part in the Society's events. Professional development programmes continue for qualified Full Members, who can also receive private referrals from the Couple Psychotherapy Service run by the Society. A journal (the *SPMP Bulletin*) is published once a year. The Society currently has over sixty members, with an increasing number outside London.

3.7 Numbers of students per intake
We generally accept four new clinical students per academic year. The total student group at any one time does not exceed 20.

4. CLINICAL AND ACADEMIC REQUIREMENTS

4.1 Personal therapy
Students are required to be in a minimum of three-times-weekly psychoanalytic psychotherapy or in analysis with a member of the Institute of Psychoanalysis, or the Society of Analytical Psychology or someone deemed suitable by the Training Committee. This must commence twelve months prior to the training.
    Conversion Training: further psychotherapy may be a requirement, at the discretion of the Training Committee.

4.2 Clinical requirements
Trainees work with a minimum of six couples during their training: two couples to be seen weekly (eighteen months minimum); four couples to be seen weekly (one year minimum); five couples for assessment. (Conversion Training students' caseload is less than the above. Details upon application.)
    Initially, trainees' cases will be shared with a senior staff co-therapist. Later they are required to undertake cases on their own, and they may co-work with co-trainees. Trainees and their co-therapists meet for weekly discussion. All cases are provided within the TMSI.

4.3 Supervision

Students receive weekly supervision until the end of the third year or until clinical requirements have been satisfactorily completed, whichever is the later.

All supervisors are TMSI staff members. The supervisor has the primary clinical responsibility for the trainee's cases.

4.4 Written work and course attendance

Papers required (4,000 words each): theory (2); infant observation; clinical; research methodology; clinical paper (9,000 words).

Professional Doctorate Students only: literature search skills paper (5,000 words); research proposal (3,000 words). The Doctoral thesis (30,000 words) will be expected to represent an independent and original contribution to the professional field.

4.5 Assessment, standards and ethical requirements

The TMSI operates an equal opportunities policy that aims to ensure that no user of its services is discriminated against on the grounds of race, colour, religion, ethnic or national origin, gender, marital status, sexual preference or disability.

Code of practice

There is a Code for staff, trainees and others working under the auspices of the TMSI. It is intended to protect the rights and interests of those using the Institute's services and those participating in its research activities. The Code derives from the principals contained within the Institute's Code of Ethics, the spirit of which should apply to all aspects of its work. Details available upon application.

Assessment

A continuous assessment process involving trainee, supervisor, tutor, seminar leaders, and co-therapists underpins the trainee's progress throughout the course of the clinical training.

Trainees are required to submit a regular self-assessment of their professional practice learning.

There is a Complaints and Appeals Procedure.

5. TRAINEE RESPONSE

(Author's note: This response was elicited from a single individual because the sheer business of this demanding course prevented the group from assembling something more representative.)

1. Why this course was chosen

1.1 What made people decide to train?

Because it was a psychoanalytic approach to couple psychotherapy.

I have trained in individual psychotherapy and I wanted to learn about working with couples, which I think needs more specific thought.

1.2 What were the aspects of this course that were most attractive?
I was particularly attracted to the co-therapy approach to the work and from which I could learn. Also that I could get couples to work with through TMSI.

1.3 What was your experience of the selection procedure?
I had a professional and a personal interview. These were what I had expected, and they were conducted thoughtfully.

1.4 Before the start of the course, how informed did you feel about each stage of the training?
I do not feel that the course requirements were sufficiently laid out before I started. This might be due to the fact that it is the first year of the course and I am the only student doing this component, the Conversion Course. I think the course does having teething problems and the link with the University of East London has made for some major changes from previous courses.

2. The atmosphere of the course
I think the atmosphere is friendly and that staff are approachable. There are just seven students and I think it is a friendly and cooperative group.

2.1 How do you feel about the way in which information is communicated?
Communication is reasonably good, although staff are sometimes unclear about what should be communicated as it is all so new.

2.2 What do you find the most confusing aspect of the training?
The students training together are on different courses and this can be confusing in being clear about what is required.

2.3 How much opportunity do you have to share thoughts and feelings with fellow trainees?
The times we are together are quite busy and we do not have much time together as a student group to discuss thoughts and feelings. To do this we need to find time outside of course time.

2.4 What do you feel about the methods of teaching?
The methods of teaching are fairly standard, with the clinical work, supervision and reading and clinical seminars.

2.5 What did you think about the way assessments were done to allow you to progress to the next stages of training?
The assessment procedure I have felt has been quite onerous and some of it not very helpful. We are assessed with grades, the marking of some of the assessments is done anonymously and this has felt both quite persecutory and unhelpful. This is all part of the new procedure, but it may be rethought following student responses. I think there is a tension between what is helpful and relevant to a psychotherapy training and what is required from an academic course.

2.6. Has the course met your expectations?
The course places more emphasis on academic work, essays, research seminars, than I had expected.

2.7 How do you feel about your future with the organisation?
It is not clear what the TMSI has to offer me in the future. Staff are employed by TMSI and I do not know what it has to offer graduates of the course who are not employed by it. I can become a member of the Society of Psychoanalytical Marital Psychotherapists when I qualify. This is a professional body and again it is not clear to me what this would offer. Hopefully, a collegial point of reference and a referral network.

2.8 What plans do trainees have for future practice and possible balance of different sorts of work in their career?
I intend to continue in my private work, but extending my work to working with couples as a part of my practice. Possibly making links to work in another setting if this were possible.

AUTHOR'S COMMENTS

The TMSI course provides some unique opportunities. The training is based at the Tavistock, itself a well-resourced learning community in which trainees can participate in a wide range of activities. The clinical work is also based there with the unusual advantage peculiar to couple work of being able to work alongside an experienced senior colleague as a co-therapist working jointly with a couple. The training is thorough and demanding of the level of engagement and depth required by many of the individual trainings in the form of thrice-weekly therapy and the study of interpersonal as well as intrapsychic aspects of couple relating.

The TMSI course offers flexibility. Although the basic course is demanding, lengthy and a solid clinical training, qualified practising therapists can negotiate a conversion course with reduced demands, recognising some of what they have already learned and accomplished. Additionally, there is the option of contributing to thinking in the work, through research up to Masters or Doctorate level.

The range and complexity of these different options suggests that an interview is needed to follow through the implications of each option. Each applicant will have to seriously think about the time and resources involved for their particular stage of development and aspirations in sorting out with tutors what they may wish, what will be demanded of them and what is possible. As the trainee response suggests, the academic demands may be high and not as yet well integrated within an otherwise strongly clinically based course.

INSTITUTE OF GROUP ANALYSIS (IGA – UKCP/PPS)

1 Daleham Gardens, London NW3 5BY
Tel. 020 7431 2693 Fax. 020 7431 7246
Training Office: Tel./Fax. 020 7431 2949
Web site: <http://www.igalondon.org.uk>
E-mail: iga@igalondon.org.uk

Membership of the Institute of Group Analysis is also available through the Diploma Courses in Group Analysis at Manchester and Glasgow.

For further information contact either:

The Administrator, Group Analysis North, 78 Manchester Road, Swinton, Manchester M27 5FG Tel. 0161 728 1633
or
The Administrator, The Garnethill Centre, 28 Rose Street, Glasgow G3 6RE Tel. 0141 333 0730 Fax. 0141 333 0737

The following entry pertains particularly to the London Qualifying Course except where reference is made to other trainings.

1. HISTORY OF THE ORGANISATION

S.H. Foulkes' first years as a psychoanalyst were spent in Frankfurt where the Institutes of Psychoanalysis and of Sociology enjoyed close physical and cultural connections. He was profoundly influenced by Kurt Lewin's work on field theory and his concepts of the dynamic whole, of figure and background, of belongingness, of tension and conflict and the idea of the group as a dynamic whole operating in a social field.

Another central influence in Foulkes' thinking was his teacher, the neurobiologist Kurt Goldstein. Foulkes developed the conviction that the essence of man is social: the individual is a part of a social network, 'a little nodal point as it were' and that the neurotic position is the result of an incompatibility between the individual and his original group.

'Symptoms in themselves autistic and unsuitable for sharing exert for this very reason an increasing pressure upon the individual for expressing them. As long as he cannot express them in a better communicable way he finds no real relief.'

It was under the further influence of Norbert Elias and his synthesis of the study of society through sociology that Foulkes was able to develop a new form of psychotherapy, bringing his individual patients together in a group to study and facilitate communication and understanding between them. He was able to test and develop this model into the first comprehensive theory of group analytic psychotherapy while working as an army psychiatrist at the Northfield Military Hospital.

In 1952, with colleagues, he founded the Group Analytic Society to further develop and disseminate group analytic ideas and, in 1971, the Institute of Group Analysis and a full training programme of group analytic psychotherapy.

2. THEORETICAL ORIENTATION AND CURRICULUM

The clinical training leads to membership of the Institute and the widely recognised professional title of 'Group Analyst'. In conjunction with Birkbeck College, London, trainee group analysts will be awarded the MSc in Group Analysis on completion of an extended dissertation.

Completion of an approved Introductory Course is a requirement for entry to the qualifying training. These usually run for 30 sessions over a year and offer an experiential group and lectures/seminars.

IGA Introductory General Courses are currently available at eleven sites around the UK – London; Manchester; Sheffield; Cambridge; Turvey, Beds; Oxford; Bath; Exeter; Southampton; Brighton and Glasgow.

The Academic Programme of the London Qualifying Course runs over nine terms on Monday evenings and Thursday afternoons.

First year

- A critical introduction to the assumptions and context of group-analytic theory
- An introduction to group-analytic method
- An outline of psychoanalytic theory from classical to contemporary including Freud, Klein, British School of Object Relations and Self-Psychology
- Foulkes and other principal theorists. Origins and method.

Second year

- Human Development: The individual
- Human Development: The group
- Relational theories in clinical practice
- The family of group therapies I
- Forensic and other special applications
- Psychopathology.

Third year

- Contemporary issues in group psychotherapy
- Clinical issues in individual and group psychotherapy
- Therapeutic communities; large groups and organisational settings
- Forensic and other special applications II
- The evolving identity of the group analyst
- Theory projects.

3. TRAINING STRUCTURE

3.1 Training committee

The Training and Academic Policy Committee is directly accountable to Council. It is responsible for the Institutes' training policy and takes an overview of the Institutes' training activities and the deployment of its resources.

3.2 Selection procedure and admission

Academic requirements: Medical and non-medical candidates with a University degree or equivalent professional qualification and experience in the field may apply. Some academic requirements may be waived for applicants with exceptional professional experience.

Prior training: Applicants are required to have completed an approved General Course prior to training.

Prior psychotherapy: Candidates are normally required to have been in group-analytic psychotherapy prior to application.

Psychiatric experience: The Qualifying Courses Committee must be satisfied that students have adequate experience of work with psychiatric patients prior to commencement of the formal part of the training.

Admissions procedure: The Director of Training is available to consult with prospective applicants. Once a written application has been received, the selection process consists of a clinical interview with a Consultant Psychiatrist member of the Institute, followed by a further interview with a Board of Assessors to whom the Consultant's report is submitted. There is an Admissions Committee that receives all the reports and arrives at a recommendation, which is submitted, to the London Courses Committee where a final decision is made. (The same procedures apply for the UK Diplomas, Manchester and Glasgow.)

3.3 Time commitment and length of training
The academic curriculum of the London Qualifying Course, beginning in September, takes place over nine terms of some twelve weeks on Monday evenings and Thursday afternoons. The whole training takes some four years, sometimes five. There are additional time commitments when students run training groups, see individual patients if necessary and attend supervision groups. Most students remain in full-time employment throughout the training.

3.4 Financial cost of training at different stages
2000/2001 Fees: £2,368 per annum, plus £308 MSc registration fee; monthly instalment option available

Supervision of individual psychotherapy: £190 per term

Selection Fees: £279

Separate personal group analytic fees.

3.5 Interruptions in training
Interruptions in training due to external conditions will be considered on their own merits and depend on individual circumstances.

3.6 Graduating and beginning a career
Qualification is at the discretion of the Council of the Institute, which receives recommendations from the London Course Committee (see section 4.4 below).

Graduation and admission to the Institute
There is an annual Graduation Ceremony for new members of the Institute. On qualification members are entitled to:

- use of the qualifications, 'Group Analyst' and 'Member Institute of Group Analysis' (Mem. Inst. GA)
- receive a copy of the Institutes' quarterly newsletter, *Dialogue*
- attend the Annual General Meeting of the Institute as a voting member
- attendance at the Institute's post-graduate events.

Members are eligible for:

- membership of the Institute's Council and Committees
- staff responsibilities in the Institute's Introductory, Regional, Overseas and Qualifying Courses
- registration as a Group Analyst with the United Kingdom Council for Psychotherapy
- full membership of the Group Analytic Society.

The Institute has an Organisational Consultancy Service and a Clinical Referral Service from which members may benefit.

3.7 Numbers of students per intake
The Institute has no policy on student numbers but, because of the limitations of space, may be constrained to defer applicants.

4. CLINICAL AND ACADEMIC REQUIREMENTS

4.1 Personal therapy
Qualifying course students undertake a twice-weekly personal group analysis with a Training Group Analyst throughout their training. They are required to have spent at least one year in this group prior to the commencement of formal training, but this period is usually longer.

4.2 Clinical requirements
Students are required to conduct two groups under supervision. The first, set up early in the training and continuing for a *minimum* of six full terms, is a once-weekly clinical group for adults. The second, conducted in the final year of training, is of shorter duration and can accommodate students' own special areas of interest.

4.3 Supervision
For the first group, students attend a weekly supervision seminar during the academic term throughout the training period and continue for as long as required by the London Course Committee. For the second group, students attend a weekly supervision group during the academic term of the concluding year with a different supervisor.

Students will need to show competence in therapeutic work with individuals. Those with insufficient experience will be required to take on patients for psychotherapy and to attend a weekly supervision seminar for the first two years of training.

4.4 Written work and course attendance
Students are required to present essays for assessment at the end of year one and year two and a theory paper of 3,000–5,000 words in term seven, which forms the basis of the MSc dissertation of 12,000 words presented at the end of term nine.

Students must present a clinical paper at the end of their training. An approved theme in group-analytic psychotherapy, based on clinical material recorded during the training period, is presented in a paper of approximately 10,000 words within twelve months of completing course requirements. Qualification is then at the discretion of the Council of the Institute, which considers the recommendations of the Panel of Readers.

4.5 Assessment, standards and ethical requirements
The Institute has available a 'Statement of Ethical Code of Practice for Group Members and Students' which details expectations of professional competency, responsibility and conduct. Council has recently established an Ethics Committee.

5. TRAINEE RESPONSE

1. Why this course was chosen

1.1 What made people decide to train?
Completion of the IGA Introductory Course and participation in a personal therapy group are prerequisites for the Qualifying Course application, so all candidates have experienced the IGA culture in theory and practice before seeking to train. Most did some research into alternatives and with personal and career development in mind. Many have contact with Group Analysts at work and so know something of the philosophy and values of the Foulkesian tradition.

1.2 What were the aspects of this course that were most attractive?
The IGA's high reputation as a mature training and an outstanding clinical course with attractive social values have traditionally influenced candidates. There is now the additional option of the combined MSc in Group Analysis at Birkbeck.

1.3 What was your experience of the selection procedure?
This involves an extensive series of hurdles, so the IGA and the applicant may experience each other several times in different situations. It can be confrontational, challenging and robust. The selection stages include assessment for training group analysis, report by the group therapist, the psychological/psychiatric assessment, the panel interview and any pre-course requirement such as the need for a psychiatric attachment and/or to give further experience with individual patients before starting the training.

1.4 Before the start of the course, how informed did you feel about each stage of the training?
A handbook and reading list are issued in the July before the course starts in September. The reading in the first year in particular is very demanding. Also, the logistics involved in finding a host institution for starting the first group under supervision in the second term need to be anticipated.

2. The atmosphere of the course

2.1 How do you feel about the way in which information is communicated?
Personal communications with and from the staff are generally warm and positive but formal written communications are somewhat of a hit-and-miss matter, giving

rise to anxiety from time to time. This may be partly due to the complexity of the interrelated elements of the training which on the London Qualifying Course amount to an individual menu of times and places which is unique for each candidate, although seminars and supervision are shared with colleagues.

2.2 What do you find the most confusing aspect of the training?
The most confusing aspect of the training is the need for coordination of the different aspects and the sheer challenge of reconciling them with work and family commitments.

2.3 How much opportunity do you have to share thoughts and feelings with fellow trainees?
During the first term of the first year the opportunity to share is difficult until people get to know each other. However, each term includes opportunities for a peer group to meet and close relationships develop with colleagues who are in the same supervision groups, regardless of their year.

2.4 What do you feel about the methods of teaching?
The teaching methods vary, although the content is always of a high standard. Traditionally there has been a lot of reading for seminars but not much writing as a course requirement. This is changing with the introduction of the Birkbeck MSc. from September 1999 which will require written work at the end of the first and second years, as well as the traditional theory paper in the third year and clinical paper in the fourth year. Emphasis is placed on learning from supervised experience in conducting a small analytic group and an applied short-term group. Together with personal therapy over the course of the training, the cumulative effect of these learning streams is to absorb a strong culture. Overall the teaching is good and the learning practical.

2.5 What did you think about the way assessments were done to allow you to progress to the next stages of training?
The organisation has operated traditionally on the basis that 'no news is good news'. The default assumption was that people would hear if they were doing badly. The policy is quite clear but the practices of individual supervisors vary considerably, and while some have begun discussing their draft or final reports with students this is not yet universal. It is sometimes necessary to prompt for direct feedback. Generally both the assessment criteria and results could be made more explicit. The recent introduction of formal progress reviews with the Director of Training at the end of the second year is a step in the right direction.

2.6 Has the course met your expectations?
Has exceeded expectations but perhaps in surprising ways. We continue to be impressed with the power of the clinical training as time goes along but nothing could have prepared us for the degree of physical exhaustion, for the investment of time, earnings and commitment. However, the training does bring lives and careers together, in ways that we are still discovering.

2.7 How do you feel about your future with the organisation?
Is perhaps best summed up as positive and cautiously optimistic.

2.8 What plans do trainees have for future practice and possible balance of different sorts of work in their career?
A wide range of options is open to qualified Group Analysts, many of whom are attracted to additional earnings from private practice and often an increased salary or enhanced career prospects for those working in the NHS when they qualify. The qualification enables graduands to broaden their career options to include clinical, management or consultancy work in business and the public service. Most Group Analysts seem to run a portfolio career, even when a career NHS post is the centrepiece, for the time being.

AUTHOR'S COMMENTS

The IGA course is not just the application of psychoanalytic ideas to the group context. It offers a course in the integration of psychoanalysis as a social context. This means treatment and learning within the group that provides a profound access to re-enactments of unconscious processes in a way that can be re-experienced and re-negotiated in both the analytic patient groups that trainees participate in as well as in the training course as a whole. Group-analysts-in-training therefore have the experience of being patients alongside other patients with whom to identify, not available in the individual trainings in quite the same way.

It is the commitment to treating the whole course and the institution within which it takes place as a microcosm of society that gives the experience its distinctive character. It also means for the trainee that there is a lot to get into the three qualifying years after the introductory course. There is also the potentially confusing situation of reconciling other demands with the course referred to in the trainee response.

Not least do trainees have to take into account the huge uncertainties involved in the experience of interviewing for and forming, two groups. In addition, the literature in the field is huge, including not just group psychology, but also psychoanalysis and analytical psychology.

The course has a reputation of being challenging, demanding but also providing an extremely supportive atmosphere, in which participation is forged across all the difficulties in such an experience. The course also insists on individual work so that graduates are prepared for every aspect of clinical work whether in private practice or in the NHS where many senior members of the IGA work with considerable recognition and responsibility.

Beyond training there is the prospect of an internationally enriching membership of a growing European membership of the Group-Analytic Society with opportunities to participate in events that aim to challenge barriers and prejudices in society of many kinds.

One of the questions worth asking is about the problems and advantages of group analysis versus psycho/analysis. Each approach may expose very different aspects of the personality, but again each may also hide aspects of the personality. The more intense individual trainings emphasise the importance of a training analysis or therapy in order to expose and work through the psychotic and narcissistic aspects of the personality. It is worth asking whether group analysis can achieve the same thoroughness. Many group analysts, like those individually trained, seek further personal therapy individually, whether linked to further training or not.

GOLDSMITHS COLLEGE, UNIVERSITY OF LONDON (UL:G – UKCP/UPA) POSTGRADUATE DIPLOMA IN GROUP PSYCHOTHERAPY, UNIT FOR PSYCHOTHERAPEUTIC STUDIES

Lewisham Way, New Cross, London SE14 6NW
Tel. 020 7919 7237 Fax. 020 7919 7236
Enquiries: 0800 0900659
E-mail: K.power@gold.ac.uk

1. HISTORY OF THE ORGANISATION

The course was established at Goldsmiths College in 1989, by a number of group psychotherapy graduates from a private institute. The basic structure has been expanded and adapted over the twelve years of the course. A number of additions were made to meet the criteria of the PP section of the UKCP and the Universities Psychotherapy Association (UPA). Over fifty graduates have passed through the training during this time, most of whom are now registered with the UKCP's National Register of Psychotherapists.

2. THEORETICAL ORIENTATION AND CURRICULUM

The Postgraduate Diploma in Group Psychotherapy provides a thorough training in the clinical, experiential and theoretical aspects of the discipline with a group-analytic orientation. There is a Foundation course for those who require this preliminary experience.

3. TRAINING STRUCTURE

3.1 Training committee
The course is offered to the public under the rules and regulations of Goldsmiths College, within the department of Professional and Continuing Education (PACE). The course is administered generally by the Programmes Coordinator for Group Psychotherapy programmes, while the course in detail is administered by the Course Coordinator. Regularly employed staff contribute to the continuous assessment process. Written work is read by the External Assessor, who in turn meets each year with the finishing year for their assessment of the course. There is also in place a Course Monitoring programme, which gathers information from the students once each term in a plenary meeting between staff and students.

3.2 Selection procedure and admission
Applicants need a first degree and/or a professional qualification in a health or social care related profession. A minimum of six months' therapy prior to an application

is also required. Exceptional candidates may lack one or other of the above. The College's Equal Opportunities (EO) policy affects all applicants for all courses. We regret to say that the building in current use is not suitable for wheelchair users, or for those unable to use stairs. The EO policy is applied throughout the course.

3.3 Time commitment per week and length of training

The length of the modular teaching programme is three years. The minimum time commitment – teaching, supervision, experiential and psychotherapy groups and training groups will total about ten hours each week. This will not include reading, library research, and travel not only to the College once a week but also to a psychotherapy group and to the student's placement(s). Some students extend their work into a fourth year in order to continue and complete supervision and/or clinical papers.

3.4 Financial cost of training at different stages

The fee for the course starting in October 2000 will be approximately £1,450, payable in three amounts through the year. This covers all College-based activity for that year, as well as the benefits of a university's resources and campus. Students will have to pay separately for their personal psychotherapy group. Extensions into a fourth year are charged at slightly higher rate than during the previous three years.

3.5 Interruptions in Training

Students may apply to the College for such interruption in studies as make continuance not possible, for example, serious illness, pregnancy, loss of job.

3.6 Graduating and beginning a career

Graduates will need to join the Universities Psychotherapy Association (UPA) as their Member Organisation through which they can be registered with the UKCP. In addition graduates are encouraged to join one or more of the following to maintain their professional involvement and for continuing professional development: the Goldsmiths Association for Group Psychotherapy, the British Association for Group Psychotherapy, the Group-Analytic Society. All three of these bodies encourage members to become involved with both their organisation and in the pursuit of research and the production of workshops. Graduates have chosen to take their new skills back into their continuing employment, to move into part-time employment and establish themselves in a mix of private and sessional work, or to set up their own therapy and consultative practices.

The degree of involvement is the individual's decision, yet it must be borne in mind that psychotherapy as with most other professions expects that its members will maintain their own personal and professional development in the years following the award of the Diploma. To study for a higher degree in psychotherapy, to take a further training, to branch out into staff team consultation and to apply group analysis to non-clinical settings are further possibilities for graduates, in addition to building a private practice alone or one with a small number of similarly minded people.

3.7 Numbers of students per intake

There is a ceiling of twelve students for each intake.

4. CLINICAL AND ACADEMIC REQUIREMENTS

4.1 Personal therapy

Applicants need to have been in personal therapy for a minimum of six months prior to making an application. Once accepted students need to enter a psychotherapy group, the theoretical orientation of which must be appropriate to the course. They attend this regularly throughout the course programme and are encouraged to stay for some time afterwards. This is in a once-weekly group, or twice weekly, if an individual chooses. There is also the experiential group, which is a part of the course programme.

Therapists are contacted twice during the course, once before the student starts to form the main clinical training group and once before the award of the Diploma. Therapists will be contacted, and are asked to contact the Course Coordinator, should circumstances occur which require this action.

4.2 Clinical requirements

Unlike with individual training, most training placements are with the NHS or other counselling or psychotherapy or healthcare organisation. The College cannot guarantee such a placement although practically no one has gone without. The course does have links to a number of regular placements throughout London and the South East of England.

4.3 Supervision

Supervision is once weekly at the College in small groups, which continue through the three years of the course programme and beyond if necessary. Additionally, each placement requires a supervision commitment from each student, which is almost always weekly: each placement bears medical responsibility for the patients involved. Together this will provide 250+ hours of supervision through the course.

4.4 Written work and course attendance

Each student has to write three essays: one on theory, one on clinical practice and one on transcultural psychotherapy. The clinical paper is 8,000 words, and based on the work done in the long-term psychotherapy training group. The others are 5,000–6,000 words. Written work is double-marked in the College and read also by the External Assessor.

The College's minimum attendance is 75 per cent. We seek 100 per cent from our students.

4.5 Assessment, standards and ethical requirements

The Code of Ethics and Code of Practice of the University Psychotherapy Association governs the course. Headings addressed are: Qualification; Terms, conditions and methods of practice; Confidentiality; Professional Relationship; Research; Publication; Practitioner Competence; Indemnity Insurance; Detrimental Behaviour.

The course is covered by the Quality Assurance mechanisms of the College as a whole. Additionally, the UPA accredits the course's professional basis. Assessment of each student is annually and on a continuing basis. The Final Examination is when students are 'examined' on essays, clinical case study, practical examination (actual clinical work) assessment of course work (including attendance).

The ability to conduct a slow-open psychotherapy group, to conduct a closed group, to manage three short-term individual clients in order to facilitate change remain the first criteria of assessment. Supervisors' reports and opinions are used here, as well as those of the personal tutor and the experiential group conductor. The ability to write at length about the work undertaken and the theories that sustain this work is also necessary.

5. TRAINEE RESPONSE

1. Why this course was chosen
People on the course typically come from a background in the caring professions. Reasons given for choosing Goldsmiths included: group therapy appealed as a way of giving their black client group greater access to therapy; the group setting is able to cope with variety in patients' backgrounds and the possibility of feedback. Someone with a teaching background had an abiding interest in groups and belief in their efficacy for learning. A residential social worker had always wanted to train, feeling that groups gave more space for reflection. The course's location in South London is a definite advantage for those living in South London and further South.

It was more affordable than other Group Trainings. It was seen to take the issues of race and gender seriously. It was recommended by word of mouth.

Selection procedure
This is by application, individual and group interview. Although nerve racking, this procedure was seen as appropriate and interesting, particularly the group interview.

The pre-course information was clear but didn't and probably couldn't really describe how much the course would impact on an individual's life. The university offers help to dyslexic students.

2. The atmosphere of the course
If there were administrative hiccups they could sometimes be experienced as devastating, but this can be seen as part of the learning process and a response to the transferences that were evoked by the levels of regression and dependency experienced in this type of training.

Confusing aspects of the course include: what issues to bring to the student experiential group and what to personal group therapy, how to link theory and practice, and having double supervision of clinical work. All these confusions, though painful, were seen as a rich source of learning.

Thoughts and feelings could be, and are, shared with fellow trainees in seminars, discussions after lectures, supervision, the weekly experiential group, the termly study days which include lectures, discussions and a large group experience comprising all three years of the course. Informal exchanges also take place in breaks.

Teaching methods are seen as appropriate and useful. They include all the above and provide opportunities to learn from experts, academics experienced group analysts and psychotherapists and each other.

Assessment of clinical work is done by self, peers, supervisors and tutors. It is fairly unobtrusive unless something is perceived as going wrong. Written papers are double marked and criteria are clear.

Comments on the course included: it was a profound experience, I see myself differently in my family network, I have grown up, it more than met my expectations, it was a fascinating, absorbing experience that has changed my life.

Future Plans: Some students go on to do the MA, many are involved with the Goldsmiths Association of Group Psychotherapists, some on the council that runs it.

Some ex-students use the training in their current jobs, some combine private practice with running groups in the NHS and other organisations.

AUTHOR'S COMMENTS

This course is one of the few with a prominent equal opportunities policy aiming to make psychotherapy explicitly available to racial minorities. Its urban and new university setting provides a community context in which the group-analytic commitment to exploring the external as well as the internal lives of patients and therapists contain the possibility of being experienced and explored in depth.

The course is a demanding one with both clinical requirements in the form of recruiting and running an ongoing group, as well as meeting university criteria for academic work.

Emphasis on peer assessment as well as tutor assessment makes for collaboration and a less hierarchical structure than in some trainings. This produces exposure and tensions of a particular kind that may enrich or compromise judgements.

TURVEY INSTITUTE OF GROUP-ANALYTIC PSYCHOTHERAPY
(TURGAP – UKCP/UPA)
MSc IN GROUP PSYCHOTHERAPY VALIDATED BY OXFORD BROOKES
UNIVERSITY

Turvey Abbey, Abbey Mews, Turvey, Beds MK43 8DH
Tel. 01234 881 617 Fax. 01234 881 742
E-mail: abbey.mews@which.net

1. HISTORY OF THE ORGANISATION

The MSc in Group Psychotherapy began in 1993 as a Diploma course at the University of Warwick. Special features of this course include its 'block weekend' structure and location in the attractive setting of Turvey Abbey, and its unique provision of weekend therapy groups composed of mixed trainee/non-trainee clients. In 1995, the course was transferred by Professor Digby Tantam to the Centre for Psychotherapeutic Studies (CPS) of the University of Sheffield. In 1998, UKCP registration in the UPA (Universities Psychotherapy Association) section was granted. In 1999/2000, due to changes in Sheffield University policy, the MSc course transferred to independent status (without instituting any major modifications to the training programme). The Turvey Institute of Group-Analytic Psychotherapy (TIGAP) was set up and established a collaborative partnership with Oxford Brookes

University as the validating academic body. Subject to final approval, this process will be completed by September 2000. Students register with Oxford Brookes University for the award of the MSc and the training progamme is run and delivered by the Turvey Institute. The process of transferring UKCP accreditation from Sheffield to Oxford Brookes is in progress.

2. THEORETICAL ORIENTATION AND CURRICULUM

The course is a four-year part-time postgraduate programme offering a full clinical and academic training in group-analytic psychotherapy. This includes a broad range of theoretical approaches to psychotherapy. Group-analytic psychotherapy was developed by Dr S.H. Foulkes during and after the Second World War. He was a training analyst at the British Psycho-Analytic Society and brought together theories from psychoanalysis, neurobiology and sociology to create a treatment model for people in groups.

Completion of an Introductory Course approved by the Institute of Group Analysis is a requirement for entry into the MSc programme. The Turvey Institute offers an Introductory Course spread over five weekends of the academic year. This includes 30 experiential group sessions, an intensive lecture/seminar programme and a Large Group experience (together with MSc students).

The academic curriculum is delivered as a modular programme, apart from the first term of the first year.

First-year students attend seminars in the Autumn term on 'An Introduction to group-analytic theory and method'.

Students then join the modular programme consisting of:

(i)   Three modules (25 hours each) which take place on the Friday evenings of the ten block weekends from January to December. These modules include lectures/seminars on key psychoanalytic concepts; key group-analytic concepts; applications of group-analytic psychotherapy.

(ii) Four one-week (five-day, 25-hour) modules which take place once a year during the last week in February. These modules cover developmental theory; psychopathology; the individual and the group; the social-psychological foundations of group therapy; professional issues in psychotherapeutic practice; research methods.

All students are assigned a tutor and offered individual/small-group tutorials.

3. TRAINING STRUCTURE

3.1 Training committee
The Training Committee is responsible for admission and enrolment of students onto the course, for delivery of the course and for internal quality assurance, and Oxford Brookes is responsible for external quality assurance and for conferring final qualifications.

3.2 Selection procedure and admission

This is a postgraduate course, but students who have equivalent professional qualifications or relevant experience may apply. Applicants must have completed an approved Introductory Course in Group Analysis prior to training. For those who have insufficient psychiatric experience it will be necessary to acquire this via a voluntary placement.

Applicants submit a letter of application together with a full CV and the names of three referees. The selection procedure consists of two interviews, a clinical interview and an academic interview. Reports are submitted to the Training Committee who make the final decisions about admission to the course.

3.3 Time commitment per week and length of training

The MSc course follows an intensive 'block training' model. The residential weekend model offers training opportunities to those whose employment excludes them from continuous weekly training.

Students attend 40 weekends (ten per year spread over four years), from Friday 5.30p.m. until Sunday 3.30p.m.

The ten weekends usually follow this pattern:

- January, February, March, June, July, September, November, December: first weekend of the month
- April: the weekend after Easter
- October: the second weekend of the month.

First-year students attend from 2p.m. on Friday afternoon for the first three block weekends, and fourth-year students attend on Saturdays and Sundays only (except when there is a large group) from January to September of their fourth year.

Four annual one-week academic modules take place from Monday to Friday during the last week in February.

Additional time commitments include setting up and running two training groups, seeing individual patients under supervision and participating in telephone conference supervision between block weekends.

3.4 Financial cost of training at different stages

Academic programme (including supervision of groups):

Course fee 2000/01: £1,950 (a full course fee is paid for each of the four years); selection fee: 1 x £80.

Fees will increase by approximately the rate of inflation each year and are payable to the Turvey Institute of Group-Analytic Therapy.

Group-analytic therapy fees: Currently £1,120 per annum, payable to The Turvey Centre for Group Therapy.

Fees may increase by the rate of inflation each year.

Accommodation:

Full board and lodging is available at Turvey for £60 per weekend (£600 per annum for the year 2000). The Secretary of the Turvey Centre can arrange either B&B or full board, either within the grounds of Turvey Abbey or nearby.

In addition, students may need to fund some supervision of individual therapy patients, if adequate supervision is not provided in their work placement.

3.5 Interruptions in training
Cases for interruption of training will be considered on an individual basis.

3.6 Graduating and beginning a career
Individuals who have successfully completed the course will receive an MSc in Group Psychotherapy (Oxford Brookes University). A Diploma in Group Psychotherapy may be awarded to students who have not submitted a dissertation but have otherwise satisfactorily completed all elements of the course.

Students are expected to continue their membership of the Group-Analytic Society (GAS) and to further their professional development by participating in seminars and workshops offered by the Turvey Institute, GAS and other group therapy organisations. The course is also a qualifying member of the European Group Analytic Training Institutions Network (EGATIN).

3.7 Numbers of students per intake
Numbers for the total student body on the four-year programme are restricted to about 25–30; that is, an average intake of five to seven students per year. Numbers may vary from year to year.

4. CLINICAL AND ACADEMIC REQUIREMENTS

4.1 Personal therapy
Students join a therapy group at Turvey, together with clients of the centre. Normally students are expected to begin their personal therapy before beginning the academic and clinical parts of the course. There are six therapy groups (one and a half hours each) per weekend; that is, 60 groups per year. Students are expected to remain in therapy for a minimum duration of four years and during that time will also participate in 20 large groups.

4.2 Clinical requirements
Students are required to set up and conduct a classical (slow-open), adult group-analytic psychotherapy group for a minimum duration of two years. They are also required to conduct a second non-classical group for a minimum of twelve sessions in an area of their choice or interest.

Students are also required to conduct individual psychotherapy with three clients: one for 12–20 sessions, one for 20–30 sessions and one for not less than 40 sessions.

4.3 Supervision
Training groups are supervised in small supervision groups during weekend blocks (four and a half hours supervision per block). Additionally, groups are supervised (in the same supervision groups) in 20 one-hour telephone conferences per year between blocks.

Therapeutic work with individuals may be supervised locally by an approved supervisor.

Students are required to remain in supervision until they have satisfactorily completed clinical requirements.

4.4 Written work and course attendance

A minimum of 80 per cent attendance is required for all aspects of the training. Failing this, students may be required to repeat academic modules or extend their time in therapy and/or supervision.

Students are required to submit theory assignments and case studies for assessment and, towards the end of their training, a clinical paper based on clinical material from the two-year training group.

Completion of the MSc will require submission of a 15,000-word dissertation.

4.5 Assessment, standards and ethical requirements

Continuous assessment takes place within the supervision groups. Annual supervision reports and assessed written work (assignments, case studies, clinical papers and the dissertation) are presented to an annual Examination Board chaired by Oxford Brookes University, with an appointed External Examiner. Guidelines for assessment are available to staff and students.

Annual reviews and other University quality assurance procedures ensure the maintenance of academic standards.

The Turvey Institute operates an equal opportunities policy and members and students are expected abide by its ethical code regarding professional competency, responsibility and conduct.

5. TRAINEE RESPONSE

1. Why this course was chosen

1.1 What made people decide to train?
Professional development: often to obtain a qualification for group work already being carried out in various settings. To study something in greater depth which has a practical application. To further enhance psychotherapeutic practice. To obtain UKCP registration.

1.2 What were the aspects of this course that were most attractive?
The block weekends facilitate access for those for whom a weekly course proves difficult, for example, for those with geographical limitations or with demanding work commitments. The weekend format provides scope for intense work and the overall community of the course (staff, students and non-training group members) provides a containing setting. The course gives a thorough grounding in group analysis with an MSc qualification. There is a strong sense of academic rigour with a critical reflective approach to the theory being promoted. This attracts a wide diversity of students from different professional backgrounds. The setting for the course at Turvey is a special attraction in itself with its peaceful rural surroundings.

1.3 What was your experience of the selection procedure?
Supportive and caring. A valuable experience in itself offering a chance to reflect on personal strengths and motivations.

1.4 Before the start of the course, how informed did you feel about each stage of the training?
A large proportion of students have completed the introductory course at Turvey so are well informed and able to support their colleagues, having been part of the overall course community. As a relatively new course there are natural teething problems as the course evolves. This makes for a dynamic course changing in response to student needs.

2. The atmosphere of the course

2.1 How do you feel about the way in which information is communicated?
The staff encourage students to be participative and critical of the course. Students are treated respectfully as adults. Almost all aspects of the training take place during the weekend so there are many opportunities/channels for communication. Mechanisms exist for open dialogue if problems arise.

2.2 What do you find the most confusing aspect of the training?
The major challenge of the course is managing the different activities over a weekend and the intensity of the experience followed by the gaps in between weekends. This, however, can provide a valuable and particular experience of managing breaks and boundaries.

2.3 How much opportunity do you have to share thoughts and feelings with fellow trainees?
A lot over the weekends and during the intensive academic module. The residential nature of the course provides plenty of scope for social interaction and reflection.

2.4 What do you feel about the methods of teaching?
A variety of lecture and more interactive methods are used. These are formal and informal, for example, in supervision. When teaching methods are good it enables an integration of theoretical knowledge, personal experience and clinical practice.

2.5 What did you think about the way assessments were done to allow you to progress to the next stages of training?
Peer group evaluation and feedback about progress and student participation in report writing are actively encouraged. This is well valued by the students. The level of written work required is demanding with high expectations. As the course develops it is hoped that the course will include more constructive criticism of written assignments to further aid learning.

2.6 Has the course met your expectations?
Yes. The course provides a demanding yet very rich and valuable experience. The consistency and authenticity of the staff group, with their mix of experience and approaches, is very containing and provides a good model for practice.

2.7 How do you feel about your future with the organisation?
Students come from all parts of the country (and from Europe). This presents some logistical problems in keeping in touch with the heart of the course in the longer

term. The ongoing large group is open for all students and graduates to attend. The course is in transition and moves are afoot to develop ways of maintaining future contact after finishing the course. The future is positive and encouraging.

2.8 What plans do trainees have for future practice and possible balance of different sorts of work in their career?
Plans to enhance existing work in a variety of settings to include NHS, prisons, voluntary organisations, private practice. The course provides a good grounding for the application of group analytic ideas in different settings and professions.

AUTHOR'S COMMENTS

The Turvey course provides a useful opportunity for training in group-analytic psychotherapy within the Foulksian tradition (see p. 29f.) and its developments, for those who are constrained by full-time work commitments. The block weekends allow for an experience of group analysis that prepares trainees for the intensity of experience of weekly groups that they will convene and run as part of this course.

Inevitably there is a different sense of continuity in the groups and it is worth asking about whether psychological continuity in this kind of experience is felt between the group sessions. It is also a very different experience from trainees being part of a peer patient group as found in the other group trainings.

However, this is a practical model used for group psychotherapy as well as for training, applicable and innovative in a busy world.

The course has moved its validating body from Sheffield University to Oxford Brookes, but that should make no difference to the course itself. It is taught by experienced group analysts and is well connected into group-analytic work nationally and internationally through the Group-Analytic Society.

WPF TRAINING IN GROUP-ANALYTIC PSYCHOTHERAPY
WPF COUNSELLING AND PSYCHOTHERAPY (WPF-GP UKCP/PPS)

23 Kensington Square, London W8 5HN
Tel. 020 7364 4844 Fax. 020 7361 4819
E-mail: training@wpf.org.uk

1. HISTORY OF THE ORGANISATION

Please see entry under Westminster Pastoral Foundation, Training in Individual Psychoanalytic Psychotherapy (p. 229).

2. THE THEORETICAL ORIENTATION AND CURRICULUM

Philosophy of group-analytic psychotherapy training
The aim of the course is to enable trainees to work with patients in a variety of group settings, and specifically in group-analytic psychotherapy stranger patient groups.

In achieving this aim the trainees on the course develop an understanding of group analytic models of group psychotherapy and learn to apply that knowledge in conducting a variety of groups. The curriculum also covers the study of psychoanalytic theory, Self Psychology, Jung, systems theory and social psychology.

The group-analytic model taught at WPF encompasses a variety of theories, although it is fundamentally based on the writings of S.H. Foulkes, a Freudian psychoanalyst/group analyst, and his followers. Group analysis is an established form of group psychotherapy based on the view that enduring and personal development and change can occur within a carefully constituted group. It is a method which draws on the therapeutic potential of every individual in the group as well as the group as a whole.

Content of the course

Seminars: The academic part of the course currently comprises seminars in three ten-week terms each year for three years. Seminars in Group Analysis take place in all three years. The first year seminar is specifically related to Foulkesian theory, the role of the conductor, and dynamic administration. Years two and three reflect a broader exploration of group-analytic theory and its application. Seminars in Individual Psychoanalytic Theory and Clinical Concepts take place in years two and three.

Mirror observation and co-conducting: During the first year trainees observe a group psychotherapist conducting an experiential student group from behind a one-way mirror for one academic year and co-conduct an experiential group on one of the WPF skills courses.

Supervised training group: Trainees are required to conduct a once-weekly psychotherapy group for adults for a minimum of two years, and a second group, which may be time limited and/or theme focused.

Individual psychodynamic therapy: Trainees are expected to show competence in therapeutic work with individuals.

Psychiatric placement: Trainees lacking psychiatric experience are required to gain experience of ward rounds and other contact with psychiatric patients.

Large group experience: There is a large group of one and a half hours' duration, once a term, for all staff and trainees on the course. The groups are experiential and are lead by an external group analyst.

3. TRAINING STRUCTURE

3.1 Training committee
The Course Organiser and the Staff team are responsible for the delivery of the course.

3.2 Selection procedure and admission

Applicants
Applicants are selected on the basis both of previous educational and professional experience and their suitability for the work of group-analytic psychotherapy.

Applicants will have completed the WPF's one-year Diploma in Applied Group-Analytic Skills, or other appropriate introductory course, or a training in counselling skills which includes participation in an experiential group run along group-analytic lines.

Admission procedure
The admissions process consists of a written application and two selection interviews.

Applicants are requested to supply the following documents: a curriculum vitae; a statement giving relevant experience of groupwork; a personal statement giving reasons why they wish to train, important life events and experience of therapy; and the names of two referees.

Equal opportunities statement
WPF Counselling and Psychotherapy is positively committed to opposing discrimination. All departments have policy documents and seek to promote and monitor equality of opportunity in all its procedures.

3.3 Time commitment per week and length of training
The length of the training is not less than four years from the time of commencing the theoretical and supervision seminars.

The course requires attendance at WPF for approximately six hours one day a week (Wednesdays) during the first three years. In addition to this time, during the first year, trainees attend WPF to co-conduct an experiential group. Attendance at supervision sessions at WPF is required until the clinical requirements of the training are met after which trainees have twelve months to submit their final clinical paper. Time for setting up and running the training groups, seeing individual clients (if required) and attending one's personal therapy group are additional.

3.4 Financial cost of training at diffent stages (1999–2000)
The current training costs approximately £1,900 per year for the first three years (of seminars and supervision). Fee levels are revised annually. For supervision only the cost is approximately £900. These fees include library membership and membership of the WPF Trainee Association.

3.5 Interruptions in training
If a trainee needs to take time out of training we will do all we can to assist in managing the break.

3.6 Graduating and beginning a career
On qualification as a group-analytic psychotherapist, graduates become professional members of the group-analytic psychotherapy section of the Foundation for Psychotherapy and Counselling (FPC). This is the graduate body, which monitors professional standards and professional development for all its members. It provides a programme of monthly scientific meetings and annual conferences as well as study days and public lectures. Through its close ties with WPF and the national network of affiliated centres, FPC is able to offer its members access to a large number of professional posts in teaching, supervising and administrating in the fields of counselling

and psychotherapy. There is also an FPC referral scheme, which uses the website and various publications to give access to the public seeking referral for therapy.

Graduates are eligible for registration within the Psychodynamic and Psychoanalytic Psychotherapy Section of the UKCP.

3.7 Numbers of students per intake
We accept up to ten trainees a year.

4. CLINICAL AND ACADEMIC REQUIREMENTS

4.1 Personal therapy
Trainees are required to be in group-analytic psychotherapy for one year before the start of the course and remain in group-analytic psychotherapy throughout their training. The psychotherapy takes place in mixed-sex, stranger groups.

4.2 Clinical requirements

Supervised training group
Trainees are required to conduct a once-weekly psychotherapy group for adults for a minimum of two years. The group is supervised at WPF. The training group is a major clinical project, which requires a sophisticated understanding and handling of individual psychodynamics, group processes and organisation/contextual dynamics. Trainees are required to run a second group, which may be time limited or theme focused.

Individual psychodynamic therapy
Trainees are expected to show competence in therapeutic work with individuals. They are required to see, on a once-weekly basis, two clients for a minimum of 40 sessions each during the course of the training in voluntary or statutory agency settings supervised by the agency or external supervisor if they do not already have this experience.

4.3 Supervision
Trainees are in supervision throughout the training until the Training Committee is satisfied with the standard of their clinical practice.

4.4 Written work and course attendance
Trainees are required to complete three written papers and a clinical paper on their training group. Upon completion of a dissertation, participants may be awarded an MA in Group-Analytic Psychotherapy (to be confirmed).

Technically, 80 per cent attendance is always required in any one year. In practice, we consider any case of difficulty individually on its merits. We are concerned with what people have learned and can do.

4.5 Assessment, standards and ethical requirements
Please see entry under WPF Training in Individual Psychoanalytic Psychotherapy Training on ethics.

Assessment is continuous throughout the training and consists of feedback from supervisors, seminar leaders and from trainees themselves. The staff formally assesses each trainee's progress once a year with reports from the supervisor and the seminar leader.

Qualification depends upon a satisfactory report from the supervisor at the end of the two-year period of conducting a group under supervision and completion of two satisfactory written papers; a theoretical paper of 3,000–5,000 words, on a topic related to group analysis; and a clinical paper of 5,000–8,000 words based on clinical material from the trainee's training group.

5. TRAINEE RESPONSE

It was not possible to obtain a response from the trainees on this course despite having made contact with a representative.

AUTHOR'S COMMENTS

This course presents a carefully thought out training in group-analytic psycho-therapy in the Foulkesian tradition (see p. 29f.). It has the advantage of being a group training in a large institution, making the recruitment of trainees patient groups an easier process. It also makes the study of group behaviour in the organi-sational context an enriching possibility on the course. This exploration follows the tradition of the large group and organisational work of the Institute of Group-Analysis rather than the approach of Bion (p. 18), whose theories are nevertheless studied. Trainees are expected to be in patient groups, whether once or twice weekly.

Two other learning opportunities are unique to this course: one is the chance from year one to observe a group being run through a one-way mirror. The second is the chance to co-conduct an experiential group on another WPF course. These apprenticeships appear to offer direct learning from senior practitioners and respect for a trainee's contribution.

2.5 Trainings in Universities and/or Connected to the NHS

CENTRE FOR THE STUDY OF PSYCHOTHERAPY AT THE UNIVERSITY OF KENT (CSPK – UKCP/PPS)

Psychotherapy Group, Institute of Psychiatry, Kent Institute of Medical and Health Sciences, Kent Research and Development Centre, University of Kent at Canterbury, Canterbury CT2 7PD
Tel. 01227 823 691 Fax. 01227 823 224
E-mail: G.N.Phillips@ukc.ac.uk

1. HISTORY OF THE ORGANISATION

The Centre for the Study of Psychotherapy, which was originally developed within the School of Continuing Education to offer formal training in psychoanalytic psychotherapy, became part of the Kent Institute of Medical and Health Sciences, within the Division of Psychiatry, in 1996. The programme was registered in 1993 with the United Kingdom Council for Psychotherapy, and since then, many graduates have completed the full psychotherapy training and have achieved professional registration. Becoming part of the Kent Institute of Medical and Health Sciences in 1996 reinforced its commitment to provision of training in psychoanalytic psychotherapy geared to the needs of the National Health Service.

2. THEORETICAL ORIENTATION AND CURRICULUM

The Psychotherapy Group programme consists of two degree courses, and a variety of stand alone modules which can be undertaken as Continuing Professional Development modules, or as parts of a degree course leading to an MA.

The *postgraduate Diploma/MA in Psychotherapy* is a two- to three-year course of lectures and seminars combined with an experiential group which aims to provide a general introduction to psychoanalytic theory as an end in itself, or as an introduction to further training. On award of the postgraduate Diploma, with satisfactory grades in the course work, students may apply to continue on to further clinical training. The MA is intended for those with existing mental health qualifications.

The *Master of Clinical Science* (MClinSci) is a three-year part-time programme of clinical and theoretical seminars, and supervised clinical practice, which includes placement in a NHS psychotherapy unit, which, upon successful completion, leads to UKCP registration. The normal prerequisite is the postgraduate Diploma, but suitable candidates with previous training in psychoanalytic studies may be considered.

All students on the MClinSci and MA programmes are required to be in personal psychoanalytic psychotherapy.

Psychotherapy training at Kent is research-led. Research modules form part of the clinical training, and further research opportunities are available.

The *Doctor of Clinical Science* (DClinSci) can be undertaken on completion of the qualifying course, MClinSci, and affords students the opportunity of developing their interest in clinical research. In addition, there is a Masters by Research and a PhD programme in Psychotherapy Studies.

Entry with accreditation of prior learning and training is considered at all stages of the programme.

3. TRAINING STRUCTURE

There is a permanent staff of four part-time Lecturers in Psychotherapy who administer and deliver most of the seminars and supervision. Additional part-time staff supplement the permanent staff, offering specialist seminars and supervision.

3.1 Training committee
The Training Committee consists of the permanent staff plus the Director of the Division of Psychiatry, of which we form part.

3.2 Selection procedure and admission
Applicants to the postgraduate Diploma/MA should hold a degree or equivalent level of qualification in a relevant field. Applicants typically come from mental health and allied professions, teaching and social work, but applications from those from other backgrounds are also considered.

Applicants for the MClinSci will successfully have completed the postgraduate Diploma, or its equivalent.

Applicants for the DClinSci will successfully have completed the MClinSci, or an equivalent UKCP recognised training in psychoanalytic psychotherapy.

3.3 Time commitment per week and length of training
Teaching on the postgraduate Diploma/MA takes place on one afternoon and evening per week, currently on a Thursday, during term time over two years. The teaching and supervision of the Master of Clinical Science takes place on a Monday. Clinical practice and supervision may involve part of another day, at the later stages of the MClinSci. The minimum period of clinical training on the MClinSci programme is three years, part-time, and while all effort is made to help the student complete within this time, often a further one or two semesters are required to complete all the clinical requirements.

3.4 Financial cost of the training at different stages

(Academic year 1999–2000)
Diploma/MA modules – £270 per unit
MClinSci modules – £310 per unit

Diploma in Psychotherapy Strides
Year 1 – £1,080
Year 2 – £1,650
MA in Psychotherapy Studies
Year 1 – £1,890
Year 2 – £1,620
Master of Clinical Science
The fees for the MClinSci will depend on the completion of clinical work, but a guideline figure for the complete three- to four-year training is £9,000 (including all clinical supervision).

3.5 Interruptions in training

Intermission during the course is permitted, in cases of illness, pregnancy or family distress in discussion with the Programme Director.

3.6 Graduating and beginning a career

All graduates of the Master of Clinical Science are registered with the UKCP through the Canterbury Consortium of Psychoanalytic and Psychodynamic Psychotherapists (CCOPPP). Professional seminars are held on a termly basis, and all members are invited to take an active part in CCOPPP's activities. A recent survey of the first ten years of the programme showed that a high proportion of graduates have gained, or changed, employment within the NHS as a result of training.

Graduates of the MClinSci follow a career as an individual psychotherapist, typically with a part-time post in the NHS, and a private practice. Some return to take further modules – for example on one-year postgraduate clinical seminar in group psychotherapy – to supplement their clinical skills. We plan to introduce further modules suitable for Continuing Professional Development in the coming years. Some graduates have taken up teaching and supervision roles in the region.

3.7 Numbers of students per intake

Numbers on the postgraduate Diploma/MA courses number between ten and eighteen per year. On the Master of Clinical Science, the normal intake is six to eight students each year.

4. CLINICAL AND ACADEMIC REQUIREMENTS

4.1 Personal therapy

Students registered on the postgraduate Diploma take part in an experiential group, and are encouraged to enter once-weekly psychotherapy if they anticipate wishing to continue training to registration level. Once-weekly therapy is required for all students applying for the Master of Clinical Science, for at least one year before commencing training. During training, students on the Master of Clinical Science programme are required to be in minimum twice-weekly therapy, increasing to thrice-weekly if they undertake a thrice-weekly training case (an elective).

4.2 Clinical requirements

Most patients seen by students in their first clinical practice module (Psychoanalytic Practice I) are NHS patients. Patients seen by trainees in the second module (Psychoanalytic Practice II) – twice weekly – are usually taken from the NHS waiting list, but may be referred through other sources. Students also see NHS patients in the context of an outpatient psychotherapy clinic, or voluntary sector provider, or a General Practice surgery, in their 'Clinical Elective' module. Students may elect to see a thrice-weekly case, on an elective basis, if their previous experience of NHS practice is sufficient to meet the requirements of the clinical elective placement.

4.3 Supervision

Supervision is conducted on both clinical practice Modules by the University staff. Additional supervision is provided by suitably qualified clinicians in the Clinical Elective placement. For the first Practice module, supervision is based on tape-recorded sessions with clinic patients, and takes place once weekly in groups or two or three students. Members of the staff, on a once weekly basis provide individual supervision of twice-weekly patients.

4.4 Written work and attendance

This must meet the university requirements. Written components of the course comprise:

- Postgraduate Diploma – 1st year: 2 essays; 2nd year: 4 essays (2,000–3,000 words)
- MClinSci: Basic requirement: Process research project; Practice I
- Clinical Dissertation (7,000 words); Practice II Clinical Dissertation (9,000 words) Self-assessment exercise.

4.5 Assessment, standards and ethical requirements

Adherence to the code of ethics and good practice is required of all students undertaking clinical training. The ethics code, based on UKCP requirements, includes statements concerning the professional relationship; the therapeutic contract; advertising; legal proceedings; health; confidentiality; medical cover and insurance; and a statement about detrimental behaviour.

There is also a set of training guidelines, which set out what is expected of the student, and what the student may expect of his or her course.

Standards in the first instance are set to meet UKCP training standards requirements. University standards for postgraduate courses govern the expected level of all academic submissions, and all courses are externally examined.

Assessment procedures

Postgraduate Diploma: All written work is double-marked according to published marking criteria, and submitted to the external examiner. Group leaders reports are used in assessing the students suitability to continue on to clinical training.

Master of Clinical Science: Assessment is summative, taking into account accumulating evidence of academic and clinical competence. All academic work is double marked according to published marking criteria and externally examined. To this are added the reports of clinical supervisors, seminar leaders' reports and the self-assessment report.

5. TRAINEE RESPONSE

1. Why this course was chosen

1.1 What made people decide to train?
The experience of individual and group therapy in conjunction with an academic/intellectual interest in the subject area prompted the decision to train. A number of students come with a counselling, medical, social work or psychology background wanting a psychoanalytic psychotherapy training. Changing and improving career prospects and being eligible for UKCP registration were some of the reasons cited for choosing this training.

1.2 What were the aspects of this course that were most attractive?
The training is university-based thereby offering both an academic and clinical qualification. An additional strength is the broad-based curriculum providing access to the perspectives of Freud, Klein, Winnicott, Bowlby, Bion and Fairbairn. Child development theory and process research forms important aspects of the training alongside clinical practice. This eclectic nature of the training is viewed positively.

The location, outside London, the course being a daytime commitment, part-time and modular was deemed advantageous, particularly for those with young children. The modular approach offers a flexible training programme, which can be important where there are a number of other commitments.

1.3 What was your experience of the selection procedure?
The selection procedure involves two to four interviewers. The issues of why the individual wants to do the training, their appropriateness and commitment were explored in each case. The consensus was the interview was fair and thorough but not arduous. One student remarked on the fact that there is no charge for the selection interview. A certificate or Diploma in Psychotherapy (usually two years) is a prerequisite to the Masters programme along with some relevant pre-clinical experience.

1.4 Before the start of the course, how informed did you feel about each stage of the training?
A handbook is provided which details the academic courses and clinical training requirements. The modular and clinical practice requirements have remained broadly similar over the past few years. However, the students consulted did comment critically on the number of changes to the programme as a result of the university and UKCP requirements, and more recently recommendations following a Quality Assurance audit.

The training is both practically and emotionally demanding. This experience is widespread amongst students and anticipated although perhaps underestimated.

2. The atmosphere of the course

2.1 How do you feel about the way in which information is communicated?
Personal experiences in relation to the communication of course related information
varied somewhat. At times the lines of communication are clear and satisfactory. On
other occasions the information is contradictory, muddled and experienced as a
breakdown in communication. Pressure on accommodation, under-resourced and
hard-pressed staff and the part-time nature of staff input on the programme were
felt to contribute to these shortcomings. Most of the students consulted feel clarity
and consistency about the structure of the course is improving but remains
challenging.

2.2 What do you find the most confusing aspect of the training?
Course meetings, held once a term, provide some space for students to feedback
thoughts and feelings regarding the programme as do the individual module
evaluation forms. All students see their personal tutor once a term and are
encouraged to use this to discuss any difficulties they are experiencing.

*2.3 How much opportunity do you have to share thoughts and feelings with fellow
trainees?*
The opportunity to share thoughts and feelings with other trainees is largely
confined to being with those enrolled on the same modules or in the same
supervision group and as such is a disadvantage of the modular approach. The fact
that there is no communal meeting area to date in addition to the recent ending of
the experiential group as a course requirement exacerbates this problem. The introduction of half-yearly clinical seminars, to be attended by all students on the Masters
programme will provide greater opportunity for dialogue within the student group.

2.4 What do you feel about the methods of teaching?
Teaching methods vary among the modules and feedback is sought from trainees in
the form of evaluation questionnaires. Methods which achieve a balance between
instruction and promoting discussion of the material are viewed most positively, as
are those which relate theory to practice in a dynamic way. External speakers are
used for the assessment and diagnosis module. This provides the opportunity to
understand how psychotherapy relates to other disciplines and its application in
practice in a variety of settings.

*2.5 What did you think about the way assessments were done to allow you to progress to
the next stages of training?*
Clinical supervision is central to this training. The quality of this is well regarded by
the students while also being personally demanding and challenging. Clinical
Practice I sessions are tape-recorded. This is anxiety-provoking but a valuable
learning tool. Individual supervisor style varies and informs the extent to which
there is mutual discussion of progress to date and outcome.

Overall satisfaction and confidence in the assessment process was expressed. One
has different supervisors for the different clinical practice modules, which provides
a range of experience and styles.

2.6 Has the course met your expectations?
Expectations of the programme and the perception of these being met or not was felt to be based on individual experience of the training, the stage the individual is at in terms of their training, personal issues and how these interact with structural issues related to the course. The experience of support through personal tutorials and the clinical supervision structure was cited and greatly valued.

2.7 How do you feel about your future with the organisation? and
2.8 What plans do trainees have for future practice and possible balance of different sorts of work in their career?
All trainees are student members of the Canterbury Consortium of Psychoanalytic and Psychodynamic Psychotherapists and bound by its Code of Ethics. Full membership is available upon qualification and provides a link in promoting ongoing professional development. Many students envisaged doing additional training following qualification. For most students the combination of building up a private practice with some NHS work as a psychotherapist is favoured. The clinical elective provides the opportunity to see patients in the private or public service sector.

In summary, student feedback on this training indicates it's strength lies in the quality of supervision provided, the flexibility offered by a modular programme, the incorporation of an academic qualification, the range of theoretical perspectives advanced to inform clinical practice and the emphasis on research in relation to clinical practice.

AUTHOR'S COMMENTS

This course has been one of the early initiators of a training in psychotherapy based in a university, alongside a training for the NHS. In recent years the development from a Diploma course to a Masters in Clinical Science and a possible Doctorate degree includes the possibilities of learning and using research methodologies. These offer a chance to contribute to the growing awareness of process and outcome research as well as to using qualitative data collection as a means to research meaning systems within psychotherapy.

The emphasis on academic and research work inevitably means that there is less focus on the theoretical and clinical aspects of complex transference and counter-transference issues that have become such a central feature of so many analytical trainings .

The modular aspect of the course offers the possibility that the training can be taken with different intensities depending on the interests and possible setting in which a trainee wishes to work. The choices include once-weekly therapy and intensive three-times-weekly therapy. This means being with fellow students who have very different requirements and depth in both their own therapy and their clinical work.

The students suggest that the modular nature of the course and the lack of coherent events that gather the whole group together make identification with a core group difficult. Nevertheless, there are some signs that this is being addressed.

Despite the mixture of student enthusiasm and anxiety about the tape-recording of sessions for supervision and assessment, this practice does raise issues about the ethics and intrusiveness of such a practice, that prospective students might want to think about.

NORTH WEST INSTITUTE OF DYNAMIC PSYCHOTHERAPY (NWIDP UKCP/PPS)

Gaskell House, Swinton Grove, Manchester M13 0EU
Tel. 0161 273 2762 Fax. 0161 273 4876
E-mail: sallyb@nwidp.com

1. HISTORY OF THE ORGANISATION

The training was set up in 1987 by a federation of NHS psychotherapy services in Manchester, Blackpool and Preston. More recently, NHS services in Lancaster and a clinic in the private sector have also been involved.

2. THEORETICAL ORIENTATION AND CURRICULUM

As a result of its federal origin, the theoretical orientation of the training represents a historic compromise between four elements: group analysis, psychoanalysis (mainly Kleinian), dynamic-interpersonal psychotherapy (especially the Conversational Model of Robert Hobson), and empirical psychotherapy research.

The training also has a special interest in psychotherapy in the public sector, and the development and position of psychotherapy in the regions.

As a prerequisite, candidates are required to complete an introductory course in group psychotherapy recognised by the Institute of Group Analysis, such as the Manchester Course in Group Psychotherapy.

Training then consists of a Foundation Course of four terms (beginning in May), followed by a Qualifying Course of six terms.

3. TRAINING STRUCTURE

3.1 Training committee
A committee of representatives from the centres involved manages the training from day to day. Trainees' progress through the course is determined by a termly meeting of supervisors.

3.2 Selection procedure and admission
Prerequisites for application are:

- completion of the introductory group psychotherapy course

- previous supervised experience in psychodynamic psychotherapy (suitable candidates may be able to arrange supervised experience in NHS psychotherapy services in the region)
- previous personal therapy at least to the level of one year in an experiential group
- academic ability to degree level or equivalent (alternatives to an academic degree will be considered on their merits)
- support of employer.

Candidates are often members of core mental health disciplines. Other candidates will be asked to obtain experience of work in mental health, and help may be available to arrange an appropriate placement.

The closing date for applications is presently at the end of September. Following shortlisting, candidates attend two interviews: one focused on professional skills and experience; one on their personal qualities. The latter is usually confidential, but if there are serious reservations about a candidate, their permission may be sought to discuss the matter with the committee of selectors.

The training subscribes to the equal opportunities policies of the UK Council for Psychotherapy.

3.3 Time commitment per week and length of training
The course requires a commitment of about 20 hours per week. This includes daytime commitments on weekdays of about one and a half days per week.

The taught course runs for three years and one term. Trainees should expect to take up to the end of a fourth year to complete clinical and written requirements.

3.4 Financial cost of training at different stages
The cost for 1999 is £2,250 for the Foundation Course and £2,250 per annum for the Qualifying Course. This includes all elements of training, including supervision, except the cost of personal therapy.

3.5 Interruptions in training
The Foundation Course is designed to stand as a course in its own right, and it is accepted that trainees may take a break at the end of the Foundation. The training will attempt to accommodate breaks due to illness, pregnancy, and so on, at other points, but some elements of the training may need to be repeated.

3.6 Graduating and beginning a career
Graduates qualify for membership of the North West Institute of Dynamic Psychotherapy (NWIDP), which is a member organisation of the Psychoanalytic and Psychodynamic Psychotherapy Section of the UK Council for Psychotherapy.

NWIDP has developed continuing professional development seminars in cooperation with the University of Manchester, the Merseyside Psychotherapy Institute and the Tavistock Clinic.

One of the principal aims of the training has been to enable graduates to work as psychotherapists in the NHS in the North West of England, and many go on to do so. Significant numbers of graduates also work in the private and voluntary sectors.

3.7 Numbers of students per intake
There is an annual intake of around six trainees.

4. CLINICAL AND ACADEMIC REQUIREMENTS

4.1 Personal therapy
Trainees must be in personal therapy throughout the duration of the course, attending a minimum of once per week. Above that minimum, in practice trainees vary widely in terms of number of attendances per week for personal therapy.

Training therapists must have completed a training at least to the standard of North West Region Diploma in Dynamic Psychotherapy, and have five years of substantial continual practice as a psychotherapist post-qualification. New trainees may therefore ask for an existing therapist to be regarded as their training therapist, and this will be accepted if the therapist meets the above criteria.

The training does not require the training therapist to provide reports on the trainee's progress in therapy.

4.2 Clinical requirements
Foundation Course:

- 120 hours supervised practice, including a minimum of 90 hours psychoanalytic psychotherapy and a maximum of 30 hours psychodynamically informed work (the latter may include a wide variety of work, considered from a psychodynamic point of view)
- 80 hours supervision
- two psychoanalytic psychotherapies conducted from beginning to end during the course
- four assessments for psychotherapy.

Qualifying Course:

- one individual therapy twice weekly for two years
- two brief focal psychotherapy cases (usually one three-month and one six-month)
- an analytic psychotherapy group conducted once a week for a minimum of two years
- a further six assessments for psychotherapy.

Most clinical work takes place within NHS or private psychotherapy clinics, which provide the trainee with a base for their work and a wide variety of cases.

4.3 Supervision
On both Foundation and Qualifying Courses, trainees are supervised in three settings:

- weekly individual supervision throughout the course
- supervision in a group of between two and four trainees, weekly during term time

- a further group supervision, running throughout most of the course, meeting at a frequency dictated by the nature of the work being supervised (this allows some flexibility in the supervision of brief therapies or psychodynamically informed work).

4.4 Written work and course attendance
Written work is as follows.
Foundation Course:

- a 2,000-word case study
- a short case summary of 400–800 words
- an 1,800-word essay on a set topic
- four assessment reports.

Qualifying Course:

- a 2,000-word case study
- a short case summary of 400–800 words
- a dissertation of 2,000–4,000 words
- six assessment reports: when taken together with the assessment reports from the Foundation Course, these should demonstrate a breadth of patients assessed and options considered.

Course attendance is on Tuesday afternoons and early evenings at Gaskell House in Manchester. The course meets for ten sessions per term. In addition to a supervision group, the course afternoon includes two sessions on theoretical and practical aspects of psychoanalytic psychotherapy. Trainees are regularly involved in presenting seminar papers.

4.5 Assessment, standards and ethical requirements
A Code of Practice for trainers and trainees deals with the provision of pre-course information, teaching, clinical work, personal and financial involvement, supervision, assessment, complaints and appeals.

Assessment of clinical work takes place through a structured discussion between supervisor and supervisee, using a set of topics for the discussion, which cover the principal aspects of supervision and therapy. Key points are then presented to the termly meeting of supervisors, which takes overall decisions as to the progress of trainees.

Written work is double-marked in accordance with marking guides, with blind marking insofar as this is possible with a small learning group.

5. TRAINEE RESPONSE

It was not possible to elicit a response from the trainees on this course.

AUTHOR'S COMMENTS

This Manchester-based course has offered for many years a training connected to work in the NHS. Most of its applicants will come from mental health disciplines. It is significant in a number of ways. The course is the only training to insist on an introductory year in group-analytic psychotherapy before individual psychother-apy training follows. There is a tradition of making analytic understandings available through the interactional 'conversational' therapy inspired by Bob Hobson (Hobson 1985). This approach emphasises engaging with the patient in possibly everyday conversation as a way of building a relationship in which patterns of interaction can be established and noted for their symbolic meaning. Teaching tapes from NHS out-patient work illustrate the approach vividly. On the course there is also a strong emphasis on Kleinian and post-Kleinian thinking and additionally an emphasis on empirical research.

This is a varied but inevitably usable learning experience for anyone planning a career in psychotherapy in the public services, particularly the NHS. The demands of the course are heavy on top of full-time posts and applicants need to be aware of its ethos and organisational context.

SOUTH TRENT TRAINING IN DYNAMIC PSYCHOTHERAPY (STTDP – UKCP/PPS)

c/o Department of Psychotherapy, 1 St Anne's Road, Lincoln, LN2 5RA
Tel. 01522 51200

1. HISTORY OF THE ORGANISATION

The South Trent Training has been organised by the NHS Psychotherapy Services in Derby, Leicester and Nottingham since 1982, with the psychotherapy service in Lincoln joining this organisation in 1987.

2. THEORETICAL ORIENTATION AND CURRICULUM

The training is committed to the aims, concepts and values embodied within the Psychoanalytic tradition. The curriculum is organised to explore this fully and to enable trainees to become specialist dynamic psychotherapists capable of substan-tially independent clinical practice within the NHS.

3. TRAINING STRUCTURE

3.1 Training committee
The Training Committee has a maximum membership of eight. Each service is entitled to select two of its personal tutors to be members of the Training Committee.

3.2 Selection procedure and admission
Trainees are usually drawn from the core NHS professions and must be employed or seconded to work at least half-time in one of the four psychotherapy services. Eligible

trainees are already expected to have completed intermediate levels of training in dynamic psychotherapy.

Trainees formally register with the training when they register with a personal tutor.

Appointments and selection committees follow an equal opportunities policy.

3.3 Time commitment per week and length of training

Most trainees work in full-time NHS psychotherapy posts. It is possible for a part-time commitment to gain approval. Full-time trainees can expect to complete the training within four to six years.

Trainees are eligible to take the South Trent Certificate in Dynamic Psychotherapy if they have completed a minimum of 1,000 hours of supervised clinical work, including at least one group of 18 months' duration and 20 supervised assessments. There should be a total of 352 hours of supervision. The Certificate Assessment Panel assess a written case analysis, a theoretical paper and a viva.

3.4 Financial cost of the training at different stages

The cost of training is born by the NHS, with the exception of the fees for a personal therapist if a trainee chooses an approved therapist from the private sector.

3.5 Interruptions in training

Interruptions in training are primarily an issue for the NHS Trust employing the trainee, and are dealt with under the Trusts policies and procedures.

3.6 Graduating and beginning a career

Graduates from the training have opportunities to gain specialist posts for trained psychotherapists within the NHS Departments as they arise, or elsewhere within the NHS.

Within a few years of qualification psychotherapists working within one of the South Trent Departments can expect to be called on to offer supervision within the South Trent Training, and many will become tutors within three to five years.

3.7 Numbers of students per intake

There is no maximum number of trainees.

The intake depends on trainees successfully securing posts within the psychotherapy services or secondments from within the Trusts.

4. CLINICAL AND ACADEMIC REQUIREMENTS

4.1 Personal therapy

Personal therapy is for a minimum period of three years, at least once weekly with an approved therapist.

4.2 Clinical requirements

Trainees are expected to have a clinical caseload normally drawn from the waiting list of the NHS Psychotherapy Services constituting South Trent Training. Trainees usually work with a variety of patients and a range of psychological problems.

Clinical work also ranges from long-term individual psychotherapy through to brief focal therapy and group therapy. Patients are normally seen at a frequency of one session per week.

4.3 Supervision

Trainees are expected to be in weekly supervision throughout their training. During training trainees have a number of different supervisors. Minimum requirements are that there be a main supervisor throughout the duration of training, normally the trainee's personal tutor, and at least two additional approved supervisors each for a minimum of twelve months.

4.4. Written work and course attendance

Trainees must attend a minimum of nine terms of theoretical and clinical seminars. Trainees are expected to consolidate their learning through a variety of further educational activities within each base psychotherapy service, as well as through the writing of a number of papers. Trainees must submit a final theoretical paper of about 5,000 words, and a case analysis of no more than 10,000 words as they sit for the South Trent Certificate.

4.5 Assessment, standards and ethical requirements

The South Trent Code of Ethics covers:

1. *General Standards of Practice*
   1.1   Clinical Standards
   1.2   Dignity and Respect
   1.3   Clinical Need
   1.4   Continuing Professional Development
   1.5   Qualifications
   1.6   Research
   1.7   Advertising
   1.8   Indemnity Insurance
2. *Confidentiality and Boundaries*
   2.1   General Principle
   2.2   Therapeutic Boundaries
   2.3   Confidentiality
   2.4   Disclosure in Supervision
   2.5   Disclosure to other professionals
   2.6   Disclosure in the face of serious risk
   2.7   Contractual obligations and judicial or other statutory proceedings
   2.8   Publications
   2.9   Teaching and Training
3. *Conduct of Trainers*
   3.1   Standards
   3.2   Individual Needs
   3.3   Boundaries and Confidentiality
4. *Procedural Obligations*

The South Trent Training approach to standards and assessment is one of a continual assessment of performance. Each NHS service is also subject to high NHS standards of conduct and disciplinary procedures, as well as an obligation towards audit and clinical governance.

Trainees must submit an up-to-date tutor's report and written reports from two other supervisors, together with a case register of all training cases, to be eligible to sit the Certificate. The Certificate is awarded by the Training Committee upon the recommendation of an Assessment Panel who have examined the trainee's final case analysis and theoretical paper and conducted an oral assessment of the candidate. Trainees must meet the requirements for being a specialist dynamic psychotherapist capable of substantially independent practice within the NHS.

5. TRAINEE RESPONSE

1. Why this course was chosen
First of all it is important to explain that South Trent Training is the training provided for the people who work in the four NHS Psychotherapy Departments of Nottingham, Leicester, Lincoln and Derby. Thus people who come on the training usually have to have a post in one of the departments first. This could be a post as a social worker, nurse, psychologist, occupational therapist, doctor, and so on, or a trainee psychotherapist post. Some posts are permanent, some posts are time limited, that is, trainee psychotherapists post of five years, Specialist Register Post (SpR) for training to be a medical consultant psychotherapist of three to four years. The SpR posts have been extended to four years, as it was not thought to be possible to do the training in three years. Thus most people choose the training because it was part of a job and the training was free. There are some people who have had links with a department as a visiting therapist, who have gone on to do the training on a part-time basis either because their work seconds them part time or, in one case, someone who is giving half-time work in the department in exchange for free training. People also talked about choosing the training because it is clinically based and that, within a psychodynamic frame, it encompasses a number of schools of thought.

Everyone felt the selection process was rigorous and difficult to get through, but seemed fair.

People varied how much they knew about the training before they started from very little to a great deal.

2. The atmosphere of the course
Most trainees felt there was a problem about communication and finding out what was happening. However, this did vary between departments some being more open than others. There is a plenary once a term (three times a year), in which everyone from the training is invited and issues can be discussed. There is a Training Committee where two senior members from each department are representatives, but there is no trainee representative on the committee. Again, feedback can vary between the four departments.

We felt the most confusing aspects of the training are the four departments working differently (Nottingham, Leicester, Lincoln and Derby) and how difficult it is for them to come together to form a whole. There are conflicts sometimes between needs of training/trainees versus being employees and the needs of the individual departments.

It was felt there is little opportunity for trainees to get together, this mostly happens when we meet at the seminars. However, when trainees are writing up their papers they no longer attend seminars and can feel somewhat isolated from other trainees. We also have a trainee meeting after each plenary. However, trainees, particularly those who are part-time, struggle to get to these meetings.

There was very positive feedback about the teaching in seminars. The trainees have some say in areas they would like to cover in seminars putting forward suggestions each year. There are three terms of seminars over a year, covering different topics with different tutors depending on the topic. Trainees are expected to do at least nine terms of seminars and many stay on and do more than this as they value the seminars very highly and feel they learn a lot.

Different departments have different ways of assessing trainees as to how they are progressing some have yearly reviews, but this is not standardised. Only at the end of training, is there a standard of submitting for the certificate by putting in a case register, two pieces of written work, followed by a viva.

There was a wide range of responses as to whether people felt the course had met their expectations from very positive responses, through to one or two people feeling very unhappy about the way the training has panned out.

Some trainees have permanent jobs and would expect to stay on as trained staff when they have successfully completed the course. With others it is less clear – most people who did not have a permanent post as a psychotherapist were wanting to find such a post.

Most trainees saw their career as a psychotherapist if jobs were available; some people (the minority) were planning to work privately as a psychotherapist.

AUTHOR'S COMMENTS

Since 1984 this course in adult psychotherapy within the NHS has offered a training with funded posts for trainees. An account of its work and vision as well as of the role of a consultant in charge of such an enterprise, can be read by its founder, Mark Aveline ('NHS Psychotherapy Services and Training Scheme', *BJP* 6:312–23, 1990). As in other trainings where there are funded posts, there is the task of reconciling being a trainee with being a responsible and/or senior employee with all the vicissitudes and conflicts of reconciling both. Not so surprising that the trainees spoke of the need for a context where such conflicts could come together.

Reading Aveline's article demonstrates the interest and popular need for therapy within the NHS and suggests how important is the contribution of courses such as this that may well proliferate in years to come. The trainees suggest that it is the range of views within a psychodynamic approach that are attractive without addressing how differences are perceived and dealt with. This might be something interested applicants might like to explore.

THE UNIVERSITY OF LEEDS PSYCHOTHERAPY DEPARTMENT (ULPD – UKCP/UPA)

MASTERS IN PSYCHOANALYTIC PSYCHOTHERAPY
40 Clarendon Road, Leeds LS2 9PJ
Tel. 0113 295 5430

1. HISTORY OF THE ORGANISATION

Established in 1974, this is the second oldest university postgraduate course in psychotherapy in the UK, the other being Aberdeen. It is distinguished by being associated with the name of Harry Guntrip who worked in the University Department of Psychiatry.

In 1987 the two-year postgraduate diploma was converted to a four-year Masters. The course has continued in this format.

The aim of the course is to develop psychotherapeutic experience and expertise among mental health professionals working primarily in the NHS within the Yorkshire region. The secondary aim has been to promote the development of psychotherapy locally.

The course is mainly reliant on local NHS consultant psychotherapists for its teaching and training with input from other professionals and from privately practising psychotherapists. The emphasis remains NHS and the course keeps in touch with changes in Health Service requirements. For instance, the development of modularisation is part of this development and change.

The impact of UKCP PP section accreditation criteria has been to require increasing commitment from students to personal therapeutic experience and individual clinical supervision. The theoretical teaching of the Masters course has always been extensive.

In addition, change in the university has encouraged the course tutors to develop modular teaching with the capacity to put on individual modules which may stand alone as well as being an integral part of the course structure enabling a wider range of health professionals to gain experience in different aspects of psycho-therapy over time.

The course is part of the Department of Psychotherapy Specialist Registrar Training Scheme and has been visited regularly by both the Royal College of Psy-chiatrists and by the British Psychological Society.

2. THEORETICAL ORIENTATION AND CURRICULUM

The course is accredited by UPA to the PP section standards of UKCP. The theoretical training includes Psychoanalytic Theory, Clinical Applications in Psychoanalytic Theory, and Psychotherapy Research, and these three modules continue throughout the four-year course amounting to about 364 hours of teaching. There is also a module on Assessment. In the second year there is a brief Dynamic Psycho-therapy module.

The first year teaching is largely didactic with increasing expectation that students will lead the teaching programme through presenting seminars. It is possible to do additional optional modules in the third and fourth year from other courses, for example, Infant Observation, Child Observation, Personality Development, Family Therapy.

Most students will have experienced an introductory course.

3. TRAINING STRUCTURE

This is a four-year Masters in Psychotherapy with the expectation that entrants will have had a year of personal therapy before beginning the course.

3.1 Training committee

This is known as the Curriculum Committee and includes four course tutors student representation, and two co-opted members, one to address issues surrounding personal therapy and one to address these issues surrounding clinical supervision. It meets four times a year and approves the curriculum for the following year, reviews individual students progress and develops a strategy for course development. It functions separately from the main Course Committee, which includes representation from the university departments.

3.2 Selection procedure and admission

Students normally have a first degree or equivalent experience, a core professional training and are working in a situation which enables them to practice psychotherapy. All applicants fulfilling these criteria are called for two interviews.

At the academic interview criteria for suitability include intellectual integrity, and openness to learning the clinical and theoretical approach of psychoanalytic psychotherapy. Students are asked to present prepared clinical work.

There is a personal interview. The criteria applied include a commitment to understanding how their own personal experience of life and value systems may effect a patient's progress in therapy, and an appropriate level of emotional investment in the practice of psychoanalytic psychotherapy.

Equal opportunities policy includes the course aim to wide representation of different professional groups and an openness to multicultural approaches. Each student has their own personal tutor.

3.3 Time commitment per week and length of training

The course takes place one half-day a week. There is expectation that half a day will be devoted to private study and supervision. In addition individuals should practice psychotherapy in the work setting one day a week.

The length of training is four years. The maximum time for a Masters Degree at the University of Leeds is six years and all clinical work and academic work must be completed and presented within this time span.

3.4 Financial cost of the training at different stages

The financial cost of the training is currently £1,800 per year for the academic course. The cost of supervision and personal therapy is arranged by students.

3.5 Interruptions in training

Interruptions in training are assessed on individual merit. A maximum two-year break in training is permissible.

3.6 Graduating and beginning a career

There is a postgraduate group, which meets annually. In addition, the Yorkshire Association of Psychodynamic Psychotherapy was set up for graduates of the course.

This now has a wider membership and provides continuing professional development.

Graduates of the course take a number of career paths, in Community Mental Health Teams, Social Services, Voluntary agencies, and so on, or go on for higher qualification to BCP level and practice specialist psychotherapy. A number of individuals have gone on to make important contributions within psychotherapy services across Yorkshire. Some individuals further their psychotherapy experience in London, or work in the private sector.

3.7 Numbers of students per intake

The maximum number of students is twelve and the minimum is four per year.

4. CLINICAL AND ACADEMIC REQUIREMENTS

4.1 Personal therapy

Personal therapy is required once a week throughout training and one year before the beginning of training. Some individuals have more frequent personal therapy experience for their own interest or requirements or wish to take on patients more frequently than once a week and will be expected to have personal therapy of similar frequency. Personal therapists must be UKCP and/or BCP accredited. The course has a list of accredited therapists who have given their CVs and/or attended an interview.

4.2 Clinical requirements

Students are encouraged to take assessed patients from waiting lists of local psychotherapy services and other organisations that have the capacity to provide training cases. Within the Leeds Specialist Psychotherapy Service each student has a named person who liaises between them and the service. The liaiser for the service facilitates the student in finding a training case.

4.3 Supervision

Supervision is required from two separate supervisors, each supervising the student on one training case of between eighteen months and two years each. Supervision takes place on a weekly basis throughout. Supervisors are UKCP or BCP accredited and have enclosed their CV and/or attended an interview. There are regular meetings for supervisors.

4.4 Written work and course attendance

There is a requirement of 80 per cent attendance on the course. Tutors counsel students if attendance poor. Written work is part of the assessment process and is required for the main academic modules as well as for supervision. In accordance with university regulations written work must be handed in on time or a 10 per cent reduction in marks occurs. Written work is double marked and discussed at the curriculum committee and reviewed at the examinations committee.

4.5 Assessment, standards and ethical requirements

The Code of Ethics is the Code of Ethics for UPA and UKCP PP Section. There is a rigorous approach to standards; tutors meeting briefly on a weekly basis to flag up any problems. The university regulates academic standards and the course requires evidence of the development of good clinical practice. Students may not enter the second year unless all five modules have been passed at 50 per cent standard. The first year may be retaken and the exam at the end of the first year may be re-sat before the beginning of the second year. The tutor role is seen as fundamental in ensuring professional development and awareness of student progress throughout the course. Student and supervisor discuss together the progress report, which is then signed by both.

Assessment procedures include ongoing assessment throughout the course, essay assignments, examinations, clinical case report, research dissertation, review of academic papers. The final assessment procedure includes an interview with the external examiner and a course tutor at which particular emphasis is based on the final case report, and the research dissertation. Recommendation may be made at this time that further clinical work with supervision, and/or further personal therapy is required before the Masters Degree can be granted.

Students are asked for their assessment of teaching and required to fill in questionnaires about the teaching for each module at the end of each semester. There is a course review meeting at the end of each semester. The criteria for assessment vary between each module. Personal therapy is not formally assessed but it is a requirement of the university that it is contained within the module structure and attendance monitored.

5. TRAINEE RESPONSE

The course is organised in conjunction with the NHS psychotherapy unit and is orientated to working within the NHS. The course offers a combination of an academic approach, combining theoretical and clinical learning, and includes a strong emphasis on psychodynamic research. One of the attractions of this training is that it is accredited by the UKCP.

Among the reasons for students' choice of the course are its central location, its clinical aspects, a wish to deepen understanding in the work of counselling or related work, hopes for career enhancement and promotion, personal gains and satisfaction. The selection procedure consists of interviews with all the main tutors who determine personal qualities and academic abilities.

The different levels of experience within the current cohort and the various work backgrounds inevitably have an impact on the nature of the student group. It is therefore worth bearing in mind that each cohort will be a different experience for all participants.

The course is particularly relevant to practitioners within the NHS but this is not seen as a barrier to using the course learning for other work places, as there are opportunities to develop in specific therapeutic areas and opportunities for discussions.

Each student was sent the description of the four-year programme briefly outlining the contents and structure. The theoretical teaching is organised around a progression from a foundation in theoretical concepts to a refinement and further learning about psychoanalytic concepts. There is a good balance of reading between contemporary and more traditional writings thus providing a stimulus and scope for broadening one's own reading. There is also an emphasis on relating the overall learning and clinical practice to the importance of psychodynamic research.

The style of teaching encourages students to discuss the given papers with minimal didactic teaching, with the exception of the research module, and an expectation of student presentations. The course is led in such a way as to promote students' self-motivation and there is appreciation of the didactic input alongside discussion. The latter is encouraged as a way of developing the reflective processes of the trainee therapists.

Students are asked to give feedback of the course components at the end of each semester as part of the university requirements. During the course, communication to students is via the teaching and personal tutors. Students are encouraged and expected to voice their thoughts and feelings throughout the course via the student representative and are given the opportunity to meet with all teaching tutors at the start and end of each year for the same purpose. Communication between peers is left for the time outside of the teaching slots.

Assessment is by ongoing assessed work and short examinations. Students are generally satisfied with the learning provided by the course and would agree that the workload is demanding. All participants benefit from the deeper learning achieved and the clinical learning which is a popular part of the programme since it allows for 'hands-on' learning. The hopes of the students are that the training will open doors for employment prospects whether they be within or outside of the NHS. Some hope for promotion; some for a career change; some for expanding private practice, and some hope for full-time work.

AUTHOR'S COMMENTS

Although it does not exclude people from other settings, this course is organised within the NHS, being based at a psychotherapy department in a major northern conurbation. As its entry states its primary task is to train staff for NHS work, which means that most trainees will already be working in one of the core mental health professions. It also means that like other courses with funded training, patients will be seen from a wider social spectrum and trainees will have to fit their training around other work.

The course has moved from a three-year diploma to a four-year Masters. It is one of those accredited by the Universities Psychotherapy Association (UPA) but also claims to use the clinical requirements of the PP section of the UKCP. This means that the course is geared not just to NHS work, but also to those who wish to develop private practice whether they have been in counselling or other backgrounds.

As in other university trainings, there is much to cover including different analytic approaches, research methods and the task of preparing presentations for many of the seminars as a prime teaching method. The broader academic interests may reduce the time and energy available for more detailed grappling with clinical theory and practice.

The requirement for training therapists that they be of UKCP or BCP accreditation leaves a wide spectrum, presumably dealing with the small number of possible trained therapists in the region. There appears to be no requirement that they be five years post-qualification as in some trainings. This might make for a student group with possibly widely different experiences of personal therapy working clinically at very different depths.

UNIVERSITY OF LEICESTER DIPLOMA IN PSYCHODYNAMIC STUDIES (ULDPS – UKCP/PPS)
VAUGHAN ASSOCIATION OF PSYCHODYNAMIC PSYCHOTHERAPISTS (VAPP)

Vaughan College, St Nicholas Circle, Leicester LE1 4LB
Tel. 0116 251 7368 Fax. 0116 251 1128

1. HISTORY OF THE ORGANISATION

The Association, the graduate body of the Diploma in Psychodynamic Studies at the University of Leicester, started in 1991 and was accepted as a training by the PPP section in 1993. In 1999 UKCP required a professional association separate from the University, so the Vaughan Association (VAPP) was formed.

Links with the Diploma remain strong, although VAPP also accepts into professional membership psychotherapists trained elsewhere, where similar standards can be demonstrated.

2. THEORETICAL ORIENTATION AND CURRICULUM

VAPP's philosophy is based on psychoanalytic and psychodynamic theory and practice, particularly understanding the conscious and unconscious dynamic that exists between persons and in each person's internal world; between past, present and anticipated future; and taking full account of the reflective process at different levels of therapeutic relationship. Stress is laid on the centrality of the therapeutic relationship in its real and its transferential aspects, and importance attached to the realities of the external world, as well as to individual interpretations existing within the inner world. Students are encouraged to question the different schools and the major proponents of theory and practice; and to be aware of difficulties achieving objective criteria, given both epistemological questions, and the capacity of the psyche to interpret 'facts', events and relationships on more than a rational basis alone.

Training starts with a Foundation Year, in which Freud, Klein and Winnicott are taught; followed by the Diploma in Psychodynamic Studies, a two-year part-time course. Its curriculum is outlined below. There are plans for a Masters year. There is a fourth year, post-Diploma, of monthly clinical and theoretical seminars. Affiliate members may then apply for professional membership and registration with UKCP, through VAPP.

Curriculum
The Diploma involves six assessed modules:

1. The task and craft of psychotherapy
2. Developmental theories
3. Developments in psychoanalytic theories
4. Motivation and relationship
5. Specialist themes
6. Practice issues.

Two further modules are not assessed: Year 1: Group dynamics; Year 2: Video role-play practice.

3. TRAINING STRUCTURE

3.1 Training committee
The Professional Board oversees VAPP. A Board of Studies sets the syllabus and assesses the progress towards the Diploma. The Continuing Professional Development Committee runs the fourth post-qualifying year, and ongoing professional development for all members through lectures and workshops. The Registration Committee assesses applications for UKCP registration.

3.2 Selection procedure and admission
The training is designed to be as accessible as possible, including to those whose age, status, gender or race sometimes puts psychotherapy training out of reach. This equal opportunities policy extends throughout and at all levels of membership.

Applicants should normally have a degree and/or a professional qualification and should normally have undertaken a Diploma-level course in psychodynamic counselling, with at least two consecutive years of counselling or psychotherapy practice. Selection is through interviews and practical assessment of existing skills and knowledge.

3.3 Time commitment per week and length of training
The training lasts four years minimum: applications for registration are then possible, although it may be longer before the right level of practice and theoretical reflection is achieved.

Foundation year: one academic session (two or three hours) a week, weekly supervision, five client hours; reading (two hours a week).

Diploma: one day a week (eight hours) for 30 weeks, plus additional weekly supervision in student's locality, personal therapy, five client hours; reading and writing, approximately three hours a week; approximately five half-days during vacations for course supervision.

Post-qualifying year: ten monthly three-hour seminars, reading and writing; weekly supervision in student's locality.

Clients' needs have priority over a student's training needs. Completion of the Diploma and requirements for applications for registration may therefore require more time. Extensions can be given for the submission of written clinical work, and completion of clinical requirements, although rarely for theoretical assignments.

3.4 Financial cost of training at different stages

The costs for 1999/2001 were:

- Foundation year: approximately £150, plus personal therapy, plus any costs of weekly supervision.
- Diploma: Year 1: £1,600; Year 2: £1,650; plus personal therapy, plus any costs of weekly supervision.
- Post-qualifying year: £250, plus any costs of weekly supervision.
- Affiliate member fees: £55 plus two workshops/lectures in the VAPP programme (approximately £30 each)
- Professional member fees (1999/2000): £55 membership, plus £65 UKCP registration.

3.5 Interruptions in training

Interruptions because of illness or pregnancy are possible, although with a biennial intake this may mean waiting to rejoin the course. Apart from a short period of absence pregnant/nursing students have sustained academic requirements and course attendance requirements, and where necessary made up missing clinical hours.

3.6 Graduating and beginning a career

Since it is expected that students will be experienced counsellors, many are already in employment throughout the course, and may add some independent practice to this. Expectations of graduates five years after graduation are better job opportunities, with some working solely as independent therapists.

VAPP actively encourages professional members in running its programme and other affairs. Affiliate and student members serve on some committees and the Professional Board. The requirement for annual re-registration, that professional members attend two VAPP lectures or workshops annually, makes for a real sense of a collegial professional society.

3.7 Numbers of students per intake

Up to twelve students are accepted on the Diploma. There is a biennial intake.

4. CLINICAL AND ACADEMIC REQUIREMENTS

4.1 Personal therapy

Students must be in individual personal therapy throughout the Diploma, and in the year preceding (normally the foundation year). They are required to attend therapy with the frequency they practise (that is, once-weekly therapy implies a professional member will, except in emergencies, see clients once weekly). The training does not require recognised training therapists, preferring students to seek a therapist with whom they can work well, and who will be challenging where necessary.

4.2 Clinical requirements
Diploma students are required to produce evidence of a minimum of 240 therapy sessions which must include one client for at least 70 sessions (or 120 twice-weekly sessions); one for at least 60 sessions; and two clients for at least 50 sessions. One case is used for a long-term case study with tapes of two consecutive sessions; and at least one client is seen for planned short term therapy.

For registration, trainees must produce evidence of two cases of a minimum of 18 months each.

Students are accepted on the course on the understanding that they are already experienced counsellors, able to recognise whom they can and cannot usefully engage with psychodynamically. Supervisors advise students where cases are unsuitable for training supervision and for assessment.

4.3 Supervision
In the foundation year students are supervised once weekly; on the Diploma they are supervised weekly in a pair on the course, and weekly individually by a supervisor external to the course, who should be a UKCP-registered psychodynamic or psycho-analytic therapist. External supervision continues weekly through the post-qualifying year, and until registration, after which time supervision arrangements are a matter for the professional member.

4.4 Written work and course attendance
Assessed work involves analysis of one session, a journal of an infant or child observation, analysis of a short-term case, an essay, a record of the mental health observation, a case study of a long-term client and a case log. The proposed MA will involve a dissertation of 20,000 words. For registration there is a further case study, and a personal statement concerning suitability.

Students must attend at least 80 per cent of the Diploma training; and at least 90 per cent of the supervision hours on the course. Attendance in the foundation year and post-qualifying year is a minimum of 80 per cent.

4.5 Assessment, standards and ethical requirements
VAPP makes available the UKCP code of practice for training organisations and trainees, and abides by UKCP training requirements. VAPP's Code of Ethics and Practice has been approved by the PPP section and UKCP. It includes the philosophy of VAPP; responsibilities to the client; responsibilities to colleagues and to the profession; and information about the complaints and grievance procedures. A Standards and Ethics Committee oversees ethical issues and complaints.

A high standard of written and clinical work is expected, particularly for regis-tration. There is equal emphasis on clinical and academic aspects. A satisfactory standard must be attained in all aspects – case analysis, essays, placement journals, case log, and so on, with the Diploma awarded either at pass or distinction level.

Assessed written work is described under section 4.4. Criteria for assessment are set out for students, and detailed instructions given for particular pieces of work.

Students are expected to receive satisfactory reports from their supervisors, and to have attendance for personal therapy confirmed.

5. TRAINEE RESPONSE

People decided to train for professional development in order to gain more rigorous theoretical and clinical expertise, leading to registration with UKCP.

Potential students were attracted by the reputation of the teaching staff, the apparent brevity and cost of the course and the final goal of being recognised by the UKCP. Other factors for some in choosing this training were the convenience of the locality and the lack of age discrimination. Many liked the fact that they were able to devote one day a week (Monday) to the training, and that weekends and evenings were not involved.

The selection procedure was very professional and well done. The process took into account an holistic view of candidates' development, maturity and clinical practice, as well as academic ability. Candidates included some already associated with Vaughan College, which was off-putting for both insiders and outsiders. The former seemed to assume that they would be automatically included (which proved not to be the case). However, this was unnerving for the outsiders.

Before the start of the course the description of the academic work was clear and concise. However the requirements regarding clinical hours and external supervision needed clarification. Some would have welcomed the chance for an informal meeting with previous course members.

The atmosphere of the course was affected by changing criteria from UKCP, causing alterations to the course requirements for written work, to which students voiced bewilderment. However, the biggest cause of confusion and upset were the changing clinical requirements for professional registration by UKCP.

Fortunately, there was good opportunity to share thoughts and feelings with fellow trainees.

Methods of teaching included lectures, seminars and student-led reading groups. Some felt a more traditional didactic approach would have been helpful on occasions. However, most agreed that an enormous amount was learned and absorbed!

The course included much written work, the marking of which some felt was too much in the hands of just one member of staff (together with an External Examiner). Supervision reports were also required from internal and external supervisors, and this system worked well.

The course met the expectations of many of its graduates. However, subsequent registration with the UKCP is proving to be a prolonged process for some, requiring a long period of supervised clinical work after the successful completion of the psychotherapy diploma.

Many remain actively involved with this training organisation, meeting at regular intervals either for committee purposes or for ongoing professional development.

Recent trainees are individually involved in training, supervision and teaching activities, and in developing counselling and psychotherapy centres.

AUTHOR'S COMMENTS

This course provides a much needed training for people in the Midlands region, although many are attracted from beyond the area. The university setting, the one-day-per-week requirement for the middle two years of the course and increased clinical requirements have made this into a more demanding course than it once was. The course seems to have wanted to hold on to its focus in training for less intensive therapy while increasing its standards for more intensive work. This is a dilemma for many courses that wish to do both.

The trainees' comments reflect the teething problems of a course in transition increasing its standards to secure UKCP organisational membership. These have included changing goal posts about clinical requirements and the need for external supervision insisted upon for UKCP recognition. This has been a familiar issue for students in many courses in the last five years of the 1990s. It is not easy to experience and future generations of students and eventually patients will benefit from the greater demands and greater clarity this will provide.

This course, like the AIP and the Site, allow the trainee to find their own training therapist without stipulating that person's experience and training as a requirement. This trusts the trainee with their own choice and yet risks them choosing a less experienced person (see comments on p. 59f.).

The course is also going through a transition with the retirement of Michael Jacobs, the course founder, and of Moira Walker, who have moved to London. It is in the process of appointing new senior staff who will no doubt affect the nature of the course and perhaps its ethos and therefore its future development remains to be seen.

THE UNIVERSITY OF SHEFFIELD CENTRE FOR PSYCHOTHERAPEUTIC STUDIES (USCPS – UKCP/UPA)

16 Claremont Crescent, Sheffield S10 2TA
Tel. 0114 222 2961/2/3/4 Fax. 0114 270 0619
E-mail: t.coldwell@Sheffield.ac.uk

1. HISTORY OF THE ORGANISATION

This course is based within the Centre for Psychotherapeutic Studies, School of Health and Related Research, University of Sheffield. The MA course was established in 1993 and replaced the previous Diploma in Psychotherapy which had run in the Department of Psychiatry for many years.

2. THEORETICAL ORIENTATION AND CURRICULUM

This is a firm grounding in adult psychoanalytically orientated psychotherapy. It is pluralist in perspective and involves core components of supervision, psychoanalytic theory, clinical practice and personal therapy.

Aims

- To develop an understanding of core areas of psychoanalytically orientated psychotherapy, both in theory and practice
- To distinguish a psychoanalytic orientation and its boundary in relation to other psychotherapeutic approaches
- To enable the application and creative use of such theory and technique in the service of good practice
- To enable trainees to work independently within an analytic framework and to reflect critically upon that framework and on their own practice.

The qualification

The Diploma/Masters training course is one of only a few such courses located within an academic setting providing a university qualification in this field at a post-graduate level. In addition, on successful completion of the training, trainees will be eligible to apply for accreditation with the UKCP.

Psychoanalytic psychotherapy

This form of psychotherapy is concerned with the exploration and attempted resolution of internal conflicts and changing states of mind which affect the individual's personal and social world. The psychotherapeutic relationship, and in particular the transference involved in it, is the primary agency through which such phenomena may be better understood and altered through the application of analytic understanding and technique.

There is no standard introductory or pre-clinical approved course. We would consider a wide range of introductory courses to be suitable.

3. TRAINING STRUCTURE

3.1 Training committee

The Training Committee for the course is composed of key members of university staff who work clinically with patients in psychoanalytic psychotherapy and who contribute to the course. A representative of supervisors to the course may also sit on the Training Committee. The Training Committee meets at least termly in order to assess trainee progress and consider all other matters of policy and practice relevant to the training.

3.2 Selection procedure and admission

Entry requirements and eligibility are as follows.

The course will be of interest to and suitable for those working in the helping professions and related fields, in particular for those who already have some demonstrable experience in fields ancillary to psychotherapy. This is likely to include workers from the fields of mental health, psychiatry, counselling, clinical psychology, social work, general practice and in some cases education. Good relevant experience and personal aptitude are clearly very important in this field, thus applicants without the usual, prior professional training may also be eligible to apply in some cases.

Normally, entry to this course is at a postgraduate level or equivalent. Special allowances may be made should experience and professional qualifications be deemed by the Training Committee to be of sufficient standard so as to exempt the student from the need for a first degree. In such cases trainees will commence the training programme at the Diploma level with a possibility of transferring to the full Masters Programme after two years subject to satisfactory academic achievement.

3.3 Time commitment per week and length of training
The training is four years part time though some students may require a little longer than four years in order to satisfy our assessment criteria. The seminars and lectures can be fitted into almost half a day a week, but applicants should expect to add clinical hours (425 over three and a half years), supervision, individual personal therapy, and tutorials to this time schedule. Reading and writing clearly also require a large amount of time. In all, applicants should plan to spend the equivalent of a minimum of one day attending seminars, supervision, tutorials, and seeing patients and to add to this time for their own therapy (usually twice a week) and several evenings for reading and writing. The course runs during normal University times, but clinical work, supervision and personal therapy run for considerably longer.

3.4 Financial cost of training at different stages
Trainees pay for their own personal therapy, and part of the cost of supervision (at the time of going to press). University fees generally increase slightly each year (for 1999–2000: £1,840).

3.5 Interruptions in training
The university normally expects trainees to complete their training course within the specified times. Exceptions are made on medical, compassionate and clinical grounds.

3.6 Graduating and beginning a career
There are facilities for further study and training at the University of Sheffield, both in terms of research and continued professional development.

Recent graduates have indicated they are working across several areas of psychotherapy: private practice, NHS and voluntary sector; some are also carrying out research in psychotherapy.

3.7 Numbers of students per intake
The Centre for Psychotherapeutic Studies runs a modest-sized training programme in a region where psychoanalytic resources are limited. We tend to take between four and eight trainees each year.

4. CLINICAL AND ACADEMIC REQUIREMENTS

4.1 Personal therapy
Students will be expected to engage in training therapy for 40–45 weeks of the year at a recommended rate of twice weekly. Therapy must be psychoanalytically orientated and with a therapist approved by the Training Committee.

The training therapist will not normally have any formal assessment role and will only be consulted as a result of extreme concern by the training committee and with due consideration to matters of boundary and confidentiality.

Fees for personal therapy are the responsibility of the trainee in negotiation with the personal therapist.

4.2 Clinical requirements

Clinical practice settings
Clinical practice may take place either under the auspices of the clinical services at the Centre for Psychotherapeutic Studies and/or in conjunction with the local NHS Trust, Department of Psychotherapy, where this is appropriate. Alternatively, and normally because of geographical factors, trainees may be able to see their training cases in their own locality in a suitable placement which is validated by the course.

Training patients
Trainees are expected to have experience of working with both men and women patients.

4.3 Supervision
Supervision is required for all clinical work undertaken during training and will be for a period of nearly two years with a first supervisor, at which point the trainees should change to a second supervisor.

Costs
Currently the Centre subsidises the first £15 of supervision costs.

Reports
The course requests a report from the supervisor at the end of the year, that is, towards the end of the Summer term. This report is an assessment report of the trainee's development and progress in relation to their clinical work.

4.4. Written work and course attendance
Students will be expected to provide six written essays of up to 4,000 words in length, fully referenced and properly presented, based on the material studied in the academic seminars during the year. Students will present a published paper on research in psychotherapy which they have read, analysed, critiqued and applied to clinical practice, in their first year of study. In addition, students will be expected to produce three fully documented case studies, written up and presented in the academic and clinical seminar series during the last year. MA students will also complete a 15,000–20,000-word dissertation, which will contribute significantly to the overall mark for the course.

Diploma students will complete four essays by the end of the second year and will be assessed on these for upgrading to the Masters programme. The extended essay will be approximately 7,000 words.

Self-evaluation
Trainees are required to complete an individual self-evaluation in the summer term of each academic year.

All trainees must pass a clinical supervisor's report reach year. No final work will be considered until this clinical assessment has been completed satisfactorily.

4.5 Assessment, standards and ethical requirements
Trainees are expected to work within UKCP agreed ethical guidelines.

All criteria for all assessments are clearly indicated in an annually updated course handbook. All academic work is doubled-marked and moderated by an external examiner appointed by the University. Such an external examiner is normally of professorial level and of high standing within the profession.

5. TRAINEE RESPONSE

1. Why this course was chosen

1.1 What made people decide to train?
In general, the students did the course in order to deepen their existing knowledge, to extend their current career choice and to develop and grow individually.

1.2 What were the aspects of this course that were most attractive?
For some it was important that the course was not too far geographically, that it offered a pluralistic and varied approach and for most that it was recognised by the UKCP.

1.3 What was your experience of the selection procedure?
The selection procedure was felt to be thorough and the interviews were found to be gruelling and daunting.

1.4 Before the start of the course, how informed did you feel about each stage of the training?
The students felt well informed throughout the training but the initial information about the rules and regulations about the graduation requirements changed several times during our training. This, however, has been well accepted by most students since it was felt that our course is relatively new and therefore needed to have a few adjustments and changes made.

2. The atmosphere of the course

2.1 How do you feel about the way in which information is communicated?
On the whole, the students felt quite satisfied with this aspect of the course.

2.2 What do you find the most confusing aspect of the training?
Some students were confused and struggled a lot with different psychoanalytic schools of thought. For example, a student may have a Jungian therapist, a Freudian

supervisor and a Kleinian lecturer, which apparently may be very difficult to get used to or to work with.

2.3 How much opportunity do you have to share thoughts and feelings with fellow trainees?
Regrettably, the students felt that they did not have enough time or opportunity to share their thoughts and feelings on any issue that may be of concern to all.

2.4 What do you feel about the methods of teaching?
The students would have liked a more structured exposition of the papers and to have had them linked more with clinical work.

2.5 What did you think about the way assessments were done to allow you to progress to the next stages of training?
Most students felt that more regular feedback from tutors and supervisors would have helped to address difficulties as they surfaced.

2.6 Has the course met your expectations?
Some students felt that the course emphasis was predominantly Kleinian but that the programme, as a whole, had very high academic standards and expectations which is what most people had wanted.

2.7 How do you feel about your future with the organisation?
The majority of students intend to move on and away from the organisation but they also expressed a wish to maintain a link and remain in contact with the organisation.

2.8 What plans do trainees have for future practice and possible balance of different sorts of work in their career?
For the future career moves, most students expressed a wish to work in as many different settings as possible, that is, NHS, private practice and teaching.

AUTHOR'S COMMENTS

The Sheffield course combines the academic standards and resources of a university setting with its own clinical service, a contact with a local NHS psychotherapy unit and a range of teachers, therapists and supervisors from different orientations. Recent years seem to have been accompanied by changing standards from which future generations will benefit.

The course's pluralist philosophy is both attractive and demanding from what some trainees report. They suggest that for some the contradictions of approach from different orientations experienced in therapists, supervisors and teachers make for a confusing learning experience, despite this having been one of the things that attracted some to the course. This suggests that the course may leave the task of integration more up to the trainee with potentially contradictory approaches being taught at the same time. As explored elsewhere in this guide, there is a difficult dilemma for courses that present theoretical viewpoints from a purely academic point of view, contrasting one with another, without the undergirding support of integrating theories with clinical work so that trainees have a clear idea why their methods of intervention make good sense by being rooted in a theory of practice.

Unlike some similar courses that produce therapists for NHS work, there is a requirement for twice-weekly therapy, above the minimum, which suggests a commitment to deeper analytic work on the course.

Appendix of Useful Addresses of Organisations Mentioned in the Text and those Related to the Field

PSYCHO/ANALYTIC, PSYCHODYNAMIC PSYCHOTHERAPY COURSES NOT YET MEMBERS OF BCP OR UKCP

South of England School for Psychoanalytic Psychotherapy (SESPP)
1 Ham Common, Richmond, Surrey TW10 7JF Tel. 020 8237 2921 Fax. 020 8237 2996

Southern Derbyshire Mental Health Trust and University of Derby, *Psychodynamic Psychotherapy in Practice*, Department of Psychotherapy, Temple House, Mill Hill Lane, Derby DE23 6SA Tel. 01332 364512 Fax. 01332 293316

Oxford University Department for Continuing Education, *Master's Programme in Psychodynamic Studies Counselling and Psychotherapy*, c/o Noel Bell, Course Administrator, Psychodynamic Studies, OUDCE, 1, Wellington Square, Oxford OX1 2JA Tel. 01865 270384 Fax. 01865 270309 E-mail: noel.bell@conted.ox.ac.uk

Southern Counties Psychotherapy, Oxford Brookes University School of Health Care, *Clinical training in psychodynamic psychotherapy and MSc in Psychodynamic Psychotherapy in the Health Service Settings*, Mental Health Department, Heatherwood Hospital, Ascot, Berkshire SL5 8AA Tel. 01344 877472

University of Lincolnshire/Doncaster Health Care NHS Trust, Psychology Department, Diana Princess of Wales Hospital, Grimsby, DN33 2BA Tel. 01472 874111 Ext. 7120

UNIVERSITY POSTGRADUATE COURSES IN PSYCHO/ANALYTIC WORK

Goldsmiths' College, University of London, MA Psychotherapy and Society, Professional and Continuing Education (PACE), Unit of Psychotherapeutic Studies, Goldsmiths' College, University of London, New Cross, London SE14 6NW Tel. 0120 7919 7205

Middlesex University, MA Psychoanalysis School of Social Science, Queensway, Enfield, EN3 4SF Tel. 020 8362 5161

Psychoanalysis Unit, University College London – MSc in Psychoanalytic Studies (non-clinical) and PhDs, Sub-department of clinical health psychology, Gower Street, London WC1E 6BY Tel. 020 7380 7899

University of Essex, Psychoanalytic Studies PhD, MPhil, MA by dissertation, MA in applications of psychoanalysis in health Care; MA in Jungian and Post-Jungian Studies, MA in Psychoanalysis in Social and Cultural Studies; PhD and MA in Philosophy and Psychoanalysis; Centre for Psychoanalytic Studies, University of Essex, Wivenhoe Park, Colchester CO4 3SQ Tel. 01206 873745

University of Hertfordshire (in collaboration with the Guild of Psychotherapists) **MA in Psychoanalytic Psychotherapy**, Marion Holt, The Guild of Psychotherapists, MA Administrator, 149 Faraday Road, London SW19 8PA Tel. 020 8540 4454. University of Hertfordshire, Health and Human Sciences, College Lane, Hatfield AL10 9AB

LIST OF COURSES IN OBSERVATIONAL STUDIES AND THE APPLICATION OF PSYCHOANALYTICAL CONCEPTS TO WORK WITH CHILDREN, YOUNG PEOPLE AND FAMILIES CHILD OBSERVATION TRAINING COURSES
(Hindle & Smith 1999)

Courses are provided by training institutes whose addresses may be found in Part Two, including: the Tavistock Clinic, the Birmingham Trust for Psychoanalytic Psychotherapy, the Scottish Institute for Human Relations, the Lincoln Centre
Organising Tutor, UBHT Teaching Care, Child & Adolescent Service, Knowle Clinic, Broadfield Road, Knowle, Bristol, BS4 2UH
Course Administrator, Leeds Community & Mental Health NHS Teaching Trust, Southfield House, Clarendon Road, Leeds LS2 7PJ
Course Administrator, Merseyside psychotherapy Institute, c/o Department Child and Adolescent Psychiatry, Alder Hey Children's Hospital, Eaton Road, Liverpool LI2 2AP
Organising Tutor, The Oxford Observation Course, c/o 12 Rectory Road, St Clements, Oxford OX4 1BW
Tavistock Course in Psychoanalytic Observational Studies. Contact Mrs Felicity Weir Tel. 01626 873228. Ringmore Farm, Higher Ringmore Road, Shaldon, Teignmouth, Devon TQ14 0HG
Other training opportunities can be found in Barnstaple, Exeter (01626 873228), Hereford, Nottingham, Plymouth, Torbay, London Borough of Newham, and the University of Kent.

LIST OF OTHER USEFUL ORGANISATIONS RELATED TO PSYCHO/ANALYTIC AND PSYCHOTHERAPEUTIC WORK

Antidote Campaign for Emotional Literacy: 5th floor, 45 Beech Street, London EC2Y 8AD Tel. 020 7588 5151
Association of Child Psychotherapists, 120 West Heath Road, London NW3 7TU Tel. 020 8458 1609.
Brighton Association of Analytic Psychotherapists, Referrals and enquiries: 01273 887334
British Association of Counselling and the UK Register of Counsellors, 1 Regent Place, Rugby, Warwickshire CV21 2PJ
British Association for Psychoanalytic and Psychodynamic Supervision, PO Box 275, Dorking, Surrey RH4 1YR E-mail: bapad@adbapps.freeserve.co.uk
British Confederation of Psychotherapists, 37 Mapesbury Road, London NW2 4HJ Tel. 020 8830 5173 Fax. 020 8452 3684 E-mail: mail@bcp.org.uk Web site: <www.bcp.org.uk>

Confederation of Analytical Psychologists, c/o Hon. Sec. Julia Paton, 30 Stormont Road, Highgate, London N6 4NP Tel. 020 8341 7746 E-mail: hugh.paton@virgin.net

European Federation for Psychoanalytic Psychotherapy in the Public Sector (EFPP) c/o Pestalozzi, Gerbegasslein 5, 4051 Basel, Switzerland Fax. +41 61 483 82 70 E-mail: pestalozzi@magnet.ch

Freud Museum, 20 Maresfield Gardens, London NW3 5SX Tel. 020 7435 2002 Fax. 020 7431 5452 E-mail: freud@gn.apc.org Web site: <www.freud.org.uk>

Forum for Independent Psychotherapists, 167 Sumatra Road, London NW6 1PN Tel. 020 7624 7431 Web site: <www.fip.org.uk>

International Attachment Network, 6 Oman Avenue, London NW2 6BG Tel. 020 482 4212. Or 1 Fairbridge Road, London N19 3EW Tel. 020 7281 4441

London Marriage Council, 180 Tottenham Court Road, London

Nafsiyat Intercultural Therapy Centre, 278 Seven Sisters Road, Finsbury Park, London N4 2HY Tel. 020 7263 4130

PIPPIN, 49 Gordon Road, Wanstead, London EN11 2RA

POPAN – Provention of Professional Abuse Network, 1 Wyvil Court, Wyvil Road, London SW8 2TG Tel. 020 7622 6334

Psychotherapists and Counsellors for Social Responsibility (PCSR) c/o Ruth Williams, 17 Glenkerry House, Burcham Street, London E14 0SL E-mail: RuthWilliams@msn.com

The Squiggle Foundation Administrator, 33 Amberley Road, London N13 4BH E-mail: squiggle_foundation@msn.com

St Bernard's Hospital, West London Psychotherapy Training Department, North House, Ealing Hammersmith and Fulham Mental Health (NHS) Trust, St Bernard's Wing, Uxbridge Road, Southall, Middlesex UB1 3EU Tel. 0208 867 5234

United Kingdom Council for Psychotherapy, 167–9 Great Portland Street, London W1N 5FB Tel. 020 7436 3002

UK Association for Therapeutic Counselling, Top floor, 30 Park Row, Nottingham, NG1 6GR Tel. 0115 9414032

Universities Psychotherapy Association (UPA) c/o Ms Cathy Matheson, Centre for Psychotherapeutic Studies, 35 Linden Walk, Louth, Lincolnshire LN11 9HT

Women's Therapy Centre, 10 Manor Gardens, London N7 6JS Tel. 020 7263 6200

Yorkshire Association for Psychodynamic Psychotherapy (YAPP), 5a Westgate, Otley, West Yorkshire LS21 3AT Tel. 01943 851110

LIST OF PSYCHO/ANALYTIC PUBLISHERS

Artesian Books Ltd, 18 Artesian Road, London W2 5AR

Carfax Publishing Ltd, PO Box 25, Abingdon, Oxfordshire OX14 3UE

Free Association Books, 57 Warren Street, London W1T 5NR. Tel. 020 7388 3182

Guilford Press, Routledge, Brunner/Mazel, Psychology Press, Accelerated Development, International Thompson Publishing Services, Cheriton House, North Way, Andover, Hampshire SP10 5BE Tel. 01264 343071

Jessica Kingsley Publishers, 116 Pentonville Road, London N1 9JB Tel. 020 7833 2307

Karnac Books Ltd, 118 Finchley Road, London NW3 5HJ Tel. 020 7431 1075, also at 58 Gloucester Road, London SW7 4QY Tel. 020 7584 3303. E-mail: books@karnacbooks.com Web orders: <www.karnacbooks.com>

Palgrave (formerly Macmillan Press), Brunel Road, Houndmills, Basingstoke, RG21 6XS Tel. 01256 302611 Fax. 01256 330688 E-mail: f.woodruffe-peacock@palgrave.co.uk. Web catalogue: <www.palgrave.co.uk>

Sage Publications, 6 Bonhill Street, London EC2A 4PU Tel. 020 7374 8741

Bookshops that specialise in psycho/analytic books

Compendium Books, 234 Camden High Street, London NW1 8QS Tel. 020 7485 8944

Karnac, 118 Finchley Road, London NW3 5HJ Tel. 020 7431 1075, also at 58 Gloucester Road, London SW7 4QY Tel. 020 7584 3303. E-mail: books@karnacbooks.com. Web orders: <www.karnacbooks.com>

Rathbone Books, 76 Haverstock Hill, London NW3 2BE Tel. 020 7267 2848

Journals related to Psycho/analytic psychotherapy
(See above for address of publisher)
Attachment and Human Development, Routledge
British Journal of Psychotherapy, Artesian Books
European Journal of Psychotherapy, Counselling and Health, Routledge
Free Associations: Psychoanalysis, Groups, Politics, Culture, Karnac
Group Analysis – Journal of the Group-Analytic Society, London, Sage
Harvest: Journal for Jungian Studies, Karnac
International Journal of Group Psychotherapy, Guilford Press
International Journal of Psycho-Analysis (Institute of Psycho-Analysis, London)
International Journal of Psychotherapy (Journal of the European Association for Psychotherapy), Carfax
International Journal of Psychotherapy (Journal of the European Association of Psychotherapy/Cross-Orientations), Routledge
Journal of Analytical Psychology (Journal of SAP), Blackwell
Journal of Child Psychotherapy (Journal of ACP), Routledge
Journal of Psychoanalytic Studies (Academic, Interdisciplinary, International and Pluralistic, eds Sheffield University), Routledge
Journal of Psychodynamic Counselling (Therapeutic counselling, organisational and group processes, use of psychodynamic ideas in different occupational settings, social and cultural issues), Routledge
Psychoanalysis and History, Artesian Books
Psychoanalytical Studies – Carfax, Web site: <www.carfax.co.uk/pst-ad.htm>
Psychoanalytic Psychotherapy – Journal of the Association for Psychoanalytic Psychotherapy in the NHS, c/o the Tavistock Clinic
Psychodynamic Counselling, Routledge
The Psychotherapy Review, PO Box 14, Teddington, TW11 8YY, Web site: <www.psychotherapyreview.com>
Winnicott Studies Monograph Series, Karnac Books

References

Abram, J. (1996). *The Language of Winnicott: A Dictionary of Winnicott's Use of Words.* London: Karnac; New York: Jason Aronson, 1997.

Abram, J. (2000). *André Green at the Squiggle Foundation.* London: Karnac.

Addenbrooke, M. (1998). 'Training: A Recent Trainee's Reflection', in Alistair, I. and Hauke, C. (eds), *Contemporary Jungian Analysis: Post-Jungian Perspectives from the Society of Analytical Psychology.* London: Routledge.

Alistair, I. and Hauke, C. (1998) *Contemporary Jungian Analysis: Post-Jungian Perspectives from the Society of Analytical Psychology.* London: Routledge.

Alvarez, A. (1992). *Live Company.* London: Routledge.

Alvarez, A. and Reid S. (1999). *Autism and Personality.* London: Routledge.

Astor, J. (1995). *Michael Fordham: Innovations in Analytical Psychology.* London: Routledge.

Balint, M. (1953). *Analytic Training and Training Analysis.* London: Tavistock, 1965.

Balint, M. (1957). *The Doctor, his Patient and the Illness* (2nd edn). London: Pitman Medical, 1964.

Balint, M. (1968). *The Basic Fault.* London: Tavistock.

Balint, M. and Balint, E. (1961). *Psychotherapeutic Techniques in Medicine.* London: Tavistock.

Balint, M., Balint, E. and Ornstein, P.H. (1972). *Focal Psychotherapy – An Example of Applied Psychoanalysis.* London: Tavistock.

Barker, P. (1992). *Regeneration.* London: Penguin.

Benvenuto, B. and Kennedy, R. (1986). *The Works of Jacques Lacan, An Introduction.* London: Free Association Books.

Bion, W.R. (1961). *Experiences in Groups.* London: Tavistock.

Bion, W.R. (1963). *Elements of Psycho-Analysis.* London: Karnac, 1984.

Bion, W. (1967). *Second Thoughts.* London: Heinemann.

Bollas, C. (1987). *The Shadow of the Object: Psychoanalysis of the Unthought Known.* London: Free Association Books.

Bollas, C. (1999). *Hysteria.* London: Routledge.

Bowlby, J. (1969). *Attachment and Loss. Vol. 1: Attachment.* London: Hogarth.

Bowlby, J. (1973). *Attachment and Loss. Vol. 2: Separation: Anxiety and Anger.* London: Hogarth.

Bowlby, J. (1977). *The Making and Breaking of Affectional Bonds.* London: Tavistock, 1979.

Bowlby, J. (1980). *Attachment and Loss. Vol 3: Loss: Sadness and Depression.* London: Hogarth.

Bowlby, J. (1988). *A Secure Base.* London: Tavistock/Routledge, 1992.

Bridger, H. (1985). 'Northfield Revisited', in Pines, M. (ed.), *Bion and Group Psychotherapy* (pp. 87–107). London: RKP.

British Association of Counselling (1998). *Code of Ethics for Counsellors.* (Address in appendix)

British Psycho-Analytical Society (1997). *Psychoanalysis Today*. (Leaflet available from British Psycho-Analytical Society, the Institute of Psycho-Analysis, Byron House, 114 Shirland Road, London W9 2EQ)

Britton, R. (1989). 'The Missing Link: Parental Sexuality in the Oedipus Complex', in Britton, R., Feldman, M. and O'Shaughnessy, E. (eds), *The Oedipus Complex Today* (pp. 83–102). London: Karnac.

Britton, R. (1997). 'Making the Private Public', in Ward, I. (ed.), *The Presentation of Case Material in Clinical Discourse* (pp. 11–28). London: Freud Museum Publications.

Brown, D. and Pedder, J. (1979). *Introduction to Psychotherapy*. London: Tavistock.

Brown, D. and Zinkin, L. (eds) (1994). *The Psyche and the Social World: Developments in Group-Analytic Theory*. London: Routledge.

Casement, P. (1985). *On Learning from the Patient*. London: Tavistock.

Casement, A. (1995). 'A Brief History of Jungian Splits', *J. of Analyt. Psychol.*, 40(3).

Casement, A. (1998). *Post-Jungians Today*. London: Routledge.

Caspari, I. (1974) 'Educational Therapy', in Varma, V. (ed.), *Psychotherapy Today*. London: Constable.

Coltart, N. (1992). *Slouching Towards Bethlehem* ... London: Free Association Books.

Coltart, N. (1996). 'Two's Company, Three's a Crowd', in *The Baby and the Bathwater* (pp. 41–56). London: Karnac.

Couch, A.S. (1995). 'Anna Freud's Adult Psychoanalytic Technique: A defence of classical analysis', *Int. J. of Psycho-Anal.*, 76(1):153–72.

Dicks, H. (1967). *Marital Tensions*. London: RKP.

Dicks, H. (1970). *Fifty Years at the Tavistock Clinic*. London: RKP.

Dyne, D. and Figlio, K. (1989). 'A Response to J. Pedder's "Courses in Psychotherapy"', *Br. J. Psychoth.*, 6:222–6.

Edgecumbe, R. (2000) *Anna Freud*. London: Routledge.

Eisold, K. (1994). 'The Intolerance of Diversity in Psychoanalytic institutes', *Int J. of Psycho-Anal.*, 75(4): 785–800.

Ellis, M. (1994). 'Lesbians, Gay Men and Psychoanalytic Training', *Free Associations*, 4(4) No. 32:501–17.

Ezriel, H. (1950). 'A Psycho-Analytic Approach to Group Treatment', *Brit. J. Med Psychol.*, 23:59–74.

Fabricius, J. and Kennedy H. (1999). 'A Profile of the Anna Freud Centre', *The Psychotherapy Review*, 1(1).

Fairbairn, R. (1952). *Psycho-Analytic Studies of the Personality*. London: Routledge.

Falzeder, E. (2000). 'Profession – Psychoanalyst: A Historical View', *Psychoanalysis and History*, 2(1):37–60.

Fisher, J.V. (1999). *The Uninvited Guest: Emerging from Narcissism towards Marriage*. London: Karnac.

Fonagy, P., Steele, M., Moran G., Steele, H. and Higgitt, A. (1993). 'Measuring the Ghost in the Nursery: An empirical study or the relation between parents' mental representations of childhood experiences and their infants' security of attachment', *J. of Amer. Psychoanalyt. Association*, 44:957–89.

Fonagy, P. and Target, M. (1996) 'Outcome Predictors on Child Analysis', *J. of Amer. Psychoanalyt. Association*, 44:270–3.

Fordham, M. (1969). *Children as Individuals*. London: Hodder and Stoughton.

Fordham, M. (1978). *Jungian Psychotherapy: A Study in Analytical Psychology*. Chichester: John Wiley.

Fordham, M. (1985). 'Integration–Deintegration in Infancy', in *Explorations into the Self*. London: Academic Press.

Fordham, M. (1988). 'Principles of Child Analysis', in Sidoli, M. and Davies, M. (eds), *Jungian Child Psychotherapy*. London: Karnac.

Foster, Sir J. (1971). *Enquiry into the Practice and Effects of Scientology*. London: HMSO.

Foucault, M. (1961). *Madness and Civilisation: A History of Insanity in the Age of Reason*. New York: Vintage/Random House, 1972.

Foulkes, S.H. (1964). *Therapeutic Group Analysis*. London: George Allen and Unwin.

Freud, A. (1936). *The Ego and Mechanisms of Defence*. London: Hogarth.

Freud, A. (1946). *Wartime: The Psycho-Analytical Treatment of Children*. London: George Allen and Unwin.

Freud, A. (1965). *Normality and Pathology in Childhood*. London: Hogarth.

Freud, S. (1905). *Three Essays on the Theory of Sexuality*. SE 7:135–243. London: Hogarth; The Pelican Freud Library 7:45–169.

Freud, S. (1914). *On Narcissism*. SE 14:69–102, and in Richards, A. (ed.) Pelican Freud Library No. 11: *On Metapsychology* (pp. 59–98). London: Pelican.

Freud, S. (1917). *Mourning and Melancholia SE* 14: 243–258, and in Richards, A. (ed.), (1984) Pelican Freud Library No. 11: *On Metapsychology* (pp. 245–68). London: Pelican.

Freud, S. (1924). *The Question of Lay Analysis*. SE 20:183–258. London: Hogarth.

Freud, S. (1940). *An Outline of Psycho-Analysis*. SE 3. London: Hogarth and Institute of Psycho-Analysis.

Garland, C. (ed.) (1999). *Understanding Trauma: A Psychoanalytical Approach*. London: Tavistock.

Geissmann, C. and Geissmann, P. (1992). *A History of Child Psychoanalysis* (English trans.). London: Routledge, with Institute of Psycho-Analysis, 1998 (originally published in French).

Gray, A. (1994). *An Introduction to the Therapeutic Frame*. London: Routledge.

Green, A. (1987). *Private Madness*. London: Hogarth.

Greenson R.R. (1978) *The Technique and Practice of Psycho-Analysis*. London: Hogarth and Institite of Psycho-Analysis.

Guntrip, H. (1968). *Schizoid Phenomena, Object Relations and the Self*. London: Hogarth, with Institute of Psycho-Analysis.

Guntrip, H. (1973). *Personality Structure and Human Interaction*. London: Hogarth.

Hahn, H. (1988). 'On Establishing the Therapeutic Alliance in an Unsophisticated Environment', *Br. J. Psychoth.*, 4:253–62.

Hamilton, V. (1996). *The Analyst's Preconscious*. New Jersey: The Analytic Press.

Harrison, T. (1999). *Bion, Rickman, Foulkes and the Northfield Experiment*. London: Jessica Kingsley.

Hauke, C. (1998). 'Jung, Modernity and Postmodern Psychology', in Alister, I. and Hauke, C. (eds), *Contemporary Jungian Analysis* (pp. 287–98). London: Routledge.

Herman, N. (1989). 'Ilse Seglow in her Time: Reflections on her Life and Work', *Br. J. Psychoth.*, 5:431–41.

Hindle, D. and Smith, M.V. (1999). *Personality Development: A Psychoanalytic Perspective*. London: Routledge.

Hinshelwood, R.D. (1994). *Clinical Klein*. London: Free Association Books.

Hinshelwood, R.D. (1998). 'The Organising of Psychoanalysis in Britain', *Psychoanalysis and History*, 1(1):87–102.

Hinshelwood, R.D. and Manning, N. (eds). (1979). *Therapeutic Communities: Reflections and Progress*. London: RKP.

Hobson, R. (1985). *Forms of Feeling*. London: Tavistock.

Jacobson, E. (1964). *The Self and the Object World*. New York: International Universities Press.

Johns, J. (2000) 'The future for psychoanalytic psychotherapy'. BCP 1999 Annual Lecture. *Brit. J. Psychoth.*, October.

Jones, E. (1957). *Sigmund Freud: Life and Work*. London: Penguin.

Joseph, B. (1989a). 'Addiction to Near-Death', in Feldman, M. and Spillius, E.B. (eds), *Psychic Equilibrium and Psychic Change* (pp. 127–38). London: Routledge, with Institute of Psycho-Analysis.

Joseph, B. (1989b). 'The Patient who is Difficult to Reach', in Feldman, M. and Spillius, E.B. (eds), *Psychic Equilibrium and Psychic Change* (pp. 75–87). London: Routledge, with Institute of Psycho-Analysis.

Jung, C.G. (1916). *Psychology of the Unconscious*. New York: Moffat, Yard & Co.

Kalsched, D. (1996). *The Inner World of Trauma*. London: Routledge.

Kernberg, O. (1976). *Object Relations Theory and Clinical Psychoanalysis*. New York: Jacob Aronson.

Kernberg, O. (1986). 'Institutional Problems of Psychoanalytic Education', *J. Amer. Psychoanal. Assn.*, 34:799–834.

Kernberg, O. (1996). 'Thirty Methods to Destroy the Creativity of Psychoanalytic Candidates', *Int. J. of Psycho-Anal.*, 77(5):1031–40.

Kernberg, O.F. (1999). 'Psychoanalysis, Psychoanalytic Psychotherapy and Supportive Psychotherapy: Contemporary Controversies', *Int. J. Psychoanal.*, 80(6):1075–92.

King, P. and Steiner, R. (1991). *The Freud–Klein Controversies*. London: Routledge.

Klauber, J. et al. (1987). *Illusion and Spontaneity in Psychoanalysis*. London: Free Association Books.

Klein, J. (1987). *Our Need for Others and its Roots in Infancy*. London: Tavistock.

Klein, M. (1932). *The Psycho-Analysis of Children*. London: Hogarth.

Klein, M. (1940). 'Mourning and its Relation to Manic-Depressive States', in Klein, M. (ed.), *Love, Guilt and Other Papers 1921–1946* (pp. 311–38). London: Hogarth, 1947.

Klein, M. (1975). *Love, Guilt and Reparation*. London: Hogarth .

Kohon, G. (1986). *The British School of Psychoanalysis. The Independent Tradition*. London: Free Association Books.

Kohon, G. (1999). *The Dead Mother*. London: Routledge.

Kohon, G. (1999) *No Lost Certainties To Be Recovered*. London: Karnac Books.

Kohut, H. (1971). *The Analysis of the Self*. New York: International Universities Press.

Kovel, J. (1976). *A Complete Guide to Therapy*. London: Pelican.

Laing, R.D. (1959). *The Divided Self*. London: Tavistock.

Lake, T. and Acherson, F. (1988). *Room to Listen, Room to Talk*. London: Bedford Press, in association with BBC Radio 4.

Langs, R.J. (1978). *The Listening Process*. New York: Jason Aronson.

Laplanche, J. and Pontalis, J-B. (1980). *The Language of Psycho-Analysis*. London: Hogarth, with the Institute of Psycho-Analysis.

Little, M. (1986). *Transference Neurosis and Transference Psychosis: Towards basic unity*. London: Free Association Books.

Livingston Smith, D. (1991). *Hidden Conversations*. London: Tavistock/Routledge.

Lomas, P. (1990). 'On Setting Up a Psychotherapy Training', *Free Associations*, 20:139–49.

McDougall, J. (1986). *Theatres of the Mind: Illusion and Truth on the Analytic Stage*. London: Free Association Books.

McDougall J. (1989). *Theatres of the Body*. London: Free Association Books.

McDougall, J. (1995). *The Many Faces of Eros*. London: Free Association Books.

Malan, D.H. (1963). *A Study of Brief Psychotherapy*. London: Tavistock.

Malan, D.H. (1979). *Individual Psychotherapy and the Science of Psychodynamics*. London: Butterworths.

Marrone, M. (1998). *Attachment and Interaction*. London: Jessica Kingsley.

Martindale, B. et al. (eds) (1997). *Supervision and its Vicissitudes*. London: Karnac.

Meltzer, D. (1967). 'The Gathering of the Transference', in Meltzer D. (ed.), *The Psycho-Analytical Process* (pp. 1–12). Strath Tay: Clunie Press, 1990.

Meltzer, D. (1979). *Sexual States of Mind*. Strath Tay: Clunie Press.

Meltzer, D. (1992). *The Claustrum*. Strath Tay: Clunie Press.

Meltzer, D. and Williams, M.H. (1988). *The Apprehension of Beauty*. Strath Tay: Clunie Press.

Mendoza, S. (1997). 'Genitality and Genital Homosexuality: Criteria of selection', *Br. J. Psychoth.*, 13(3):384–94.

Michels, R. (1999). 'Psychoanalysts' Theories', in Fonagy, P., Cooper, A.M. and Wallerstein, R.S. (eds), *Psychoanalysis on the Move* (pp. 187–200). London: Routledge, with Institute of Psycho-Analysis.

Miller, E.J. and Rice, A.K. (1967). *Systems of Organisation: Task and Sentient Boundaries and their Boundary Control*. London: Tavistock.

Miller, L., Rustin, M.E., Rustin, M.J. and Shutleworth, J. (1989). *Closely Observed Infants*. London: Duckworth.

Milner, M. (1987). *The Suppressed Madness of Sane Men*. London: Routledge.

Mitchell, S.A. (1994). 'The Origin and Nature of the "Object" in the Theories of Klein and Fairbairn', in Grotstein, J.S. and Rinsley, D.B. (eds), *Fairbairn and the Origins of Object Relations* (pp. 66–87). London: Free Association Books.

Molino, A. (1997). Interview with Joyce McDougall. *Freely Associated* (pp. 53–92). London: Free Association Books.

Mollon, P. (1993). *The Fragile Self: The Structure of Narcissistic Disturbance*. London: Whurr.

Morgan, M. (1995). 'The Projective Gridlock: A form of projective identification in couple relationships', in Ruszczynski, S. and Fisher, J. (eds) *Intrusiveness and Intimacy in the Couple* (chapter 2). London: Karnac.

Mowbray, R. (1995). *The Case Against Psychotherapy Registration*. London: Trans Marginal Press.

Nitsun, M. (1996). *The Anti-Group*. London: Routledge.

Obholzer, A. and Roberts, V.Z. (1994). *The Unconscious at Work*. London: Routledge.

O'Connor, N. and Ryan, J. (1995). *Wild Desires and Mistaken Identities*. London: Virago.

Ogden, T.H. (1982). *Projective Identification and Psychotherapeutic Technique*. New York: Jason Aronson.

Olivier, C. (1980). *Jocasta's Children*. London: Routledge, 1989 (originally published in French).

O'Shaughnessy, E. (1999). 'Relating to the Superego', *Int. J. of Psycho-Anal.*, 80(5):861–70.

Palmer-Barnes, F. (1998). *Complaints and Grievances in Psychotherapy*. London: Routledge.

Parsons, M. (2000). *The Dove that Returns, the Dove that Vanishes – Paradox and creativity in psychoanalysis*. London: Routledge.

Pedder, J. (1989). 'Courses in Psychotherapy: Evolution and current trends', *Br. J. Psychoth.*, 6:203–21.

Pedder, J. (1996). 'Psychotherapy in the British National Health Service: A short history', *Free Associations*, 6(1) No. 37:14–27.

Perelberg, R.J. (1999). 'A Core Phantasy in Violence', in Perelberg R.J. (ed.), *Psychoanalytic Understanding of Violence and Suicide* (pp. 87–108). London: Routledge.

Pestalozzi, J. et al. (eds) (1998). *Psychoanalytic Psychotherapy in Institutional Settings*. London: Karnac.

Pines, M. (1998). 'A History of Psychodynamic Psychiatry in Britain', in Pines, M. (ed.), *Circular Reflections* (pp. 183–208). London: Jessica Kingsley.

Pokorny, M. (1995). 'History of the United Kingdom Council for Psychotherapy', *Br. J. Psychoth.*, 11(3):415.

Postle, D. (1995). 'The Alchemist's Nightmare – The Annexation of Psychotherapy', *Int. J. of Psychoth.*, 3(1):53–83.

Pritz, J. (1998). 'Austrian Psychotherapy Law and Some Consequences', *European J. of Psychotherapy, Counselling and Health*, (April) 1(1):135–40.

Randall, R. (1995). 'Does Psychotherapy need "NVQs"?', *Br. J. Psychoth.*, 12(1):98–102.

Rayner, E. (1990). *The Independent Mind in British Psychoanalysis*. London: Free Association Books.

Rayner, E. (1999). 'The British Independents: A brief history'. Website of BP-AS and Institute of Psycho-Analysis, <www.psychoanalysis.org.uk>

Rey, H. (1979). 'The Schizoid Mode of Being and the Space-Time Continuum (Before Metaphor)', in Magagna, J. (ed.), *Universals of Psychoanalysis in the Treatment of Psychotic and Borderline States* (pp. 8–30). London: Free Association Books, 1974.

Riesenberg-Malcolm, R. (1999). *On Bearing Unbearable States of Mind*. London: Routledge.

Roberts, J. and Pines, M. (eds) (1991). *The Practice of Group Analysis*. London: Routledge.

Robertson, J. and Robertson, J. (1989). *Separation and the Very Young*. London: Free Association Books.

Rosenfeld, H. (1965). *Psychotic States*. London: Hogarth.

Rosenfeld, H. (1987). *Impasse and Interpretation*. London: Tavistock, with the Institute of Psycho-Analysis.

Roth, A. and Fonagy, P. (eds) (1996). *What Works for Whom?* London: Routledge.

Ruszczynski, S. (ed.) (1993). *Psychotherapy with Couples: Theory and Practice at the TMSI*. London: Karnac.

Ruszczynski, S. and Fisher, J. (eds) (1995). *Intrusiveness and Intimacy in the Couple*. London: Karnac.

Ryle, A. (ed.) (1995). *Cognitive Analytic Therapy: Developments in Theory and Practice*. Chichester: John Wiley and Sons.

Samuels, A. (1985). *Jung and the Post-Jungians*. London: RKP.

Samuels, A. (1993). 'Object Relations, Group Process and Political Change', in Samuels, A. (Ed.), *The Political Psyche* (pp. 267–86). London: Routledge.

Sandler, J. (1962). 'The Hampstead Index as an Instrument of Psychoanalytic Research', *Int. J. of Psycho-Anal.*, 43:287–91.

Sandler, J. (1976). 'Countertransference and Role-Responsiveness', *Int. Rev. of Psycho-Analysis*, 3:43–7.

Sandler, J. (1987). 'The Background of Safety', in *From Safety to Superego* (pp. 1–8). London: Karnac.

Sandler, J. (1988). 'Psychoanalysis and Psychotherapy: Problems of differentiation', *Br. J. Psychoth.*, 5:172–7.

Sandler, J. and Sandler, A.M. (1998). *Internal Objects Revisited*. London: Karnac.

Sandler, J., Dare, C. and Holder, A. (1973). *The Patient and the Analyst*. London: Allen & Unwin.

Scarlett, J. (1991). 'Getting Established: Initiatives in psychotherapy training since World War Two', *Br. J. Psychoth.*, 7:260–7.

Schermer, V.L. and Pines, M. (eds) (1994). *Ring of Fire*. London: Routledge.

Shamdasani, S. (1999). 'The Compulsion of Self-Control', in Greenberg, S. (ed.), *Mindfield: Therapy on the Couch – A Shrinking Future?* (pp. 61–5). London: Camden Press.

Sinason, V. (1992). *Mental Handicap and the Human Condition*. London: Free Association Books.

Skynner, R. (1989). *Explorations with Families: Group Analysis and Family Therapy*. Edited By J.R. Schlapobersky. London: Methuen.

Steiner, J. (1993). *Psychic Retreats*. London: Routledge, with Institute of Psycho-Analysis.

Stewart, H. (1992). *Psychic Experience and Problems of Technique*. London: Routledge, with Institute of Psycho-Analysis.

Strachey, J. (1969). 'The Nature of the Therapeutic Action of Psycho-Analysis', *Int. J. Psycho-Anal.*, 50:275–92.

Suttie, I. (1935). *The Origins of Love and Hate*. London: Kegan Paul.

Symington, N. (1996). *The Making of a Psychotherapist*. London: Karnac.

Tantam, D. and Van Deurzen, E. (1998). 'Creating a European Profession of Psychotherapy: The European Certificate of Psychotherapy', *European J. of Psychotherapy, Counselling and Health*, (April) 1(1):121–34.

Taylor, D. (ed.) (1999). *Talking Cure*. London: Tavistock.

Trist, E. and Murray, H. (eds) (1990). *The Social Engagement of Social Science*. London: Free Association Books.

Turkle, S. (1992). *Psychoanalytic Politics – Jacques Lacan and Freud's French Revolution* (2nd edn). London: Free Association Books.

Tustin, F. (1981). *Autistic States in Children* (revised edn). London: Routledge, 1992.

UKCP (1998). *National Register of Psychotherapists* (p. xvii). London: Routledge.

Van Deurzen, E. (1998). *Paradox and Passion in Psychotherapy*. Chichester: John Wiley.

Wallerstein, R.S. (1992). *The Common Ground in Psychoanalysis*. New Jersey: Jason Aronson.

Winnicott, D.W. (1965). *The Maturational Processes and the Facilitating Environment*. London: Hogarth.

Wright, K. (1991). *Vision and Separation: Between Mother and Baby*. London Free Association Books.

Chart of Requirements for Psychoanalytic Psychotherapy Trainings

No. Name	Place	Orien-tation	Org	Introd. Or pre-clinical Courses	Years incl. Introd. course	Requirements (to train)	Tng Anlys	Training Patients	Written Work (other than clinical reports)	Fee (£) p.a. without sup'n
Individual Adult Trainings										
1 ARBS	N8	PI	UKCP PPS	1y assoc prog	1asoc+3 = 4	Assoc prog 1y+placement	@1 assoc yr+ @3 tng	2 clinical placements 2ps @ 2 (1y+6mo)	2 placement papers+ Final clinical paper	Y1:1380 Y2+:1400
2 AGIP	N19	PI	UKCP PPS	No	4 to 5	deg.equ.	@2+tng+1yr prior	24+18@ 2+ other cases	2 + final clinical paper	1400 (3yrs)
3 AIP	N6	PI	UKCP PPS	No	5–6	30–60.th=200. counselling course/exp	@2+tng.	24+18 @ 2+ 3–5 others	Several,one rel clin wk to theory	1200–300
4 AJA	NW3	J	UKCP APS	1 y pre-clin	4	30.deg,6 mo. Half dy clin placemnt	@3.tng+150hrs prior	2y+1y @3 M+F	Stge1 short paper+final clin. paper	720
5 BAP-P-A	NW2	K/I/CF	BCP	No	4 to 5	deg.equ. 1y th.	@ 3 tng+1y prior	24+18 @ 3 M+F	Inf Obs paper + Reading-in pap=7k3	Y1: 128 To Y5:789
6 BAP-J	NW2	J	BCP	No	4 to 5	deg.equ. 1y th.	@ 3 tng+1y prior	24+18 @ 3 M+F	Inf Obs paper + Reading-in pap=7k	4777 for 4 yrs
7 BAP-Conv	NW2	CF/IF	BCP		2–3	Child psychotherapy training	Frequency not specified	24+18 @ 3 M+F	Reading-in pap=7–8k	1290
8 CSP	Cambridge	F/OR	UKCP PPS	No	4+	Letter of applic'n:4 resource issues-time, emotion, intellect & money	Rel'td to dev & Clin wk 1 y prior	Diff durations & frequencies Some intensive	Encouraged, not specified, Final paper	140
9 CAPP	NW3	Att	UKCP PPS	No	4	1 y th,exp hlpng prfs +traumtsd ps	@ 2 by 2nd yr +1 yr prior Professional	2y @ 2 + 6 others	Long contract,portfolio incl. Clin/th papers+ final paper	2000+
10 CFAR	SE15	Lac	UKCP PPS	Prelim yr	4	Introd to Lacan lectures	Lacanian analysis+ 1y prior	Not specified	2clin + 2 other papers	Y1:400 Y2/3:1195
11 CPP	NW2	CF/K/IF	UKCP PPP	No	4–5	Deg or equiv	@3 tng+1y prior	24+18 @ 3	Short termly paper + Clinical paper presented	Y1–3:1395 Y4: 885
12 GUILD	SW19	PI/Ph	UKCP PPS	No	4	30.clin exp, deg or equiv with exceptions	@2+tng	2x18mo@ 2+ M+F	Theory 3k+ final paper	930

No.	Name	Location	Orientation	Body	Pre-clinical	Years	Entry	Training	Duration	Assessment	Cost
13	IGAP	W3	J	UKCP APS BCP	1.5y Candidacy	1.5+3=4.5	deg equiv	@ 3.tng+150 hrs prior	2y+2x1y@x3	Exams+orals+Presented thesis 15–20k.+1 paper	510 + exams 400
14	Inst.P-A	W1	CF/K/IF	BCP	No	4+	Deg+ prof tng & exp. under 40 usually	@ 5 tng, 18 mo prior	2 yrs+1 yr @ 5	Optional	£255
15	IPSS	N6	P-A/ Soc Crit	UKCP PPS	1Yr Exploring Psychoth	4	Dip overlaps MA(Univ Lon)	@ 2 tng, 1 yr prior Tng	2 @ 2 (1 for 18 mo)	Dip 2x2k+10k clin+15kclin.More MA	Y1/2: 2424 (Incl sup'n) Y4: 500
16	LINC	SW4	CF/IF/K	BCP	No	4+	Deg+ prof tng & exp.	@ 3 tng, 1 yr prior M+F	24+18 @ 3	Inf obs+qualifying paper	Y1:1365 Y2/3: 1095 Y4: 945
17	LCP	NW5	PI	BCP	Foundation Course 4 +		Deg or equ, Foundation course or equiv.	@ 3+ tng+iy prior	24+18mo @ 3	Theory 5k. Inf obs 5k + 2 longer clinical papers	1300
18	NIASP	Belfast	P-A	BCP		5+	Deg or Prof Qual	@ 4–5 per wk for 4 yrs 1 yr prior	140 hrs clinical exp + 2y @ 3– 5+1y@ 3–5	250 hrs theory & clinical seminars @ Queens Univ. Belfast. Reading-in paper	
19	NEATPP	Newcastle	F/K/OR	BCP	No	4	Deg equiv+ post-grad clin wk+1yr intr 'grad. thinking'+qualities	@ 3 tng+1y prior	3(24+18+12) mo@3–5	Case reports+ Reading-in paper	1350
20	PA	NW3	Philos Phen F/OR	UKCP PPS BCP	Introd. Yr.	Int+3+	prof qual+exp with psychiatric patients	@ 2+tng,1y prior	2x18mo@ 2	th 8k+Qual. Paper presented	Y1: 600 Then: 750
21	SIHR	Edinburgh	F/OR		diff profns	3+	prof qual+exp	@ 4 tng	2+1 yr @ 3+	Not specified	900
22	SIPS	Bristol	PI	UKCP PPS	No	5	25.rel exp,deg or prof qual	@ 3 tng+1y prior	24+18 @3	4: work discussion, theory, inf obs, clinical paper	Y1: 500 Then: 1200
23	SITE	N6	Critical P-A	UKCP PPS	No	4	rel exp+deg orl prof qua	@ 2 tng + 1y prior	2x18mo	1 th + 1 clin + final paper 8k	690
24	SAP	NW3	J	BCP	1 y pre-clin	1+3=4+	deg equiv.psych.1yx2pats	@ 4/5.tng+6mo prior	2+1yrs @ 4/5 M+F	Clin pap, case presentation 8k	500–200
25	TAVI Adult	NW3	F/K/OR	BCP	Optional Foundation course time+(3 if in P-A Psychoth.	4 full- Foundation course time+(3 if child traind)	deg+prof qual+exp	@3 tng SAP or Inst.P-A analyst or equiv exp.	24+18 m @3 + assessments + group	Presentation of tutor assessments gathered by student+final paper	Couns: 4000–1700 Psychoth: 1700
26	WMIP-F	Birmingham	F	UKCP PPS	No	4	Deg/prof equ	@ 2 tng,1 yr prior	2+1Yr @ 1 M+F	3x(4k)+qualifying paper (10k)	1,600
27	WMIP-J	Birmingham	J	UKCP PPS	No	4	Deg/prof equ	@3 tng, 1 yr prior@2	18@3.12@2. 12@1	Annual essay. Inf obs. final clinical essay	Cost divided by numbers.
28	WMIP-K	Birmingham	K	UKCP PPS	2 yr pre-clinical courseincl child obs	4+	Deg/prof equ	@ 3 tng,1 yr prior	3(24+12+12) @ 3	Portfolio of casework letters +qualifying paper	pre-clin:1000 clin: 6000+

355

Chart of Requirements for Psychoanalytic Psychotherapy Trainings *continued*

No. Name	Place	Orien-tation	Org	Introd. Or pre-clinical Courses	Years incl. Introd. course	Requirements (to train)	Tng Anlys	Training Patients	Written Work (other than clinical reports)	Fee (£) p.a. without sup'n
29 WPF	SE15	PI	UKCP PPS	Cert/Dip Csk Dip Psy C	2–4 Coun +2+Psyoth tng.	25,Grad equ.couns intro cse+exp	@ 3 tng	24 @3+ 18@2/3	7modulesx2k+final paper	1.700–2.500
Child Trainings										
30 AFC	NW3	F	UKCP ACP	No	4 (1st yr ch probation)	Post-grad wk in psych field+exp with	@ 5 tng.	3 child analyses+ 6 child or parent cases	2 obs +th & resrch if 1st yr MSc. If PhD 2 pa.+ dissertation	Y 1: 2675 1200–800
31 BTPP	Birmingham	K/OR	UKCP ACP	2 yr pre-clinical course incl child obs	4+	Public sector/5 NHS trainee posts £18.500+expenses	@ 3–5 tng	3 ch@ 3–4(2y+1y+1y) +others	Portfolio of casework letters +qualifying paper	pre -clin:1000 clin:6000+ incl sup'n
32 BAP Ch	NW2	CF/IF	UKCP ACP	Ext MSc if no deg	4 to 5	deg or higher deg in rel subj	@ 3 tng BAP/ACP approved analyst/therapist	3 ch @ 3+other cl wk with children + parents	Inf obs, 2 clinical cases, work with parents. reading-n paper	1–2: 1195– 3–4: 955
33 FAETT	N5	P/A+Ed	UKCP PTCS	1 yr	4	Qualified teacher+ 2yrs exp.	@1+ 6 mo prior	Child & Guid. Placement	9	1,200 incl supervision
34 IP-A Ch	W1	CF/K/IF	BCP	No	5+	Deg+ prof tng & exp. under 40 usually	@ 5 tng, 18 mo prior	1 child + 1adolescent @ 5		
35 SIHR Ch	Edinburgh	K/OR/ Att	UKCP ACP	2 yr 'Th skills with children & young people'	2+2/3=4/5	prof qual+exp with children	@ 3 tng	2 ch+1 adolesc@x3 +other clin exp	Theory 5k Client papers Clinical paper up to 10k	2500–3000 incl sup'n
36 TAVI Ch	NW3	F/K/OR	UKCP ACP	2 yr child obs course	4+	Deg/prof equ Some regional posts	@4/5 + 6 mo prior	2ch+1 adolesc@ 3 + org consultation	Masters in P-A Psychoth Portfolio+clin paper 8–12k	1.100
37 SAP Ch	NW3	J	UKCP ACP	No	4 to 5	Deg/prof equ_2 yrs+ wk with children	@4–5 tng	6(2 @ 4+adoles@ 3+1 parent+ 2 ch @ 2)	Qualifying paper	Y1:171 Y2/3:141 Y4:74

Couple & Group Courses

38 TMSI	NW3	PI	UKCP PPS	No	4	Relevant professional qualification & experience	@3+ tng,1 yr prior	2couples x18mo. 4x1y. 5 assessments	Inf obs pap+3yrly ps+qualifyng clin paper	3,000 Clin tng - 4.500 for last 2 yrs of PhD £2,676 incl. MSc
39 IGA	NW3	G-A	UKCP PPS	Introd cse(regional/Lon)	4+	Relevant professional qualification & experience	g'p@2 tng+1y prior	2y g'p+1 y g'p	MSc thesis 12k + 2 essays+clin 10k	1450
40 UL:G	Lewisham	G-A	UKCP UPA	No	3 +	30.deg/equiv.exp in core professions,	@1 or 2 weekly group	2y g'p x1 weekly	3 : clinical 8k, trans-cultural 5k, other 5-6k+ MA dissertation+15-20k	
41 TURGAP	Turvey	G-A	UKCP UPA	Prelim Cert.if tng not related	Dip.+MA =4+	post-grad or equiv	Weekly group	1 weekly gp+ 12 session gp+3 inds	3 pa (2x3/4k+1x2/2.5k) + final dissertation	1950+ accom + therapy
42 WPF Gp	SE15	G-A	UKCP PPS	No	4+	1 y dipl in gp w'k skills or equiv	60 gps. P.a.	2y @1 g'p+ limited or themed gp	Th 3-5 k+ clin 5-8k	Y1-3:1900 Y4: 900 Incl sup'n

Courses affiliated to Universities and/or NHS

43 CSPK	Canterbury	PI	UKCP PPS	2 yr post grad diploma	3 to 6	1 yr th,+Dipl in Psychoth equivalent	@ 1 + 1y prior	2y @x2/3+	Dip: 6 papers 2-3k MClin Sci: Process research project+2 clinical dissertations 7k+9k	Dip:1080-1650 MA 1890-1620
44 NWIDP	Manchester	G-A/P-A(K)/I-P	UKCP PPS	Group Psychoth course+4 terms foundation	1Fnd+2Ac+ 1=4	deg equ. Man G'p cse or equiv+clin exp	@'1+ tng.+ prior 1y gp th	2y@2+2brief +g p+6Assts	Case 2k+4-800+ 6 assessments + Dissertation 4-6k	2250
45 STTDP	Nottingham, Lincoln, Derby, Leicester	P-A PPS	UKCP	No	4 to 6	Core NHS profns,	@1 for min 3 yrs gp=pt time	1khrs/18 mo ass't psychoth clinic	1 case analysis. th. Pap+ oral	NHS posts
46 ULPD	Leeds	P-A	UKCP UPA	Certificate to Diploma to Masters	4	Deg in Med. Psychol. Soc Sci. Nursing+clin exp+introd course	@1 tng 1 y prior	(24+18mo) @1	5 incl research dissertation(+viva)	1800
47 ULDPD	Leicester	P-A	UKCP PPS	Adv cert Dip couns.U Leic	Foundation +2	Deg/prof qual+ Adv Cert/dip couns +exp	tng+1yr prior =frequency of later work/any therapist	70hrs @1 or 120 @2 + 2x50	2x2k+5kclininica1+ placemnt obs + 6-7k theory	1600-1650 Y3:250
48 USCPS	Sheffield	PI	UKCP UPA	Prelim Cert.if tng not related	Dip.+MA =4+	post-grad or equiv	@1-2 tng	3ps100+75+ 75hrs +=425 hrs	6x4k+7/8k Dip or 15-20k MA dissertation	1840

Chart of Requirements for Psychoanalytic Psychotherapy Trainings *continued*

No. Name	Place	Orientation	Org	Introd. Or pre-clinical Courses	Years incl. Introd. course	Requirements (to train)	Tng Anlys	Training Patients	Written Work (other than clinical reports)	Fee (£) p.a. without sup'n
Courses that may seek membership of UKCP/BCP in the future (addresses in appendix)										
49 SCPT	Oxford Brookes (NHS) Ox.Berks. Northants.	P-A	UPA affil.	No	3		@ 2 tng+1 y prior	700 hours 5 per week 12 k	2 clinical + 1 disseratation 10–	
50 SESPP	Richmond	CF/K/IF	Discuss-ing with BCP	No	4	Deg/prof equ./ 25–55		2ps(M+F).@ 3	Reading-in paper	£2,400
51 ULINC	Lincoln & Grimsby	P/D& P/A	UPA affil.	1st y certificate	Cert+dip= 2+2 MSc= more papers/ seminars	Deg/prof exp	Y1: @ 3, Y2: @ 4 1 yr prior	480 hrs 80 hrs supervision	MSc includes research + clinical paper	Y1: 390 Y2-4: 525
52 OUPSP	Oxford (University cont ed dept)	PI	UPA affil	Post-grad cert in Psychodynamic counselling	4		Experiential groups	Placements	Dip: 2 case studies+3x3k reports M.St:2 theory 3k. clin 4k. spec. interest 5k	Dip: 1925 M.St: 1305+
53 DERB	Derby	P-A	UPA affil	Introductory	3+		Y1: Group Y2+ Group or Individ	Cert: 80 hrs Dip: 200 hrs MA: 500 hrs		Staff paid for by Health Authority

Key

Prof. Org.=Professional Organisation: ACP=Association of Child psychotherapists, APS=Analytical Psychology Section,BCP= British Confederation of Psychotherapists, UKCP=United Kindgom Council of Psychotherapists. UPA=Universities Psychotherapy Association, appl.=applying to, affil.=affiliated to

Orientation: CF=Contemporary Freudian. IF=Independent Freudian. K=Kleinian, OR=Object Relations, G-A=Group-analytic. Pl=Pluralist. Att =Attachment. Lac=Lacanian, Crit or Soc Crit=Critical approach to philosophical, sociological and linguistic pre-suppositions of psychoanalysis. I-P=Interpersonal. P-A=psychoanalytic. PD=psychodynamic

Other Columns: Assts=assessments. Coun=counselling.Coun Sk=counselling skills course. exp.=experience. rel exp=relevant experience. tng=training or during training, cl or clin=clinical. k=1000 as in 1kwords=1000words. pres=presentation. inf=infant. ch=child. obs=observation. th=theory or theoretical. distrn=dissertation. prof(ns)=profession(s). ap=applied for, deg=degree. dip=diploma, ext=external, repts=reports. PG=Post Graduate. equ=equivalent. @ 3=at 3 times per week. 6ps or 6=6 patients. adolesc=adolescents. wk=week. found=foundation, anal=analysis, min=minimum.

This data was drawn from course brochures and entries in this book. Courses are frequently changing requirements and costs. so this information should bechecked with specific trainings.

Index of Names and Key Words

(References to training organisations are not included.)